THE BEST OF

100 Years

of Great Writing

EDITED BY J. I. MERRITT

WITH

MARGARET G. NICHOLS

AND THE EDITORS OF

FIELD & STREAM MAGAZINE

A FIRESIDE BOOK
Published by Simon & Schuster

FIRESIDE
Rockefeller Center
1230 Avenue of the Americas
New York, NY 10020

First Fireside Edition 1996
Published by arrangement with Lyons & Burford, Publishers, Inc.

FIRESIDE and colophon are registered trademarks of Simon & Schuster Inc.

Manufactured in the United States of America

1   3   5   7   9   10   8   6   4   2

Library of Congress Cataloging-in-Publication Data

The Best of Field & Stream : 100 years of great writing
/ edited by J. I. Merritt, with Margaret G.
Nichols and the editors of Field & Stream. — 1st Fireside ed.
p.   cm.
Originally published: New York : Lyons and Burford, 1995.
Includes index.
1. Hunting.   2. Fishing.   3. Outdoor recreation.   I. Merritt, J. I.
II. Nichols, Maggie.   III. Field & stream.
[SK9.B47   1996]
799—dc20   95–52846
                                                                  CIP
ISBN 0-684-81831-0

Contents

v

"The Soul of the American Outdoors"

J. I. MERRITT

THIS BOOK CELEBRATES a hundred years of outdoor writing in the pages of *Field & Stream*. The magazine has changed beyond measure since the first edition of what was then called *Northwestern Field and Stream: a Journal of the Rifle, Gun, Rod and Camera* rolled off the presses in St. Paul, Minnesota, but one constant in *Field & Stream*'s long history has been strong writing. The articles chosen for this anthology reflect that tradition. Many of them, too, echo themes as old as stories of any kind.

For most of his million-plus years on earth, man lived by hunting, fishing, and foraging for wild seeds and plants. At some point he invented spoken language and began telling stories of the hunt around campfires. He also "wrote" stories on the walls of caves and canyons in drawings and pictographs that have survived over time. Some ten thousand years ago, after man tamed a few animals and plants, he started down the slippery road toward civilization and all that goes with it, including taxes and traffic jams. But among civilization's benefits was writing: now man could record his deeds in words as well as pictures for peers and posterity. Hunting and fishing were some of the earliest subjects to be immortalized.

Xenophon, a soldier, historian, and member of the rarefied circle of Athenians that included Socrates and Plato, wrote a treatise on hunting in 400 B.C., making him the first outdoor writer. Like the works of so many of the type today, his treatise is descriptive and instructional (what editors call "how-to"), concerned with the tools and tactics for bagging various game of the rugged Greek countryside. He writes about nets, snares, javelins, and spears for the hunting of hares, deer, boars, bears, leopards, and lions. Xenophon tells us what to look for in good hunting dogs and how to train and care for them. He writes about them with admiration and affection, but also with an exasperation familiar to any owner of a hunting dog:

> Some start in pursuit of the hare with great speed, but relax for want of spirit; some run on, and then miss the scent; others run senselessly into the public roads, and so lose it, and show the utmost reluctance to be recalled. Many, abandoning the pursuit, turn back through dislike of the hare, or from longing for the society of their master... Some run after anything in uncertainty, while others fancy strongly that they are getting on a track.

For Xenophon, hunting also has its philosophical and moral dimensions. It is an "art": one blessed by the gods, he tells us, and whose skills and discipline promote virtue. No one can claim to be liberally educated who is not a hunter. Hunting improves health, makes for a better citizen and soldier, and prevents those pursuing it from lapsing into "viciousness or excessive pleasures of the senses."

With the revival of classical learning in the late Middle Ages and early Renaissance, this emphasis on the morality and ethics of hunting resurfaces in works like *The Art of Falconry*, by Frederick II, one of the ablest of the Holy Roman emperors. Frederick's thirteenth-century chivalric code equated virtue with nobility, and falconry was the noblest sport for the demands it makes on a falconer's knowledge of birds of prey. In the fourteenth century, a French nobleman, Gaston de Foix, wrote *Livre de Chasse*, which in 1406 was translated and expanded by Edward, Duke of York, as *The Master of Game*, the first book in English on hunting. Edward, one of Henry V's "band of brothers," died at Agincourt—a hero, we like to think, although he may have smothered in his armor; at any rate, in a 1909 edition of *The Master of Game*, kindred spirit Theodore Roosevelt extolled him as "a mighty lord and mighty hunter." Edward covers some of the same ground as Xenophon, but lavishes more detail on hunting dogs, whose specialized breeds—greyhound, alaunte, spaniel, mastiff—had begun to proliferate by the late Middle Ages. Also like Xenophon, he argues that hunting makes for a happy and virtuous life, free from idleness and lust, and pleasing to the Almighty: "All good habits and manners come from it, as well as the health of a man and his soul."

Fishing, like hunting, began for utilitarian purposes and evolved into a leisure pursuit with the rise of civilization. Prehistoric fishermen fashioned gorges and hooks from bone and ivory. Seven thousand years ago in the Middle East, copper fish hooks were among the first metal tools forged by neolithic smiths, and hooks of bronze and iron followed. No one knows when a fisherman first came up with the idea of leveraging a fish with a pole, but by the second millennium B.C. fishing rods were appearing on Egyptian tomb art. In China, angling was already an ancient pastime by the sixth century B.C., when Confucius worked through his moral philosophy while fishing for carp with a silk line and cane pole. By the twelfth century A.D. the Chinese were storing their lines on reels, but "winches," as they were called at first, didn't come into general use in Europe for another six hundred years.

The first work in English on fishing, *Treatise on Fishing with an Angle*, was published in 1496 but written much earlier in the century, probably not long after *The Master of Game*, whose virility it gently mocks. This extended essay is attributed to a nun, Dame Juliana Berners, who dismisses the chase as "too much work. The hunter must run all day and follow his hounds, laboring and sweating . . . He blows on his horn till his lips blister; and when he thinks it is a hare, very often it is a hedgehog." By contrast, the angler—even one who goes fishless—at the very least will have "his wholesome and merry walk at his own ease, and also many a sweet breath of various plants and flowers . . ." Angling makes for a joyful spirit, good health, a long life, and a contented soul.

Berners tells her readers how to build rods, make hooks, and weave lines from horsehair; the proper way to rig floats and sinkers; where and when to fish and the right baits and flies for various conditions and quarry. Izaak Walton covered some of the same ground 157 years later in *The Compleat Angler* (1653), a book that went through six editions in his long life (he lived to age ninety). Since Walton's day *The Compleat Angler* has appeared in more than 450 editions; among books in English, only the Bible and *Pilgrim's Progress* have been published more often.

Subtitled "The Contemplative Man's Recreation," Walton's work is an extended idyll, discursive and pastoral, filled with natural history and learned references to Scripture and classical writers; if occasionally pious, it is never pompous. The sweet-tempered Walton was a prosperous hardware merchant who lived through a tempestuous period in his nation's history, but his prose holds no hint of the civil war and religious strife raging all around him. In his rambling account of streamside picnics and encounters with milkmaids, the taking of fish becomes incidental to the pleasures of the English countryside and the companionship of "good-natured plain" fishermen.

Two centuries after Walton, "outdoor writers" were filling the pages of magazines in England and America. In the United States, the seemingly endless numbers of fish and game and a vast wilderness attracted sportsmen, adventurers, and those who saw nature's bounty as a source of income. Most stories about the outdoors were rambling descriptions of adventures afield, but a few writers—most notably Henry William Herbert, an expatriate Englishman who went by the pen name "Frank Forester"—recognized the dangers of unbridled enthusiasm and called for stricter game laws and a sporting code.

In the two decades prior to the Civil War, the prodigious Herbert wrote more than a hundred articles and a dozen books on hunting and fishing, and he can rightly claim title as America's first outdoor writer. The main outlet for his pieces was the country's first outdoor magazine, the *American Turf Register and Sporting Magazine*, launched in 1839 by New York sportsman William T. Porter. (As the title suggests, the *Turf Register* also covered horse racing.) Other periodicals devoted to field sports, natural history, and conservation came along in the years following the Civil War, an era marked by rapid economic growth and an accelerated exploitation of nature. The first of these journals, which appealed mainly to hunters and fishermen, was the monthly *American Sportsman*. It debuted in 1871, and with the others it editorialized against logging that wreaked havoc on watersheds, factories that fouled air and rivers, and market hunting that threatened entire species.

Forest and Stream, a New York-based weekly tabloid that appeared in 1873 and ran until 1930, when it was absorbed into *Field & Stream*, became the most influential sporting journal of its day, thanks to its crusading editors—initially Charles Hallock, then George Bird Grinnell. Hallock pushed for uniform game laws based on habitat rather than state boundaries, the management of forests for the benefit of wildlife, the protection of watersheds, and the restoration of fisheries harmed by commercial exploitation and pollution. Grinnell, who took over the editorship in 1880, founded the National Audubon Society and (with his friend Theodore Roosevelt) the Boone and Crockett Club, the country's first two national conservation organizations. As editor of *Forest and Stream*, he preached conservation until his retirement, in 1911. Meanwhile, his predecessor, Charles Hallock, came out of semiretirement in 1896 to edit the magazine that celebrates its hundredth year with the publication of this book.

The magazine was known as *Northwestern Field and Stream* when it appeared in St. Paul, Minnesota, in 1895. The fledgling journal, which consisted mostly of articles reprinted from other publications, made little impact, and it might have passed into oblivion had it not been taken over a year later by an enterprising local sportsman named John R. Burkhard. The new publisher had a vision to make it a national magazine, and he moved in that direction from the start by broadening the magazine's editorial scope and readership. He renamed the magazine *Western Field and Stream* ("A Journal for the True Sportsman," with a purpose to "Preserve, protect, propagate—not only for ourselves but for those who come after") and hired as its first editor Charles Hallock, who since leaving *Forest and Stream* had pursued several careers as an inventor, author, prospector, and farmer.

The first issue with the new title appeared in April 1896. In February 1897, Burkhard dropped "western" from the title, and by the following March he had relocated the magazine to New York City, to be closer to its advertising base. Hallock continued to contribute to the magazine, but the editor's job passed to Henry Wellington Wack, who used the pen name "Mark Biff". (For the record, the name "Field and Stream" had first appeared in 1874. The Chicago journal bearing that title changed its name several times and was called *American Field* when it went out of business, in 1900.)

From the beginning, *Field & Stream* sounded a clarion call in behalf of wildlife. It editorialized for conserving resources through shorter seasons and smaller bag limits, and made the case for uniform game laws, an end to market gunning, and a "universal gun tax or license" to pay for conservation measures and enforcement. (At the time, few states required hunting licenses.) Then as now, the appeals for conservation were made in an editorial context that focused on outdoor recreation. Most articles were upbeat, and informal to the point of being folksy, like letters between friends. The contents of the May 1896 issue are typical. They include a story about hunting and fishing along the upper Mississippi, a piece by "Mark Biff" on hunting moose in Minnesota, and an offbeat treatise by naturalist Elliott Coues on the uses of buffalo chips. A department aimed at sportswomen—titled "The Modern Diana"—offers a leisurely travelog about Wisconsin's Yellow River. Other departments cover fishing, photography, canoeing, and dogs. The issue features a poem ("Sweet May! Come Back Again!"), reports by various gun clubs on their activities, and such odds and ends as accounts of "Boer Marksmanship" and the killing of a giant alligator in North Carolina.

Despite an extraordinary growth in industry and population since the Civil War, the United States in the late nineteenth century remained a mostly rural society. In the year of *Field & Stream*'s founding, about 70 million people were scattered across the contiguous states and territories (the current U.S. population is nearly four times that). At twenty-three people per square mile, the population density was close to Nebraska's today. There were no automobiles or paved roads to speak of. Although railroads had given sportsmen access to remote areas, most hunting and fishing still took place within a walk or horseback ride from home. It was an era of unbridled capitalism, for good or ill; but it was a time of opportunity, too. For a fledgling enterprise like Burkhard's, finances were touch-and-go—reputedly, after moving to New York, he and his wife were too poor to afford housing, so they slept on cots in the back office. But by its tenth anniversary *Field & Stream* was fat with advertising and appeared to be prospering.

In the fall of 1906, an energetic and ambitious young man named Eltinge F. Warner joined the staff as general manager. A native of St. Paul, Warner had graduated from Princeton just five years before. He had been working for another magazine in New York and was eager to run his own show, and in 1907, after Burkhard's untimely death, he bought a controlling interest from the publisher's widow.

A cigar-champing autocrat of the old school of publishing, Warner owned the magazine for the next forty-four years. No man had a longer association with *Field & Stream*, and no one had more to do with its becoming the nation's leading sporting journal in circulation, advertising, and influence—a pinnacle it reached within a decade of his taking charge. A snapshot of Warner from this period shows him in a hunting camp, sitting on a stump with a rifle across his knees. He is squarely built, with a thick moustache, and looks more at home in the woods than in any office. His emphatic personality left its mark. Hugh Grey, the last editor to work with Warner, remembered him as "an entertainer, an evangelist, and a sound businessman. The businessman never prevailed: if Warner had to take an unpopular position . . . he took it boldly. If an advertisement was at all dubious, he rejected it violently. He cried out time and again that springtime shooting of waterfowl was a crime against decency—and this at a time when many of his readers were enjoying spring shooting."

A.J. McClane, *Field & Stream*'s long-time fishing editor, dined out on stories about Warner, a "dapper little trapper who somehow reminded me of a Groucho Marx with the spending habits of a J. Paul Getty." Warner hired McClane one morning in 1947, fired him before lunch after McClane left the office on his coffee break, then rehired him that afternoon. Warner was an accomplished slight-of-hand artist and practical joker, as McClane found out when he accompanied him and several friends on a hunting trip. Placing a fifty-cent piece under a hat, Warner bet a buddy that, when he snapped away the hat, McClane could slap his hand on the coin faster than the eye could see. McClane obliged—and squashed the egg his boss had slipped in place of the coin.

In the course of his long career, Warner's business interests greatly expanded. He produced movies, published the influential *Smart Set* (edited by H. L. Mencken), and headed a magazine chain. But *Field & Stream* remained his first love, and he used it to promote a range of conservation causes. He fought for forests and the protection of Pacific fur seals, and against pollution and the shooting of nongame birds when market gunners were killing robins and other songbirds by the barrel. He opened the magazine's pages to noted conservationists like Gifford Pinchot, William T. Hornaday, and Aldo Leopold. Observed Van Campen Heilner, who wrote and edited for the magazine for decades: "Warner proved that sportsmanship and conservation are two facets of the same thing."

For the first decade and a half of Warner's reign, the magazine evolved under the guidance of editors S. D. Barnes (1908–10), Warren H. "Cap" Miller (1910–18), and Hy S. Watson (1918–24). The multifaceted Watson not only edited but wrote and illustrated articles, and even painted a number of covers. Milestones of the period included the first *Field & Stream* fishing contest (1911) and the serialization of Zane Grey's instant classic of the American West, *Riders of the Purple Sage* (1912–13). (Grey was a regular contributor of fishing articles. But the editors took broadly their mandate to publish "outdoor" writing, including fiction and poetry.) On the conservation front, from 1910 to 1917 *Field & Stream* served as the official publication of the Camp Fire Club of America, an activist group whose membership claimed such towering figures as forester Gifford Pinchot, naturalist Ernest Thompson Seton, and Theodore Roosevelt.

In 1918 the magazine began carrying the Bulletin of the American Game Protective Association. The bulletin's editor, Ray P. Holland, was soon contributing articles to *Field & Stream* under the byline "Bob White." This was still the era of the six-day work week, but Hy Watson, *Field & Stream*'s editor, routinely toiled on Sundays and holidays, too. Perhaps as a result, his tenure ended abruptly in the spring of 1924, when he suffered a nervous breakdown. Warner replaced him with Holland, a straight-laced Kansan who ran the editorial side for the next seventeen years.

The forty-year-old Holland had solid editorial skills and a deep knowledge of hunting and fishing, but what most impressed Warner was the editor's moral authority. Among conservationists, Holland had achieved near-legendary status for his efforts as a U.S. game warden to enforce the Migratory Bird Treaty Act, enacted in 1916, which established federal control over the shooting of ducks and other migratory birds and effectively outlawed market gunning and spring shooting. But the states saw the act as an infringement of their sovereignty, and Frank W. McAllister, Missouri's attorney general, flouted it by shooting ducks out of season in the spring of 1918. When federal warden Holland heard that McAllister and some powerful friends were hunting at a private club, he staked out the place and caught them with ninety-three ducks in their possession. A series of counter-moves followed, including a suit filed in a federal court by the State of Missouri claiming that Holland had acted unconstitutionally. *Missouri v. Holland* made its way to the U.S. Supreme Court, which in 1920 decided for Holland—and for wildlife.

Holland kept *Field & Stream* in the forefront of conservation. In his first year as editor, the magazine established the Field & Stream Conservation Council, a ten-member board dedicated to the creation of a national waterfowl refuge system to be funded by "duck stamps," which waterfowlers would be required to purchase along with their state hunting licenses. The council happily retired itself after the system—and duck stamps—became reality in 1934. In that same year, the magazine began a conservation department devoted to the "Square Circle," a loose organization of hunters and fishermen who spread the word about conservation and sportsmanship.

Editorially, *Field & Stream* continued to evolve. It started departments on camping (including car camping) and boating. The stately travelogs of earlier days gave way to more focused pieces emphasizing how-to. True-life wilderness adventure remained a staple.

Like others before and since, Holland discovered that editing a major outdoor magazine doesn't leave enough time for being outdoors. So in 1941, he took early retirement for the stated purpose of getting in more hunting and fishing. The editor's job passed to David M. Newell, a genial Floridian and a longtime contributor to the magazine. Newell was skilled at both writing and art, and like Hy Watson he occasionally illustrated his own pieces. But he too tired of his deskbound existence in Manhattan, and in 1946 he returned to his beloved Florida. Over the years he continued to contribute articles to the magazine.

Warner filled the vacated editor-in-chief's chair by promoting the managing editor, Hugh Grey. A native of eastern Massachusetts, Grey had started his career with several Boston-based outdoor magazines and had worked for *Newsweek* before coming to *Field & Stream* in the late 1930s. He proved an inspired choice, guiding the magazine for twenty years—the longest tenure of any top editor in *Field & Stream*'s century of publishing.

When Grey became the editor, the magazine's offices were at 515 Madison Avenue. He remembered that "El," as everyone called Warner, asked artist Arthur D. Fuller to paint the doors of the men's and women's rooms, respectively, with portraits of a pointer and a setter. Warner so loved his sly joke that when the offices moved to another floor of the building, he insisted the doors go, too. Neither restroom had a sign—the paintings were the only clues about which was which, but anyone working for an outdoor magazine presumably knew bird dogs, or learned fast. But what about visitors? Grey recalled his father's dropping by and asking directions for the men's room. His son pointed down the hall and explained the system. "He saw the first door with a dog on it and went right in." It was, of course, the ladies' room.

The booming post-World War II economy fueled the magazine industry. By the time Grey retired, in 1966, a typical issue of *Field & Stream* was stuffed with advertising and ran to more than two hundred pages. Color photos and paintings by top artists and illustrators took over from the old black-and-white graphics. Grey sent writers to exotic regions like South America and East Africa to report on hunting and fishing frontiers. He also had a sharp eye for talent and attracted major writers as regular columnists, including Robert Ruark ("The Old Man and the Boy"), Corey Ford ("The Lower Forty"), H.G. Tapply ("Tap's Tips"), and the incomparable Ed Zern ("Exit Laughing").

Through all these changes, *Field & Stream* continued to speak out in behalf of the sportsman's environment. In the late 1940s it ran articles warning about the dangers to wildlife of the insecticide DDT—fifteen years before Rachel Carson's *Silent Spring*—and acted as an early warning system on many other issues, among them the increasing threat to fish and fishermen from water pollution, the dangerous overharvesting of offshore and coastal fish, and the serious drop in numbers of breeding ducks.

In 1951, after forty-five years in the harness and 540 issues of *Field & Stream*, Eltinge Warner sold the magazine and retired. In a farewell to readers, he noted that the "passage of time is measured in many ways. All of them are too slow when we are young, too fast as we grow older." It was the end of an era, but *Field & Stream* continued to flourish under a series of corporate owners: Henry Holt and Company (later Holt, Rinehart and Winston; 1951–72), CBS Publications (1972–88), and Times Mirror Magazines (1988–present). Following Grey, the magazine's editorial direction was in the hands of veteran outdoor journalists Clare Conley (1966–72) and Jack Samson (1972–81), who added Bob Brister (shooting), Bill Tarrant (gun dogs), Ken Schultz (fishing), Patrick F. McManus (humor), George Reiger (conservation), and Gene Hill (Hill Country) to the list of regular contributors.

Field & Stream's current editor, Duncan Barnes, took over in 1981. Prior to joining the magazine, Barnes, who grew up in New York State and majored in English at Dartmouth College, wrote about the outdoors for the St. Petersburg (Florida) *Times* and *Sports Illustrated*, and was editorial director of the Winchester Press. During the past fourteen years, he has built on the magazine's tradition of strong writing and has sought to create an equally strong artistic presence in its pages. Under the direction of award-winning designer Daniel McClain, the finest in sporting art and photography are used each month to make as compelling and colorful a statement as the articles they illustrate.

One thing that hasn't changed from the magazine's first issue to the present, says Barnes, is the absolute necessity of conservation:

"Without being overly preachy, it's important to keep reminding readers that the resource must come first—that without sound stewardship of our land and waters, there won't be any hunting and fishing. *Field & Stream*'s readers benefit from our writers' technical expertise, but most readers know there's more to hunting and fishing than bagging a buck or filling a live-well with bass. We stress the outdoor *experience*, which goes way beyond how many fish you catch or the size of an elk's rack. Hunting and fishing are about connecting with nature, yourself, and others. They're about enjoying the sight of an osprey plucking a fish from a river on a day when you've gone fishless, or the pleasure of following a good dog through a cornfield with your child or dad or an old friend, whether or not you get any birds.

"As this collection of great writing from its hundred-year history shows, *Field & Stream* has always provided not just information, but adventure, nostalgia, humor, philosophy, tradition, and good old-fashioned yarns. In this rich mixture of entertainment, education, and visual splendor, you'll find the soul of the magazine . . . and the soul of the American outdoors."

January 1995

Editor's Note

Putting together this treasury of the best of *Field & Stream*, we tried to include as many old favorites as possible. But inevitably some popular writers had to be left out. So, although you'll find such past regulars as Gordon McQuarrie and Frank Dufresne, you won't find Arthur McDougall, author of the Dud Dean series; W. C. Tuttle and his Rudolph the Barber; or a number of other fine authors who entertained readers over the years. The choices were difficult, and we regret having to make them at all. But we're sure you'll agree that what we did include is great stuff, a memorable collection of good reading and a fascinating look at the scope of "outdoor writing" over the years.

Song of the Angler

A. J. McCLANE

*To a fisherman, the sounds of a river and pounding surf are as musical
as any symphony, and twice as compelling.*

EOPLE OFTEN ASK me why I enjoy fishing, and I cannot explain it to them because there is no reason in the way they want
meanings described. They are asking a man why he enjoys
breathing when he really has no choice but to wonder at its truth.
Psychologists such as Dr. Ronald Ley (*Why Anglers Really Angle*, February
1967) have tried to explain its mystique in terms of behavioral conditioning,
but this is as oddly misleading as his comparison of angling to golf. There are
also pundits who believe that the rod provides an outlet for our hostilities,
our frustrated egos, or our competitive instincts, or that it symbolizes the
primitive feelings of man in his search for food, *ergo* the need to kill. To a degree I believe all these qualities exist in every participant in any sport, and if
so, healthfully so, as it is far more harmless to vent one's spleen on a trout
stream or a golf course than on one's fellow man. However, if this assumption
is logical, then the rationale of *angling* is still without explanation.

The chirping plague of analysts who have invaded every chamber of
the mind from the bedroom to the tackle room has missed one thing—angling
is a robe that a man wears proudly. It is tightly woven in a fabric of moral,
social, and philosophical threads which are not easily rent by the violent climate
of our times. It is foolish to think, as it has been said, that all men who fish
are good men, as evil exists on all of life's paths; but to join Walton's "company
of honest men" requires first the ability to accept a natural tempo of misfortune not only in the allegory where failure is represented by the loss of a fish
(or success by its capture) but in life itself. In the lockstep slogan of young
radicals thumbing their noses at their world, reality is no longer realistic; but I
would argue that life is a greater challenge than death, and that reality is as close

as the nearest river. Perhaps an exceptional angler doesn't prove the rule, but then anglers are exceptional people.

Lord Fraser of Lonsdale is not only a peer, but he wears the robe of an angler as well. He is a skilled fly-fisherman, and when last we visited together, he caught a 35-pound salmon which was the biggest in the camp for many weeks. What's more, he could charm the socks off Willie Sutton, and I have heard him spellbind a roomful of strangers with tales of his life in South Africa, while sipping rare wines, naming each chateau and its vintage. This introduction would be fatuous were it not for the fact that Lord Fraser is totally blind. Both of his eyes were shot out in the First World War. A profoundly intellectual man, Fraser has developed his other senses to a point that most of the people who sat with him that night had no idea that he was unable to see them; yet later he could summarize the physical characteristics of each person as though he was describing a rare burgundy.

I don't know if you have ever tried wading (unaided) and fly fishing a stream while blindfolded. I cannot do it, and I would probably lack the guts if I *had* to do it. Fraser's explanation for his ability to do this is that he can hear all things around him: the changing tempo of deep and shallow water, the curling smack of a rapid against a boulder, even the roll or rise of a fish. His ear for the music of angling is incredibly keen. Is this Dr. Ley's behavioral conditioning? In terms of a compensatory development of the senses, perhaps, but it does not explain *why* a man, even a blind man, enjoys angling.

The music of angling is more compelling to me than anything contrived in the greatest symphony hall. What could be more thrilling than the ghostly basso note of a channel buoy over a grumbling surf as the herring gulls screech at a school of stripers on a foggy summer morning? Or an organ chorus of red howler monkeys swinging over jungle stream as the tarpon roll and splash in counterpoint? I have heard them all—the youthful voice of the little Beaverkill, the growling of the Colorado as it leaps from its den, the kettledrum pounding of the Rogue, the hiss of the Yellowstone's riffles, the sad sound of the Orinoco, as mournful as a G chord held on a guitar. These are more familiar to me than Bach, Beethoven, and Brahms, and for my part more beautiful. If there are three "B's" in angling, they are probably the Beaverkill, the Broadhead, and the Big Hole.

Big-game angling has quite another music. The hull creaks and the outriggers clap as the ship comes into the wind while the sea increases the tempo as she turns from stern to bow. Then the frigate birds scream at a ball of bait and you know the marlin are below. As the ship lurches over the chop her screws bite air in a discordant whine and the mullet trails *skitter flap skitter flap* until the pitching hull sounds like the soft rolling of drums.

At last one note assails the ears, the *snap* of white linen pulled from the outrigger. Now the water explodes in a crescendo of hot engines roaring into life before you lean into a quarter ton of shoulder-rocking fury. And in that ageless walking leap which follows no path in the ocean the angler hears the most exciting sound of all—the wailing of a reel as stark and as lonely as a Basin Street clarinet.

But my protracted maundering leads us away from Dr. Ley's hypothesis which he reinforced with the learned E. L. Thorndike's thesis of punishments and rewards. What *are* the rewards of angling? A dead fish? A trophy? At some point perhaps, but then it takes years to become an angler.

There are tidal marks in our development. In the beginning, when one is very young and inexperienced, fish are measured in quantity. Then, only quality becomes important. Eventually even record fish lose their significance unless they are of a particular species, and ultimately the size doesn't matter provided they are difficult to catch.

The latter condition is fairly easy to find in these days of declining resources. Trout in the upper Beaverkill, for instance, are generally ½-pound in weight, but they can be the most demanding kind. The water is diamond clear and at the shadow of a passing bird or the glint of sun against rod they instantly vanish under the nearest boulder. You must work with a leader of cobweb diameter and have enough control to drop your fly in a teacup target through a maze of overhanging limbs. There are large trout in the stream, of course, wise old browns which you might catch a glimpse of once in awhile, usually in a pool that everybody believes has been emptied.

Recalling the years when anglers gathered at the old Gould cottage on the Beaverkill—a temple now fallen to death and taxes—which Arnold Gingrich described in his wonderful book, *The Well-Tempered Angler* (you can even smell the waders drying in the rafters)—one man comes to mind who knew perhaps a bit more about the rewards of angling than most of us.

Ellis Newman could cast a fly line to 90 feet with his bare hands. I saw him make three measured casts with tournament tackle, each of which fell short of 200 feet by inches. I doubt if a more polished caster ever lived. He had neither the time nor the inclination to compete in games (except for the pigeon shooting circuit which he did for money). We often fished along opposite banks of the Beaverkill, or alternated pools, just for the pleasure of each other's company.

One day, when the mayflies were on the water, Ellis caught and released several good browns below the dam, one going about 3 pounds. At the top of the next run we met a young boy who proudly displayed a 9-inch brook trout. Ellis admired it so much that I thought we were looking at the biggest squaretail captured since Cook hit the jackpot on the Nipigon in 1914. When the lad asked Ellis if he had any luck, he looked very serious; "Oh, I caught a few, but none were as *pretty* as yours."

Ellis worked with underprivileged children and handicapped people at his own expense. And the expense was appreciable. He designed Rube Goldberg wheelchairs and tractor-driven bucket seats for fishing and for hunting as well, and he even developed a method of running steel cable through a string of boulders to build "necklace" dams on his eroding Beaverkill. Ellis never waited for the fulmination of a new idea to die down before putting it into practice, and the people who loved him may be consoled with the reflection that angling would have suffered a greater blow had he regarded each new venture carefully.

Arnold Gingrich became, as Charley Ritz once called him, "that terrible fishing machine" in the sense that he was on a first-name basis with every trout in the stream. He would appear with smaller and smaller fly rods, considering any stick over 2 ounces as heavy tackle, and any leader above 7X suitable only for salmon. But the publisher of *Esquire* magazine is a tremendously energetic individual and the piston-like style of casting with flea rods was duck soup for him.

Arnold earned his robe in my eyes the first time we angled together; in releasing a tired trout he held the fish underwater gently, almost lovingly, stroking its belly and talking to it. He is a master of conversation and, so help me, at times the fish swim away with an impossible but perceptible grin on their faces. Arnold has that passionate blood fire, typical of anglers, which no psychologist (nor wife who hears her husband stumbling out into an April blizzard at 4 a.m.) has satisfactorily explained.

One morning I was crossing the Swinging Bridge Pool and happened to look down; there stood Arnold in an icy torrent banging away with a little dry fly. Something was protruding from his mouth. I didn't recall that Arnold smoked cigars.

"When did you start smoking cigars?" I called. He pulled the bulbous object from his mouth and examined it as though he didn't know it was there.

"Oh. That's my stream thermometer."

"Your *what*?"

"I'm sick. I have a fever."

"Then what are you doing in the river?"

"Oh hell, it's only 99.8 If I break 100, I'll go to bed."

Whenever somebody asks me why I enjoy fishing another thing that comes to mind is what it means in terms of friendships. General Charles Lindeman was always impeccably dressed, cologne lashed, and wearing his stiff upper lip as Counsel to the British Ambassador in Washington. During the years we fished together he had a running verbal duel with Charles Ritz for reasons which only an Englishman would feel about a Frenchman and vice-versa. There was no evil lurking beneath this play of wit; it had the woolly camaraderie of barracks talk. When Lindeman stepped into the river, Ritz would ask him, "Where is your gaff, old boy? *All* Englishmen carry gaffs." Although a stranger would think that the General meant to hang Ritz with his old school tie, they were really fond of each other.

This good-natured combativeness continued until we stopped to lunch on the bank of the Stamp River one noon. A sudden change came over the General. For a moment he became misty-eyed. He told us that he had sat in this very spot with his young wife a half-century before and made his life's plans. Now she was buried in France, a geographical anomaly which he made no attempt to explain except to refer to a wartime plane crash. Later that day, while I was beaching a steelhead, I saw Ritz crawling along the bank picking wild flowers. Swearing me to silence he carefully packed a bouquet in his duffle bag. "I know the cemetery outside of Paris. I will take these to her. She would like that."

Lindeman didn't know what he had done, and despite my old friend's deserved reputation as one of the world's great anglers, I would embarrass him now by saying that Charles Ritz wears his robe because he is a truly kind and loving man. The General is gone, and it wasn't until his death a few years ago that a certain irony became apparent in our secret when he learned that General Lindeman had been Chief of the British Secret Service.

The only psychologist I have ever met who knew anything about anglers was Dr. J. H. Cooper of Kansas City, Missouri. He made sense because he invented the marabou bonefish jig, which reveals him as a practical man. We met, as anglers so often do, through his giving me a duplicate of his lure at a time when I was having lousy fishing at Andros Island.

Have you ever noticed how often anglers tend to share their good fortune? I have seen this happen many times among perfect strangers who simply meet on a stream. I remember a man who, after landing a beautiful rainbow trout below the Fair Ground Bridge on the East Branch of the Delaware, turned to a bug-eyed kid holding a 98-cent telescopic fly rod, and snipping the March Brown pattern off his leader gave it to the boy. "See what you can do with it, son." That's all he said. I was that boy and I can't tie a

March Brown on my leader today without blessing my Good Samaritan.

Before you conclude that the author has broken loose from his moorings and is bobbing impotently on a sea of virtue, let me reassure you that the world is full of narrowly shrewd self-seeking people, blind to God and goodness, and for all I know, Dame Juliana Berners could have been some piscatorial Mary Poppins or a grosser wart on the face of society than Polly Adler. But I would be untrue to my craft if I did not add that although we live in a curiously touchy age when Mom's apple pie, the flag, and the Boy Scout's oath are losing currency, these still make a better frame of reference than Harvard's pellet fed rats or Pavlov's dogs.

Psychologists tell us that one reason why we enjoy fishing is because it is an escape. This is meaningless. True, a man who works in the city wants to "escape" to the country, but the clinical implication is that (no matter where a man lives), he seeks to avoid reality. This is as obtuse as the philosophical doctrine which holds that no reality exists outside the mind.

Perhaps it's the farm boy in me, but I would apply Aristotelian logic—the chicken came before the egg because it is real and the egg is only potential. By the same reasoning the fluid content of a stream is nothing but water when it erupts from a city faucet but given shores it becomes a river, and as a river it is perfectly capable of creating life, and therefore it is real. It is not a sewer, nor a conveyor of barges and lumber, although it can be pressed to these burdens and, indeed, as a living thing it can also become lost in its responsibilities.

So if escapism is a reason for angling—then the escape is *to* reality. The sense of freedom that we enjoy in the outdoors is, after all, a normal reaction to a more rational environment.

Who but an angler knows that magic hour when the red lamp of summer drops behind blackening hemlocks and the mayflies emerge from the dull folds of their nymphal robes to dance in ritual as old as the river itself? Trout appear one by one and the angler begins his game in movements as stylized as Japanese poetry. Perhaps he will hook that wonder-spotted rogue, or maybe he will remain in silent pantomine long into the night with no visible reward.

And that, Professor, is why anglers *really* angle.

October 1967

The "Ferocious" Commuter

A.J. McCLANE

*By accident and design, and to the delight of anglers, the plucky bronzeback
has spread far from its ancestral waters.*

I REMEMBER THE RIVER in spring with its rosy-fingered dawns
mirrored on hemlock-shaded pools when bankside cobwebs were
spangled with luminous dew; and in the fall, when the sun fell like a
golden melon over the edge of the world, as it does before evening's
chill, lighting the forest floor where maple leaves are soon limned with frost.
And in drought summers, when great boulders lay bare and the riverbed
looked like some prehistoric backbone twisted in a hundred sinuous curves.
There was only one daily train into our town, and after it departed, the sta-
tionmaster, Dan Todd, often invited me to ride his handcar, to help pump the
machine down the tracks. The railroad followed the river, and in many places
we had a bird's eye view of the water from its high banks.

Dan was a nut fly fisherman, and just the sight of swallows or cedar
waxwings dancing over a riffle was reason enough to stop and try a few casts.
Although occupying the same pools, smallmouth bass were a kind of
sideshow on the East Branch of the Delaware—brown trout were the stellar
event—but the spectral forms of bass rising to a hatch of mayflies or stone-
flies, or a bounty of flying ants, was to a teenage addict worth pumping another 5 miles. I was immune to the salmonid syndrome (the idea that bass
were inferior to trout extended all through traditional New England until recent years), and to me the bronze acrobat was maybe not as smart as the
brown trout but more endearing for that reason. But if smallmouth fishing has
a modern genesis, it began with the American railroads, for *Micropterus dolomieu*
was at one time a regular commuter with a finfull of one-way tickets.

According to fossil records, the earliest known fishes go back to the
Ordovician Age, about 400 million years ago. A group that eventually evolved

from the existing herringlike and salmonlike Clupeiformes with their soft-rayed fins—and this was about 60 million years ago—became the Perciformes with fins supported by both soft and spiny rays. This physical transition was the origin of thousands of marine and freshwater species, including the sunfish family. Exactly where or when a percoid fish became a genuine smallmouth bass is not known, but in a modern form it appeared in the Great Lakes during the late Pleistocene glaciation about 20,000 years ago. Its original range in the memory of man was limited to the Great Lakes and parts of the Mississippi basins in North America extending from northern Minnesota and southern Ontario eastward to Quebec, and from Minnesota south to northern Alabama and eastern Oklahoma.

The smallmouth first appeared in print in 1664 when Pierre Boucher published his *Histoire Veritable et Naturelle de la Nouvelle France*. Of course, "New France" was the province of Quebec, bordering the St. Lawrence River, where the abundant bass was known by the Algonquin Indian name *achigan*, which means "ferocious." In French-speaking Canada it is still called *achigan à petit bouche*. But elsewhere its distribution was a slow process of transplanting the fish beginning in the mid-1800's; Connecticut in 1842, Massachusetts in 1850, Maryland in 1854, New Jersey in 1866, Maine in 1869, Vermont and Pennsylvania in 1870. Railroads followed all the big river systems and bass were often dumped off trestles by angling hobbyist engineers in the genre of Dan Cahill, who originated the Cahill fly pattern.

Trout fishing in a modern sense did not exist in that era. Eggs of the western rainbow trout were only shipped to eastern hatcheries in 1877 and the brown trout didn't arrive in America from Germany until 1883, so a great void was being filled by the smallmouth before the turn of the century. The smallmouth did arrive in New York as early as 1825, but by accident rather than intent. It was naturally dispersed at the completion of the Erie Canal, giving the fish access to the Hudson River watershed.

None of these introductions was more fruitful than the journeys made by General William Shriver, who delivered a total of thirty small bass in a perforated tin bucket hung in the water tender of a locomotive in 1854—from West Virginia to the Chesapeake and Ohio Canal. The canal drained into the Potomac where, in the following decade, the smallmouth population boomed and spread through 200 miles of that river system including the fabled Shenandoah. This was the seed stock for some enthusiastic Pennsylvania anglers who caught them at Harper's Ferry and transported live-boxes full to Lord de la Warre's namesake river. As a result, the Delaware soon became one of the most productive bass streams in the East. In these pristine habitats, the smallmouths often weighed 5 to 7 pounds, according to the *Baltimore Sun*, with 4-pounders more or less commonplace.

Fishing of this kind no longer exists. Declining water quality took its toll; the fish marinated in a mixture of pesticides, coal dust, mercury, fertilizers, acid mine drainage, PCBs, acid rain, and God-knows-what-all, and the survival of the smallmouth in many Eastern waters is a miracle in itself. The all-tackle world record has been on the books for thirty-five years now, and it may well represent a climax weight for the species. In July of 1955, David L. Hayes caught a 27-inch-long, 11-pound 15-ounce smallmouth in Dale Hollow Lake, Kentucky. The only other bronzeback approaching that size taken in recent years was a 10-pound 8-ounce fish from Hendricks Creek in Kentucky. And the only other states reporting big smallmouths in the last decade, that is to say bass over 8 pounds, are Tennessee and Alabama. In northern waters, a 5-pounder is an exceptional catch, and it may take ten or twelve years to grow to that size (a fourteen-year-old Maine smallmouth is the oldest on record).

Some years ago, biologists tried an experiment in intrageneric hybridization, crossing smallmouth bass with the largemouth, and the result was more *achigan* than the Algonquins had in mind. Dr. William Childers, reporting on bass genetics, observed that hybrids occasionally bit swimmers, actually lacerating the flesh, and several fish attacked a woman, striking her in the head and chest, driving her from the pond. The hybrids also attacked a dog in shallow water, and while Childers was inspecting a bass nest for eggs, the guarding male bass bit his leg.

Dubbed the "meanmouth bass," it is debatable which parent produced the mean genes. Either species will, when big enough, eat just about anything that will fit in its jaws. However, favorite foods of the smallmouth include crayfish, insects, salamanders, shiners, sculpins, madtoms, darters, tadpoles, frogs, and the occasional field mouse. Forage availability is the determining factor; bass in the Shenandoah River for example, feed heavily on the abundant madtom, while bronzebacks in Maine's Big Lake gorge on insects, especially mayflies. Red-bellied dace can be an important food in one river, while the common shiner means chow-time in another.

For my part, the best of all smallmouth fishing is with the fly rod. There is a great variety of lures that will take fish: cork and balsa popping bugs; streamers like the Muddler, Zonker, and Woolly Bugger; dry flies and nymphs of all kinds; hair bugs that imitate frogs, mice, crayfish; and even some basic saltwater patterns. For years I have been fishing for bass with inverted hook bonefish flies that are virtually snagproof. One of the most effective patterns for me has been the epoxy-weighted Crazy Charlie, white- or pink-winged with strips of silver flashabou. For most fishing, I do well with three lures; a Queen Bee popper, a Black Woolly Bugger, and a Crazy Charlie, all on No. 6 hooks.

In lakes during those hot-weather periods when smallmouths retreat to deep water, I take along an ultralight spinning outfit and use grubtails, marabou jigs, spinnerbaits, and sonic plugs or rattlers. I prefer small lures with plenty of wiggle or vibrating action in weights from ⅟₁₆ to ¼ ounce. Maybe it's an antique in the eyes of my peers, but I still use a 5½-foot *fiberglass* rod that weighs just 1½ ounces. In my opinion, space-age graphite and its composites are too stiff and too fast for casting ultralight lures; in the process of our building better mousetraps, only the mice have prospered.

On rivers, one can reach fishable depths of 4 to 6 feet with a sinking fly line and still have fun, but when working blind in lakes where bass are often down 12 feet or more, casting and retrieving becomes a laborious process, and long lengths of heavy taper handicap the spirited play of the fish. With a 4-pound-test monofilament on ultralight, I can comb the shoals, ledges, and dropoffs with a featherweight rod and enjoy the tug and pull of even a modest-sized bass.

Any roll call of the best smallmouth waters must include the James, Shenandoah, and Susquehanna Rivers, the South Branch of the Potomac, Lake Champlain, Rainy Lake, the Quetico Wilderness areas, parts of the St. Lawrence, parts of the Connecticut River, the upper Penobscot River (between, this is for real, Dassadumkeag and Mattawamkeag), Norris Lake, Pickwick Lake, and Dale Hollow Reservoir. My angling year includes a considerable variety of gamefish, but I haven't missed at least one lengthy smallmouth trip in over four decades. I like the spring season best, fiddlehead and apple blossom time, when a bronzeback in the shallows will spring panther-like at a surface lure, then make a rocketing jump; such a simple act but always a startling experience no matter how often it is repeated. It is about as explicable as the electric pulse of sound through silent space.

September 1990

Izaak Walton:
His Friends and His Rivers

RODERICK HAIG-BROWN

Behind the simple prose was a man as complex as his times.

W HEN WALTON PUBLISHED *The Compleat Angler*, he was sixty years old. He was a mature, wise, gentle fisherman who had developed a calm and deeply philosophical attitude toward his sport. Reading his book, one imagines him a charming old man, a ready friend, not unlearned, yet quite simple and remote from the great world. And one is entitled to the opinion, for Walton himself says of his book: ". . . the whole Discourse is, or rather was, a picture of my own disposition; especially in such days and times as I have laid aside business . . ."

The qualification is an important one, for Walton was the intimate friend of some of the truly great minds of his time. A devout Protestant and staunch Royalist, he lived through some of the most troubled political and religious years of his nation's history. He was a craftsman and a businessman, of whose formal education we know little or nothing. Yet he wrote a lot of good and important things besides *The Compleat Angler*.

Altogether, it is dangerous to form too simple a picture of just what manner of man he was. Perhaps his capacity for friendship, based on a tranquil and tolerant nature and deep understanding, is the key to him. Unfailingly sincere he was; simple, he cannot have been.

So far as anyone knows, Walton was the son of unpretentious country folk, small landowners perhaps, in Staffordshire. He moved to London, as an apprentice ironmonger, when he was seventeen or eighteen, and was admitted to the guild as a full-fledged craftsman when he was twenty-five. For the next twenty or thirty years he carried on his trade, in small shops in or near Fleet Street, and found time to build the experience from which he wrote *The Compleat Angler*.

It is tempting to wonder just what manner of store he kept and what manner of iron he wrought. Did he, perhaps, forge fish hooks, the Pennells and Limericks and offsets of his day? Was he the original prototype of the hardware-sporting goods dealer of North America? There is no direct evidence of this, yet it was in his business years that he entered into close friendship with some of the great men of his day, several of whom are known to have been keen anglers. In his little store he would have made and sold such small things as hinges, locks, latches and weathercocks. Occasionally he may have undertaken larger work, such as wrought-iron gates or railings.

In *The Compleat Angler*, Walton puts little emphasis on tackle, but this is natural enough, for his tackle was quite simple, and he had advanced far beyond the youthful stage where enthusiasm for tackle almost obscures angling itself. There can be no doubt that he had more practical skill with his hands than most of his friends, or that he was able to help them in many little mechanical problems. Walton was a 30-year-old ironmonger, with strong literary interests, and with growing skill and experience in the art of angling.

Among Walton's closest friends during his business years were several who were twenty or thirty years older than he, and who died nearly fifty years before him. Sir Henry Wotton was an ambassador and poet, Provost of Eton College, a famous man and an angler. Dr. John Donne, an enormously popular preacher and a poet who powerfully influenced later poets, so precociously brilliant that he entered Oxford at eleven years of age, was known as a difficult and exacting man, yet Walton became his intimate and adoring friend. He was also an angler. Michael Drayton, often known as the river poet, was an intimate of Shakespeare and Ben Johnson as well as Walton, and he too must surely have been an angler. John Hales, scholar and fellow of Eton College, known as "one of the clearest heads in Christendom," was Walton's friend, and fished with him.

It requires no stretch of the imagination to see such men meeting in Walton's shop to discuss with him literary, political and religious affairs of the day, forgetting his comparative youth as they drew upon the reserves of faith and cheerfulness that were so strongly in him. It may have been they were attracted a little by the chance to pick over a batch of hooks fresh from the forge or test out a new rod butt bound with hoops of iron. Certainly there would have been some seventeenth-century equivalent of "The Thames is hot right now, out by Waltham Cross," and envious attention to Walton's accounts of great fish hooked on his latest trip to the wilds of Staffordshire or Derbyshire.

These men were men of the world, involved in large affairs and not without strenuous ambitions. The times they lived in were difficult and dangerous times for men of ideas and ambition. Donne had been in prison and had known extreme poverty. John Hales was thrown out of his fellowship at Eton for refusing to take a seventeenth-century loyalty oath and died in poverty. Sir Henry Wotton once fell into severe disfavor during his foreign service, and was arrested for debt when he was Provost of Eton. Drayton had seen the whole edition of his first volume of poems destroyed by order of the Archbishop of Canterbury.

It was a harsh time in which to think vigorously, but Walton had standards of religious faith and earthly loyalty that seemed to grow stronger all through his life. He knew, perhaps more fully than any other man ever has, the sources of fulfillment and freshness that were to be found in the countryside and in his gentle art. No doubt he talked as easily and gracefully as he wrote. It is not very difficult to believe that his powerful friends found him at once stronger and more rewarding, surer in his assessments of life and living, than they were themselves. And it is unlikely that ever, in all their discourses together, they could have suspected him of a false or insincere word.

Donne, Drayton and Herbert all died before Walton was forty. Sir Henry Wotton went not long after them. They left Walton, with other friends, to live on into far more troubled times of revolution and religious persecution. For all his serenity and strength, Walton must have been forced to test and search his conscience many times.

In 1649 he saw his king executed. He himself was living in Clerkenwell, only a few doors from Cromwell's house, where the death warrant is said to have been signed. In 1651, at the time of the battle of Worcester and only two years before *The Angler* was first published, he was in Stafford, no doubt quietly fishing the Sow and the Trent. Shortly after the battle he visited a Mr. Milward, a Royalist friend who was imprisoned in Stafford. Milward handed to Walton a ring known as the lesser George, which belonged to the King, and asked him to deliver it to Colonel Blague, who was imprisoned in the Tower of London. Walton did exactly that, and Blague escaped from the tower and returned the lesser George to the King in France.

To understand the full meaning of this, it is necessary to remember the importance that men of those days set upon such symbols of office and power. Cromwell's regime deliberately destroyed the ancient crowns of England, including St. Edward's crown, as though by so doing the return of kings could be prevented. Nearly forty years later, the last despairing act of Judge Jefferies, after the abdication of James II, was to throw the privy seal into the Thames. Men were hung, drawn and quartered for far more trivial offenses than Walton's. Yet it is certain he went about it with a calm mind and conscience, secure in the conviction that what he did was right and necessary.

One wonders what precautions he took, for he must have been known as a Royalist. It would be satisfying to believe he went out beside the Thames with grasshopper or minnow (the latter by preference, for Thames trout are big and hard to persuade) and caught himself a great trout. Then, having dressed it as he dressed the chub, "making the hole as little and near to the gills as you conveniently may," he slipped the lesser George into the fish's belly and carried it safely to his friend the colonel in the Tower. But it seems more likely that, secure in the armor of a clear conscience and a simple courage, he just walked through the guards with the jewel in his pocket.

This is sometimes referred to as "the only known adventure" in Walton's long, quiet life. Yet clearly it was not. Having the friends he had, holding the beliefs he held, he must often have been in danger. It is known that he moved from Chancery Lane in 1644 because it was "dangerous for honest men to be there." We know, too, that many of his friends, perhaps the majority of them, were highly placed churchmen, at a time when churchmen were always in trouble.

Two years after *The Compleat Angler* was first published there was much religious persecution, and the clergy were banished from London. Walton quietly records that he met Bishop Sanderson in London that year "in sad-colored clothes" and spent an hour with him in a tavern where "he made to me many useful observations of the present times, with much clearness and conscientious freedom." Some of the conversation is recorded in Walton's *Life of Sanderson*, and the words were directly against recent state orders and against "the unhappy Covenant . . . brought amongst us." If we know of these two incidents through records so casual as to have been little more than chance, plainly there must have been others.

Yet Walton, for all his convictions, was truly a quiet and inoffensive man, too deeply sincere ever to look for glory, too honest a Christian ever to provoke trouble, too calm and reasonable ever to be contentious. In this at least, we may safely trust his book's picture of his own disposition. His choice of rivers, his choice of angling methods and ways, closely matched the happy serenity of his character.

There is little doubt that Walton was a great walker, as must have been most of the anglers of his day. It has been suggested that he kept a horse in London and rode it out to his fishing. But even so, he must often have walked. He is walking when he meets the fowler and hunter of his book, and they walk for many a mile after the meeting. Walton thinks nothing of a mile or three or four along the stream to a favorite fishing place: "We are not yet come to a likely place; I must walk a mile yet before I begin." But I think he walked them easily and companionably, talking if he was with friends, looking about him and noting everything if he was alone. He was happiest with quiet streams and quiet fishing, though Cotton taught him to love the wilder Dove, and he himself wrote of Hampshire, which he knew well: "I think [it] exceeds all England for swift, shallow, clear and pleasant Brooks, and store of Trouts . . ."

Much of *The Angler* is written of the Lea, near Waltham Cross and Tottenham and Ware. In Walton's day it was a wonderful stream, wandering gently among lovely meadows, with "primrose banks" and "honeysuckle hedges" to sit down upon or under, altogether a perfect place for Walton's method of catching a trout on a hot summer evening. "Get a grasshopper, put it on your hook, with your line about two yards long, standing behind a bush or a tree where his hole is, and make your bait stir up and down on the top of the water." A good place, too, for drifting quill or cork over a quiet, smooth roach "swim," or for leaving a rod to fish for itself, which, Walton says, is "like putting money to use; for they both work for the owners when they do nothing but sleep, eat or rejoice . . ."

But even in Walton's time industrialization of the Lea had begun. Sir Hugh Mydleton's canal was in course of construction; much building followed it, and then pollution. The charm of the countryside is largely gone, and little of the stream would now be recognizable to Walton, though the river still holds a fair supply of coarse fish and an occasional trout.

Like the Lea, the Trent, river of Staffordshire, Walton's home county, has been greatly changed since his time by industrialization and pollution. Once "the most famous coarse fishery in England and a salmon river of value," it has been slowly restored in this century to produce fair fishing, which is still improving. Its tributary, the Sow, which flowed through Walton's property at Shallowford and where he may have fished as a boy as well as in later life, is now preserved by an angler's association, and holds perch, pike, roach, chub, dace and trout—an assortment that could hardly have been exceeded in the seventeenth century.

Walton fished the Thames, even as many of his followers fish it today. It is changed, of course, perhaps in many places beyond his recognition. But one place he would surely know: the bend below the playing fields at Eton, called "Black Potts," where he fished through many an afternoon with Wotton and John Hales. There are chub there still, and roach and dace and pike, perhaps even a fine trout or two. For the Thames still yields some enormous browns to a devoted fraternity of Thames Trouters.

The Kentish Stour still holds sea trout, but whether they are the great "Fordidge trout" of which Walton wrote I do not know. Walton called them "the rarest of fish, many of them near the bigness of a salmon, but known by their different color; and in their best season they cut very white." If they were rare in Walton's day, perhaps they are still rare—but not unknown.

Walton spent much of the last thirty years of his life near Winchester. He worked quietly on his *Lives*, and certainly fished as keenly as ever. Marston imagines him on the Itchen, near Shawford, and I certainly hope it was so, for the Itchen is a lovely stream, full of trout and grayling. Walton would have hunted them with worm or minnow or grasshopper, as the season directed; but no doubt he fished the natural mayfly when the big ephemera was up, dapping it skillfully over the deep pools, wafting it ahead of him on the wind over the shallows. And he must have tried, often enough, the wet-fly techniques he would have learned from Cotton on the Dove.

The Itchen is still a fine trout stream, broad and clear and weedy, one of the classic dry-fly streams of England. I saw fine trout rising freely along it during the war years, and once, as I crossed a foot-bridge near Shawford, I knelt and scooped up a great swatch of weed that was caught there. It was crawling with handsome, healthy fresh-water shrimps, pale gray and brilliant, the sure abundance of feed that grows big trout. It is not unlikely that the Itchen today, like the Test and a few other well-preserved south-country chalk streams, holds more trout and bigger trout than in Walton's time.

I have said little of Charles Cotton and his Derbyshire Dove. Cotton was thirty-seven years junior to Walton, who had been a friend of his father. He was traveler, soldier, poet, courtier and man of the world, yet a dear and close friend of Walton's later years. Cotton was full of Walton's own sincerity and gentleness and friendliness, and Walton must have found him a refreshing and enlivening companion.

Cotton's stream, the Dove, is, like Cotton himself, lively and strong and bright, carrying the wildness of the Derbyshire hills. Walton traveled north to visit his friend, perhaps to discuss with him the great translation of Montaigne that Cotton was later to undertake, certainly to fish and to discuss Cotton's addition to *The Compleat Angler*, which was published with the fifth edition in 1676. It is the most famous friendship in the history of angling, and one of the most touching of all times.

In 1674 Cotton built the little square fishing house on the banks of the Dove that is the true shrine and tabernacle of modern anglers, with its famous interlacing of initials I.W. and C.C. over the doorway and the inscription "Piscatoribus Sacrum, 1674." The fishing house has been through many vicissitudes and restorations, yet it stands today with the exterior just as it was in Cotton's time. I hope it will always so stand, sacred to fishermen and especially to the memory of two fishermen. There is reason to believe that it will, for, with much of Dovedale, it is now the property of the National Trust of Great Britain.

As for the Dove itself, the footbridge and the slippery cobblestones are gone. Little stone weirs across the stream are new. Pikes Pool is unchanged, with the tall rock still breaking the water, and all the essential beauties of the stream and its valley are as they were. Walton and Cotton would recognize the beloved place, notice the changes, and be well pleased by the gentle treatment of almost three centuries. May all anglers and very honest men find the way there once before they die.

May 1953

The Truth About Izaak Walton

An irreverent look at the "real" meaning of the world's most famous fishing book.

O N A N U M B E R of occasions I have tried, out of a sense of duty aggravated by a suspicion that my literary taste buds might have been defective on previous attempts, to read Izaak Walton's *The Compleat Angler* beyond, oh, say page 25 or 30. It was no use. By the time I had endured the compulsively dreary discourse of Piscator, Venator, and Auceps through a dozen pages I was bored so stiff that my wife had to call the children to help get me out of the chair and up to bed. As a result I suffered from an habitual feeling of moral, intellectual, and spiritual inferiority, and would slink abjectly from the room whenever my fellow anglers commenced to boast of the number of times they had read this hallowed tome or the number of editions of it they had accumulated in their sporting libraries.

Recently, however, it occurred to me that although most of these friends referred to Izaak Walton on terms of easy familiarity, it was possible that none of them had any actual knowledge of the man. I thereupon took it upon myself to investigate the background of the author, and his work, with results that astonished me and will, I have no doubt, astonish you. Here, then, are the true facts about this much-discussed but little-known book and its author (to be read at your own risk, if you cherish illusion).

First, the man who called himself Izaak Walton was in reality an adherent of Charles II named Matthew Hornaday, who, so far as is known, never fished a day in his life or cared to. He was, in fact, scornful of all outdoor sports or games, although there are records indicating that he occasionally bowled at St. James Green in London until caught cheating in a minor tournament and expelled from the club.

Second, the book *The Compleat Angler* has nothing whatsoever to do with fish or fishing. It is, in every detail, a turgidly tedious political allegory intended not for the amusement or instruction of anglers but simply for the advancement of the Caroline cause and the confusion of the forces of Cromwell. The gist of Hornaday's thesis is the fundamental illegality of the Cromwellian regime, in the furtherance of which viewpoint he assumed the pseudonym of "Walton," which is, quite obviously, a backwards spelling of "Not law"! Similarly the name of Charles Cotton, purportedly the collaborator who appended the book's later sections on fly fishing, is a heavy-handedly humorous reminder that he is "pulling the *wool* over the eyes" of the disestablishmentarian authorities.

Hornaday was an admirer of the English theological writer Richard Hooker (1553–1600), whose two-volume *Laws of Ecclesiastical Polity* dealt lengthily with the controversial problem of the role of the established church and its relation to the civil government and to royalty; Hornaday chose the angling allegory as an obfuscatory reference to the theologian, since a fisherman is, of course, a hooker of fishes.

Quite naturally the book abounds in veiled or disguised references to ecclesiastical and political figures of 17th-century Britain; the famous admonition on the handling of the frog as bait, for example ("Use him as though you loved him . . . that he may live the longer"), often cited as an instance of the author's compassion, is in fact a clumsily obscured incitement to anti-Cromwellian insurrection, in which the word "live" is, of course, "evil" spelled backwards, and which—if we attach to its front and back the two inner letters of "frog" and again spell it backwards—becomes "Oliver."

After I had made this discovery it further occurred to me that some of the current literature ostensibly devoted to shooting and fishing might in fact be this same insidious sort of political propaganda. It did not, therefore, greatly surprise me to find in an article on fishing in Europe a reference to having watched a blue bird flit along the bank while fishing a German river ("Elbe jay"=LBJ!) nor to notice that the current Abercrombie & Fitch catalogue of used guns lists several elephant rifles.

October 1964

Roger's River

RALPH D. CONROY

The two young fishermen exchanged only a few words that day, but three decades later, the memory of one man haunts the other.

THERE ARE FLEETING incidents in our lives which we unwittingly carry with us to discover and examine anon, like burdocks plucked off wool trousers after a day afield. Such was the case with a young man whom I shall call Roger.

In that time, there were very few of us who donned packs and stout shoes and walked away from the roadheads to spend a day and night and longer encamped by a trout stream or remote lake. If you had done so, you had an excellent chance of finding yourself very much alone. Those were the days before the ubiquitous machine had ripped and churned its way to the very entrails of the land.

Backpacking, at least in the East, was considered, if it was considered at all, a minor lunacy. Good equipment was scarce. What was available was army surplus. The tent, as often as not, was of the open-faced Whelen type, home-sewn and without netting. Citronella was still the standard mosquito deterrent. Elvis had yet to cut "Heartbreak Hotel," young girls wore penny loafers, and, I am told, crinolines beneath their skirts. Though it didn't seem so then, I suppose it was a gentler, slower time.

Even so, the herding instinct was very strong. To wander alone any distance from the herd, or rather to be caught doing so , made one an instant curiosity, which very often led to irrevocable social ostracism.

The summer after graduation from high school I acquired a middle-aged six-cylinder Chevrolet, which was reliable, commodious, and used gasoline with discretion. I would pack it with duffel and head north to fish some stream on which there was a good chance of being alone. I had taken the precaution of allowing friends to convince themselves I had a girlfriend or two in Maine and Vermont. Girls, of course, were accepted cause for any amount of idiocy. It was on such a jaunt that I first found Roger's River.

I had been driving along a dirt road on the outskirts of a small Vermont town. We called those neat New England settlements, nearly always dominated by a church spire and village green, Holstein towns, after the tradition of painting the houses white and the shutters black.

Alongside the road, in an indentation, there was an ancient cast-iron kettle. It must have held 50 gallons and might have once been used for scalding pigs. A small, ingeniously crafted stone aqueduct carried a steady stream of water from a small stone springhouse several yards up an embankment to the lip of the kettle. The water plunged nearly a foot downwards in a tiny falls to the kettle below. The kettle's bottom was paved with leaves and gravel. The water was marvelously clear and sweet. A few inches below the rim a heart-shaped hole allowed the overflow to drain. This water was piped beneath the road to where the land fell steeply away amidst huge drift boulders, conifers, and a scattering of great gray beeches.

It was very cool and very quiet alongside that spring. I unwrapped a loaf of homemade bread, sliced off two thick pieces with my sheath knife, and built a sandwich from the loaf of bologna I had bought along the highway. I took out a small bottle of beer and dropped it unopened into the kettle to cool, then topped the sandwich with a slice of Bermuda onion. A freshening breeze stirred the tree tops, and the road was very hot and dusty where the sun dappled through the leaves. There was no traffic, and the spring water pouring into the kettle the only sound.

After lunch I was still reluctant to leave that spot, which I had already come to regard as very special and very mine. I put the empty bottle and top into the car's trunk. I had learned that young drivers with out-of-state registrations were quite often stopped by the constabulary, and in such encounters it did absolutely no good to have an empty beer bottle alongside. I took another drink of water and decided to have a closer look at the springhouse.

It sat squatting over moist ground, the good cedar shingling still sound though turning green with a patina of moss. A sturdy plank door on the uphill side, which swung on long barn hinges, was padlocked shut. I backed away, and saw the cornerstone in the traditional place on the southeast corner. Some sprigs of spruce had obscured it.

I read the date aloud, "Eighteen fifty-six."

"Five years before the Civil War," a voice behind me said.

The sound spooked me, and turning too quickly, I stumbled and nearly fell. Standing, leaning on a cudgel and wearing a pack and short hiking pants was a deeply tanned young man, perhaps five years older than myself. His leg muscles were finely developed, as were the muscles of his arms and chest. He had sandy brown hair and very bright dancy brown eyes. He grinned at my discomfort.

"I didn't mean to startle you," he said, but his eyes showed differently.

"I was just leaving," I said awkwardly. "Can I give you a lift anywhere? My car's right down there near the kettle."

"Not a chance," he said. "I'm sorry, I don't mean it like that. But thank you. You're not from around here?"

"No. I'm from Massachusetts," I said.

"Oh, I go to school there."

"Where?"

"Cambridge."

"Oh. That's the other part of the state. Where did you come from, just now, I mean?" I asked.

"There's a river back in there. About 3 miles. The trail there takes you in."

"Are there any trout?"

"Yes," he said. "You drove over it back in the valley. That's where most people fish it."

"But not you?"

He grinned. "No, not me."

He made excuses, and I watched him walk down the trail, cross the road, and set out bushwacking down through the beeches. I wanted to tell him that I understood exactly how he felt, that I had a pack in the trunk of my car.

But I didn't. In fact, though I came to know him well, those were the only words we ever spoke.

It was not until much later that summer when the swamp maples had already begun turning and dropping leaves that I managed to return to that spot. I had joined the army, and the following week I was scheduled to report to Fort Dix.

I parked the Chevrolet next to the kettle and packed in to the river. It wasn't a river at all, I discovered, but a good-size stream. On a grassy knoll, below which the river turned back on itself, I found Roger's campsite. There were a ring of stones and a small stack of firewood, and some saplings were tied together in a lean-to frame. There were no papers or tin cans. A heavy cast-iron skillet hung from the branch of a spruce. The knoll provided a fine view, both upriver and down. It was a neat, well-kept camp.

For a few moments I thought of making camp there, but instead, I hiked downstream about a half mile till I found a flat spot alongside a small, cold feeder brook. I made my camp there. I did not want to take his spot. Perhaps I would meet him again while fishing the river, and if he invited me, I could move camp easily.

By the time my camp was secure it was twilight. I hauled up some rocks from near the stream to make a fireplace and laid in what squaw wood I could find. Twilight was fading as I joined the rod, and tied on a large White Miller dry fly. I put on shorts and sneakers and began fishing upstream. Within a half hour or so I had collected a half dozen small brook trout, which I saved for breakfast. The night was clear, but cooling, when I stopped on a rock spit along thin, flat water to clean my fish.

I was working my knife blade along the belly of the sixth trout when the sound of a harmonica cut the damp night air. I stood up, walked back along the spit, and up the embankment. Through the trees a fire was flickering in the night. He was playing "Red River Valley" in a slow and mournful time. I stood there in the darkness of the trees, letting the ballad and the music of the stream wash over me. Then, taking up my fish and rod, I stumbled downriver through the starlight to my own camp.

I had planned to rise very early the next morning and fish my way upstream to his camp. By the light of the night fire I peeled and sliced potatoes and onions. I knew he had a skillet, so there would be no sense in lugging along my own. I had the trout and could take a couple more before I dropped in on him for breakfast. "Red River Valley" had always been my favorite song.

But the night was cold and I shivered long into it in my blankets before sleep came. I awoke once just before first light and fell back to sleep. When I awoke again the sun was high and hot on the canvas. Too hungry to wait, I breakfasted on the trout and potatoes. It was late morning when I tugged on the wet sneakers and began fishing upstream toward his camp.

I fished a Light Cahill, my father's favorite fly, and took a couple of small trout, which I released. I was working my way upstream through a long pool that I had missed the previous night. At the head of the pool there was a small falls above a good hole, flanked on the one side by an overhanging rock and on the other by shallow water. In those days I was too impatient to fish wisely and ignored the tail of the pool, instead positioning myself to cast to its head beneath the falls.

I must have cast twenty times or more—sometimes into the falls itself, sometimes into the foam below, occasionally to the flat on the edge of the pool. Casting very often to the same spot is like driving an automobile long distances over straight and undistinguished roads. The mind, after a time, atrophies.

Then, on a cast that had gone into the falls, submerging the fly, I had a strike. The fish came from somewhere deep in the pool with startling swiftness and took with a suddeness and power I had never before experienced. The rod flexed downward and began pumping with a separate life. The fish was running hard downstream toward me. The line bellied behind it in the slow current, but it was running with such force that the rod was still flexing. The reel shrieked for me to do something as the big fish continued to run out line. I did nothing but grip more tightly to the cork rod handle.

The trout broke water once, coming up thick-bodied, showing color and size, 15 yards below me, splashing the water once in a heavy boil that left absolutely no doubt as to its power and strength. The fish had moved downstream and past me so quickly that when it rolled, looking as big as a man's thigh, I did not at first realize that it was the same fish. Somehow, I thought the trout must still be above at the head of the pool where it had struck. And then, as suddenly as it had struck, the fish was off.

I clambered out of the water and lay among the sweet ferns on the bank, feeling the coolness of the earth come through the khaki shirt. A quarter of an hour later I began to regain my breath.

After a time I walked back to my own camp. In late afternoon I broke camp, and hiked back along the river, stopping for a long look at the hole where I'd held for a few seconds the one great fish of my life. I knew it could last me forever.

The coals from Roger's fire were sodden when I arrived, but otherwise there was little sign that anyone had camped there the previous night. The memory of the fish was still tight in my belly, so it mattered less that I had missed him.

I wrestled off the pack and sat next to the small stone fire ring. I could see that he'd gathered fresh wood to replace that which he'd burned. Beneath a separate pile of kindling laid close to the base of the spruce that held the skillet, I spied a small piece of white, lined paper. I picked it up. It had been torn from a spiral notebook. He had written carefully with blue ink and a fountain pen:

Air temp: 72 degrees at 3 p.m.

Water: 66 degrees deep, 68 on surface, no hatches.

Sky clear, high clouds, no wind. Fished Red Quill tied on no. 18 hook. Released four, kept three. Fished weighted brown nymph, released nine.

Below that there was another entry written in a more careless hand:

Oh, I know the sound the river makes,

By dawn, by night, and by day.

But can it stay me through tomorrows,
That may find me far away?

There were additional lines, but they'd been scratched over. I folded the paper carefully and placed it in my fly box. Then I slung on the pack and hiked out to the car. I had the odd feeling I was leaving more than a river behind.

Two months of army basic training followed by a stint in an advanced training school, and I found myself in Korea.

Though the war was long over, there were long nights of patrol edging the demilitarized zone. There were also pretty girls and the occasional leave for rest and recuperation in Tokyo, Seoul, or Hong Kong. And there were books, as well as lots of time to read.

Fishing was a long way off, but it came flooding back when I found and read "Big Two Hearted River," by Hemingway. Winter nights as I lay shivering in my bag, I would think back to my own river, the great trout, and the man I had met so fleetingly there. I began thinking about him quite often, especially the lines he'd scribbled and left on that pad. The note was locked in my fly box some 6,000 miles away, but the words were locked just as tightly in my mind. Had he been going back to school? I didn't think so. But if not, where? Did he read? Had he read "Big Two Hearted River?" Who had taught him to fish? Did he tie flies? Did he shoot birds in the fall?

Finally the time passed. We spread Inchon Harbor astern the troop ship and eighteen days later, after stops in Yokohama and Pearl, we raised the Golden Gate. Three thousand miles farther east it was the same tight New England country, exactly as always.

A week later, in a borrowed car, I was heading north through the brightly dying leaves of an early autumn. The kettle was unchanged, the water pouring sweet and clear as yesterday. My body was hard and the pack light. I skimmed easily over the hard-packed trail to the grassy knoll below which the river turned back on itself.

Perhaps you can't go home again. Instead of the neat camp I remembered, the site was littered with shards of red and green plastic and burnt cans. At the water's edge there was a deflated inner tube. The skillet was gone, as was the lean-to frame. There was no firewood. Within the tree line there were several shredded plastic garbage bags. Broken bottles littered the opposite shore, testimony that someone had better marksmanship than sense.

I turned downriver to my own place. The camp had been untouched, but its magic was gone. I never jointed the rod, never unrolled the new down bag. I hiked back out to the car and drove into town.

At the filling station I described the man I sought. There are no towns so close knit as small New England towns. I took the attendant's directions.

At the house, a man, older than I had expected, answered my knock. I told him my mission.

"The missus is sleeping now," he explained. "She's taken it pretty hard, don't you know. But come along and let me show you his room. We keep it just the way he left it."

I followed him up the steep stairs. The ceilings were low on the second floor as they are in the old Cape Cods. He led the way into a small square bedroom.

"You know, he always wanted a bamboo rod," he said. "And with his first pay that's what he bought." In the corner, alongside a small desk, was a 7-foot rod in a new leather case. "It's a shame he never even got to use it," his father said, his eyes dampening.

The room held model airplanes. Behind a pair of crossed snowshoes on one wall were the spread tail feathers of a partridge. A Browning Sweet Sixteen and a Model 1894 Winchester hung from a horizontal rack above the single bed.

"Were you good friends?" he asked.

"I knew him from the river."

"Yes, you told me that. Roger loved that river."

I walked across the room to the bookcase confident of what I would find there. I was not disappointed. I told his father that I must be leaving, that I had a long way yet to travel.

"I don't fish," he said. "He had no brothers or sisters. Will you take the rod?"

I told him that I thought the rod belonged there in his room. We shook hands, then, at the door, he slipped something into the pocket of my jacket.

I drove straight to the filling station and in the attached variety store bought a packet of plastic garbage bags. I knew I could not leave his camp like that.

As I got back into the car the station attendant came up to the car window. "Did you find it all right?

"Yes, thank you," I said. "Do you know how it happened?"

"His helicopter went down the week he was to leave Korea."

That night as I camped in his place on his river, I put my hand into the pocket of my jacket and brought out his harmonica.

August 1990

Mecca

NICK LYONS

To fish the Green Drake hatch on the Beaverkill, it's best to be a true believer like old Hawkes.

THERE WAS NO spring that spring. March lingered into mid-April; late April was a wintry February; and by the end of May you might have been convinced that, since not even the Quill Gordon had arrived, God was taking a special vengeance on fly-fishers. On all except me.

Emergence dates would be postponed; few trout would be taken in the fly-only stretches I haunted; June—unless God became ungodly vengeful toward fly-fishers—would be perfect. While small clusters of distressed anglers grumbled in the tackle shops, I gloated. June was the only time I would be free, and June would be perfect. Even Brannigan was morose. I was serenely gleeful.

All winter I had corresponded from the city with Mike Brannigan, a lovable white-haired Irishman, a fanatic like myself but one who had taken the plunge and now lived chiefly—and blissfully—for fishing. What other way is there? Brannigan constantly wrote me of his friend Hawkes, a knowledgeable old Catskill trouting genius whom I had never met. But Hawkes was more than knowledgeable, more than a rumor: he was a myth. In an increasing number of understated and sometimes unconscious ways, the old trout fisher—and, in off seasons, cellist—began to emerge from Mike's letters as a figure of outrageous proportions. He had, so far as I could tell, a special formula for dyeing leaders to within a chromophore of the color of eight different streams at a dozen different times of the year. He no longer kept emergence tables, but could tell—by extra sensory perception?—not only which fly would be hatching on a particular day, but at what time of the day, even to the hour, the fly would emerge. And in what numbers! Of course I believed none of it. Who would? It was all the fiction of that wild Irishman. Brannigan was obviously a madman, more afflicted even than I, who had lost two jobs because of his trout neurosis, and almost a wife. He was given to exaggeration, fantasy, mirage, and fly-tying. I had only almost lost my wife.

But I was curious. Who wouldn't be? And I had asked four or five times, covertly, whether or not Hawkes would fish with us when I got away for my one week alone in June.

"Rarely fishes any more," wrote Brannigan. "Most streams have become rather easy for him; most hatches too pedestrian. Says he only fishes the Green Drake hatches—says there's still something to be learned there."

The Green Drake, yes—the most exciting and mysterious of them all. *Ephemera guttulata Pictet*, yes—which brought the lunkers, the old soaks, out of the deep pools, which emerged in massive and manic hatches, sometimes for only a few days, perhaps a week. Sometimes the circus occurred on the Beaverkill as early as the first week in June; but, according to water temperatures, no doubt, it could be delayed for several weeks. Yes—to fish the Green Drake hatch on the Beaverkill this year with Hawkes, that was an ambition worth the twelve months of brooding and scheming. To return to the Beaverkill, which I had not fished in ten years, with the old myth himself, yes—it would be Mecca, a vision to hold me throughout another long dry city winter.

But there was no adequate imitation of *Ephemera guttulata*—that was common knowledge. White Wulffs took a few fish; dyed light-green hackle flies took some; the attempts at exact imitation took very few; and, in the spinner stage, there was the adequate waxy-white and funereal Coffin Fly.

So I experimented that spring, to wile away the wait, and finally, in mid-May, accomplished what to my mind was a major innovation, a contribution of staggering dimension to the angling fraternity. I called it the Pigeon Drake, after the pigeon quill body I had used after a long quill had fluttered down to me, quite mystically, at the very moment I was thinking about this fly one dreary lunch hour. That quill was a portent, and I promptly sent my older sons out to collect me several dozen in the park at a penny per quill. They brought in ninety-seven, but I only used thirty in my experiments, and ultimately only made four or five usable flies.

The result is hard to describe. It was not a small fly, nor a particularly neat fly. The tip of the quill, through which I had inserted exactly three stems of stripped badger hackle for the tail, had to be strapped firmly to the shank of a No. 12 hook. Peering up through specially purchased contact lenses from the bottom of a filled bathtub at numerous flies floating there—the door had to be locked to keep out my skeptical wife and distracting children—I observed that the white impala wings of the Wulff flies, sparsely tied, closely resembled the translucent wings of the Green Drake (and many other naturals, which perhaps explains part of their extraordinary success). I dyed pure-white hackle in green tea for the hackle. The pigeon quill body, however, is what made the fly; it was natural, translucent, and would cock slightly upward if properly strapped to the shank. Frankly, it was the work of genius, and I could not wait to fish it with Mike and Hawkes on the Beaverkill—Mecca.

But it rained the first three days of my week's vacation, and all I could do was take Brannigan's abuse that a man who had not been out on the streams *once* by June 9 was a fallen man, fallen indeed—a man given over to mercantilism and paternalism and other such crimes and moral diseases as were destroying the world, or at least sensitive practitioners of a noble sport. "These are dangerous years for you, Nick," he advised me. "Worse will lead to worse."

The fourth day was Brannigan's one day of work, his one day of homage to mercantilism and paternalism, and since Hawkes was not to be heard from, had, apparently, disappeared, I went out glumly to a small mountain stream nearby and surprised myself by having a delightful day catching 7- and 8-inch brookies and browns on tiny No. 18 and 20 Coachmen and Adamses, dry. It was fun watching the spirited streaks as trout shot out of their cover and gulped the little flies; it was real sport handling them on 6X tippets. But it was not Mecca.

That night I could bear it no longer. Indirections lead to indirections, and I, a mercantilist, had no business being subtle. "Mike," I said, "it's the tenth of June. There have been no reports that the Green Drake hatch has started and it's due momentarily. Don't you have *any* idea where Hawkes is? Can't you simply hunt him up and ask him if he'll go to the Beaverkill with us to-morrow?"

Brannigan roared. "Sure. I know where Hawkes is. But you just don't ask him like that. It takes some engineering, and some luck. He's got to ask you."

"Dammit. What is he, Mike, a saint?"

Mike smiled and sipped at his fourth beer in a leisurely way.

"Did you make the damn guy up?"

"All right. All right. I suppose I can find him. But I can't promise a thing."

Two days later, the night before I had to leave, after two days of mediocre fishing in the Esopus, Brannigan said simply, "Hawkes is going to-morrow; said we could come if we want to."

I tried to answer calmly. Though I still didn't believe a word about Hawkes, not a word of it; a myth is a myth, and it comes with ineluctable power, a power elusive and haunting.

The next morning at 8:00 Brannigan was at his garage arranging his tackle, selecting from his six fly rods the best for the day.

"Hawkes thinks there might be a Green Drake hatch this evening," the bright white-haired Irishman said, "but then again that there might not."

Already a hedge; the tricks of the prophets, the ambiguities of the mediums. He didn't exist. Not the Hawkes I'd dreamed about.

Then, as I got out my gear and piled it beside Brannigan's, Hawkes arrived in his '46 Dodge. His gaunt lined face was that of a saint, or of a gunman. His eyes were deep set, his fingers were long and thin and obviously arthritic. He was old—old as a wilting pine that bears few greens anymore. He walked stiffly toward us.

"Brannigan, old Branny, so this is our young friend," he said, extending his bony hand. "Has he made all the necessary preparations? If he is to be admitted into our little club he must agree to will his ashes to us, that we may sprinkle them upon the waters of the Beaverkill."

Brannigan tried to suppress a smile. I tried, gently, to remove my hand from Hawkes' firm but friendly grasp.

"The Beaverkill," he continued, looking warmly at me, smiling, "home of Gordon and Darbee and Dette: Mecca. Tell me, Nick, do you face the Beaverkill every morning and every evening at sunset? Do you pray to the gods?"

"Of course he does, Hawkes," said Mike. "Now let's get started. This will be his only real day of trout fishing for the year."

"Very curious," said Hawkes, shaking his head. "One day of trout fishing. I'm sure our young friend has the burdens of the world upon him, then. Nevertheless, one day of real fishing can be enough. Especially at Mecca. It can be made to serve the whole of the year."

I smiled—an embarrassed, naive smile that spread and spread all day, until my cheeks hurt, on that long unforgettable drive to Mecca.

The drive to the Beaverkill should have taken no more than an hour. It was nine o'clock, and I had all hopes of catching the late-morning rise. But it took about an hour for us merely to pack Hawkes' old Dodge, an immaculate, impeccably ordered vehicle, with each object in its proper place: rods, waders, vest, extra fly boxes, net, and Jack Daniels whiskey. There was a holder for his pipe above the dashboard, neat disposal bags, and four cans of beer neatly packed into the ample glove compartment. Hawkes placed each of our items of equipment carefully into the car, with such measured movements that he might have been giving them permanent homes. As he picked up each piece of tackle he would contemplate it for a moment and then comment on its appropriateness to the sport. "Branny, you know that felt is best for the Beaverkill—and yet you bring hobnails. Curious. Is there a special reason for that, Branny? Do you know something you're not telling? Have reports reached you of great mountains of silt and mud being washed into it? You surely would not be using them simply to impress the pedestrian likes of Nick and I—to taunt us with the fruit of some large sale of flies to a posh New York City tackle shop?"

And then, when the felt waders were brought out from Brannigan's garage, after another five minutes of slow, meticulous scrutiny, "I suppose you know that the glue you've used won't last the day. But the Irish are knowledgeable men, and if you've failed to use the preparation I gave you last winter I'm sure you have your reasons."

At eleven we set out. Too late for the morning rise—but still early enough for a long day on the river. We wouldn't even have to stop for lunch, I thought, hopefully: pick up a sandwich or two for the vest, and hit the stream as soon as possible. I had a raging fever to be on the stream.

The old Dodge scrunched slowly out of Brannigan's pebbled driveway, made the semicircle onto the tarred road, and started, with incredible slowness, west—to Mecca.

Hawkes opened and closed his long arthritic fingers deliberately around the wheel. "This is a day not to be rushed," he said. "It is going to be an experience, an event. It must be savored."

"Come off it, Hawkes," said Brannigan.

Hawkes stopped the car abruptly. Smack in the middle of the highway. Without taking his eyes away from the windshield in front of him, he said, with dead seriousness: "If this is to be a day of cynicism, of doubt, of feverish behavior by an unruly Irishman, I would be most happy to turn around, return said Irishman to his own car, and make my peace elsewhere. I have my doubts that the Green Drakes will appear anyway; the temperature dropped to 52 degrees night before last—which, I take it, the less sensitive scholars of the streams *did not notice*—the barometer is falling, if slowly, and the moon was not to be seen last night. My fingers are tight, I have a telltale itch along my right thigh, and this *could* become a highly dubious proposition all the way around."

"OK, OK, Hawkes. I apologize. Please—let's go."

"You're tense, man. Sink into the day. Don't force it. The electricity of such feverish thinking is transmuted imperceptibly but ineluctably to Mr. Brown Trout. The result you can well guess."

My smile spread, my cheeks ached. Three miles down the road Hawkes stopped at a gas station, got out, and asked the attendant about the composition of the gasoline. Hawkes put a drop on his fingers, smelled it, touched it gently to his lips, smiled, and wiped his fingers carefully on some paper toweling. "It is quite possible after all, gentlemen, that the Green Drake *will* make his appearance this afternoon. Very curious."

We started out again and this time Hawkes was silent, thoughtful, meditative for five minutes. Several times he stopped the car at small mountain creeks, got out of the car, scrutinized the water, threw boysenberries into the eddies, and began to hum quietly. "Boys," he said, nodding, "it's really going to be a day. This is going to be an event."

Three more miles down the road, feeling immeasurably dry, he had to get a small bracer at a roadside tavern. We each ended having three tall beers apiece. Another mile, feeling too wet, he had to relieve himself, and did so, in a conspicuously high arc. Half a mile farther and he stopped abruptly, whistled a long clear whistle, not a wolf whistle, and watched a young blonde farmgirl carrying a child walk slowly across a field of knee-high corn shoots. "It is a day of poetry, of cosmic stillness," he informed us. "She is the Madonna agrarianistically developed."

When I noted, unobtrusively, that it was now 2:30, he advised: "There are lessons to be learned on a day like this. Let it not be rushed; let it be savored. It is a day composed on the celestial lyre. An event. We need only stop at the Blue Goose tavern, my dear Nick, and we will get to Mecca in good time. Branny, where is that oasis?"

Mike did not remember, but several inquiries proved that it was seven miles out of our way, up an unpaved road. No matter. It was impossible to fish the Beaverkill during the Green Drake hatch without first stopping at the Blue Goose. It was a ritual. Part of the sacraments. The Blue Goose was a holy place, a temple pilgrimages were made to.

It looked like a cruddy overaged bar to me. We stayed an hour, but only two miracles occurred: the floor rose 3 inches on my fourth beer, and I was able to walk out. We took a six-pack with us and were on our way, due west, over the last little mountains, pilgrims, pioneers, seekers of the holy Mecca.

We arrived in Roscoe at 5:30, still in time for a long evening's fishing, but Hawkes thought we should look up Bishop Harry Darbee before heading for the stream, to seek his blessings as well as his advice. "It is advisable," he said. This could not be done directly. It was first necessary to head for the Antrim Lodge, to the cool dark cellar for a few stronger snorts than we'd had. Hawkes invoked us each to empty two double shots of Jack Daniels, which done he launched into a series of incisive questions of the good bartender. But when that dispenser of firewater said that the water had been high and that a few men had been in that very afternoon with limits they'd taken on spinning rods, Hawkes became violent and Brannigan had to grab his arm, even hold his mouth, as he shouted, "Coffee grinders! Hoodlums! Saracens!"

Darbee was not to be found, but Walt Dette was home, and Hawkes conned him out of a dozen hackles from a natural blue dun after an hour of talk about the breeding of this rare bird. When Dette said the Green Drakes had not appeared, Hawkes smiled quietly, nodded confidently to us.

Seven o'clock we hit the stream. Not ten miles downriver where Dette told us to go, but at a spot directly below Junction Pool. One look at the water, after that interminable drive, and I had insisted. Hawkes shrugged. It did not make much difference, he said.

Once parked, Mike and I suited and set up hurriedly. Hawkes sat back and puffed at his pipe. "Long as you two have the St. Vitus Dance you might as well indulge it. Go on. Git, you two. Takes an old man like me a while to get into the proper frame of mind for this holy stream. It is not something to be rushed."

We wasted no time. Brannigan headed downstream, I up—and we were flailing away wildly at the waters for a full twenty minutes before Hawkes, on stiff legs, puffing contentedly on his pipe, ambled to the spot on the stream nearest the car. Fish were beginning to rise steadily just at that moment, and the large pale-green duns began to rise in swarms from the water. I switched from a Cahill to a No. 12 Pale Watery Dun, and then to a White Miller, a White Wulff, and then to an imitation Drake. All in rapid succession. Nothing. Something was missing. My mind was beer-fogged, my casting was sloppy, I was wobbly, and something important was trying to press itself out of my unconscious. Below me, Brannigan, fishing nymphs dead drift, took nothing.

Hawkes waded out a few feet, stood stark still like a heron, fixed his glasses, took the temperature of the water, tested it with his hand, peered long into the swirling duns, the many dimples of rising fish, and selected a fly from his single aluminum case. I could not see which he chose. It took him a full minute to afix it, but when he had he looked at the water again, clipped off the fly and started the process again. He pulled the leader tight, clipped off the end bit, ran the leader through his mouth six or seven times, and peeled off line.

I was staggered when his first cast brought a strike only moments after the fly had alighted. Deftly he played an 11-inch brown, drew it closer until it turned belly up, and then neatly netted it.

The scene was unbelievable. The sun was several feet above the treeline now, and seemed to hang—luminous and diffused—ready to drop at any moment. The hatch was fantastic, the large pale-green drakes thick as locusts, heavywinged and fat. Leisurely, two- and even three-pound trout stalked them, inches beneath the surface. It was like a slow-motion film. They would cruise, like sharks, their dorsal extended above the waterline, and heavily suck down the fallen drakes. Everything took place on the surface—methodically, devastatingly. There must have been fifty trout cruising in that long, flat pool—many, no doubt, denizens of the large lakelike pool several hundred yards downstream. They were in no hurry. For them it was an event, an annual feast some of them had no doubt partaken of for four or five years. My hands and limbs were shaking.

Hawkes' next cast brought another strike, but it was short, and he retrieved the line quietly, without a ruffle of the surface.

I made a full twelve casts before he cast again, and this time the rise to his fly—which I could not see—was not short. While playing what was obviously a 2-pound trout or better, he called softly for me to come to his position. I scampered through the water like a water buffalo, convinced that he had both the right spot and the right fly, and scurried to his side just as he netted a fine 18-inch brown, broke its neck, and creeled it.

I was frantic. There could not be more than another thirty-five minutes of visibility. Wildly I tried four or five different flies, my back cast slapping the water behind me noisily. Hawkes did not frown. He did not take his eyes from the water. I had never seen such intense concentration.

Then I remembered—*how could I have forgotten?*—and my entire body shook with excitement as I did: the Pigeon Drake.

I was so unhinged that it took five tries before I got the leader through the eye of this miraculous fly, and when I jerked the knot tight the line broke. I tried again and this time managed. The Pigeon Drake hung convincingly from my line.

Carefully I false cast out 15, 20 feet of line. I felt calm and confident now, as icy and knowledgeable and canny as Hawkes. Then I released the last few feet of line, shot them through the guides, and happily, expectantly, watched the fly drop to the water.

It landed like a shot pigeon. But immediately one of those slow-motion monsters glided ominously toward it. I watched, heart a drum, while the dorsal neared. The spotted back and each and every aspect of the awesome body of this fine brown were clear to me as he moved, inches below the surface. Then he stopped, the fly not 4 inches from his nose. The trout was motionless, but not tense. "Take it. Take it, you old soak," I whispered. I twitted the fly. "Take it," I murmured again. Once more I twitched the fly, and this time the movement did it. When the reverberations in the water ceased, the fly began to sink, like the City in the Sea, majestically down. Unmistakably the trout turned its nose up. It did. I'll swear to it. And then, with noble calm he glided toward a natural nearby, and took that. It had been a sneer—the sophisticated sneer of a wise-acre sophisticated trout if I'd ever seen one. And it finished me. Dejectedly I retrieved my line, clipped off the fly, dropped it into the water—where it promptly sank like a stone—reeled in my line, and dismantled my rod.

In the remaining half hour of visibility Hawkes calmly took three more fish, the largest a full 20 inches, minutes before darkness set in.

The drive home, after Hawkes had finished three almost raw hamburgers and two cups of black coffee, took exactly sixty-two minutes. Hawkes did not particularly race along the road.

All the way back I had visions of those swarms of greenish duns rising from the flat pool, fluttering clumsily, falling back, drifting downstream and being leisurely sharked down by slow-motion monsters. Brannigan had caught nothing; I had caught nothing; three anglers we met had taken one small trout between them; innumerable trout-fishers throughout the East take nothing during the massive Green Drake hatches; but Hawkes had taken six in about an hour, using no more than a few dozen casts. Alas, I can only further the myth about Hawkes: I certainly cannot disprove it.

He evaded all our questions for the first forty-five minutes of that quick drive home, with a skill to dwarf Falstaff's.

"Yes, it did seem like the Green Drake, *Ephemera guttulata Pictet*, was the major hatch."

"You're not saying they weren't taking those duns, are you?" asked Mike pointedly. "I saw them take a dozen myself."

"Exactly what were you using?" I asked.

"How, how, how! An extraordinary question. Not at all an easy question to answer, my dear Nick. There are a dozen subtle factors involved that . . ."

"Come off it, Hawkes," said Brannigan.

". . . that the unenlightened Irishmen who slash the streams—and whom it has been my misfortune to fall in with during my decline—would scarcely understand. Brannigan, Branny old boy, did you see the innocence, the absolute simplicity of that farmgirl holding her child this afternoon? The Madonna—no less."

"Will you simply tell us what fly you were using?" Mike insisted.

"A question impossible to answer, beyond my power to answer. Ah, but did you see the colors of the sun settling below the treeline, the ochers, the magentas, the great song of the heavens? You must scatter my ashes there, Branny. It is so written."

We were silent while he dropped us off at Brannigan's house, carefully unloading all our tackle—this time without comment. He asked if we'd like a fish apiece (though not the two trophies).

We both said no.

Then he got back into his car stiffly, turned over the motor, looked at us both with those ancient and shadowy eyes, smiled, and said: "It was an event, gentlemen—was it not? We have been to Mecca. And it will last longer than these six trout, which I shall dispatch shortly—the least part of our trip."

"You won't tell us what you took them on?" I asked.

"You've missed the point. Nick," he said, taking my hand in his bony fingers, "until next year . . ."

With that he drove off, around Brannigan's graveled circle and up the road. On the highway we could see the old Dodge pause. Hawkes leaned far out of the car, looked up at the moon, and said something loudly which we did not hear.

"Perhaps it *will* last longer," said Mike, putting his arm around my shoulder and smiling broadly there in the moonlight. I started preparing for the long trip back to the city, for the long year.

"Perhaps," I said.

And it has.

November 1968

How I Didn't Fish the Little Lehigh

ED ZERN

The writer's encounter with his father's friend turns a fishing trip into a time warp.

A LONG TIME AGO I was thirty years old and lived in Philadelphia with my wife Evelyn and our three-year-old son Brook. During the trout season I would spend nearly all of my weekends at Analomink on the Brodheads Creek in the Poconos, staying at Charlie Rethoret's Hotel Rapids and fishing the Brodheads, the Bushkill, the Paradise, and a few other streams in the area. When someone asked me one time if I ever fished the Little Lehigh I said no, because I hadn't, but it occurred to me that perhaps I was in a rut, albeit a pleasant one, and should broaden my horizons. So early the next Saturday I drove north toward the Little Lehigh, figuring if I didn't like it I could always continue on north and east to the Brodheads.

When I stopped to get gas, and looked at the road map to check my route, I noticed I'd pass within about 20 miles of the small town my father, who had died fifteen years before, had come from, and where I hadn't been since I was six. In my mind's eye I could see the large white frame house where my grandmother had lived, and the white picket fence around it, and I could see the horse chestnut tree beside the house and the sweet-shrub bushes, and the swing on the front porch. I also had a strong feeling that if I got to the town I'd be able to find the hill on which the house had stood, with the house still on it, without asking directions. So I detoured toward the town, as the map indicated, and got there about 10 o'clock.

The town was (and still is, I suppose) a small one, of about 5,000 people, mostly Pennsylvania Dutch as my father had been, but it boasted a town square with a Civil War monument in the center, and I parked my Ford roadster in the square. It was a mild, sunny day, and I decided to see if I really could find the old house without asking directions, partly because my grandmother

47

had moved from that town to Philadelphia some twenty years before, so that few people were likely to remember her and be able to tell me where she had lived. Also, as I drove into the town I still had the feeling I could find it unaided, and the feeling got stronger as I parked the car; *Surely*, I thought, *all I have to do is walk down the main street about three blocks, turn right up the hill and there would be the house.*

I had walked about a block, past dry-goods stores selling cheap work clothes and bakeries selling shoo-fly pies, when someone called "Ed!" I turned and saw it was an old man, wizened and gnomish, in his eighties or perhaps his nineties, leaning on a cane and peering at me. One reason my son is named Brook is that brooks have always had a special importance to me; the other is that sometimes it seems every third person is named Ed, and I spend too much of my time finding out that it's some other Ed being hollered at. But there was no doubt about it: the old man meant me, although I felt sure I hadn't ever seen him before. There are lots of Eds, I thought, and was about to explain to the gaffer that he had mistaken me for someone else when he tottered toward me and croaked, "You're Ed Zern, aren't you?"

I admitted I was, and thought perhaps the old man had worked around the fraternity house grounds when I was at college—there had been a succession of elderly gardeners, mostly drifters and all forgettable.

"Haven't seen you for five, six years!" the old man said, and I mumbled something inane. "You haven't changed a bit, though," he went on. "I'd of knowed you anywhere. Let's see now, you went to Penn State, didn't you?" I said that was right, and he contemplated me thoughtfully and then cackled, "I heard you got married! Heard you had a little boy! Ain't that right?"

Again I admitted it was right, and was about to ask him how he knew me when he said, "Let's see now, Ed. You married a girl from Bloomsburg, didn't you?" and I understood. My mother had been born and raised in Catawissa, a village near Bloomsburg, and had met my father while he was an undergraduate at Penn State and she was a student at Bloomsburg's small college. And I look, or looked then, like my father, whose name was Edward.

:"Tell me, Ed," the gnome said, "how's that little boy? Smart, I'll bet, like his daddy! Ain't that so?"

I stared at him, not knowing what to say. What little boy? What daddy? I couldn't tell him he had slipped a forty-year cog in his memory, but should I tell him the little boy was smart? It seemed immodest. "I guess he's smart enough," I said.

"What's he going to be when he grows up, heh?" the old man croaked. "A writer like his pa, I'll bet." My father was a mining engineer, and although he had become the editor of a group of engineering publications after a long career as a university professor, I had never thought of him as a writer.

"The newspaper ain't been the same since you went away to college, Ed," the old man chuckled, and I remembered my father telling me how he had earned a dollar a week, or it may have been 50 cents, by writing for the town paper while he was in high school; I think I hadn't really believed him, until now.

"I hope he'll be a writer," I said, and probably blushed; I knew damn well he *had* become a writer, mostly of fishing and hunting stories, or at least the child the old man was talking about had become that; the child I was talking about, or should have been, my son Brook, might or might not become a writer or President of the United States—I hadn't given it much thought. (He did become one of those.)

"Tell me, Eddie," the gnome said, "what are you up to these days? Where are you living?" I tried to decide: should I say Philadelphia, which was where I lived, or should I say West Virginia, which is where the man the old man thought I was had lived when his son, I, had been three years old? Should I tell him I had sold my soul to a Philadelphia advertising agency for a fairly tasty mess of potage, or should I tell him I was head of the School of Mines at West Virginia University? I wasn't able to concentrate on the problem, because I had a frightening feeling that at any moment the old man would suddenly get his memory back on the track and, realizing I had to be some sort of impostor, start whacking me with his cane.

"Ed," he said, squinting at me, "I recollect your father. A fine man. You sure look a lot like him. I'll bet your little boy looks like you, don't he?" By this time I was too panic-stricken to keep straight which little boy was which and who looked like whom, and blurted, "He sure does. Look, I've got to be going but it was nice talking to you." Then I hurried back to the square, got in the Ford roadster, and got the hell out of there.

A mile out of town I stopped and looked at the map to see which way the Brodheads was, because not being absolutely sure if I was I or my father or my son, or even what state I lived in, I needed to be someplace where I could regroup and shake off the feeling that I had just blundered into some sort of H. G. Wells time-space trap and might never get out.

When I got to the Brodheads two hours later Charley found a room for me and after a martini and lunch I changed into fishing clothes and got into my Anderson waders and out on the river as fast as I could. The sun was too bright on the water and I spent most of the afternoon sitting at the Bend

Pool watching a few small trout splashing at stragglers from the Hendrickson hatch, and hoping something over 6 or 7 inches would show up, and by the time the sun had hunkered down behind a Pocono and a few decent fish began moving, I had pretty much figured out who I was, and when and where, and even managed to take a respectable 15-inch brown from the little eddy on the far side of the pool. It rained hard that night, and when I found the Brodheads up 3 feet and muddy after breakfast I packed it in and drove back to Philadelphia.

Maybe some day I'll get up the courage to try the Little Lehigh again. I hear it's a nice little river, and that old man would be at least 110.

August 1979

Midnight Stripers

RUSSELL CHATHAM

Fishermen will go to extremes to keep their secret about a great spot.

URBAN LIFE HAS never been known to dull people's urge to go fishing. In any town there is always a subculture, an armature upon which any number of casual and some not-so-casual friendships are based, that has only and particularly to do with fishing. Early in the morning in San Francisco, for example, you frequently see people loading tackle into their cars. Most will be staying close to town, fishing from piers or beaches. Others will be going to the waterfront to take a boat out on the bay for bass, or the ocean for salmon.

Some of the men work at City Hall, some are Montgomery Street brokers, bankers, or executives. Others work in department stores, shops in the Japanese Trade Center, the Department of Public Works. Some are unemployed and live in old hotels south of Market. It doesn't matter. A phone call to one of those with a secretary hard to get past will be put through twice as quickly if it's about where they hit the stripers yesterday than if it has to do with actual business.

Too little has been said about finding one's sport close to home, probably because most of the sportsmen who are getting the press are men of means, or professionals who earn a living by visiting the exotic and the distant either as tournament anglers or as journalists.

Inasmuch as that is true, brochure esthetics and magazine promises invariably fail to compare with the rich skein of knowledge which is one of the results of simply paying attention at home.

There is a shallow arm of San Francisco Bay, which for twenty years was under ten minutes from my home. The place is so spartan, so unappealing in the light of day, so geometric and seemingly perverse, that it was, and still is, overlooked entirely by fishermen. Point it out to a trout fisherman and he will want to throw up.

As a striped bass fisherman I see it differently. Not for a moment excusing the damage done by industrial disregard, when I look, I see a fishing hole where you can catch bass up to 30 pounds twelve months of the year by fly casting from shore.

There is room for two fishermen—if they are close friends. This is one of those intricate, precise situations that remind you just how thin is the line between failure and success. In this instance, success means fishing one exact edge of current at a critical moment of tide, at a certain hour, and from one particular angle. It has long been a matter of the gravest importance to me that absolutely none of this data fall into the hands of anyone who has ever even thought of owning a fishing rod.

A look at the tide and current tables gives us our starting point: low tide. From there my friend and I—he fitting the description closely—determine the part of the flood we must catch, and at what time. It appears that we will be finished fishing and home by midnight, looking into a comfortable fire.

My companion and I pull off the freeway and park near a commuter bus stop. It is nearly dark as we slip over a low embankment and start the 600-yard walk to where we will fish, through weedy, uneven marshland, acres of debris. It is not an altogether pleasant stroll, but a necessary ruse to escape detection.

My friend has gone to the trouble of buying black industrial waders and a black parka. He wears a black cotton turtleneck shirt and a black wool watch cap. He has even painted his fiberglas fly rod flat black. I wonder aloud why he hasn't taken commando tactics to the limit and done his face in soot. His only response is that I am going to someday give the whole thing away by wearing loud clothing such as my dark green sweater.

Oddly, even the flies we use are black feather streamers. Although in this instance the motive is to show the striped bass something they *can* see.

The cool evening air is still. It is not, however, in any sense quiet, and we must talk in voices loud enough to be heard above the heavy drone of nearby traffic. The surrounding landscape is complicated, inorganic, industrial; piers, bridges, and docks give way to frontage roads, restaurants, service stations, office buildings, apartment houses, and a vast array of night lights.

Shortly, we reach a complex of pilings only a few yards from the muddy bank. The tide is at its utmost ebb, so we sit down on a large pipe (in all likelihood sewer) to wait for the tide to come in.

Nearby is a curved exit ramp that most cars seem to take a little too fast. As we sit, one takes it entirely too fast, there is the improbable screech of rubber against asphalt, and someone buys the farm. Within minutes the highway patrol is there, red and yellow beacons flashing, reflecting off the water and freeway abutments like a sixties Fillmore Auditorium light show. A tow truck tacks into place near the twisted metal and broken light filaments. Police radios crackle loudly in the night.

Nearby there is a patch of marsh that appears intact, the light green grasses lush and dense. At its edge a wooden structure, built at the turn of the century, still stands. Something old does remain. The years laminate their influence upon the countryside, but certain places are covered more slowly than others, some not at all. It is a bit like fattening a picture over the underpainting; paint and repaint, yet in the end certain areas are finalized by being left alone.

You get out of the habit of rifling through the pages of time, perhaps because your mental health rests in some large measure on coming to terms with present situations. So it takes a while to occur that I am sitting mere yards from where my mother and her family lived in 1915.

They lived on a houseboat, one of many that lined the little slough. My grandfather, Gottardo Piazzoni, a painter, did many sketches of the arks, the bay, the surrounding hills. Rich little paintings, soundly constructed, sensitive in every detail, they record moods of solitude, peace, and warmth; summer moonrises, giving no notice whatsoever of the coming of freeways and the Army Corps of Engineers.

But come they did. The two lane blacktop, wooden drawbridge, and arterial stop were replaced by ten lanes and soaring overpasses, some so many-leveled and complex they became known as mazes.

Dissatisfied with intimate, serpentine creeks and sloughs, the Corps dredged and straightened every mystery out of them, leaving bare, evenly beveled shores unfriendly to herons and mallards, but perfect for the backyards of townhouses and condominiums. They gave the landscape a giant manicure, polishing it with shopping malls, and a seemingly endless number of fast-food establishments.

The tide begins to move. In the wake of some pilings, distant lights glint off tiny folds in the current. As the water gains momentum, bits of food will be dislodged and small forage fish disoriented. And when the tide reaches a particular pitch we will see the first feeders explode out on the dark edge of the channel.

Night flying birds glide in and out of the light, gulls mostly. They have adapted to the surprise appearance of power lines and their feet conform perfectly to bridge railings.

Near us, a small fish hops erratically from the water, being chased by a striped bass. My friend lands a cast in the feeding lane and has an immediate taker. His fish pulls strongly to one side, giving me room to cast to other bass, which have begun to feed. My streamer is seized and we are now both connected to struggling fish. When we land them we make a bed of rushes and hide them.

The bass feed wantonly, visibly reckless as they slash into a buffet of bright silver smelt. Inside of two hours, four more stripers are hidden in the reeds. Of the six, the smallest will weigh at least 15 pounds, the largest about 25. This is our lawful limit; in this case around 75 pounds of fillets, delectable roe, and court bouillon. In any quarter it is an impressive catch, the more so to have been taken by the difficult craft of fly casting.

This evening perhaps 10,000 speeding cars have passed within yards while we fished in a solitude as complete in its way as that of the Brooks Range. To keep it that way, maybe soot on the face is not going too far at all.

We decide it's late enough to bring the car over so we won't have to carry the fish so far. When they are safely in the trunk, we go back for our rods and waders. The effort is cut short by a nudge from my companion.

"There's someone coming."

I see the figure moving toward us along a pedestrian walkway. It seems preposterous to make a run for it, like fugitives. Besides, he's now close enough that if he is a warden or member of some other arm of the law, we'd be seen, thus arousing his deepest suspicion. We quickly decide to simply walk casually along as if it were the most natural thing in the world to be wandering around by the freeway at 11 P.M. with armloads of fishing tackle.

"I think we're safe," I say inconspicuously when the man nears. "He looks drunk as a skunk to me."

And indeed he is, passing us at full stumble. But his reaction is delayed, and it takes him several seconds to turn and call out.

"Hey! You guys!"

We freeze, then slowly turn around.

"You been fishin'?"

"Uh . . . sort of."

"Get any?"

"No."

"Yer doin' it wrong. It's the wrong night. C'mere. Yer gonna think I'm blowin' smoke at ya. You think I'm blowin' smoke at ya I know, but I've seen 'em THIS BIG!"

He is jabbering, holding his hands outstretched to indicate a large fish.

"Now, I'm drunk. I been drinkin'. Okay. But I swear I'm not makin' this up. I've seen 'em by those pilings. Listen: come back right here on the second full moon."

My friend and I look at one another.

"I know, I know," he goes on, holding out his hands as if he were supporting a panel of plywood with his fingertips and forehead. "You guys think I'm blowin' smoke at ya. Believe me now, second full moon of the summer. Warm night. Be here. See, the mosquitos fly down by the water to keep cool then the big fish are there waitin'. They just jump up an' grab 'em."

We laugh and agree to take his advice, enthusiastically convincing him we don't think he's blowing smoke at us. Seeing we have taken him seriously, he is openly pleased. We promise to return at the time of the second full moon, whatever that is, but only if he promises to let this wonderful news remain our secret. We shake hands and he goes on his way, humming.

We are at the car and have just put away the rods and boots when suddenly, headlights beam over us, then a spotlight.

"Good Lord, it's the police," I say, with that momentary sinking feeling in the pit of the stomach that peace officers always seem to provide when they are going to question you.

"Be cool, it's nothing."

The car pulls up and two officers get out.

"Sheriff's Department," the first says. "Everything all right?"

"Yes sir."

"What are you doing down here?"

"Oh . . . well . . . uh, we just thought we'd stop for a little air, walk around, look at the water, you know, *get outside*."

"Here? You boys have some identification?"

We give him our driver's licenses. The second officer goes to the patrol car to check them.

"Funny place to be getting air, isn't it?" The deputy says, looking directly at us, then scanning the surrounding area.

"Officer," my friend begins earnestly, "maybe we'll get into less trouble if we just level with you. We were shooting pool at that bar about five blocks from here when we decided to step out and smoke a little number. You know? Didn't think we'd be bothered down here."

"You have any more stuff in the car?"

"One joint was it."

The second officer comes back with our licenses.

"These check out okay."

"You guys get out of here now," the first officer tells us.

We climb in the car and start away.

"Why did you tell him *that*?"

"Look," my friend explains, "a lot of cops like to fish. They're like firemen. They all fish and hunt. Suppose those two deputies happened to be fishermen. If they found out about our spot they'd go crazy. They could even time their rounds so they could get in a few casts right during the best part of the tide. That would be it. You know how touchy this place is. I had to tell them something to completely satisfy their curiosity."

"What if they arrested us for drugs?"

"We don't have any do we? And we hadn't done any either. If they were actually going to take us in or something like that, then we would have had to tell the truth. But they didn't."

March 1977

Not Far From Sundown

ARTHUR GORDON

For the old man and his dog, it was a farewell journey, and the way it ended was a kind of miracle.

THE OLD MAN came out of the Medical Arts building and walked slowly down to his car where the small black dog waited, paws on windowsill, ragged ears up, brown eyes following every movement. A welcoming tail thumped the upholstery.

"Move over, Andy," the old man said. He sat for a while gripping the wheel with hands that were thin but still strong. He looked up at the fierce sunlight gilding the weathervane on the courthouse down the street. "Ever had a cardiogram, Andy? Well, don't."

He had had others, of course, but this was the first since the blackouts had started, annoying little lapses, very quick, where darkness seemed to come at him from the outside corners of his eyes and everything faded but then gradually brightened again. He had said nothing to Martha—why alarm her?—but since she was away for a few days visiting the grandchildren he had decided to let the doctor check it out.

Now he almost wished he hadn't because the verdict was discouraging. No undue stress or excitement. No exertion. Specifically no more solitary expeditions down the lonely windswept beaches. "I know it'll be tough," the doctor said, "for you to give up surf fishing and messing around with boats. But slow-down time comes to all of us. Besides, you've already caught most of the fish in the sea, haven't you?" One of those questions designed to make you feel better that just make you feel worse.

"I suppose the man is right, Andy," the old man said. "But it's pretty annoying when a bunch of electric wires can tell you what to do. Look at that weathervane. Southeast wind; high tide around noon. One more little excursion won't make much difference, probably; why don't we try it before Miss Martha gets back and tells us we can't?"

In the little tidal river the skiff was riding 30 yards offshore. The old man flicked his surf-rod so that the 3-ounce sinker arched out and the leader wrapped itself around the anchor line close to the bow. He reeled in slowly until the keel of the skiff touched bottom, then looked at the dog sitting at the water's edge. "Come on, Andy," he said, "be brave. You may not be able to swim, but you can wade, can't you?"

Andy stood up, touched one paw to the water, then sat down again, looking dejected.

The old man sighed, picked Andy up, and deposited him in the boat. "Not only are you a coward," he said, "you are also the ugliest dog on the Eastern seaboard. Even your tail is hideous. How did I ever get stuck with a wretched beast like you?"

Andy looked up with soft brown eyes and wagged his hideous tail. He knew a compliment when he heard one.

The dog, just a stray which had been found half starving beside a road some years ago, went everywhere the old man went, even in the boat, although it was clear that some unknown early trauma had left him with a profound fear of water. Once the old man tried to overcome that fear by placing the dog on a tiny sandbar with a rising tide and the boat not 10 feet away. Years ago he had watched a mother raccoon teach her offspring to swim in such a manner, crossing a creek herself and then calling back to them until they found the courage to follow. But the misery in Andy's brown eyes as the water rose was more than he could stand, and in the end he placed the dog back in the skiff, where he sat immovably like a misplaced black fireplug until they were home and the old man carried him safely to shore.

Now he sat in just such fashion as the skiff drove through the chop in the middle of the river and then on through the network of creeks on the far side where terrapin skittered down the muddy banks into the still green water and mullet swirled and the great blue herons soared up and away. Ordinarily the old man paid little attention to such familiar things, but on this day he watched them with a certain intensity, as if trying to impress the images on his memory.

They came at last to a broad estuary flowing eastward through the barrier beaches with leaping tongues of surf on either side where it met the sea. A short distance above this entrance was a little cove, and here the old man anchored the boat, placing Andy carefully ashore and watching him chase sandpipers, barking wildly. He never yet had caught one, and never would, but the old man understood how he felt. A dream is just a belief in possibilities and this was Andy's dream.

He circled back at last to bark even more fiercely at a horseshoe crab, stranded on its back in a shallow pool. Seeing this, the old man paused. "Don't be rude to that crab, Andy," he said. "His ancestors were on this earth long before yours or mine. Besides, if we speak nicely to him and help him out, the sea-gods may reward us." He picked up the grotesque creature by its armored tail, feeling the life vibrating within it still and carried it back toward the estuary with the dog pacing uneasily alongside. "Your mistake, Andy," he said, "is treating this crab as if it were an it, instead of thinking of it as a you. Try to get the notion through that head of yours that every living creature is a you, just as you are. Took me a long time to figure that out, but it sort of binds things together somehow. So let's just say, 'Good luck to you, old crab,'" and he tossed it out into deep water while Andy stared, bemused.

On then through some shallow dunes where the sea-oats nodded to their own shadows and across the broad beach, blinding white in the sun with scattered driftwood and bundles of marsh grass and bleached sanddollars. Two hundred yards offshore, gulls were mewing and diving where a school of mackerel were tearing up some baitfish. No other human being was in sight, no houses, no manmade thing except far off against the dunes the rusted engine of a wrecked shrimp boat. The old man knew that very few beaches like this could be found anywhere, and that this one could not remain untouched for very long, but he tried not to think about it.

Near the water's edge he put his gear on the sand and sat down beside it, waiting for his heart to cease its pounding. Ahead of him was a shallow lagoon or slough with the tide easing into it and beyond that a narrow sandbar where the green rollers broke with a sound like muffled thunder.

Andy came up, panting, and the old man poured some water from a small thermos and gave him a drink. "Nice day, isn't it, Andy? Nice friendly day. Nobody's trying to run us off today. But that was a queer business last year, wasn't it? Scared you, I know, and it spooked me too. Yessir, it did."

They had been fishing in this place on a bright autumn afternoon, wind and tide favorable, water so clear you could see schools of mullet stacked up in each wave as it curled over to break. The old man had made a few casts, at peace with himself, at peace with everything, waiting to see what the sea had to offer. Andy was sitting, tired of chasing sandpipers, content to wait as long as necessary.

Then without warning the sun seemed to grow dim. The green water turned the color of lead. The wind died, but the air seemed colder. The birds vanished. A ringing silence settled over everything. Waist deep in the warm water the old man felt the hair on the back of his neck tighten. He looked quickly, left and right, for a shark's fin, and then behind him. Nothing. But the feeling of isolation and dread grew stronger. On the beach Andy had crouched down suddenly like a dog expecting an undeserved blow. *This is nonsense*, the old man thought, but a deeper part of him knew that it was not. Something invisible was surrounding him, crowding in, something very powerful and very threatening. That something was laying claim to the special solitude of this place, and it didn't want to share it with any human being. Or any dog, either.

The old man had tried to close his mind against a rising tide of panic. He started backing up, reeling in, but suddenly the line was slack. He felt no strike, no tug, nothing, but he knew the hook and leader and sinker were gone. He turned then and splashed back to the beach where Andy was still crouched beside the tackle box. He scooped up his gear and started back to the skiff, the dog close at his heels, angry with himself for fleeing but with a sense of almost-terror that was stronger than his anger. He put the dog in the boat, snatched up the anchor, cranked the engine, opened the throttle wide and roared westward up the estuary. And he did not look back.

His pulse seemed to be running smoothly and evenly now so he reached for his tackle box and took out a pair of pliers. "If this is the last roundup, Andy, why don't we even the odds a little bit?" Picking up the hook at the end of the long leader he carefully mashed the barb flat. "May cost us a fish or two, but that's all right." He took a piece of cut mullet and inserted the now barbless hook so that the needle point went through the skin at one place and came out at another. He stood up a bit stiffly. "If you had an ounce of fidelity in you," he said to Andy, "you'd swim this lagoon and join me on the bar. But I know you won't. Why couldn't I have had a noble retriever named Rex instead of a misbegotten mutt?" Andy lay down and put his nose on his forepaws. He judged words by tone, not content, and knew that all was well.

The old man waded across the lagoon, climbed the short steep bank on the far side, and moved into the surf until the breakers swirled about his knees. The silver scales of the mullet glittered as the line soared out into deeper water. In a short time, now, the bar would be covered and the lagoon would be 5 feet deep. But the old man knew he had an hour of fishing before that, perhaps a bit more.

For 10 minutes he waited, feet braced against the thrust of the waves, cap brim pulled down over his eyes to lessen the sun-dazzle. A flight of pelicans came by, coasting downwind. Beyond the breakers the gleaming black backs of two porpoises surfaced and disappeared. The wind blew and the foam seethed softly and the tide moved in.

Abruptly, with a tremendous shock, something seized the bait. The rod bent almost double, then sprang erect again as a black-tipped shark, close to 5 feet, exploded into the air in a frenzy of spray, threw the hook, and was gone.

The old man felt his heart lurch with the sudden rush of adrenaline. He waited until it seemed quiet, then reeled in slowly. As he rebaited the hook, he noticed that his hands were trembling, so he waited until they were still before making another cast. Then he moved back six paces and waited again, because some instinct in him knew that the shark was only a prelude.

He knew this with certainty, and so he was not surprised when something picked up the bait gently and stealthily and started moving out to sea. He had disengaged the brake on the reel and was controlling the line only with his thumb, so he was able to apply pressure very gradually. But the pressure made no difference; the line kept moving out until he knew he would have to begin to fight the fish before it was all gone. So he flipped on the brake and struck hard.

It was like setting the hook into a runaway freight train. The reel gave a metallic screech; the line was ripped off despite the drag. The old man felt the tremendous pressure on his arms and shoulders and he knew that pressure must be maintained if he was going to land the fish. By aiding the drag with his thumb—and getting it burned—he managed to slow the first tremendous straightaway rush, but he knew that somehow he would have to turn the fish eventually. If it began to swim laterally, he might be able to move with it and eventually begin to recover some line. As it was he could see the linen backing through the few turns of monofilament that were left on the reel, and so he began to walk forward, following the fish. The water rose to his shoulders, a wave lashed him across the face and knocked his cap off. He still held the rod high and the strain was becoming unbearable when, far out, he saw the long dark shadow of his adversary silhouetted inside a towering roller, saw too the angry flash of a great bronze tail that could belong only to an enormous channel bass—stag bass, redfish, a fighter by any name.

The old man decided that he would either turn the fish or break the line. He put most of his remaining strength into a desperate heave, and the head of the fish swung round and it began to swim parallel to the beach, moving toward the point where the mouth of the lagoon met the incoming tide. The old man knew that he would never be able to land such a fish in the heavy surf. His only chance was to maneuver it into the lagoon itself. And after 20 minutes that is what he did, backing up slowly, hearing his own breath come in gasps, gaining 10 feet of line and losing 20, always keeping the tension on the fish until finally he could see it in the calm waters of the lagoon, where it made two or three last convulsive runs and then rolled over on its side, fins and tail moving faintly.

The old man waded forward slowly, feeling his knees tremble, keeping the rod tip high and the line taut. He came to the great fish and knelt beside it, knowing the mixture of triumph and regret that comes at such a time. He saw that the hook was embedded in a corner of the wide mouth, not far down the throat as he had feared. He said in a murmur, "You're pretty tired, aren't you, old fish? Believe me, so am I." He reached forward and removed the hook, but the exhausted bass made no lunge for freedom. It lay there, its yellow eye regarding its captor remotely.

"You'd like deeper water, wouldn't you?" the old man said finally. He put his rod down on the bottom of the lagoon—something he hated to do—and slid his arms under the passive fish. He eased its great weight gently out to a point where the water was 4 feet deep. He cradled it in his arms just under the surface where the sunlight glinted on the gill-plates, opening and closing, and the mother-of-pearl flanks and the massive tail with its two black spots. He waited, and gradually the fish righted itself as its strength came back. Finally it pulled away and began to swim, slowly at first, then faster and faster, toward the mouth of the lagoon and the open sea.

The old man stood up and watched it go. He turned, intending to look for the rod he had left underwater, but suddenly he felt dizzy and knew he had better get back to the bar while he could. He was within 3 feet of it when the darkness swept over him and he fell face down on the dry sand with his legs and feet still in the waters of the lagoon.

How long he lay there he did not know. Finally a shallow wave swirling across the bar slapped him in the face and he raised his head, choking and gasping. The darkness receded then and he came up on one elbow, glancing back toward the beach where his tackle box and spare rod rested tranquilly above the high-water mark. There was no sign of Andy, but when the old man sat up and scanned the now choppy waters of the lagoon, he saw a small black head moving toward him, ears flattened, eyes showing white with fright, submerged altogether now and then, but still coming, still swimming, closer and closer until the old man was able to reach forward and draw the shivering little animal into his lap. "Well done, Andy," he said. "I don't know how you thought you could help me, but I thank you for trying."

They sat there quietly for a little while. With his coat slicked back and his brown eyes, Andy looked almost like a baby seal. The old man could feel the dog's heart hammering furiously through his ribs. "Well, come on now," he said. "Better go back before it gets any deeper. Don't be afraid. I've got you and you've got me. We'll make it all right."

And so they did, the old man moving slowly through the current with one arm around Andy and one hand cupped under his chin, holding his head up until they came safely to the beach and made their way back to the skiff and home together. The old man wondered if from now on Andy might be a swimmer, but when they came to their final anchorage and he invited his companion to jump over and wade ashore, the invitation was declined. "Never mind, Andy," the old man said, carrying him to dry land. "We've had a good day. A very special kind of day."

That evening when he called Martha as he did every night when they were separated, the old man said nothing of what the day had held. It would keep until she got home. In fact, he thought, as he climbed wearily into bed and switched off the light, he might not tell anyone. Somehow it all might stay more intact if he didn't. He would know and Andy would know and that would be enough.

Andy was tired too. He went over to his scrap of carpet in the corner and lay down with a boneless thump. The old man smiled as he heard him sigh. He closed his eyes, then, and at once against the blackness inside his eye- lids the great bronze fish swam through green and gold depths, striped now by shadow, tail and fins moving silently, remote and untroubled in the element where it belonged. Farther and farther away it moved, growing smaller and smaller until with a final mother-of-pearl flicker it was gone, and sleep came down like a benediction, and the long day was over.

November 1991

Big Tuna

ZANE GREY

In the days of linen line, a legendary angler hunts for horse mackerel off Southern California.

I T TOOK ME five seasons at Catalina to catch a big tuna. And the event was so thrilling that I had to write to my fishermen friends about it. The results of my effusions seem rather dubious. Robert H. Davis, editor of *Munsey's*, replies in this wise: "If you went out with a mosquito net to catch a mess of minnows, your story would read like Roman gladiators seining the Tigris for whales."

Now I am at a loss to know how to take that compliment. Davis goes on to say more, and he also quotes me: "You say 'the hard diving fight of a tuna liberates the brute instinct in a man.'—Well, Zane, it also liberates the qualities of a liar!"

Davis does not love the sweet, soft scent that breathes from off the sea. Once on the Jersey coast I went tuna fishing with him. He was not happy on the boat. But once he came up out of the cabin with a jaunty feather in his hat. I admired it. I said: "Bob, I'll have to get something like that for my hat."

"Zane," he replied, piercingly, "what you need for your hat is a head!"

My lucky day came after no tuna had been reported for a week. Captain Dan and I ran out off Silver Canyon just on a last forlorn hope. The sea was rippling white and blue, with a good breeze. No whales showed. We left Avalon about one o'clock, ran out five miles, and began to fish. Our methods had undergone some change. We used a big kite out on three hundred yards of line; we tied this line on my leader; and we tightened the drag on the reel so that it took a nine pound pull to start the line off. This seemed a fatal procedure, but I was willing to try anything. My hope of getting a strike was exceedingly slim. Instead of a flying-fish for bait we used a good sized smelt, and we used hooks, big and strong, and sharp as needles.

We had not been out half an hour when Captain Dan left the wheel and jumped up on the gunwale to look at something.

"What do you see?" I asked, eagerly.

He was silent a moment. I daresay he did not want to make any mistakes. Then he jumped back to the wheel.

"School of tuna!" he boomed.

I stood up and looked in the direction indicated, but I could not see them. Dan said only the movement on the water could be seen. Good long swells were running, rather high, and presently I did see tuna showing darkly bronze in the blue water. They vanished. We had to turn the boat somewhat, and it began to appear that we would have difficulty in putting the bait into the school. So it turned out. We were in the wrong quarter to use the wind. I saw the school of tuna go by, perhaps two hundred feet from the boat. They were traveling fast, somewhat under the surface, and were separated from each other. They were big tuna. Captain Dan said they were hungry hunting fish. To me they appeared game, swift and illusive.

We lost sight of them. With the boat turned fairly into the west wind the kite soared, pulling hard, and my bait skipped down the slopes of the swells and up over the crests just like a live leaping little fish. It was my opinion that the tuna were running inshore. Dan said they were headed west. We saw nothing of them. Again the old familiar disappointment knocked at my heart, with added bitterness of past defeat. Dan scanned the sea like a shipwrecked mariner watching for a sail.

"I see them! . . . There!" he called. "They're sure traveling fast."

That stimulated me with a shock. I looked and looked, but I could not see the darkened water. Moments passed, during which I stood up, watching my bait as it slipped over the waves. I knew Dan would tell me when to begin to jump it. The suspense grew to be intense.

"We'll catch up with them," said Dan, excitedly. "Everything's right now. Kite high, pulling hard—bait working fine. You're sure of a strike. . . . When you see one set the bait hook quick and hard."

The ambition of years, the long patience, the endless efforts, the numberless disappointments, flashed up at Captain Dan's words of certainty, and, together with the thrilling proximity of the tuna we were chasing, they roused in me emotion utterly beyond proportion or reason. This had happened to me before, notably in swordfishing, but never had I felt such thrills, such tingling nerves, such oppression on my chest, such a wild eager rapture. It would have been impossible, notwithstanding my emotional temperament, if the leading up to this moment had not included so much long-sustained feeling.

"Jump your bait!" called Dan, with a ring in his voice. "In two jumps you'll be in the tail-enders."

I jerked my rod. The bait gracefully leaped over a swell—shot along the surface, and ended with a splash. Again I jerked. As the bait rose into the air a huge angry splash burst just under it, and a broad-backed tuna lunged and turned clear over, his tail smacking the water.

"Jump it!" yelled Dan.

Before I could move a circling smash of white surrounded my bait. I heard it. With all my might I jerked. Strong and heavy came the weight of the tuna. I had hooked him. With one solid thumping splash he sounded. Here was test for line and test for me. I could not resist one turn of the thumb-wheel, to ease the drag. He went down with the same old incomparable speed. I saw the kite descending. Dan threw out the clutch—ran to my side. The reel screamed. Every tense second, as the line whizzed off, I expected it to break. There was no joy, no sport in that painful watching. He ran off two hundred feet—then marvelous to see—he slowed up. The kite was still high, pulling hard. What with kite and drag and friction of line in the water that tuna had great strain upon him. He ran off a little more, slower this time, then stopped. The kite began to flutter.

I fell into the chair, jammed the rod-butt into the socket, and began to pump and wind.

"Doc, you're hooked on and you've stopped him!" boomed Dan. His face beamed. "Look at your legs!"

It became manifest then that my knees were wobbling, my feet put-tering around, my whole lower limbs shaking as if I had the palsy. I had lost control of my lower muscles. It was funny; it was ridiculous. It showed just what was my state of excitement.

The kite fluttered down to the water. The kite-line had not broken off, and this must add severely to the strain on the fish. Not only had I stopped the tuna but soon I had him coming up, slowly, yet rather easily. He was di-rectly under the boat. When I had all save about one hundred feet of line wound in the tuna anchored himself and would not budge for fifteen min-utes. Then again rather easily he was raised fifty more feet. He acted like any small hard-fighting fish.

"I've hooked a little one," I began. "That big fellow—he missed the bait, and a small one grabbed it."

Dan would not say so, but he feared just that. What miserable black luck! Almost I threw the rod and reel overboard. Some sense, however, pre-vented me from such an absurdity. And as I worked the tuna closer and closer

I grew absolutely sick with disappointment. The only thing to do was to haul this little fish in and go hunt up the school. So I pumped and pulled. That half hour seemed endless and bad business altogether. Anger possessed me and I began to work harder. At this juncture Shorty's boat appeared close to us. Shorty and Adams waved congratulations, and then made motions to Dan to get the direction of the school of tuna. That night both Shorty and Adams told me that I was working very hard on the fish, too hard to save any strength for a long battle.

Captain Dan watched the slow steady bends of my rod, as the tuna plugged, and at last he said: "Doc, it's a big fish!"

Strange to relate this did not electrify me. I did not believe it. But at the end of that half hour the tuna came clear to the surface, about one hundred feet from us, and there he rode the swells. Doubt folded his sable wings! Bronze and blue and green and silver flashes illumined the swells. I plainly saw that not only was the tuna big, but he was one of the long, slim, hard-fighting species.

Presently he sounded, and I began to work. I was fresh, eager, strong, and I meant to whip him quickly. Working on a big tuna is no joke. It is a man's job. A tuna fights on his side with head down and he never stops. If the angler rests the tuna will not only rest, too, but he will take more and more line. The method is a long slow lift or pump of rod—then lower the rod quickly and wind the reel. When the tuna is raised so high he will refuse to come any higher, and then there is a deadlock. There lives no fisherman but what there lives a tuna that can take the conceit and the fight out of him.

For an hour I worked. I sweat and panted and burned in the hot sun; and I enjoyed it. The sea was beautiful. A strong salty fragrance, wet and sweet, floated on the breeze. Catalina showed clear and bright, with its colored cliffs and yellow slides and dark ravines. Clemente Island rose a dark long barren lonely land to the southeast. The clouds in the west were like trade-wind clouds, white, regular, with level base-line.

At the end of the second hour I was tiring. There came a subtle change of spirit and mood. I had never let up for a minute. Captain Dan praised me, vowed I had never fought either broadbill or roundbill swordfish so consistently hard, but he cautioned me to save myself.

"That's a big tuna," he said, as he watched my rod.

Most of the time we drifted. Some of the time Dan ran the boat to keep even with the tuna, so he could not get too far under the stern and cut the line. At intervals the fish appeared to let up and at others he plugged harder. This I discovered was merely that he fought the hardest when I worked the hardest. Once we gained enough on him to cut the tangle of kite-line that had caught some fifty feet above my leader. This afforded cause for less anxiety.

"I'm afraid of sharks," said Dan.

Sharks are the bane of tuna fishermen. More tuna are cut off by sharks than are ever landed by anglers. This made me redouble my efforts, and in half an hour more I was dripping wet, burning hot, aching all over, and so spent I had to rest. Every time I dropped the rod on the gunwale the tuna took line—zee—zee—zee—foot by foot and yard by yard. My hands were cramped; my thumbs red and swollen, almost raw. I asked Dan for the harness, but he was loath to put it on because he was afraid I would break the fish off. So I worked on and on, with spurts of fury and periods of lagging.

At the end of three hours I was in bad condition. I had saved a little strength for the finish, but I was in danger of using that up before the crucial moment arrived. Dan had put the harness on me. I knew afterward that it saved the day. By the aid of the harness, putting my shoulders into the lift, I got the double line over the reel, only to lose it. Every time the tuna was pulled near the boat he sheered off, and it did not appear possible for me to prevent it. He got into a habit of coming to the surface about thirty feet out, and hanging there, in plain sight, as if he was cabled to the rocks of the ocean. Watching him only augmented my trouble. It had ceased long ago to be fun or sport or game. It was now a fight and it began to be torture. My hands were all blisters—my thumbs raw. The respect I had for that tuna was great.

He plugged down mostly, but latterly he began to run off to each side, to come to the surface, showing his broad green-silver side, and then he weaved to and fro behind the boat, trying to get under it. Captain Dan would have to run ahead to keep away from him. To hold what gain I had on the tuna was at these periods almost unendurable. Where before I had sweat, burned, throbbed and ached, I now began to see red, to grow dizzy, to suffer cramps and nausea, and exceeding pain.

Three hours and a half showed the tuna slower, heavier, higher, easier. He had taken us fifteen miles from where we had hooked him. He was weakening, but I thought I was worse off then he was. Dan changed the harness. It seemed to make more effort possible.

The floor under my feet was wet and slippery from the salt water dripping off my reel. I could not get any footing. The bend of that rod downward, the ceaseless tug, tug, the fear of sharks, the paradoxical loss of desire now to land the tuna, the change in my feeling of elation and thrill to wonder, disgust and utter weariness of spirit and body,—all these warned me that

I was at the end of my tether, and if anything could be done it must be quickly.

Relaxing I took a short rest. Then nerving myself to be indifferent to the pain, and yielding altogether to the brutal instinct this tuna fighting rouses in a fisherman, I lay back with might and main. Eight times I had gotten the double line over the reel. On the ninth I shut down, clamped with my thumbs and froze there. The wire leader sang like a telephone wire in the cold. I could scarcely see. My arms cracked. I felt an immense strain that must break me in an instant.

Captain Dan reached the leader. Slowly he heaved. The strain upon me was released. I let go the reel, threw off the drag, and stood up. There the tuna was, the bronze and blue-backed devil, gaping, wide-eyed, shining and silvery as he rolled, a big tuna if there ever was one, and he was conquered.

When Dan lunged with the gaff the tuna made a tremendous splash that deluged us. Then Dan yelled for another gaff. I was quick to get it. Next it was for me to throw a lasso over that threshing tail. When I accomplished this the tuna was ours. We hauled him up on the stern, heaving, thumping, throwing water and blood, and even vanquished he was magnificent. Three hours and fifty minutes! As I fell back in a chair, all in, I could not see for my life why any fisherman would want to catch more than one large tuna.

May 1919

Silver Savage Aboard

HART STILWELL

Fishermen get more action than they bargain for when a big tarpon crash-lands in their boat.

UCKSHOT AND I drove onto the sand-bar at the mouth of the river and sat for about nine seconds watching a show being staged on the other side of the stream. Hundreds of tarpon were constantly lunging and flashing and blasting the surface, beating the life out of mullet. During those nine seconds I am sure the same ideas came to both of us. We thought, "Only a mad man would put a skiff in that river, with the current racing out and the big breakers only two hundred yards away. Anything could happen. We're both family men, and it isn't fair to take foolish chances."

While we were thinking those thoughts one actor in the life-and-death drama near the far side of the river put on a specialty act for us. The actor was a tarpon.

He took after a mullet with such determination that he wound up on solid land and had to wriggle his way back into the water. But that didn't slow him down—away he went, hunting more mullet.

"Did you see what I saw?" I asked Buckshot.

"I saw," he replied.

"Well, what do you say?"

"The same thing you say."

Without wasting any more strength on words, we piled out of the car, unhitched the trailer, and slid the skiff into the water. Then we began moving crab-wise toward the center line of the river. The little motor would barely push the skiff against the current. When we reached midstream, I eased the anchor over. It wouldn't hold; so Buckshot held the boat in position with the motor and kept the motor in position by hooking his left leg over the handle.

70

That left both his hands free, and we knew, from long experience in battling the silver king of the Gulf, that he was going to need both hands, probably in a hurry. Tarpon that are schooled up and feeding may refuse to take plugs, but that's when they're feeding on menhaden or other small fry. When they're banging mullet around, the odds are a hundred to one they'll do the same with a plug.

If you're wondering why we didn't go upstream a bit, cross to the other shore, and cast from the bank, I'll tell you. We were fishing the Rio Grande. The other bank was Mexico, and the law said we could go to the center line and no farther.

When our floating plunkers settled to the water, tarpon pounced on them like cats catching mice. Before I had time to tighten my line my plug was up in the air with a tarpon rattling it around. He tossed it ten or fifteen feet to one side, where another tarpon latched onto it the instant it touched the water. That one bounced and shook free.

For almost two hours the tarpon gummed our plugs and we thrilled to the surging power of the great gamesters on the line. They were all small tarpon. We didn't see a one that would top five feet, which suited us fine. On our light casting tackle anything under 4½ feet was a "catching tarpon," one that put on a fine show but wasn't utterly unreasonable about giving up. A 6-footer might have tied us up for an hour or more. We even forgot those things that might happen to us.

Then out of nowhere came a crusty old grandpa tarpon with scars of battle on his scales and meanness in his soul, and before Buckshot could do anything about it the mighty warrior had the plug in his mouth. Buckshot struck and set the hooks. Sure, he knew he shouldn't have. But you try not striking a tarpon when he hits your plug!

The tarpon's first jump was straight up—fourteen feet by Buckshot's estimate, seven feet by mine. That's about right for such estimates. He always looks twice as high to the man who's got him on the line. The next time the tarpon jumped he came aboard. He just raced to the boat, took off on a flying leap, and landed in the midst of a mass of tackle boxes, gas cans, oars and other odds and ends.

From a sitting position I made what I considered a first-rate leap. I went over the side near the bow and hung onto the gunwale. Buckshot made a more spectacular leap, for not only did he go backward over the stern, but he held onto his gear.

The tarpon took charge. He set about trying to dismantle the boat, and as he flailed and thrashed and banged he worked himself toward the bow until his head stuck out from under the front seat. His scales kept him from sliding backward and the seat held him in the boat, even though he swung his tail back and forth in a mighty effort to get overboard. He was trapped.

I could distinctly hear two sounds in addition to all those made by the tarpon: the roar of the waves toward which we were moving at a fair clip, and the sputtering and spitting of the little outboard. The tarpon had given it a bath as he came aboard, and one cylinder was missing.

I eased the anchor out of the boat and let it down. It didn't do much good, but I figured it might hold a bit later, when the river mouth widened and the current eased off. We continued moving, not quite so fast but steadily enough to cause the short hair on my neck to start palpitating. All that time, which was actually only a few seconds, we were moving just inside a submerged sandbar that projects from the Mexican side of the river northeast into the Gulf, breaking the force of the big rollers.

When we reached the end of that bar, the waves would hit us in full force. And as they built up to a peak on nearing shore one of them could roll us up like the filling in a hot tamale. On we moved. Something had to be done; so I eased my head up above the side of the boat to survey the situation. I found myself looking squarely into the huge eye of a mighty tarpon, and I didn't like what I saw. He didn't either. He promptly set about trying to tear the boat apart, and I fully expected one of the planks to fly loose and bang into me.

"Do something," Buckshot shouted at me.

"Do what?" I asked.

"Stab him in the eye," Buckshot yelled. "Hurry! We're almost in the big rollers."

"Okay."

I pulled out my fish knife and poised it above the big eye of the tarpon. Fortunately he lay still for an instant.

"Stab him!" Buckshot insisted at the top of his lungs.

"I can't."

"Why not?"

"He's looking at me."

"Oh, oh, for the love of heaven!" he raged. "Why do I fish with such people? Stab him when he's not looking at you."

"But he keeps staring at me."

"All right, then just hang on a few minutes and it won't make any difference. We'll all drown together."

I felt the boat rise to a small swell. We were getting out where the bar was fading away. The next swell would be bigger, the next still bigger. Between us and shore was the main current of the river; we were on the outside edge of it now. And when we got in those swells—

I steeled myself to stab the tarpon in the eye. But just as the knife was descending I deliberately deflected it and hit the bony head without doing any damage. I know I was being sentimental and squeamish to the point of absurdity. In fact, Buckshot was busy explaining all that to me. He was telling me things about myself I had never even suspected. But I have worked up a warm bond of affection for the silver king as a result of many years' fishing, and to deliberately stab one in the eye . . .

Another wave, much larger than the last, sent the skiff skyward. Suddenly the warm bond of affection for tarpon snapped. "Okay," I figured, "I'll get the job done, and right now."

I got set, and that time I would have done it. But Buckshot began shouting a different tune. "Hold it! Don't kill him," he said. "I've got the motor going. Get the anchor up. Quick!"

I listened, and what I heard was sweet music. The whine of that outboard was as lovely and soul-stirring as the choral ode to joy in Beethoven's Ninth. But I couldn't get the anchor up. I had to cut the rope. We were making headway against the current even though Buckshot and I held the boat back some. For the current there was less than half as strong as it was where we had been fishing; it eased off as the river blended into the Gulf.

As we moved upstream, parallel to and in the protection of the submerged bar, the current became swifter. Finally we were simply standing still, even though both of us were trying to help by paddling and kicking. Buckshot started edging crabwise across the river, but the current caught the bow and swung it about so sharply that we lost twenty yards before he could get the boat headed upstream again.

Finally, after carefully surveying the situation, Buckshot sang out: "Hang on! I'm heading for shore."

He headed straight for the American side, not for the river bank but for the beach north of the river. At its mouth the Rio Grande curves sharply northward, and along the beach toward which Buckshot headed only a mild surf was running, because it got what was left of the waves after they crossed the submerged bar.

We went racing northeast with the current, but the little motor was pushing us steadily northwest, toward shore. And we got into the edge of the breakers not more than thirty feet short of the really rough surf, where the waves swept in with full force. Buckshot had calculated nicely.

A swell caught us and sped us toward land and entirely out of the current. My feet touched bottom and I tried to stand. Another swell pushed us forward and I lost my footing. Then a big roller, curling up at the top, came boiling in over the stern, drowning out the motor and emptying barrels of water into the skiff.

The tarpon had a sudden and somewhat violent revival of spirit. Now he had what he'd been needing for quite a spell—some water. It freshened him up and gave him something to lean into. The results were surprising. One end of the front seat gave way and popped up in the air right in front of my eyes, then I felt something hard and cold and slimy scrape my face, and the tarpon was gone.

I was sitting on sandy bottom. I got up and began pulling the skiff onto the beach. Buckshot stopped me. He was shouting: "Get the line loose! Get the line loose!"

For a moment I could do no more than stare at him. He caught me completely by surprise—he was standing in the surf, bouncing with the swells, fighting that tarpon. The idea that he might ever fight it left my mind the instant the fish came aboard. But during all those hair-raising seconds and minutes when Buckshot was in the water, he was hanging onto his tackle and looking forward to a battle.

But his line was caught on the seat. I reached out and freed it.

That was a long, stirring battle. If the tarpon's temporary residence in the boat took much fight out of him, I couldn't tell it. He moved up the coast, and Buckshot moved with him. I went along to furnish advice and make comments, none of which were appreciated. We were three-quarters of a mile from the skiff when I finally caught the leader and slid the huge fish out onto the sandy beach.

I measured him, eased the plug out, and pushed him back into the water. He swam away.

"Well, you've set a new record on casting tackle for these parts," I said to Buckshot. "Six foot seven inches."

"Too bad I can't count him," Buckshot lamented.

"Why not? There's nothing in the rules about tarpon that jumps aboard being disqualified."

"It's not that," he replied sadly. "It's you—you touched the line." He said it as though I had deliberately done something unethical.

I began to steam. "What the devil!" I stormed. "You asked me to, didn't you?"

"Yes, but it looks like you could have pushed the seat down, or maybe pulled it up and got the line loose. Couldn't you—" He stopped then. I guess he saw how hard I was struggling to hold myself in check.

"You know," I said, "if you were down in the bottom of that skiff, banging your head against the sides, and I raised up and looked you in the eye, why, I'm downright positive I could—"

"Don't say it," Buckshot broke in. Then he began laughing. It was a fine joke in his opinion. "You know I wouldn't try to count a tarpon that went boat-riding between jumps. Let's get back to that school before they quit feeding."

"Suits me," I said, and off we went.

May 1952

The Early Days

BYRON W. DALRYMPLE

Once upon a time, not all that long ago, "roughing it" was part of any angler's vocabulary.

IT'S FUNNY HOW far we've come in the past forty years or so. The other day an unhappy angler in his twenties was telling me about the indignities he'd suffered during a recent bass fishing trip. The guide's boat had only a "piddly 50-horse motor," no trolling motor, and the high front fishing seat screeched when he turned around to cast.

His lodge room was dark, the mattress too hard; they never gave him enough towels, and the restaurant steaks were tough. The last straw—the ice machine broke down.

I tried to look sympathetic. But I was remembering fishing camps of the 1930s, 1940s, and early 1950s. His tribulations amused me.

On my first fishing trip outside my home state, I drove 400 miles of bumpy narrow pavements interspersed with washboard gravel to reach a place in northern Wisconsin a friend had told me about: Bearpaw Cabins and Bar on Black Bear Lake, which my friend said swarmed with smallmouths.

"You'll like Bearpaw," he told me. "Dandy place. Everything there you'll need."

The place consisted of four tiny, weathered log cabins. Mine had a sag-springed bed, the mattress ticking stuffed with dry corn husks. When I turned in my sleep their rattling woke me up. There was a straight chair with a frayed wicker bottom, and a potbellied, sheet-iron stove. An ax was stuck in a woodpile out back. On cool nights I chopped kindling for a fire. A board with a brace beneath it was nailed to one wall. On it was a granite-ware wash-basin and a broken saucer with a cake of yellow soap. A bucket on the floor beside it invited the occupant to pump wash water at the nearby well. A thin, tattered towel hung on a nail nearby. As my friend had said, a dandy place. A little privy down a woods path had soft green moss growing on the roof, and an old Sears catalog on the seat.

A scrawled sign over the bar door said: "Eats." Owner Arne Jensen spoke with a Scandinavian accent. "You find da oudhouse aw right?" Bullet-headed and blocky, Arne wore a faded plaid flannel shirt with buttonless cuffs and coarse-weave, shagged pants over heavy work boots.

"You wanna ead?"

There was no menu. I sat at the bar waiting for Arne to bring my food. It was a fried meat patty with dark rye bread. He drew a mug of room-temperature beer. Although it was summer, the meat was obviously fresh venison. As I ate the patty, I found two deer hairs. I showed them to Arne.

He shrugged. "Dry mead. Gotta have somethin' to hold it together."

My cabin cost $1 a day; the boat was 50 cents extra, the motor another dollar. We went to the dock, Arne carrying a tiny Caille Twin. I remembered Caille magazine ads: "$39.50—pay as you fish." The boat was a homemade wooden rowboat. Arne got in, tilted it to one side, and bailed out a couple of quarts of water with a tomato can, saying it leaked only a little.

He pointed to the anchor, a big rock tied to a frayed rope. "Doan drop it on da boad boddum."

The day was delightful. The bass were willing. The little motor pushed the boat almost as fast as I could have rowed it. Bearpaw was more than a "dandy" place. It was great!

That evening Arne fixed me a bourbon and water. He brought a chunk of ice in his hand to drop into the glass. Arne had a large icebox, typical of that period. Ice was cut from the lake in winter, the blocks stored in a wooden shed and covered with several feet of sawdust from a nearby mill. You dug out a block, carried it to the pump, and washed off the sawdust.

Today health departments would be horrified at such procedure. As I stared at the ice chunk in my drink, I saw a tiny minnow frozen in it. I showed it to Arne.

"Kinda priddy, ain't it?"

Bearpaw was typical of fishing camps of that period anywhere across the Northern states. I vividly recall my first fishing trip farther South. It occurred in the early 1940s, a guided spring float trip for walleyes on the Meramec River in the Missouri Ozarks. I'd been directed down a narrow, dusty side road to a riverside farm where the owner floated fishermen in his homemade johnboat. Near his house was a rickety, native stone cabin, weather-stained and aged. The overalled owner—spare, lanky, with bony face and bobbing Adam's apple—came out, grinning, to meet me. Behind him six stairstep youngsters gathered on the stoop. After a handshake, I remarked on his fine brood.

He grinned again, looked toward them and said, "Seems like every spring but this'n's been too wet to plow."

His name was unforgettable: Leander Tuttle. He led me to the old stone cottage. The screen door was missing a hinge, the screen partly torn loose. There was a wood stove inside, the stovepipe leading to a crumbling stone chimney. He showed me an iron skillet and a few utensils in a cupboard, indicated the flat stove top, and said I could cook my vittles there. He'd fetch wood.

"They's been a pair of hooty owls roostin' daytimes in the chimley," he said. "I reckon they'll move when you build a fahr."

Electricity had not yet reached Leander's farm. A kerosene lamp sat on the small table. Beside it was the usual wash basin, soap saucer, and water bucket with tindipper. I inquired about an outhouse.

"They's a privy out back," Leander said. He grinned again. "Best toilet they is. Never gets out of fix."

That brought to mind a cabin I'd had in the late 1930s. There was a toilet, beside it a bucket, and on the wall above it a handlettered sign: "Flush with water fetched from lake."

He showed me to the old bed, proudly pointing to the sheets, telling me his "woman" made them. Faded yellow printing showed: "Bright Gold Brand Cornmeal."

"Purtiest sacks she ever saved up."

The place suited me just fine, and that afternoon, floating the river with Leander in his johnboat made it all the better. Every few minutes one of us caught a walleye. Leander used a cane pole, and it amuses me to remember my tackle. The rod was solid steel, square, and tapered, the guides soldered on. The reel had no level-wind. I had to thumb the black cotton line back on when I retrieved. We used fluted spinners I'd brought, with feather trebles. Leander sliced pieces of home-cured bacon from a chunk he'd brought, insisting that one wrapped onto the treble would attract walleyes by the salt trail it left. I didn't argue. It worked.

Another classic camp at which I stayed was at a central Florida lake I found during a mid-1940s winter. I arrived after dark. The cracker owner came out of his house carrying a flashlight. As he showed me to my cabin he kept sweeping the light over the ground.

"Lotsa moccasins crawling around h'yar at night," he said.

We entered the cabin using the flashlight. In the middle of the room he pulled a dangling string. A 25-watt bulb with a pull-chain switch hung from a cord through the ceiling. As the light came on there was a rustling sound.

"Mice?" I asked.

"Naw. Palmetto bugs." (Translation: cockroaches an inch-and-a-half long scurrying for cover.)

The cot springs here sagged so low they barely missed the floor. The mattress beat the corn-husk one I'd slept on long ago in Wisconsin. This one was ticking stuffed with Spanish moss. It sunk into a U when I lay down. I almost had to climb up the side to get out of bed. The place did have a bathroom of sorts. There was a toilet with a broken seat, the bowl rust-colored, and a washbasin with only a cold-water tap. There was no bathtub or shower.

The three narrow windows were equipped with old-fashioned green spring-roller pull-down shades. They had a certain appeal to one's gambling instinct. Readying for bed, I'd pull each shade clear down till it would catch. Then I'd take off my clothes, reach for my pajamas and, as I stood there buck naked, *zip*! One shade would fly up. My instinct would be to race to pull it back down, but by then another would have shot up. Finally, I got smart enough to pull the light chain before undressing.

The place did have a table, and an ancient refrigerator that screeched and rattled when the motor was running. It also leaked. There was a permanent puddle in front of it, with trickles running across the floor. Most intriguing, a huge toad lived beneath it. The critter would sit in the puddle and stoically watch me. I mentioned the toad to the owner.

"Lordy, son," he said, "don't mess with that toad. Hit keeps the pesky earwigs whittled down."

Frankly, looking back, I don't recall having been much bothered by any of those long-ago cabins, but I do remember reveling in the great fishing that came with them. There may have been inconveniences and discomforts to put up with, but there was abundant space and quiet as well—and the bass were beyond belief! Besides, we didn't think of corn-husk mattresses and such as hardships then. That's simply how things were, back in the early days, not all that long ago.

July 1992

Adrift with a Ditty-Bag Nut

ROBERT H. DAVIS

In the Maine woods, a city man has a memorable encounter with a "child of nature."

CLEAR LAKE, MAINE, 1914.—A cloudless day. Not a ripple stirred the bosom of the pond. The whole world was at peace. No sound broke the silence except the occasional splash of a black bass leaping into the ozone and throwing a back somersault in the shadow of the overhanging foliage. A kingfisher, dropping apparently from the clouds, struck the water full-breasted, pronged a minnow, and dashed back to his watchtowers in a shower of rainbows.

Idly I lay dreaming where I had thrown myself among the fragrant ferns and wildflowers.

A footfall sounded in the bracken. My ear, attuned to woodcraft and the strange noises of the forest, had not deceived me. I rose to greet a stranger who came trudging through the verdant drapery with the easy stride of an outdoor man.

He was thin of countenance, sparse of body, but tremendously well put together. A pair of blue eyes nestled under shaggy brows. The mouth was firm and straight, the nose long and thin. His hair was set well back from his forehead. His complexion was ruddy and rich as the autumn tints. His bearing was that of a conqueror.

Over his right shoulder hung a small waterproof bag about 8 inches wide and 6 inches deep. Inserted into the back of his bag, next to his body, was an old-fashioned case-knife edged on both sides and ground to a sharp point.

"Which way, stranger?" I inquired.

"Nowhere in particular," he answered. "Just roaming around through the woods studying the trees and polishing off a 20-mile walk, more or less.

"I see you are one of us," he continued, as his glance fell upon a small, double-edged woodman's brush-hatchet that I had driven into a nearby white birch tree. "Here's where we put up the ditty-bag." He removed the kit from his shoulder and hung it over the ax.

"I don't get you, Bill," said I, my face indicating that his cryptic observation was beyond me.

"Why? I supposed every woodsman knew the ritual of the ditty-bag."

"Well, I don't, for one," I ventured, with an appealing look.

"Simplest thing in the world," he continued. "Every outdoor man of any experience carries in the ditty-bag all that is necessary to sustain life and to make a journey across the continent. When he halts on the march for the night he sinks his tomahawk into a tree, hangs his ditty-bag across the blade, and makes himself comfortable. Don't you carry one?"

I made bold to inform him that I was stopping at a boarding-house about a mile down the shore of the lake which was good enough for me to halt at when I was in the halting business.

"I wouldn't be caught dead in one of those," he replied. "Only city men hang around those joints. I'm a child of nature. Do you see that bag hanging there? It carries cooking utensils, fishing-tackle, medicine—"

"Oh, you *do* get sick occasionally."

"Not me. I have medicine in case I run across some poor metropolitan boob whose health is on the bum. I never paid a doctor's bill in my life."

I never paid a doctor myself unless forced to; but that was none of his affair, so I kept my mouth shut.

"Ask for something necessary to comfort and I'll take it right out of that little bag hanging over the tomahawk there. Just name anything you want, and if I haven't got it, it doesn't exist." His confidence in that ditty-bag was magnificent.

"Now, if you don't mind," he babbled along, "I'll snake a couple of bass out of this lake and throw a meal into you that will make your hair curl. Where's the best fishing?"

Inasmuch as I wanted to see how this cove worked under normal conditions, I took him through the woods to a little bay where the small-mouth red-eye was an easy proposition from the shore. He carried his ditty-bag and I carried my tomahawk. Along the march he cut a willow rod, trimmed it artistically with his case-knife, and he was ready for business by the time we got to the rocks. Here he opened the mysterious bag and let me gaze into its vitals. It looked more like a junk-shop than anything I ever saw. From its recesses he extracted a hank of fishline, a sinker and a rusty snell hook upon which he impaled a perfectly good grasshopper. He liked his work very much.

"If that isn't a high-class, up-to-date fishing outfit, I'll eat it," he commented, walking out on a fallen tree which stretched far into the pool. He managed to get his line out, after which he jabbed the willow rod into the dead branches and returned shoreward to await further developments. In the meantime he went deeper into the ditty-bag and brought forth something that looked very much like a sausage wrapped in canvas.

"What do you call that?" I asked.

"Pea soup, concentrated pea soup, carrying a high percentage of bacon and its own pepper and salt. There's enough there to feed six men six days, three plates of soup a day for each man; eighteen plates of soup a day in all; one hundred and eight plates of pea soup per week. Can you beat it? You cannot!"

From the ditty-bag he then handed out what resembled a collapsible pie-plate, which, when opened, contained two other plates, making three in all. Count 'em! The handle was detachable and seemed to be a combination of knife, fork, spoon, and monkey-wrench.

Presto! He produced four steel rods, each 8 inches in length. These he drove into the ground so as to make a 4-inch square. Next he gathered some dried birchbark and a few chips and started a roaring fire with a tinder-box he took from the bag. He snatched a pan of fresh water from the lake, set his pie-plate over the fire, shook a few pinches of dust from his canvas sausage, and sat down to let nature take its course.

Suddenly the float on his bass rig went under. The child of nature slid out on the log with an agility that was truly commendable. I have seen some deft angling in my day, but I never saw anybody who could yank a bass out of his native heath and hurl him back into the timbers like this man. It must be a great surprise to a good, game black bass to bite a grasshopper and the next instant find himself doing a Zeppelin at a 60-foot elevation in a spruce-laden atmosphere.

The bold outdoor man pounced upon his prey without any prologue whatever, kicked him twice behind the ears, and then flashed the trusty case-knife for the finishing stroke. In one minute he had that fish cleaned and ready for the pan. During the interval the pie-plate range had heated up and the pea soup was singing a merry roundelay in effervescent ecstasy. Much to my astonishment it began to thicken up and presently assumed the proportions, characteristics, and quality of a first-class kite paste; after which it was set to one side on some hot coals and allowed to simmer.

"What do you intend to fry your fish in?" I inquired rather impatiently, with the secret hope that the ditty-bag dope was about to go bang.

"Salt pork," he replied with that bravado common to the gambler with a card up his sleeve. "Here it is, wrapped up in the oil-silk." He made a few passes and flashed a strip of salt pork upon his bewildered spectator. Its close resemblance to a hunk cut out of a cork bath-mat must not be considered here, because it really was pork—that is to say, it was *once*! At all events, it greased the pan, and the fish sizzled when it hit it.

In the third pan my frontiersman made some tea out of what looked to me like brick dust. It might have been plain, ordinary rust from the junk which made up the contents of the bag. Anyhow, it stained the water and when poured did not defy the laws of gravitation.

In the meantime the bass continued to burn, notwithstanding the fact that he turned it over three times alone, while the pea soup settled down into the unmistakable texture of a first-class, A-1 Portland cement.

The moment for banqueting was upon us. The outdoor man selected two large skunk-cabbage leaves from an adjoining bog, upon which he dished up the fish. Then, with his patent spoon, he split the soup into two portions— cracked it, I mean. It should have been served with a cold chisel.

Once again the man flipped the bass for its finishing brown and slid a half portion on my cabbage leaf. No outdoor man of standing can afford to decline bass at any time. Therefore, I passed up the soup and made overtures to the fish.

"Wait a moment," he counseled. "I forgot the salt."

In the depths of his miniature warehouse he located a small, flat tin box. The fact that it contained quinine instead of salt is a mere detail. He shook some on the fillet.

For the next 5 minutes the ditty-bag man was occupied with spitting black bass and apologies all over the landscape. In his confusion he knocked over the tea, a performance that awakened my deepest gratitude. He was perfectly willing to brew another dose, but I protested on the ground that the pea soup was rich enough to support human life in any climate. Secretly it was my intention to make a forced march back to the boarding-house, upon which he had looked with such disdain, and eat a plate of upstate Maine hash, with some rough army beans on the side, and, if possible, an entire New England pie.

I suggested that we clean up the dishes and start back over the trail for a square meal. I explained to my host that I was strong for ditty-bag chow, but, worked in an office all my life, was unaccustomed to violence at the table, and was prone to indigestion unless I paid some attention to regularity in my diet.

"I will admit," replied the culinary nut who had so valiantly offered to practice his simple arts upon me, "that this dinner hasn't been what you might call a big success. It is due to conditions over which I have no control. I have been on the road now for two months and my stock of provisions is running low. You should have seen me when I left Deal Beach, New Jersey. I had everything in its place and the whole kit weighed 9½ pounds."

"And you never really get hungry for good home cooking?" I asked of him. "A large stew, for instance, with real potatoes and onions and big parsnips swimming around in the gravy? Or a nice brown pot-roast, with a splash of creamy mashed potatoes stacked up on one side and some yellow turnips steaming in the foreground?"

He spit out another tongue-full of quinine and fixed his eye on the cold, imperturbable pea soup with an expression of malignant hatred.

"Don't you ever sit down in the quiet of the woods," I continued, "and speculate on the beauties of an old-fashioned bread pudding with raisins stuck in the custard? Haven't you ever awakened at night and visualized a pumpkin pie, with a slab of cheese leaning against the crust . . ."

The man pulled up the four pegs that constituted his cooking apparatus and hurled them with muttered curses into the ditty-bag.

"How about a plate of homemade ice cream smothered in preserved peaches?" I urged. "Or a chocolate cake, with frosting made out of real sugar and fresh eggs . . ."

He rose from the wreckage of his gastronomic nightmare and gazed into the deep recesses of the woodland.

It would have been an ill-considered action on my part to dwell at any greater length upon the misfortunes through which we had just passed. Kindness and charity seemed especially apropos under the circumstances. So, therefore, I went to his side, humming a blithe tune, hooked my arm in his and gently urged him southward in the direction of the Chow House.

Finally we came into a zone of that delicate aroma which emanates from burning wood performing heroic functions in a cook-stove.

My companion elevated his nostrils to the wind and sniffed a solo. The subtle perfume of broiling porterhouse floated through the lambent air.

The child of nature set himself for a hundred-yard dash as soon as he had determined the direction whence came the eau de cologne of home cooking.

"Lead me to it!" shrieked the apostle of the ditty-bag. And straightway he busted through the bracken, mounted the steps leading to the camp dining-room, and staggered into paradise.

Night had fallen. With his pipe comfortably filled and the gutta-percha clamped between his front teeth, the outdoor man sat on the veranda of my cabin and gazed at the stars. We talked of the starving Franklin Expedition, the Greeley trek, the march of Father Junipero through the northern wilderness, and other great human dramas in which starvation played a conspicuous part.

"They must have had a hell of a time. Hunger is a terrible thing." His voice trailed away as the drowsiness of satiety came upon him. His head fell gently upon his breast. Slowly he knocked the ashes from his pipe, stood up, waved adieu to the Milky Way, and staggered to the hay.

I followed shortly thereafter, thanking whatever gods there be that I had been chosen to rescue this poor ditty-bag nut in the most awful hour of his tragic existence.

I struck a match, held it aloft, and gazed on his recumbent figure gracefully sprawled over a bunk to which he seemed to be soldered. The voice of a whip-poor-will echoed through the distant treetops. Peace hovered over the world.

Thank God there is no copyright on sleep!

On the morrow, about 4 o'clock, I woke up to find the poor boob bending over a fireplace blowing softly on some hot coals underneath a little basin of birch-bark in which he was trying to boil pea soup without burning the utensil.

What's the use!

There are certain kinds of lunatics upon whom civilization has no influence. The ditty-bag nut is one of them.

Again I turned into my pillows for additional slumber. At 6 I reawakened. The wild man was still breathing upon the coals. I estimate that it would have taken two years to warm the pannikin of pea soup at the rate he was exhaling his precious breath.

I coughed. He turned a soot-smeared face upon me and smiled. Once before, in a New Jersey insane asylum, I saw a similar expression upon the face of a man who thought he had discovered perpetual motion.

March 1915

A Woman Through Husky-Land

FLORENCE A. TASKER

In the days before DEET, an intrepid sportswoman paddles and portages across the Far North.

IT IS ONE thing to spread out before you a large map of North America and carefully follow the stubby point of a pencil into unexplored and barren parts; another, to spend five months in completing a journey of over four thousand miles into these unexplored regions of our wonderful continent; and it is still another to be at home safe and sound, glad that you are alive and vowing never to do such a thing again.

I scarcely remember just how or when I came to promise the other member of my family to be a second party on a canoe trip to Hudson Bay and then across the northern Labrador Peninsula to the waters of the Atlantic. But I surely must have promised, for some time in the early spring, instead of planning pretty organdies, batistes, ginghams and several white linens which I remember that I had in mind, I found myself fashioning the stoutest short skirts and loose, homely gray flannel blouses—and besides these, about fifteen heavy canvas bags.

We were to leave Philadelphia in early June, and expected to return in November or December. Necessarily, we must prepare against both warm weather and cold—perhaps bitter cold. By the last of May everything was in readiness for the start. With the exception of provisions and a Peterborough canoe, which had been ordered to meet us at the starting point in Canada, everything had been gathered together. There were two balloon silk waterproof tents, an air mattress and eiderdown quilt; an aluminum cooking outfit, a medicine case, a small surgical box, camera, prism binocular, .405 Winchester rifle with fifty rounds of ammunition, 20-gauge Parker shotgun with two hundred rounds, waterproofs, pneumatic pillows or canoe seats, fishing rod and tackle, charts of the Labrador coast and astronomical tables, sextant, glass artificial horizon, pocket chronometer, thermometers, hypsometer, two axes and a miscellaneous assortment of small articles. It was necessary, you may well understand, to keep the weight down as far as possible, and we went as light as a fair degree of comfort and safety would permit.

On June 11 we arrived at Missanabie, Ontario, a small town on the Canadian Pacific Railway, north of the "Soo," where we were joined by George Elson, who was one of the men we had engaged. Almost everyone had heard of George Elson, the third man of the famous expedition on which Mr. Hubbard starved to death in the dreadful wilderness of Labrador. By dauntless perseverance George got out and sent back help to Dillon Wallace, or he undoubtedly would have met the same fate as Leonidas Hubbard. It was this same George who, with three Indians, guided plucky Mrs. Hubbard last year when in a record-breaking trip she was the first white person to successfully complete the work her husband gave his life in attempting. Our other man was Job Chappies, a full-blooded Cree. The canoe which lay at Missanabie was, as has been said, a Peterborough, canvas-covered, eighteen feet long, thirty-nine inches wide and sixteen inches deep. This, the largest we could procure, would seem a small craft for four people and a large outfit, would it not? And so it was; but even with a few inches of freeboard, we managed to the end of the trip.

We camped a mile across the lake from Missanabie for nine days, and never in the five months we spent outside the pale of civilization, did we feel the keen pangs of homesickness and depression as while camped near that unpleasant place, having our first taste, and a tiny taste too, of what the mosquitoes held in store for us.

But finally, on the ninth day, the canoe was loaded, and with a last dim look at the only railroad we were to see for a long time, we dipped our paddles and the little canvas Peterborough began her hard, faithful cruise toward the North.

The Moose or Missanabie River route from the railroad to the Moose Factory is a public thoroughfare. All summer, men, white and red, and mosquitoes, big and gray, are busy there. We encountered them all; Indians laboring with freight canoes, young railroad surveyors and even a few prospectors. None were going our way but the mosquitoes, and they never lagged nor tired. Always they escorted the canoe, unless a fresh breeze drove them off, and a swarm always awaited us no matter where we camped. There are about thirty-seven portages down the river, the longest being two miles, about three really magnificent rapids, and aside from them, no beauty whatever to speak of. There is a dispute about the distance from Missanabie to Moose Factory, but a safe average is three hundred and fifty miles. This trip we made in fifteen days, three of which were spent in camp owing to rain.

On one of these rainy days there came along the portage on which we camped eight of the most forlorn specimens of young manhood I ever hope to see. Two of the number were suffering from the dreaded scurvy, and one was so crippled and emaciated that he had to be carried over every portage. They were all Canadians and in a pitiable condition; some were hatless, some without coats and one with the soles completely worn off his shoepacs. All contributed what they could to the comfort of the two sick men and tried to be cheerful. A lump of fat, mildewed flour and black tea comprised the larder they carried. We replenished it as best we could, and they set on their way against stream to the railroad one hundred miles away. Whoever is responsible for the rations dealt out to the corps of young men going into that tangled wilderness to survey for those northern railroads, would, I should think, really be quite proud to see the little band that we saw—heartsore, footsore and ill-fed, struggling with their very lives to get out to civilization, away from mosquitoes and to where there was something better to eat than dog food. When these fellows learned that we were bent on sport and adventure, they uttered no sound—simply in a body raised their eyes and threw up their hands and looked, without the sound, like a pack of howling wolves.

There was no other event worth mentioning on our way to Moose Factory; we saw no game but caught a few fish that were acceptable additions to our monotonous bacon, biscuits, beans, rice, dried fruit and tea. Many of the rapids we shot were very dangerous, and the wonderful quiet of the forest awed one; yet how tame it all was compared to what we were to encounter across the bleak wilds of Labrador! Fifteen days from Missanabie we rounded the island of Moose Factory, and were received hospitably by the factor in charge and his wife. Everyone has heard of Moose Factory, one of the oldest forts of the Hudson Bay Company, where several hundred years ago they and the French or opposition company came together in mortal combat, and where even today the two companies are still in a war of words and threats.

One night we looked in at a dance of the élite of the community— and a great affair it was. Shy, comely squaws left their babies in the arms of the older women and gave themselves to the intoxication of a "square dance." Their soft moccasined feet beat a dull tattoo in time with the wail of a fiddle and the sickening thud of a drum which I am sure must have been a relic of that battle of English and French, before mentioned. Between the spasms of dancing, and while the orchestra mopped its brow on red cotton, great mugs of spruce beer and lumps of cake were passed around to the panting participants. And that night long after we had tented ourselves and fought savagely with a few hundred mosquitoes, we heard the thump of the dancers and the subdued cries of the tortured fiddle.

The next morning a stream of smoke was seen out towards the bay and a cry of "*The Inenew!*" went up. She is a small seventy-five-ton steamer that carries supplies to out-of-the-way posts on James and Hudson Bays, and we were depending upon her to carry us and our outfit to Great Whale River, which is her most northerly point on the one trip of the year. So when the anchor was dropped and Mr. MacKenzie, the Commissioner of the district, came ashore, we made the request and laid our plans before him, whereupon he set about to dissuade our going on such a foolish undertaking. At the last, we won out, and the next day were all packed into the close quarters of the *Inenew* and started on our seasick way. For five days I lay in my bunk, not daring to lift either head or voice, unless when that miserable little craft rose to a mountainous wave and then settled herself nearly to the bottom of the bay. Oh! It was a wretched time, and the morning that the commissioner called in to know if I would like an egg, I then and there determined to enlist every effort to have a new commissioner appointed in his place.

On August 2 we landed at Great Whale River. After establishing ourselves in the carpenter shop there for a few days, all four of us set to work renewing the outfit, patching provision bags and clothing. As we found that when everything was in the canoe she was too low in the water for safety, we also secured here another canoe to carry a part of our outfit. And now we met with another obstacle. Our original plan had been to work our way up the eastern coast of Hudson Bay to a northerly point, turn east into Lake Minto, and pass from this into the Leaf River, which from the map should bring us out to Ungava Bay. By George's interpreting, and the aid of pencil and paper, my husband tried to find Indians who could help us up the coast and into Lake Minto, but after two days' hard work of persuasion we had to give it up as impossible. None of the natives knew anything of Lake Minto nor the Leaf River, and they absolutely refused to go further north than a point called Richmond Gulf. From this point we were told we could strike east, and by portages, rivers and lakes, finally enter the Larch River, which would carry us to Fort Chimo, Ungava Bay. This trip had been made over twenty years ago by A. P. Low, the well-known geographical surveyor of the Canadian Government.

So, as we had no idea of giving up a journey thus far in progress, we closed our ears to all dissuasions and warnings of the factor at Whale River and of Commissioner MacKenzie, scribbled a few letters home, and on August 4 started again on our journey. We took with us two Cree Indians,

Noonoosh and Jimmie, who had been engaged to help us up the coast, but who would go no further north than Richmond Gulf. At Great Whale River we had been able to secure a few cans of beef, about a hundred pounds of salt pork, a good quantity of flour and more tea. As an excellent substitute for sugar we had brought with us six bottles of crystallose, and at this post a native offered us five dollars for one little bottle.

Both canoes were heavily laden, allowing a very few inches of freeboard; but, nevertheless, we shipped very little water and made good progress, keeping within easy access to the shore most of the time. In five days we made Richmond Gulf, and this was considered remarkable progress. A number of large islands—great masses of rock they are, without a shrub upon them—lie a mile or two from shore, making quite a smooth channel for two days' travel. Then we swept through a narrow passage into the great Hudson Bay. At any place along the coast we could land our canoes. Everywhere there is rock; the shore, smooth as glass and rounded from the action of the waves, slopes gradually for about a mile to a great, almost perpendicular, wall. Down from these walls, here and there, trickle thin streams of fresh water, which empty themselves into the salt, so that we had very little difficulty in procuring water for our tea. For fires we used mostly drift-wood, as we were nearly upon the edge of the tree limit and the timber was dwarfed and scarce. We encountered any number of seals and several schools of white whales. One afternoon we met a canoe coming towards us out of the mist that seemed always to shroud the coast. It proved to contain a good-sized Indian family in a state of semi-starvation. Their sunken cheeks and poor forms told more than their Cree jabber to George or Job; so we were not long in doling out supplies, and they put ashore at once for a feast.

On the fourth shining, glittering morning, when all hands were busy with the paddles and we were all quietly rejoicing in a stiff breeze that kept away the ever-present mosquitoes, the keen Indian eyes suddenly detected motion on the shore. The men pulled rapidly for the shore, and in a few minutes all could see that the queer form was human and that it was frantically beckoning to us and running like a crazy thing. With some misgivings my husband and I stepped ashore to come face to face and hand to hand with the wildest little Eskimo in all the northland. An old, wrinkled face, half-hidden by a great black shock of matted hair, and the tattered skin garments, all bespoke starvation again, and George delved into the recesses of our store to once more administer to the beings that God has planted in Labrador. The little man started back over a rise of rock, all the time talking, and beckoned us to follow. There down in a groove were his habitation and family, the latter consisting of a girl of about eighteen and a boy of fourteen; the former, a cone-shaped hut, made of short branches with several filthy skins thrown over them. Not a crumb of food was in sight, nor a kayak, gun, nor fish-net.

Their poverty gnawed at my heart. This winter I can think of them only as corpses hidden under the drifts of snow and ice, for there they were sixty miles from Great Whale River, with no boat and no food and nothing to get food with. As we turned to get into the canoe again we pointed to the northeast and said "Chimo." At this the little man grasped our hands again as if he never meant to let us go, for he recognized the word of "welcome" in his own language and seemed to understand. The maiden led her little brother back to their loathsome hut, but the father stood and looked and waved until a sharp rock hid him from view. When the snow melts away from the rocks next summer the seagulls will screech and scream and bring their neighbors to the glorious find they have made.

There was no beauty anywhere. I was tempted to believe God had had no hand in the piling up of Labrador; but since God did make it, then I know it was in the evening of the sixth day.

We crept carefully through the rocky gateway that opens into Richmond Gulf, and as the swift current swept us on and on, it seemed as if the high granite wall on either side of the narrow channel must close over our heads. Seagulls resented the intrusion into their tomblike dwellings and circled above, screeching wildly. Then came the time for Noonoosh and Jimmie to leave us. They were paid well and liberally provisioned. All the Indians we had seen told us we would have no end of game in the interior, and with that in view we were generous with our salt pork.

So we were left, in the literal sense of the word, to "paddle our own canoe" through a rough and barren land with nothing to guide us but a crude map that we could not rely upon too trustfully, and my husband's knowledge of astronomy. On those five hundred rough miles across the Labrador peninsula, one day was much like another. There was little sunshine, a great amount of rain, and the remainder of the time was divided between humidity or stinging wind; but *always*, be it understood, except upon two days and nights, we were driven almost to madness by the untiring mosquitoes. The thermometer must actually reach the freezing point before they disappear. Each morning came an early breakfast, then camp was broken, and in a few moments the canoe was neatly loaded and we were all in our places.

There were countless rapids, so forbidding that the outfit and canoe had to be carried around them. And the portages! Shall I ever forget the tangled roots and slippery, mossy boulders, or the heavy swamps that caused me many downfalls. There were no trees, to speak of—but the alders and willows wrapped their outstretched arms so clingingly to my portions of the outfit and so snapped and tore at my head-net, that the disposition I was developing was not of the sweetest.

In many places the brook trout fishing was excellent, which was fortunate, as our supply of salt pork was gradually diminishing, together with our other supplies, excepting tea, of which we happily had a quantity. When the sun would permit, at noon my husband made his observations; but this could not be done daily, as the weather was fitful and rainy. Night observations had to be almost abandoned, for a candle, lighted to level the artificial horizon, was immediately snuffed out by the swarms of mosquitoes. This part of our story has been doubted by many people, but we can go still further and tell that many times, when we had gone into the tent for the night, we called out to the men to know if it were not raining, for the thousands of taps on the tight walls of the tent sounded exactly like rain. I think I may be safe in saying that it took us at least an hour each night to defend ourselves for a restful sleep. The sod cloth must be carefully packed down with moss or pebbles (according to where the tent was pitched) and the net snugly drawn; then I had ready a thread and needle to sew up no matter how tiny a hole in the delicate mesh, for the hum of the pests on the outside was murderous.

Oh! It was weary going. Many times, after an all-day's rain, we made camp with numbed fingers and yearned for a fire before which to dry and warm ourselves and as often as we tried to light one, just so often we were driven into the shelter of the tent to get away from the nagging, irritating bites. But we stopped for nothing; no rain was hard enough to keep us a day in camp; and each day we were grateful that no sickness held any of the party down. Hourly we expected to run into hundreds of caribou, and hourly we were disappointed. One morning, when we were about three weeks from Richmond Gulf, Job exclaimed: "Ah tik! Ah tik!" which George told us was "caribou." With feverish haste we put ashore and, about a mile away on the top of a high ridge, we could see an animal running frantically 'round and 'round. Job was off in a minute with the .405 and some cartridges, and by the time George had dinner ready, we could see him hurrying down the hill with the animal on his shoulders. It was such a tiny fellow—not much larger than a dog—that I felt remorse for the shot, but when Job told me that he had been tortured by mosquitoes on the hill, I felt we had been humane and ate my share of the game with a relish. This was our only taste of fresh meat in nearly three months. When we had quite finished the caribou, and as George announced at different meals the last appearance of rice, cornmeal or dried fruit, we had a few misgivings and a great desire to reach Fort Chimo.

The rapids became fiercer and longer and the river wider, so, with re-newed hope that Ungava Bay could not be very far away, we sped on with two broken paddles. The river which we hoped was the Larch turned muddy; if the fish were there they would not bite, and our larder was reduced to bis-cuits, tea and a few beans. These latter we barely cooked, owing to our haste. Just how many mosquitoes we consumed, too, it would be hard, indeed, to determine. We never sat down to a meal that each of us did not have a smudge; while we lifted the headnet just long enough to admit of one hur-ried forkful. There was no time to shake off the pests nor count them; so they all went down, and while one was endeavoring to swallow the dose there would come a puff of smoke, and our meals became a sputter and a choke.

Job was a careful bowsman; he always went ashore before we reached a rapid, and from the highest point made a survey of the rushing water. It all seems now as if those rapids were one mighty churn from an unseen power, but one stands out in my mind as most terrifying. Job had made his survey and came back to his place; with a few words to George that sounded assuring, we sped out again and were in the swift current. The canoe gave a powerful lurch, and Job seemed fighting with the water. Before us was an enormous wave about five feet high, as nearly as I could guess, and the canoe sped to-wards it. Was a rock on its other side? With a hoarse yell, Job cried: "Sit low!" and as we crouched in the bottom of the canoe, clutching the one remaining air-cushion as well as the gunwales, we shot through the wave and beyond into quieter water. If our little craft had once struck a rock, drowning would have been our easiest death, for to be cast ashore on such a rocky barren, where there is no vegetation, would have meant a long-drawn-out, merci-less end. But thank God! In all the long and dangerous way we did not strike a rock.

George's good nature was unfailing, and he did much with his quaint tales, and quainter way of telling them, to relieve the monotony and cheer us on a cheerless way. When we had come quickly and safely through a perilous rapid, he would look back to the swirling mass and say, "My! That was quite dangersome!" At all times he was willing, kind and faithful.

On September 3, just a month from the time that we had left Great Whale River, we turned a sharp bend in the river to see spread before our joyous eyes the little red roofs of Chimo. When in midstream, cutting diago-nally across the river, we could readily see by using the glasses that we were observed from the shore. There was a great hurrying and scurrying of men, women, and children, all recognizing a strange canoe. We fired a salute and were answered by a volley of shots. Few can realize, I suppose, the mingled feelings that we experienced. Here, at last, the working part of our journey was done. Whilst we had endured no real hardships and had no mishaps, we had had many privations, with no real sport nor comfort. And now it was at an end. We had come across a bleak and solitary country successfully, and that was enough.

February–March 1908

Nothing to Do for Three Weeks

GORDON MacQUARRIE

Alone in the bush, a "pine-knot millionaire" refines the art of solitude.

I LEFT LONG BEFORE daylight, alone but not lonely. Sunday-morning stillness filled the big city. It was so quiet that I heard the whistle of duck wings as I unlocked the car door. They would be ducks leaving Lake Michigan. A fine sound, that, early of a morning. Wild ducks flying above the tall apartments and the sprawling factories in the dark, and below them people still asleep.

The wingbeats I chose to accept as a good omen. And why not? Three weeks of doing what I wished to do lay before me. It was the best time, the beginning of the last week in October. In the partridge woods I would pluck at the sleeve of reluctant Indian summer, and from a duck blind four hundred miles to the north I would watch winter make its first dash south on a northwest wind.

I drove through sleeping Milwaukee. I thought how fine it would be if, throughout the year, the season would hang on dead center, as it often does in Wisconsin in late October and early November. Then one may expect a little of everything—a bit of summer, a time of falling leaves, and finally that initial climatic threat of winter to quicken the heart of a duck hunter, namely me.

On the highway cars with hunting-capped men and cars with dimly outlined retrievers in back seats flashed by me. I had agreed with myself not to go fast. The day was too fine to mar with haste. Every minute of it was to be tasted and enjoyed, and remembered for another, duller day. Twenty miles out of the big city a hunter with two beagles set off across a field toward a wood. For the next ten miles I was with him in the cover beyond the farmhouse and up the hill.

In this leisurely mood I turned in at a certain small village not far

95

from the big city and in the growing light saw what I had phoned ahead for the previous day. It was a flitch of lean home-smoked bacon, where I could reach it behind the screen door of the locked butcher shop. No use to awaken Mr. Klippel before breakfast. And certainly no use to go north for three weeks without that pungent, smoky chief ingredient of breakfast.

There are rites that are performed to fill up the soul of man as well as his belly. One hundred and twenty miles north of the big city I stopped at Mr. Pennybacker's roadside stand and bought a bushel of Bailey Sweets. Never heard of Bailey Sweets, I suppose. Not many have. They are smallish red apples, smaller than a Jonathan and redder. They do not keep like some apples. They are sweeter than a Tallman Sweet. The experts call them old-fashioned apples and give them little attention. They are just what the hunting man needs to fill up his pockets before starting out.

Most of that still, sunny Sunday I went past farms and through cities, and over the hills and down into the valleys, and when I hit the fire-lane road out of Loretta-Draper I was getting along on my way. This is superb country for deer and partridge, but I did not see many of the latter; this was a year of the few, not the many. Where one of the branches of the surging Chippewa crosses the road I stopped and flushed mallards out of tall grass. On Clam Lake, at the end of the fire lane, there was an appropriate knot of bluebills.

The sun was selling nothing but pure gold when I rolled up and down the hills of the Namekagon Lake country. Thence up the blacktop from Cable to the turnoff at Drummond, and from there straight west through those tremendous stands of jack pine. Then I broke the rule of the day. I hurried a little. I wanted to use the daylight. I turned in at the mailboxes and went along the back road to the nameless turn-in—so crooked and therefore charming.

Old Sun was still shining on the top logs of the cabin. The yard was afloat with scrub oak leaves, for a wind to blow them off into the lake must be a good one. Usually it just skims the ridgepole and goes its way. Inside the cabin was the familiar smell of native Wisconsin white cedar logs. I lit the fireplace and then unloaded the car. It was near dark when all the gear was in, and I pondered the virtues of broiled ham steak and baking powder biscuits to go with it.

I was home, all right. I have another home, said to be much nicer. But this is the talk of persons who like cities and, in some cases, actually fear the woods.

There is no feeling like that first wave of affection which sweeps in when a man comes to a house and knows it is home. The logs, the beams, the popple kindling snapping under the maple logs in the fireplace. It was after dark when I had eaten the ham and the hot biscuits, these last dunked in maple syrup from a grove just three miles across the lake as the crow flies and ten miles by road.

When a man is alone, he gets things done. So many men alone in the brush get along with themselves because it takes most of their time to do for themselves. No dallying over division of labor, no hesitancy at tackling a job.

There is much to be said in behalf of the solitary way of fishing and hunting. It lets people get acquainted with themselves. Do not feel sorry for the man on his own. If he is one who plunges into all sorts of work, if he does not dawdle, if he does not dwell upon his aloneness, he will get many things done and have a fine time doing them.

After the dishes I put in some licks at puttering. Fifty very-well-cared-for decoys for diving ducks and mallards came out of their brown sacks and stood anchor-cord inspection. They had been made decent with touchup paint months before. A couple of 12-gauge guns got a pat or two with an oily rag. The contents of two shell boxes were sorted and segregated. Isn't it a caution how shells get mixed up? I use nothing but 12-gauge shells. Riding herd on more than one gauge would, I fear, baffle me completely.

I love to tinker with gear. It's almost as much fun as using it. Ship-shape is the phrase. And it has got to be done continuously, otherwise order will be replaced by disorder, and possibly mild-to-acute chaos.

I dragged a skiff down the hill to the beach, screwed the motor to it, loaded in the decoys, and did not forget to toss in an old shell box for a blind seat and an ax for making a blind. I also inspected the night and found it good. It was not duck weather, but out there in the dark an occasional bluebill skirled.

I went back up the hill and brought in fireplace wood. I was glad it was not cold enough to start the space heater. Some of those maple chunks from my woodpile came from the same sugar bush across the lake that supplied the hot biscuit syrup. It's nice to feel at home in such a country.

How would you like to hole up in a country where you could choose, as you fell asleep, between duck hunting and partridge hunting, between small-mouths on a good river like the St. Croix or trout on another good one like the Brule, or between muskie fishing on the Chippewa flowage or cisco dipping in the dark for the fun of it? Or, if the mood came over you, just a spell of tramping around on deer trails with a hand ax and a gunnysack, knocking highly flammable pine knots out of trees that have lain on the ground for seventy years? I've had good times in this country doing nothing more adventurous than filling a pail with blueberries or a couple of pails with wild cranberries.

Before I left on this trip the boss, himself a product of this same part of Wisconsin and jealous as hell of my three-week hunting debauch, allowed, "Nothing to do for three weeks, eh?" Him I know good. He'd have given quite a bit to be going along.

Nothing to do for three weeks! He knows better. He's been there, and busier than a one-armed paperhanger.

Around bedtime I found a seam rip in a favorite pair of thick doe-skin gloves. Sewing it up, I felt like Robinson Crusoe, but Rob never had it that good. The Old Duck Hunters have a philosophy: When you go to the bush, you go there to smooth it, and not to rough it.

And so to bed under the watchful presence of the little alarm clock that has run faithfully for twenty years, but only when it is laid on its face. One red blanket was enough. There was an owl hooting, maybe two wrangling. You can never be sure where an owl is, or how far away, or how many. The fireplace wheezed and made settling noises. Almost asleep, I made up my mind to omit the ducks until some weather got made up. Tomorrow I'd hit the tote roads for partridge. In the low years they never disappear completely, but they require some tall walking, and singles are the common thing.

No hunting jacket on that clear, warm day. Not even a sleeveless game carrier. Just shells in the pockets, a fat ham sandwich, and Bailey Sweets stuck into odd corners. My game carrier was a cord with which to tie birds to my belt. The best way to do it is to forget the cord is there until it is needed; otherwise the Almighty may see you with that cord in your greedi-ness and decide you are tempting Providence and show you nary a feather all the day long.

By early afternoon I had walked up seven birds and killed two, pretty good for me. Walking back to the cabin, I sort of uncoiled. You can sure get wound up walking up partridge.

This first day was also the time of the great pine-knot strike. I came upon them not far from a thoroughfare emptying the lake, beside rotted logs of lumbering days. Those logs had been left there by rearing crews after the lake level had been dropped to fill the river. It often happens. Then the river-men don't bother to roll stranded logs into the water when it's hard work.

You cannot shoot a pine knot, or eat it, but it is a lovely thing and makes a fire that will burn the bottom out of a stove if you are not careful. Burning pine knots smell as fine as the South's pungent lightwood. Once I gave an artist a sack of pine knots and he refused to burn them and rubbed and polished them into wondrous birdlike forms, and many called them art. Me, I just pick them up and burn them.

Until you have your woodshed awash with pine knots, you have not ever been really rich. By that evening I had made seven two-mile round trips with the boat and I estimated I had almost two tons of pine knots. In even the very best pine-knot country, such as this was, that is a tremendous haul for one day; in fact, I felt vulgarly rich.

An evening rite each day was to listen to weather reports on the radio. I was impatient for the duck blind, but this was Indian summer and I used it up, every bit of it. I used every day for what it was best suited. Can anyone do better?

The third day I drove thirty-five miles to the lower Douglas County Brule and tried for one big rainbow, with, of course, salmon eggs and a Colorado spinner. I never got a strike, but I love that river. That night, on Island Lake, eight miles from my place, Louis Eschrich and I dip-netted some eating ciscoes near the shore, where they had moved in at dark to spawn among roots of drowned jack pines.

There is immense satisfaction in being busy. Around the cabin there were incessant chores that please the hands and rest the brain. Idiot work, my wife calls it. I cannot get enough of it. Perhaps I should have been a day laborer. I split maple and Norway pine chunks for the fireplace and kitchen range. This is work fit for any king. You see the piles grow, and indeed the man who splits his own wood warms himself twice.

On Thursday along came Tony Burmek, Hayward guide. He had a grand idea. The big crappies were biting in deep water on the Chippewa flowage. There'd be nothing to it. No, we wouldn't bother fishing muskies, just get twenty-five of those crappies apiece. Nary a crappie touched our minnows, and after several hours of it I gave up, but not Tony. He put me on an island where I tossed out half a dozen blackduck decoys and shot three mallards.

When I scooted back northward that night, the roadside trees were tossing. First good wind of the week. Instead of going down with the sun, Old Wind had risen, and it was from the right quarter northwest. The radio confirmed it, said there'd be snow flurries. Going to bed that windy night, I detected another dividend of doing nothing—some slack in the waistline of my pants. You ever get that fit feeling as your belly shrinks and your hands get callused?

By rising time of Friday morning the weatherman was a merchant of proven mendacity. The upper pines were lashing and roaring. This was the day! In that northwest blast the best blind was a mile run with the outboard. Only after I had left the protecting high hill did I realize the full strength of the wind. Following waves came over the transom.

Plenty of ducks moved. I had the entire lake to myself, but that is not unusual in the Far North. Hours passed and nothing moved in. I remained long after I knew they were not going to decoy. All they had in mind was sheltered water.

Sure, I could have redeployed those blocks and got some shooting. But it wasn't that urgent. The morning had told me that they were in, and there was a day called tomorrow to be savored. No use to live it up all at once.

Because I had become a pine-knot millionaire, I did not start the big space heater that night. It's really living when you can afford to heat a 20-by-30-foot living room, a kitchen, and a bedroom with a fireplace full of pine knots.

The wind died in the night and by morning it was mitten-cold. What wind persisted was still northwest. I shoved off the loaded boat. Maybe by now those newcomers had rested. Maybe they'd move to feed. Same blind, same old familiar tactics, but this time it took twice as long to make the spread because the decoy cords were frozen.

A band of bluebills came slashing toward me. How fine and brave they are, flying in their tight little formations! They skirted the edge of the decoys, swung off, came back again and circled in back of me, then skidded in, landing gear down. It was so simple to take two. A single drake mallard investigated the big black cork duck decoys and found out what they were. A little color in the bag looks nice.

I was watching a dozen divers, redheads maybe, when a slower flight movement caught my eye. Coming dead in were eleven geese, blues, I knew at once. I don't know whatever became of those redheads. Geese are an extra dividend on this lake. Blues fly over it by the thousand, but it is not goose-hunting country. I like to think those eleven big black cork decoys caught their fancy this time. At twenty-five yards the No. 6's were more than enough. Two of the geese made a fine weight in the hand, and geese are always big guys when one has had his eyes geared for ducks.

The cold water stung my hands as I picked up. Why does a numb, cold finger seem to hurt so much if you bang it accidentally? The mittens felt good. I got back to my beach in time for the prudent duck hunter's greatest solace, a second breakfast. But first I stood on the lakeshore for a bit and watched the ducks, mostly divers, bluebills predominating, some redheads and enough regal canvasbacks to make tomorrow promise new interest. The storm had really brought them down from Canada. I was lucky. Two more weeks with nothing to do.

Nothing to do, you say? Where'd I get those rough and callused hands? The windburned face? The slack in my pants? Two more weeks of it. . . . Surely, I was among the most favored of all mankind. Where could there possibly be a world as fine as this?

I walked up the hill, a pine-knot millionaire, for that second breakfast.

February 1956

Burt's Gun

WILLIAM G. TAPPLY

The Parker double wasn't the only legacy the old man left him.

ICK SNAPPED THE little shotgun to his shoulder and led an imaginary woodcock across my living-room wall. "Comes up nice," he said. He rubbed his thumb along the side of the safety, where the bluing has worn shiny. "Not exactly mint."

"No," I said. "She's traveled many miles."

"Still…a Parker double. Twenty-gauge. What's her grade?"

"VH."

Rick nodded and cocked an eye at me. "For sale?"

I laughed. "Hardly. It's an heirloom."

"But I thought…"

"Oh, Dad's still very much alive. It wasn't his. Belonged to an old guy I used to hunt with. Name of Burt Spiller."

"Not *the* Burt Spiller?"

"Himself," I said.

"The 'Poet Laureate' of the ruffed grouse," mused Rick. "All those great stories. You knew Burt Spiller?"

"Like I said. I hunted with him."

Burton L. Spiller was born in 1886 in the seacoast town of Portland, Maine. Seven years later he blasted a grouse from the lower branches of an oak tree with his father's hammer-action 10-gauge double. The bruised shoulder and nosebleed he suffered from the recoil failed to discourage him, and he tromped the New England meadows and woodlands for more than seven decades before he took off his hunting boots for the last time at the end of the 1964 season.

Burt Spiller may well have invested more hours—and surely more seasons—in grouse hunting than any man in history. When he was a teenager Burt accepted the invitation to join up with two local market hunters. Grouse were abundant in southern Maine in those days. The three skilled and dedicated gunners moved fifty or more grouse on a typical day's hunt. But if Burt discovered the tricks by which men can outwit grouse, his two years as a commercial grouse hunter also taught him "the difference between a sportsman and that reprehensible thing I was fast becoming," as he said in his first published story, "His Majesty, the Grouse," which appeared in FIELD & STREAM half a century ago. So he "bought a registered bird dog and became a sportsman."

My first ten years of grouse hunting were Burt's last ten, and we shared them. Every October and November Saturday morning for the decade between 1954 and 1964, Dad and I pulled up in front of Burt's house in East Rochester, New Hampshire. His gun and shooting vest waited for us on his front porch. Burt always had his boots laced. "I'm ready," he'd grin.

I was fourteen and he was nearly seventy when I began hunting with him. His only concession to age was the hearing aid he wore, one of the old-fashioned kind with a little button in one ear and wires running to a battery pack in his shirt pocket. It must have been a terrible handicap for a partridge hunter. "I can hear the birds flush," he explained, "and I can hear you when you yell 'Mark!' But I don't know where to look."

So Burt didn't shoot very often. He didn't seem to mind. Even on the good days, when the woodcock flights were in the Bullring and Mankiller covers, and when the Henhouse and Long Walk In covers each held a brood of grouse, and when Dad and I might go through a box of shells each, Burt's gunbarrels often remained clean. Yet when we dropped him off at his house at the end of the day he'd always say, "A wonderful hunt. See you next Saturday."

When he could see a flying partridge, though, Burt Spiller was a master wingshot. Once during the first season I hunted with him, he and I were strolling down an old logging road together on the way out of our Orchard Hillside cover. The tall beeches along either side of the road still held their leaves, and evergreens hugged close to the ruts we were following, so that it seemed as if we were walking through a green-and-gold tunnel. The hunt had ended, and our guns hung at our sides. Somewhere off to our left Dad and our hell-for-leather setter, Duke, were taking their own route. We could hear the dog's bell and Dad's occasional shouts to him.

Then he yelled, "Mark! Your way!"

I was standing slightly behind Burt, so I could see his gun come up as the grouse darted across the 10-foot opening of the roadway 30 yards in front of us. When Burt shot, the bird crumpled, its momentum tumbling it into the hemlocks. We found it stone dead. Burt picked it up and stroked its breast feathers and fanned its tail.

"I'm sorry," he said to me. "I should have let you take him."

I couldn't have made that shot once in a hundred chances. Burt knew that, I'm sure.

He had hands like a blacksmith's—which he once had been—cracked and hardened from digging and sorting the gladiolus bulbs that he raised commercially, so his skin looked like the bark of a lightning-struck apple tree. But when he rubbed his finger alongside the trigger guard of his beautiful Parker, or stroked the ruff of a warm grouse, one could imagine him fashioning sweet-singing violins—which was something else he did.

He's best remembered, of course, for the stories he crafted. Their themes were all similar: the hero was usually "Thunder King," the grouse, often the dog, and only rarely the man. Before I ever hunted with him I had read all of Burt's tales I could lay my hands on, so I knew him even before I met him. And I felt he knew me, too. "Other boys of my acquaintance," he wrote in "His Majesty, the Grouse," "might content themselves with slaying elephants and lions and other inconsequential members of the animal kingdom, but I wanted none of that in mine. Nothing but the lordly pa'tridge would satisfy me."

Or me.

Burt was an old-fashioned man. He refused to profane the Sabbath by hunting, even though New Hampshire law allowed it. Neither Dad nor I ever heard him utter even the mildest curse, or speak critically of another, or express anger. He was a teetotaler and a devoted family man. But he had a wry Yankee sense of humor. He enjoyed a joke, especially if it was on him.

From the top of the hill along the road between the Schoolhouse and Tripwire covers near the little township of Gilmanton Iron Works stretches a magnificent vista of the southern New Hampshire countryside. In the fall it's washed with crimson and gold. Sparkling lakes and ponds nestle among the foothills of the White Mountains. Dad always pulled over to the side there and nudged Burt, who'd grin in anticipation of their joke.

"That's where we'll build our cabin when we get old," Dad would say, pointing to a spot under an ancient sugar maple. "We'll watch the seasons go by, gamble a lot, and have all the wild wimmin and rye whiskey we want."

"Especially the whiskey," Burt would always say.

When I first began to hunt grouse and woodcock, it was a deadly serious business of finding and flushing and shooting. I measured the success of the hunt by the numbers. I was a teenager, and I didn't know any better. It took several seasons of hunting with Burt Spiller and Dad, and the rereading of Burt's stories, before it came into perspective for me, so that I could say at the end of every day, "A wonderful hunt." And mean it.

On the first Saturday of October 1964, Burt and Dad and I stepped from the car at our First Chance cover. First Chance was a short hunt. "Just right for getting out the kinks," Burt always said. A grouse lived there, and a few native woodcock usually twittered away before we were done.

We slid our shotguns from their cases and crammed our vest pockets with shells while Duke whined and strained at the end of his check cord.

"Let me heft your gun, Bill," said Burt.

I handed him the Savage single-shot 20-gauge that had cost me more hours of lawn mowing and weed pulling than I care to remember. Burt lifted it to his shoulder and swung it against the sky.

"Feels good," he said. "Mind if I try it?"

I shrugged. "Sure. Go ahead."

"Here," he said. "You carry mine. If you don't mind."

He placed his Parker in both of my hands. "I don't mind," I said. I didn't understand why he'd want to try my Savage. It wasn't much of a gun. But I couldn't turn down the opportunity to carry that beautiful Parker just once.

We climbed a stone wall and crossed a frosted meadow until we came to an alder run. A stream trickled through it. Beyond rose a hillside overgrown with apples and briers. Burt followed the field edge, Dad slogged the mucky alder bottom, and I kept pace on the hillside, praying for a chance to try Burt's gun.

We found the grouse at home in First Chance that day. He scuttled ahead of the dog until he was pinned at the edge of an opening ahead of me. I came up quickly behind Duke's point. The Parker felt light in my hands. The bird exploded from under a clump of juniper, angled up to the tops of the alders, then slid swiftly back toward the old orchard. The Parker, I discovered that morning, shot exactly where I aimed it—in that case, several feet behind the fleeing partridge.

When we got out of the car at the next cover, Burt picked up my Savage. "I didn't get to shoot it back there," he said. "Mind if I try it again?"

I hesitated, then took his Parker, "Okay." I said.

We carried each other's gun for the rest of that Saturday. And when we dropped Burt off that afternoon, he left the Parker in the car and took the Savage with him. "You use it," he said. "I won't be hunting tomorrow."

Thus did Burt Spiller's gun pass into my hands—in Burt's way, without ceremony, without giving me the chance to say "thank you," and therefore without his needing to acknowledge that he had indeed bestowed upon me a priceless gift.

Later that season—Burt's last in the woods, as he may have suspected—we were hunting Tripwire, a hellish hillside of bramble and blowdown. The woodcock, by then, had moved south. Grouse were scarce. Dad and I plowed through the thick of it, while Burt took the only route his seventy-eight-year-old legs permitted, the old roadway several hundred yards off to our right. Duke roamed somewhere ahead of us. Then we heard the rumble of a flushing grouse.

"Damn that dog!" muttered Dad. Then he yelled, "Burt! Mark!"

Many seconds seemed to elapse before we heard Burt's shot. "He got him!" said Dad.

"Aw, come on. How can you tell?"

"You can tell by the sound of the shot," Dad replied, smiling. "You wait."

We cut back toward the roadway and came to it behind Burt. He was trudging ahead of us, his old legs slowly taking him up the incline of the road. My Savage hung at his side from his right hand. A ruffed grouse dangled by its legs from his left.

Burt quit hunting at the end of that season. He lived for nine more years, raising gladioli and carving violins and writing more tales of the outdoors. I like to think that he savored a special memory of his last grouse, which he shot with my gun.

And when he died in 1973, that old single-shot Savage came back to me with Burt's instructions: "For Bill's son."

"So actually," I told Rick, "I own two of Burt Spiller's shotguns."

"Not for sale, eh?" nodded Rick.

"No way," I said. "But if you take special care of it I'll let you borrow this book."

From my bookcase I slid my copy of *Grouse Feathers*, by Burton L. Spiller, Crown's facsimile reproduction of the Derrydale original.

Rick opened the book and peered at the inscription. "I can't read it," he said.

"Burt was eighty-six when he wrote it," I said. "His hand was pretty shaky. It took me a while to decipher. Here's what it says."

And I read Burt Spiller's words to my friend:

To Bill—
While listening in on grouse conversations
This is, I find, their chief complaint:
Not only do you always bust 'em,
But often bust 'em where they ain't.
From Burt.

"Did you?" asked Rick.

"Did I what?"

"Bust 'em where they weren't?"

"Couldn't then, can't now," I said. "I'm a lousy wingshot, even with Burt's gun. Actually, that inscription is one of the last—and most far-fetched—pieces of grouse-shooting fiction Burt Spiller ever wrote."

November 1982

You Have to Know Them

BURTON L. SPILLER

A grouse hunter's success depends on being in the right place at the right time.

I T HAD RAINED during the night, a real old New England gully-washer, but early morning brought a clearing sky and a gentle west wind. A morning like that, in mid-October, is made especially for grouse hunters; so I did not bother to phone Gene. Instead, I drove over to his home and found him sitting on the doorstep, his coat and gun resting across his knees and a pointer cuddled under each arm. Many years of hunting together has made us psychic in a small way. He knew that I would drive over. I knew that he would be ready to go. What need of a telephone?

All summer we had been zealously guarding our "A" stamps so that we might have at least a few days in some of our favorite covers in the White Mountain foot-hills. Conserving gas on this particular morning, we chose to go by the shortest possible route, although it meant about ten miles of washed-out and rutted dirt roads. Half-way through one agonizing stretch we came to an extensive swamp. From the slopes surrounding it the rain had converged until the swamp was nearly awash.

Bumping and splashing through the deep ruts, we at last rounded a corner and came to abruptly rising ground. Through the mud-splattered windshield I caught a glimpse of a sumac-clad knoll and behind it a growth of scrubby young pine, and at that instant Gene said, "Whoa!"

I stabbed the brake so hard that a dog catapulted from the back seat into the front. "What did you see?" I demanded. "A water-buffalo?"

He grinned. "Let's look this place over. It ought to be good for a bird or two."

The knoll looked good enough, I thought, as I got out of the car. Its sumac and blackberry vines meant that the sort of feed which grouse like could be found there. The sun was shining warmly, too, on the side-hill, but we had already passed a score of likelier-looking spots. Without much enthusiasm I snapped the gun together and dropped in a couple of hulls.

Old Rap and the pup had been doing a limbering-up exercise up the road, but now they came tearing back. Twenty feet in front of the car the old dog swerved and leaped the ditch like a thoroughbred taking a hurdle. Watching, I actually saw him stiffen in mid-air. He struck square-footed and stayed there, head and tail high, the magic of hot grouse scent making him youthful and dynamic once again. In the center of the road the pup stopped sharply to honor his old man's point. Gene was coolly feeding shells into the pump. Hitching our sleeves up at the wrists, we went in.

Whir-r-r-r! A grouse rose a scant three feet from the ground and went darting in and out among the sumacs. I missed her cleanly with the first barrel, but caught her with the other, and like an echo to my shots Gene's 20-gauge spat venomously twice. In the momentary hush that followed I caught the sound of a spasmodic drumming of wings upon the rain-soaked leaves.

"Did you get yours?" Gene asked.

"Yeah."

"All down in this alley, too," he said. "I busted a pair of 'em."

The dogs retrieved the birds, and then gave the knoll a quick once-over without again striking scent. We were back in the car in less than ten minutes.

"How did you know the birds were there?" I asked him when we were again bouncing along the muddy rutted road.

He gave me a pitying glance. "Anybody ought to know that," he said. "Birds are still using the swamps. Well, they aren't using that one today unless they've grown web feet. They had to be some place, and this was the likeliest-looking spot."

I believe that incident summarizes the secret of successful grouse hunting. I care not what may be any man's ability with a scatter-gun. If he doesn't know his birds, any good grouse hunter will wipe his eye five days out of every six and he will never suspect he is a victim of anything but his own abominable luck . . .

For sheer skill and daring in hurtling full speed through thick cover, no other upland bird deserves to be mentioned in the same breath as ruffed grouse. With his accelerator pressed to the floorboards he will flash in and out among the tree trunks and a miscellany of smaller stuff without brushing so much as a wing tip; yet I know of no other game bird, unless it be the pheasant, who so thoroughly dislikes to fly. He will wander from roosting place to feeding ground in the early morning, then loiter and peck his meandering way to some exposed side-hill for a dust bath and a bit of idle sunning. Then, as the afternoon wanes, he will retrace his steps, feeding ever more briskly as the long shadows begin to fall until he has reached his chosen roosting place for the night.

If unmolested, he will follow that routine for days and, with the exception of his ascent to and descent from his perch, will never once take wing. He knows the same reluctance to fly when he hears an approaching hunter, unless he happens to be in an exposed position or one in which he fancies he is cornered, when he will usually take wing at once. His preference, however, if he is in cover thick enough to hide his movements, is to steal quietly away from the area which he thinks lies within the hunter's line of approach, but before he moves he wants to know quite definitely where the danger lies.

He is jittery, for experience has taught him that he is scheduled for a few unpleasant moments, but instinct also tells him that he is practically invisible so long as he stays on the ground. He is considering the possibility of flight, but he will not ordinarily take wing if he knows exactly where you are and feels that you have not yet quite crossed the line that he has mentally designated as the last inch of safety for him . . .

Grouse, like other creatures of the wild, have fixed habits. To remain alive is their chief concern, and after that comes their desire for food. Their roosting place at night—and this is especially true during the fall season—is a thick growth of evergreen, and in northern New England they seem to prefer pine and hemlock. In my experience, it is impossible to have a good grouse cover without such a background.

Some of the very best grouse covers I have ever found in my wanderings have become absolutely barren when the pine was removed from them. One in particular, a four-mile strip through a mountain valley was, if I ever saw one, a grouse hunter's paradise. In it, one glorious day, I flushed to my certain knowledge more than a hundred birds; but the pine that flowed down to it from the mountain-sides was removed, and that was its finish. I went through it again last fall, with two good dogs, without finding even one lone bird.

From their roosting places grouse move in the early morning hours toward their feeding grounds. They eat lightly and intermittently throughout the day until about two hours before dusk, when they begin to feed in real earnest. Gradually their crops grow round and hard as they distend with the gorged food, until they become almost as large and cylindrical as baseballs . . .

Knowing then the feeding habits of grouse, and remembering their characteristic disinclination to fly unless disturbed, one should be able quite accurately to tell where the birds in any cover will be at varying times through the day. In the morning they are most likely to be found along the edges of thick, coniferous growth. If flushed, they will almost invariably fly toward this shelter; therefore, when two men are hunting together, one should choose a course that will keep him between the dog and the wood. He will be in the proper place if the dog points game, and also in the best possible position to intercept the occasional wary bird that takes wing immediately he hears the approach of hunters.

Under certain conditions grouse will travel long distances to feed upon a choice delicacy. I have known them to travel down the long slope of a pine-crested ridge, across the valley floor (a boggy morass that formed an almost impenetrable barrier to humans), ascend the steep slope on the opposite side, and there gorge upon the meaty white-oak acorns that could be found only in that one restricted area.

There was a time, not so many years ago, when any apple tree with fruit on it, in even the scantiest of covers, was almost certain to have a grouse either in or beneath it. I remember one wise old dog over whom we hunted for many years who would, on general principles, begin to tighten up and walk stiff-legged whenever he came within sight of one. I supposed he had figured that the law of averages would make him right more often than wrong—and it did—but for the past two or three years I have noticed that the fruit seems to have lost much of its former attraction.

I examine the crop of every grouse I take, and only rarely now do I find a trace of the forbidden fruit. I'm sorry about it, for those parts of eastern New Hampshire and southern Maine where I do the most of my grouse hunting are plentifully sprinkled with abandoned farms on which apple trees are far more numerous than grouse.

I know of no other one thing that helps more in finding grouse than the practice of dissecting the crops of the daily bag. What one learns thus is truly "inside information" which cannot be disputed. If I find the birds are feeding largely on thorn plums or barberries or acorns or dried blueberries, I make a mental survey of the covers I know that abound in whatever food the autopsy discloses and hunt them at once. It usually pays big dividends.

There is a lot of both kinds of luck in hunting any species of game, and I am grateful for all of the right sort that comes my way; but my greatest thrill comes when I feel that I have outsmarted a wary old bird that has fooled me on other occasions. If the knowledge I have gained from long association with a cover leads me to believe that a pair of grouse may be found at some particular spot within it, and if my judgment tells me they will fly in a certain direction when flushed, and if I arrange to be there at the moment of their crossing, then the fact that I may miss them both does not disturb me a bit or detract from the success of my day. I have matched my cunning against the super cunning of a ruffed grouse, and I have succeeded in outwitting him. I know there will be other grouse in other covers on other days, and if I am wise enough to remember my schooling I'll be in the right place to intercept some of them as they rocket back toward the shelter of the pines.

October 1945

Song of the Woodcock

Timberdoodle's music on the wing is a lover's serenade.

UNLESS YOU HAVE heard it yourself you may find it hard to believe that the woodcock, that long-billed, bug-eyed eater of earthworms, can sing a song as sweet as a nightingale's. Yet a singer he is, and anyone who lives away from the city almost anywhere in the northeastern quarter of the country can hear him trill any evening in the early spring when he performs his antic mating dance.

Look—no, listen—for him in a grassy clearing hard by a fringe of alder or aspen, just as the light begins to fade. If there are woodcock in the area, you will first hear a series of loud, nasal, insect-like buzzing sounds usually spaced from 20 to 30 seconds apart. Most observers describe this call as a "peent," but you may think it sounds more like "bzzzzt!"—not exactly like, but suggesting, the cry of a nighthawk. The buzzing call is made from the ground as the male woodcock struts about before launching his little body into flight. If you are close enough, and listen very carefully, you will hear, just before each buzz, a soft, gurgling two-note quaver that sounds like "turkle" played on a distant flute, and barely audible to the human ear.

After buzzing several times from the ground—all this, of course, for the benefit of a female lurking coyly in a nearby thicket—the woodcock suddenly takes wing and spirals high into the sky with the wing-twitter so familiar to all upland gunners. You can see him plainly against the dimming skylight, rising in ever-narrowing circles until he reaches a height of from 200 to 300 feet, twittering all the while.

Then, at the very top of his flight, the woodcock begins to pour forth his heartful of song while he swoops and dives toward earth. As he descends he fills the air with joyful chirpings, an aria of soft, liquid, musical notes that seem to gush out of him as an expression of utter ecstasy, and as sweet and melodic as any bird song man has ever heard.

Tumbling close to earth, the woodcock ends his song and flutters to the ground, usually very near the spot from which he launched his flight a minute or two before. Soon he starts buzzing again, and repeats the entire performance, with its sweet outpouring of song, often a dozen times or more during an evening. Should another male encroach upon his courting ground you will hear him warn the intruder away with a burst of harsh cacklings much like those made by a flushed cock pheasant.

And if you are very lucky and enough light remains, you may even witness the climax to this strange mating ritual, when the enraptured female comes out into the field and awaits the return of the flighting male—thoroughly wooed and eager now to be won.

April 1972

Love Me, Love My Dog

H. G. TAPPLY

An Emily Post of upland shooting etiquette.

MY BIRD DOG will never win any field trials. He hunts at only one speed, full throttle. When he hits bird scent he usually slams on the brakes too late and flushes the grouse or woodcock far beyond shotgun range, and then if the mood is upon him, chases it to hellengone out of the county. I hunt him with a loud bell and a long check cord, and I yell at him a lot, often profanely.

In short, ol' Buck and I are not always perfectly mannered in the bird field, and if I should invite you to hunt with us you might not be favorably impressed with our behavior, which is usually most disgraceful when we have company. Think and say what you like about me, but if you should entertain negative thoughts about Buck, I would thank you to keep them to yourself. If you couldn't find something kind to say about him I would prefer you said nothing at all and pretended not to notice his transgressions, which is simply a matter of good manners when you hunt with another man's dog.

If you own a dog yourself you will certainly follow the Golden Rule and do unto other dog owners what you would have them do unto you if they were hunting behind *your* dog. But if you don't own a dog, and are invited to hunt with someone who does, here are a few basic rules that, if followed, should lead to another invitation, assuming you wanted one:

Never criticize the dog's work, even though the owner does. That's his privilege, not yours. Besides, even the best of dogs have an off-day occasionally, and this may be one of them.

Don't try to handle the dog. You'll only confuse him—and he probably won't take orders from you anyway.

Never shoot at rabbits or squirrels or running birds when you are hunting behind a pointing dog. To most owners, that is a cardinal sin.

If the dog fetches in a bird you've shot, don't insist that he deliver it to you, or try to take it from him. Most dogs retrieve only to the boss.

Remember that the man who owns the dog plays the part of the host, and that you are his guest. Let him run the hunt as he sees fit, so that you both will have the best opportunity to find game and to benefit from the dog's work.

If the owner calls you in to a point, don't run and don't dawdle. Then wait for him to flush the bird unless he asks you to do so, and take the shot only if the bird breaks to your side.

And if, at day's end, you have bagged more birds than he has, think twice before you brag about it, because whether you realize it or not, he has probably managed things so that you got all the best chances.

October 1971

How to Hunt Chukars

ED ZERN

The almost-invention of the drinking man's diet.

ONE OCTOBER ABOUT ten years ago Ted Trueblood invited me to come out to Idaho and shoot chukar partridge with him and his wife Ellen and his setter Joe, and I went. From Ted's house in Nampa he and Joe and I drove southwest to the Owyhee Reservoir and the high-desert country in a 4-wheel-drive station wagon, down cattle trails and steep draws, through brush that would have clawed the tracks off a Sherman tank, until we came to a 14-foot boat stashed on the shore of the reservoir. We rassled the boat into the water, loaded guns, gear, grub, and Joe into it, clipped a 10 hp outboard motor onto the stern, and ran down the reservoir about five miles to the mouth of a dry-bed canyon.

By the time we got there and beached the boat it was getting dark and we were both tired and hungry, so while I lugged a small tent out of the boat—there was another tent hidden there under a tarp, from an earlier trip, and we wanted two because Ellen was joining us later—Ted built a fire and broiled some steaks. When they were about ready I hauled the guns and ammunition and a case of bourbon whiskey out of the boat, opened a bottle and poured us each a drink. It tasted about as good as whiskey can taste, and so did the steaks.

When we had finished supper and washed the dishes it was pitch dark, and Ted said we could finish unloading the boat in the morning. So we pulled it up onto the steep shingle, finished setting up the tents by lantern light, and blew up our air mattresses. Ted was in a wall tent about 10 by 14 feet, and I was in a smaller pyramid tent nearby. Before turning in we each had another pull at the jug, and Ted said there might be a bit of wind during the night and not to let it bother me. I said I wouldn't, and we retired to our respective tents.

117

About 4 o'clock in the morning I was wakened by what sounded like somebody howling bloody murder and shooting off a .45 pistol outside the tent. I thought, sure enough this is the wild west, but when I got up and went outside I saw by the rising moon that it was just the wind shrieking and snapping the flaps of my tent, cracking them like a mule-skinner's whip. It was some wind. There were tumbleweeds and small trees and stuff blowing across the desert floor, and when a rock about the size of a mushmelon came rolling by I grabbed it and hammered the pegs of my tent even deeper into the ground.

Then I looked over to where Ted's tent was supposed to be, and it was gone. I walked over there, leaning against the wind and saw it hadn't really gone, it was just flat on the ground, except for a large lump in the middle of the canvas and a smaller lump beside it. I could see that the large lump was Trueblood lying on a cot, and the smaller lump was Joe. At first I thought they had suffocated, and felt awful, because alone and without a dog it's hard to have good chukar shooting. But when I looked carefully I could see the canvas rise and fall slightly as they breathed.

I figured I had done most of the tent-pitching and obviously hadn't done it very well, so it was my responsibility to put it back up, and anyway Trueblood couldn't get out from under the canvas until I raised it. So I spent the next 45 or 50 minutes heaving and hauling on the ridge-pole and end poles and hammering tent pegs into the ground, waiting for momentary letups in the gale to snub guy-ropes tighter and catching my breath while the big gusts roared by. Finally I got the tent pretty well set up again, staggered back to the pyramid, and collapsed into my sleeping bag. I didn't know why Trueblood and Joe had lain there feigning sleep, but I was too pooped to ask them.

In the morning I got up and found the sun shining, the air calm, and Trueblood just poking his head out the flaps. "Good morning," he said. "Sleep well?" I looked to see if he was kidding. "How did *you* sleep?" I said. "Like a log," he said. Then he said, "I guess I was wrong about the wind. Usually it blows pretty hard for a couple of hours every night, this time of year. When it does, I can't sleep worth a darn."

I thought okay, Trueblood, have your little joke, so I said I had slept well too. "We'd better bring up the rest of the stuff from the boat," Ted said, and so we walked down to the water. When we got there we saw the boat was upside down on the bank and all the food had blown into the water, which was riled and cloudy. Also the bank went off steeply and most of the stuff had slid down into deep water and disappeared. There was something white showing in a shallow spot, and Ted scooped it out with an oar. It was a slab of salt pork, and it was the only food we had.

"By golly," Ted said, "there must have been some wind after all." I could tell he wasn't kidding, and so I told him how I had got up and found his tent collapsed on top of him and had spent a large part of the night setting it up again, while he and Joe had slept like babies. Trueblood knew I was making this up, of course, because he never sleeps well when the wind blows. "Furthermore," Ted said, "Joe always sleeps with one eye, one ear, and his nose wide open. He wakes up when a wildcat walks by a hundred yards downwind." I showed Ted the blisters on my hands and tried to find the rock I had used to hammer tent pegs, but it had blown away. To this day he doesn't believe me.

It was a good thing I had taken the whole case of whiskey and the ammunition out of the boat, because for the next four days, until we went back to pick up Ellen, we lived on whiskey, chukar partridge, and enough salt pork to provide cooking fat and salt. We had chukar partridge for breakfast, chukar partridge for lunch, and chukar partridge and whiskey for dinner. Sometimes we didn't have any lunch because we didn't have any chukar partridge or because we were too busy hunting. We walked about twenty miles a day, mostly straight up or straight down, either trying to find birds or trying to get them to fly after we had found them. Usually they ran ahead of us like rabbits, to Joe's disgust and ours, and we had scruples about shooting any bird on the ground.

At the end of four days I had lost a dozen pounds and felt better than I had felt anytime in the previous ten years, and although I didn't realize it at the time, we had invented the low-carbohydrate, high-protein diet (or so-called "drinking man's diet"). If we had thought to patent it, or write a book about it, we might both have become so filthy rich that by now we would be too gouty and wracked by riotous living to go hunting anymore, and perhaps sometimes it pays to be slow witted.

May 1977

When a Man's Thoughts Are Pure

HAVILAH BABCOCK

Recipe for a perfect day: bobwhites, a good dog, a good friend, and someone to welcome you home.

MY DIVERSIONS ARE hunting, fishing, and vegetable gardening, and teaching is my trade. How, I often ask, could a man be divided up more pleasantly? Teaching has brought me so much pleasure that I could list it as a pastime too. I may not have everything I want, but what I haven't got I can do without, which makes me rich. I don't covet my neighbor's maidservant, his ox, nor yet his ass.

I have been hunting and fishing most of my remembering days, and I enjoy these diversions as much now as ever. But as a man grows older his concept of a good time changes. So does his idea about what constitutes a successful hunting or fishing trip. When I was younger the measure of success was what I brought back.

I still like to bring home something to grace the dinner table when I go hunting or fishing, and I can imagine no finer reason for going. The world was made to be lived in as well as looked at, and nature's supermarket is well stocked if you don't mind its self-service feature.

But the size of the bag is no longer the sole criterion. I find, as I acknowledge the passing years, that the incidental gains—fringe benefits, they are called nowadays—are becoming more important, and I am growing more aware of the little extras that set a day apart and make the memory of it more fragrant.

I have often said that the bobwhite is America's most superb game bird, and that the pursuit of this gallant little fellow is the pastime of a scholar and a gentleman. I may not fit either of these categories, but few men have pursued *Colinus virginianus* longer or more ardently than I, yet I am sometimes baffled by his quirks and whimsies. Where, for instance, does he go when he isn't there? How does he manage at times—even in territory where he is

120

known to exist in great plenitude—to be completely unfindable?

There are days, indeed, when a poor, disheartened hunter might almost conclude the species has become extinct, as with head bowed and spirits adroop he homeward plods his weary way. But what is this his sharp eye catches which quickly assures him that the species is not extinct, and that a sizable bevy was in recent occupancy and may even now be in the environs? Nothing other than a quail roost.

Such a roost is always an object of interest and curiosity to me. The pattern of droppings is distinctive and unique, and the bedding habit of quail is evidence of the innate cunning of the wild. Perhaps his manner of roosting is one way of coping with his enemies. Groundling that he is, Bob must be prepared from darkness to dawn for sudden alarms and instant flight. Only through the alertness of every member of a covey can it be forewarned of lurking peril. Such alertness is achieved by roosting in a complete circle, with tails in the center and heads turned outward to spy out danger.

And a tight circle it is. On frosty mornings quail are inclined to lie abed, and I have seen a bevy of fifteen in a knot that the crown of my hat would have covered. No wonder a covey seems to explode when startled! But I have never seen birds collide on takeoff, each being a missile aimed along its own path.

The close circle also imprisons the scent arising from the family discharge. If uncurbed, such effluvium might prove a fatal giveaway to nocturnal marauders. I have often suspected that quiescent animals have some unexplored ability for withholding body scent, that something beyond mere immobility is involved. Certainly a dog may pass within two feet of a bedding covey without detecting its presence.

An experienced observer can estimate the size of a bevy by its roost, but a companion of mine who fancies himself an expert in this field of deduction once allowed himself to fall into a trap. Or more accurately, he was pushed into it. The owner of a commercial quail hatchery had brought me a bag of quail manure for my vegetable garden, and when I looked at the great profusion of "sign" a malicious idea popped into my head.

The following day I sneaked off to a swamp where we sometime hunted, and where my companion had called attention to a cluster of roosts. When I left, there reposed on what poets call the forest floor a quail roost such as no mortal eye had ever beheld. The next day my companion, with a little maneuvering on my part, discovered the planted evidence, and his voice boomed through the woods.

"Great balls of fire! Come here quick!" Down on his knees, he was pointing dramatically at the wondrous pyramid. "Have you ever—in all your born days?"

"How many would you say?" I prodded, helping him admire the phenomenon.

My companion picked up a stick to aid his calculations, but withheld his hand from demolishing so wondrous an edifice. "I'm coming back with my camera," he explained.

Then, with the half-closed eyes of a connoisseur appraising a chef-d'oeuvre, he surveyed the miniature pyramid from different angles and awesomely intoned, "I'd give it as my considered opinion that this covey had in the neighborhood of 150 birds!"

But in a moment he recovered from his trance, jumped up and sputtered, "Goshamighty! That's impossible!"

Throughout the afternoon he shook his head in puzzlement and mumbled unhappily to himself. I hope it is needless to say that I never confessed the swindle. But my companion got his revenge without being aware of it: for three days straight he dragged my unhappy carcass through that swamp in quest of the phantom covey.

Another sure sign that "Kilroy was here," and one which always brings me quiet pleasure to come upon, is a bevy's "wash," or dust bath. In loose woods earth on the sunny side of logs such curiosities are most likely to be found. They interest me not only because they advertise the presence of birds in the neighborhood but because I carry a mental picture of what happens in such communal baths.

I have lain in the brush and watched an entire bevy, one after another in orderly fashion, perform its fluttery ablutions. I have seen them stand in a sort of anteroom, busying themselves with idle chatter, while waiting their turn for the shower; and once inside, each bather disported himself with such spirit that its small body was almost swallowed in a miniature dust cloud. Although birds appear to enjoy the exercise, dust-bathing is a cleansing rite rather than an idle sport. As all observing hunters know, birds engage in such "washing" to suffocate the lice and other mites on their bodies.

What is more beautiful than a pointing dog? And what hunter is so impassive that he can contemplate one without a quickening of pulses and a surging of hope? "Statuesque," a pointing dog is often called, but no statue, however exquisite, can hold a candle to the real thing. I would like my dog to point with head and tail aloft, to be the fashion plate that finicky field-trial judges demand that he be. But if he didn't point like an all-time champion, even if he dropped to the ground and bellied forward like a base-born cur, I would forgive him and he would still be my dog, because that was the kind I hunted with when I was a boy. My first dogs were all groundlings and "pumpers," as we called them, and great self-advertisers.

I could hear one pumping up the ground fifty yards away, but if there was a covey in that end of the county, and I didn't run out of time, he would find it. In dry weather such a dog was a godsend, picking up and working a trail that an air-minded aristocrat would have missed or disdained to follow. Truth to tell, with quail becoming denizens of the deep-tangled wildwood in many areas, such a dog might be a godsend today.

When old Boss, the brag dog of my boyhood, finally snorted and pumped his way to the environs of a covey, he would flop down and begin praying. The nearer he got, the more he debased himself, dragging his carcass along the ground as if every movement would be his last. And on every covey rise old Boss had a nervous breakdown. So did I; how I ever got my growth I don't know.

Even now a dog that bellies down and goes into histrionics on point sends my blood pressure away up. But there is a thing or two to be said for such earthlings. Certainly they prolong the agony and the ecstasy longer than dogs that race up and slam on the brakes, although this may not be a favor. And in defense of trailing it might be argued that Bob belongs to the infantry, too, traveling mostly afoot, and that ground scent is the basis of bird hunting. I am in favor of any dog that will find and hold a bird until I get there. If he looks like Abercrombie & Fitch, fine and dandy; but if he is a lazy homespun character that points with his tail at half-mast, at least he points. After all, what makes a dog a bird dog is what he does about birds.

"How does a bird dog's sense of smell compare with that of other hunting dogs?" I am sometimes asked. Having hunted birds all my life, and nothing but birds, I have no basis for comparison. But two peculiarities have long puzzled me. First, how a dog's acuteness of smell can vary so much— from detecting the presence of birds fifty feet away to being blithely unaware of a skulker under his very nose. Second, how does a dog distinguish the direction from which birds have come from the direction in which they have gone? A good dog will infallibly trail *toward* birds rather than away from them.

A covey's daily neighborhood meanderings might embrace half a mile, and over a variegated terrain, yet a dog can intersect the trail at almost any point and without apparent effort make the right turn. I have often heard dogs accused of backtrailing, but I have seen this happen only a few times, and almost never by a first-class dog.

"Sometime a dog will backtrack on purpose," a shooting companion once told me. "When I was a boy I was a great possum hunter, and I often bragged that Jumbo, my possum dog, never backtracked. But one night Jumbo got chewed up by a ferocious bull possum that had moved into our woods. And for a solid month—until the old boy recovered his nerve—Jumbo back-trailed that big possum every time we went hunting. And with a hurrah that echoed through the hills! Yes, sir," laughed my companion, "Jumbo became an expert on where that possum had been, and not once did he make the mistake of trailing in the right direction!"

One day last season while dawdling over my noonday snack I chanced to see a bevy of quail scurrying across the path ahead. Such a sight would ordinarily have galvanized me into motion, but not that day. Having within one bird of my requirements, and being of a mind to humor my legs a bit and perchance catch a little shuteye, I merely grinned and leaned back against a friendly stump.

An hour or so later I released my dogs from the car and watched with more than passing interest as they picked up the trail and unerringly set off in the right direction. Not a moment's hesitation, no awareness of having solved a problem.

Does the explanation lie in some subtle exhalation from the birds themselves, or in some uncatalogued sense that nature installed in dogs? I suppose there is no percentage in pondering the imponderable. Having been a guest of nature off and on for forty years, I have come to one conclusion: whoever put things on this earth of ours and started them off evidently knew what he was doing.

No dissertation on the pleasures of hunting and fishing should leave out the titillating effects of good conversation. A great beguiler of time and abridger of distances is conversation, for what so shortens a trip as good talk? The charm of good conversation lies in its spontaneity and disrespectfulness, the way it rambles without apology from one topic to another. Lay down rules for the conduct of a conversation and you wind up with a conference, which is a swapping of ignorance and an exercise in mutual boredom. The first requirement of good conversation is that nobody should know what is coming next.

Good conversation, of course, demands good companionship. A man may work alone, but it is improbable that he will get much playing done without the companionship of others. Bird hunting is one such social pastime. Companionship is, in fact, half the hunt and may go far toward redeeming a bad day. Certainly it should be listed among the pleasures of hunting, but tastes in companionship may vary.

I want a companion to be friendly, but not too friendly; to be talkative, but not too talkative; to have a good dog, but not quite as good as mine; to have a sense of humor without being a humorist—and for God's sake, not a punster! I also want a companion who is a good shot, but not too damned good. The first rule of companionship in hunting is not to embarrass the other fellow.

Surely not the least of my pleasures in hunting and fishing is getting back home. And having somebody there who is glad I'm back and is interested in the kind of day I've had, someone to call out, "Any luck?"

"More luck than I'll probably ever know," I *could* answer. "My companion and I have been handling guns all day, I have driven 150 miles over dangerous highways, and I am still alive. If that isn't luck, I don't know what is. Just getting back home can be an achievement. Many people don't."

I *could* say that, but I don't. This is a time for relaxation, not morbid moralizing. So I'll say, "Yes, a wonderful day. There will never be another exactly like it."

"Any birds?"

"Yes, I brought back some and left some, and it is possible that those I left gave me as much pleasure as those I brought home. There is only one thing you can do with a dead bird, you know—eat it."

December 1964

A Bird Like Christmas

DATUS C. PROPER

The nimble ringneck, nature's ornament, reminds a hunter of the season at hand.

YOU NEVER HUNT alone when you take your dog along. At least, you never feel alone if you have a dog who likes to hunt with you. There are dogs who don't care for human interference, and they are happier than their people, because the dogs get to hunt birds while the people spend their time hunting dogs. Hunting birds is much more fun than hunting dogs.

When Trooper and I were younger, it took us awhile to decide that we could get more birds when we were both hunting in the same acre. This realization brought about a compromise. For my part, I agreed to stop hunt- •
ing according to the principles of Euclidean geometry. Some time before Trooper I had persuaded myself that a square field should be hunted in a pattern with 90-degree angles, missing no corners or tangles of briars, and that every pheasant would run all the way to the end of a hedgerow. I was better at geometry than at smelling pheasants. Trooper explained that the way to find birds was to look where his nose was pointing, or a few yards farther on. Trooper is a German shorthaired pointer who failed geometry, but nothing is wrong with his nose.

Trooper's discovery was that I shoot better than he can. I don't shoot as well as a lot of the boys at the skeet range, but they seldom come hunting with us; and between me and Trooper there is no comparison. Trooper has now become the opposite of gun shy, whatever you call that. The skeet range makes him unhappy because with so much shooting there are bound to be dead pheasants all over the place, yet I never let him out of the car to retrieve.

I forgot to tell you that Trooper is also a retriever when he's allowed to be. He's delighted to bring me half of every pheasant he finds—the bony half, which is dry and hard to swallow anyhow. Clearly a fair deal, when you consider that with all the loops he runs, he probably hunts 30 miles to my 10. Trooper has never understood why I make him point dead instead of practicing his retrieves. But he bears no ill will, and when he hears my gun go off—even at mile 28—his old joints stop aching and he runs like a puppy to the place where the bird ought to fall, frequently arriving at about the same time. His hope is that the pheasant will try to run. Trooper is allowed to retrieve runners. My wife cooks some abbreviated pheasants that we'd be ashamed to serve to guests, but at least we don't leave many wounded birds out there for the foxes.

Take one day last season, for instance. It was the third Saturday in December, and we weren't hunting for Christmas dinner, because a rooster for that occasion had already been hanging in a cold corner for a week, building up flavor. We just wanted a bird to justify the week's sitting around; to go with a bottle of red wine, for New Year's; and to keep the place looking right after Christmas dinner. A cock pheasant has every color you could want for the short days. You could deck out a balsam fir with his feathers and they'd look prettier than the ornaments your kid made at school.

I was, however, a little concerned about the weather forecast—the gusty northwest winds, not the part about the chill factor of 10 below zero. Cold I can dress for, and Trooper doesn't care as long as he's dry, running, and finding a sniff of pheasant now and then. But holding a pheasant (or any other bird) is tough for a dog when it's windy.

Turned out the day wasn't as bad as it sounded to the disc jockey in his heated booth. The wind didn't blow all the time and the storm coming through from Montana had beaten the haze, giving us a Montana sun instead of the distant orange, fluorescent glow that sometimes passes for daylight here in the mid-Atlantic.

You're a hunter, I guess, so I don't have to tell you what it feels like to whistle up your dog and hike off across the fields after a week of commuting through a dingy city. A step becomes a stride, and fields that were cramped in the green four months ago now stretch on to the sky in corn stubble and yellow grass. Winter fields are endless, for a fellow with hunting permission, even if he has to turn corners and climb barbed-wire fences to keep from reaching a stopping point. And it is a little spooky—if you believe that humans and other animals are far apart—to see that your dog shares your stupid grin. His ears flap back, he runs in unprofitable circles, and he clears tall rosebushes at a single bound.

Trooper's first hedgerow had some splendid smells, and I reckoned we'd find birds in it, because last year we had shot a rooster right here and found two hens killed by a goshawk that had eaten only the intestines and pieces of thigh—just the bits that Trooper prefers. Perhaps the other predators have figured out something that humans are too squeamish to understand.

Trooper got a little carried away by whatever he was smelling and beat me to the end of the hedgerow. I saw a flicker of something bright running out ahead of him and thought, *oh, indecent dog, you are going to bust the bird*. But Trooper didn't. He didn't even bust the fox, which is what had been making the smells. She—must have been a she, to be in that kind of mood—came running back to play. She flirted her long tail and dared him to chase her. He did.

In another corner of the field, where the fox had not been, Trooper found the correct smells. They were in the only decent patch of grass around, and pheasants do love tall grass. We had a point.

Now, Trooper is not a dog who just stands there when a bird is encountered, waiting for someone to come up and do the necessary. His eyes bug out; he nearly stops breathing; his tail stands up and quivers; his body emits wavelengths that say: *shut up and sit still, bird, till the boss comes up and makes you into a Christmas decoration*. Mostly they do sit still, when Trooper is that close.

Seven of them sit this time. I can't blame Trooper for pointing hens, and he doesn't blame me when I fail to shoot as they flush, one after another, leaving a hunter undergoing withdrawal symptoms. I have never tried any other drug that required withdrawal, so I don't know much about cold turkey, but it can't get much shakier than hot hen pheasants.

You hear of dogs that grow surly if the boss fails to get off a shot, or misses, but Trooper just figures it's a chance to do the thing all over again. So off we rush, hoping the hens will lead us to where the cocks are hiding. It usually doesn't work, but it's as good as any other idea I have, and at least hens can be counted on for abundant winter points. The other good thing about them is that they will still be around in spring to produce eggs, half of which will contain incipient roosters. Maybe that's why I can hunt pheasants right through the holidays and find just as many the next year.

Some of the hens have, I think, lit in a brushy hedgerow. Thither I go. Elsewhere Trooper goes. I whistle. He persists in sniffing around the edges of a woodlot that is clearly too thin to shelter pheasants. Clearly to me, that is. Guess who is right. Before Trooper can locate and point, a rooster swirls out of the trees at full flap, heading toward the field we just abandoned. I told you I was a slow learner. We go back to Field One and hunt it for half an hour, finding only a hen who flew that way at the first flush. The rooster has, no doubt, gone several fields farther—a nasty habit roosters have after the first bangs of November.

Then we walk. And walk, and walk. Both of us are a little weaker of knee than we were at sunup, but I am not at the hallucinatory stage yet, so the pheasants had better watch out. As a pheasant hunter I have fewer talents than Trooper, but I do have long legs, toes that point straight forward, and a disposition to follow them until the matter of New Year's dinner had been resolved.

A possible resolution appears, at last, in a high, dense, bramble patch that has grown over a fence bordering corn stubble. We come up from the downhill side and Trooper points. There is no way over the fence without a long detour, so I have to come up from below and behind Trooper, which is precisely the wrong way to approach a dog pointing pheasants. With both adversaries on one side, the bird naturally flushes on the other, and there is no shot to be had through the bramble jungle. The cock stays low for 50 yards, then rises toward dim horizons—snowy ring resplendent below evergreen head, red wattles rampant, orange breast aflame, tail pennants flouting the idiot with a shotgun. No wonder that bird is still alive on December 21. But I think there is a way to get him surrounded next weekend: Trooper will come up from below again, while I will cross the fence well back from the brambles and tiptoe in from the top.

Which makes this a good place to observe that pheasant hunting is a different thing from pheasant shooting. Pheasant shooting is what we do (with luck) during the first hours of opening day, or (with money) on shooting preserves, or (with an airplane ticket and much money) on the other side of the Atlantic.

As to the shooting part, I can manage to miss under most circumstances. When, after a lot of hunting, a shot that I can make does offer itself, I am not disappointed. I am, on the contrary, profoundly thankful that Trooper found the pheasant and then stopped to wait for me. There are enough of the other kind of shots, at 40 yards through the woodlot, with my left foot in the greenbriars.

Pheasants have been hunted, one way or another, for millennia, and by now they do it all. They run, and they stop. They flush wild and they sit tighter than woodcock, while hunters walk past. Mostly pheasants do what's best for their survival, given recent experiences with men and dogs. If they happen to make a long, sneaky trail for Trooper to puzzle out, and if at the end of that trail they hide away where no one has found them before, then he and I think we're doing something which is about as good as hunting gets. Hunting, not just shooting.

Of course, there are also days like the Saturday last season, when we were limping toward evening without a feather in the game pocket. I was limping, at least. Trooper was still ranging, but it was near sundown when he went on point, off in the distance. Before I could get close a covey of bobwhites flushed and passed me, almost out of range, headed for an impenetrable patch of second-growth woods. I took a shot with the left barrel, and while nothing fell, I thought that one bird landed too soon, in thick grass at the edge of the woods. On the remote chance that it had been hit I ran to the spot and stood there while Trooper hunted dead. I didn't want to spoil any scent by moving around. Then, after a few minutes, I slumped on a limestone outcrop while Trooper kept at work. When he finally locked up, his nose was pointing down at the ground. I walked in to pick up what I thought would be a dead 7-ounce quail, and out flushed a 3-pound cock pheasant in excellent flying condition. I was ready: had been for a long time.

By now, it seemed clear to me that there was no bobwhite around, but Trooper did not want to leave the tall grass. Probably just wanted to enjoy his recent triumph: another of his defects, like sticky retrieves. So I sagged onto the soft rock again. And Trooper pointed again. When I reached him he broke point, ran 30 yards, and pointed a second time. I trotted up and he went off 50 yards to a third point. Poor old dog had been running so long that his overheated brain was producing fantasies. But this time, when I circled in from the side, the fantasy jumped into the air and cackled off, setting sun flickering through fanned-out wing feathers. We headed for the car with two big birds bulging my game pocket so it felt like Santa's pack, and now both of us could afford to limp.

Those two roosters had held still for walking, running, waiting, grass-kicking, shooting, cussing, whistle-blowing, bell-ringing, and dog-calling. All of it took place within a few yards of the birds—sometimes a few feet. They did not move until the dog had them accurately located. You can figure how much chance I'd have had without Trooper.

But that, I suppose, is merely practical. Nothing tastes better than a pheasant, but Trooper and I really hunt together because we have the same cells down the middle of our backs. When he is pointing something close, a ridge of hair along his spine ruffles. My back hairs fell out during the late Pleistocene, but the cells where the hair ought to be still work fine; so there I am, out in the suntanned field backing my pointer. He makes mistakes, but he doesn't lie. Something is going to happen when I take a few steps. Probably it's a hen; maybe it's the farmer's cat; and once or twice a day it's a big bird decorated like a Christmas tree.

December 1986

Growing Up

NORMAN STRUNG

Born under a skyscraper's shadow, they sought the wild world that began where the pavement ends.

DIX, ROY, RONNIE, The Burm, and me. We were city kids, born in the shadows of skyscrapers, so the hunger we shared was remarkable. None of our parents cared about the wild world that began where the pavement ended, yet we were drawn to hunting and fishing as naturally as specks of steel seek the poles of a magnet.

Although the greening of sportsmen on the streets of New York seems improbable, dogged desire and city savvy found us meeting the challenge in original, if slightly illegal, ways. By the time we were ten years old, we were regularly bagging squab and squirrel.

Guns inside the city were unthinkable, but slingshots were silent and easy to hide, and marbles made cheap, accurate ammunition. Pigeons and squirrels were perpetual beggars in local parks, and all it took to draw them into lethal range was a dollop of peanut butter smeared on the tip of your shoe.

Bean a squirrel in the head at arm's length with a smooth cat's eye or aggie and there was meat in the pot and another hide to adorn a bedroom wall. The technique was not without its hazards, however. If your aim was low, you clipped your foot and hobbled for a week. I once lost a nail off my big toe.

Fishing required equivalent environmental adaptation. Many of the city's drainage sumps and park ponds had populations of carp and goldfish. You could catch the smaller ones on pin hooks with doughballs, but the trophies we lusted for fed on floating bread cast upon the waters by the same kind folks who fed the squirrels. We tried different brands of bread, searching for one that was tough enough to hold a hook when waterlogged; but only bagels filled the bill, and the fish wouldn't touch them. Then The Burm perfected his "butcher lure," a matchbook-sized chunk of foam rubber, laced with wire and treble hooks. A carp couldn't sniff at the contraption without getting caught.

If there was a mecca for us in the city, it was Oakland Lake, a half square mile of freshwater out in Queens. It had trees along the shore, it was fed by mossy springs, and it was stocked regularly with put-and-take trout.

Every spring weekend we would take the long bike or bus ride out to Oakland and stroke its waters with spinning gear, losing precious lures, and catching few trout. Then we hit upon a scheme to replenish those lost lures.

The hatchery truck always dumped its load of trout in the same place, and the pressure around that spot was enormous. The simple-minded fish would hang around there for days. One afternoon we stretched a rope between two bus stops and anchored them underwater within casting distance of shore. The next weekend we harvested sufficient terminal tackle to see us through several seasons.

By the time we had entered our teens, we had all conned apprehensive parents out of shotguns for Christmas, and our bait-casters had matured into fiberglass shafts and Mitchell 300's. We had also discovered the rules of thumb—a motorist is a sucker for a kid with a fishing rod; don't hitch with more than two companions; and when you hitch with a gun, keep it cased and hidden. Our thumbs opened up the lands and lakes that lay east and north of the city, on Long Island and in Westchester County.

Although we had expected it to be otherwise, we found that fishing and hunting there was like the city—crowded, ugly and competitive. There was one notable exception, however: the clubs that lay behind cyclone fences and posted signs. It didn't take us long to succumb to their shameless wink.

To an adolescent stoked on the pages of outdoor magazines and starving for their promise, the clubs were an Eden. Gaudy pheasants pecked gravel on the well-trodden paths, rabbits darted into warrens in the greenbriar, and mallards nested along the shores of streams. And in those streams, fat trout—fed on pellets, familiar only with artificial flies—simply slobbered after a night crawler. The temptation was too great. We entered the estate of poachers in order to embrace paradise.

As might be expected, our flirtation with illicit game, and those that protected it, was as clumsy as the gangling kids we were. One of our most regularly visited fishing holes was a cement culvert, known simply as "the tubes."

The tubes flowed under a highway on Long Island, and a headgate had been built on its upstream end, backing up a large pond onto the property of an exclusive sportsman's club. The culverts were large enough in diameter to waddle through, which got you under a stout fence topped with barbed wire. Then, when you reached the headgate, there was a 4-foot pocket below the falls with just enough room for a snappy backcast. You could pop your head above lake level, periscope the pond to see if it was empty, and if it was, fish to your heart's content. It was strictly a one-man operation, however, so we would line up behind one another down in the tubes and take turns.

There was only one flaw to the tubes. Unless you kept a sharp lookout to the far right and left, it was possible for a crafty keeper to creep along the fence unseen and get in back of you. There he waited for your next cast. He would catch your rod on the back snap and snip 6 to 8 inches off the tip.

Another of our favorite targets was a stocked pond that lay behind a high board fence along a major artery to the city. The highway department had installed guard rails on the road shoulder that gave you an extra 3 feet when you stood on them. It was just enough height to lob a cast over the barrier and into the water beyond.

One morning we each took a post, and proceeded to yank trout after flopping trout onto the green grass of the roadside. It must have been quite a show, for according to the bemused keeper who ordered us down from our perches, we had backed rush-hour traffic into the next township as cars slowed to witness the spectacle.

It was a game of cat-and-mouse between us and the club employees, most of whom were possessed of a supreme sense of humor and justice. When you were caught, a snipped tip was the first penalty. If you were caught a second time, you could expect confiscation of your equipment, but you could get it back by a personal appearance and an apology. Later, when The Burm acquired that dream of all youth, personal transportation in the form of a '48 Pontiac, we learned that flattened tires or toothpicks in door locks were also a part of the deal if your parking place was discovered. They seemed to enjoy the game as much as we did.

As might be hoped, we began to mature as sportsmen as we matured in years. The thrill of easy marks where we could catch quick limits subsided, and we forsook the tubes and the fences for a more sophisticated approach— camouflage clothing and a sense of timing.

On weekends, you were free to wander just about anywhere inside a club before 7 A.M. Wednesday afternoons were the worst times to fish. Doctors and lawyers usually took that half day off. We traveled together and compared notes at day's end, but each of us started to fish and hunt in different directions. I discovered the joys of fly fishing. I learned how to tie crude flies, and actually returned some fish to the water.

Not that I had completely lost my roots planted in the New York hustle. I always kept a few of the biggest fish, and on the way into the city would have The Burm stop off at Oakland Lake where I would clean them. Four or five fat trout always drew "ohs" and "ahs" from the weekend crowd, and the inevitable question: "What did you catch them on?" At which point I would open a fly box stuffed with Woolly Worms, the only pattern I was capable of tying, and sell them for 75 cents each.

I must also confess to the onset of conscience. I couldn't verbalize that what we were doing was wrong, for we didn't view it as poaching. Limits and seasons were scrupulously observed, licenses were bought, and nongame animals were never taken. We weren't exactly poachers, just takers of the king's game, Robin Hoods. Yet I became aware of the burden of the trespasser—that the solace you seek by entering private lands is subverted when you have to watch over your shoulder.

That fall, Dix shot his first deer and nearly gave a gamekeeper a heart attack. We had all passed our sixteenth birthday and were eligible for a big-game license. Rifle hunting was beyond our reach, for it required a long journey upstate, but deer could be hunted with a bow right across the city line in Westchester. We directed every free moment to archery.

One rainy Sunday afternoon, Dix sent an arrow through a young doe. He had been up a tree, just inside the border of posted property, and the mortally wounded animal ran deeper within. Afraid to lose his new recurve, he hid it in a tree, and rounded up Roy, who was hunting nearby. They entered the club with sheath knives drawn to retrieve the animal.

Although they wore our standard camouflage uniform and tennis shoes, it wasn't enough of a disguise to elude a sharp-eyed keeper who was patrolling the property. But before he could intercept them, they saw the deer. Her head was still up, so they dropped to a crouch and slowly approached the dying animal.

"Now," Dix hissed, and the two youths jumped on her. Blades flashed, the doe kicked and struggled, the three rolled in the mud and leaves, and Roy was able to finally end her suffering by cutting her throat. When the two arose, they discovered they were not alone. The keeper stood before them, ashen-faced and white-knuckled.

"My God," he whispered. "Do you boys always hunt deer like this?"

Dix got to keep the doe, too. After hearing that the animal had been wounded on the other side of the fence, the man pulled himself together and told them he'd let them go this time, but if a similar thing happened, they had better get someone from the club before they entered the property.

"Neat guy," Dix nodded as we drove home that night, all of us exuding pride at Dix's kill.

"Yeah, he was," someone else chimed in. "When you think of it, most of those keepers have been pretty straight with us."

The enemy was quickly becoming the role model.

The next spring we discovered the Beaverkill and all of us were bowled over by its gentle beauty. It was on a weekend when spring was at its greenest. We fished the public section in the morning, but soon became disenchanted with three small trout and anglers at your elbow. We searched out the quick-fix promise of private waters.

We scattered upstream from a little hamlet along the river, each of us looking for a thatch of woods that could not be seen from the road. I had The Burm drop me off at a bridge. The place was just too delightful for me to have to look over my shoulder.

I had heard that bridges were considered a public right-of-way. That you could fish from them, or under them, without being guilty of trespass. I slipped into the slow, slick waters between the abutments and unlimbered my fly rod, drinking in the nodding maples, the serpentine gentility of the stream, and began to cast.

"Hey fella . . ."

I stepped from the shadows and looked upward. An older fisherman with a fly-studded hat looked down. "You're not allowed to fish there, son. This is private."

"Under a bridge? I thought you could fish from under a bridge anywhere . . ."

"Not exactly," he smiled. "Law says you can fish *from* the bridge, but then again, it doesn't stop me from throwing rocks in the water if you try."

I shrugged my shoulders, reeled in my line, and climbed up to the roadway. "Is there any place around here where I *can* fish . . . I mean away from people?"

The man shook his head. "Not unless you belong to one of these clubs. Where you from, anyway?"

"The city."

"A city kid, huh? Couldn't tell it by the way you handle a fly rod. That's different, too. Most kids your age not only poach us to the poorhouse, they do it with minnows or worms or spinning lures."

"No kidding?" I muttered, feigning shock as I recalled that we had all three baits in The Burm's trunk.

"Tell you what. Go ahead and fish from the bridge if you want. I'll square it up back at the club." The man turned to walk away.

"Mister, what does it take to belong to one of these clubs?"

"Well, about $800 a year, and you've got to be invited to join by another member. If you're interested, drop by the clubhouse later and I'll show you around. I think everyone would welcome a decent young man like yourself."

I stood on the bridge until The Burm picked me up, weighing his words, my wants, and the world that lay before me. I never fished on the wrong side of a posted sign again. Instead, I headed for Montana the following fall.

April 1984

The XIVth of John

NASH BUCKINGHAM

A daughter's wedding stirs a goose-hunting memory.

ROM MY GOOSE pit on the upper plateau of old Ship Island bar, I used to gaze longingly up and across the tawny Mississippi at a finger-like sand ridge jutting from Arkansas. Under varying river levels my glasses revealed it sometimes as mainland; at others, peninsula, or again, a mere knob in a blur of dun.

Frequently, that first season, I observed heavy goose traffic avail itself of an apparently unshot landing field. Strange to say, the odd formation seemed proof against that dismantling to which floods subject river bars. Beyond this barrier, fancy pictured a shallow lagoon, with no telling how many unmolested duck lakes, turkey woods and fur pockets across the rough beyondage of Walnut Bend. There must needs be, I figured, some resistant reef guarding the bar's upper neck—some tight lining to absorb current rip and eddy suction.

This was years ago. Gas boats were few and far between, though Ed had a crazy one. But save for the stately packets and their stodgier river kin the only powered craft were the occasional steam yachts of an annoying idle rich. To explore that distant goose concentration camp became little short of an obsession.

At that time there were practically no goose hunters among the members of the duck club. I was the reputed and smiled-at "crazy man" who made long drives, lay out nights, or shivered all day in clammy sandholes waiting for fool geese.

Ours was a made-to-order wilderness. Sixty square miles of dense and varied game haunt! Behind Bordeaux tow-head lay an old river bed. Its three miles of meander was spotted with hidden ponds, mallard and goose holes de luxe. Just below its reunion with "Old Miss" we had general headquarters at Ed's house-boat.

No potentate every governed a more bountiful and carefree domain than Ed. Nor did any captain of industry ever finger a wider assortment of apparently aimless but somehow remunerative enterprises.

Ed was steamboat agent. Government light-keeper and insurance salesman. He was deputy sheriff, magistrate and benign political over-lord. By turns and terms he was gravel and cement manufacturer, photographer, portrait painter and critic of national affairs. He dwelt ever upon the brink of some great invention.

In addition to activities as ferryman, farmer and amiable usurer, he dealt in fur and cotton. His talents as mortician, doubling in white or black, were profound and widely utilized. As chief mourner, orator, residuary legatee, executor with or without bond, referee in bankruptcy or umpire out of same, Ed's versatility was astounding. First, last and all the time, however, he was river-fisherman, squirrel-turner and lazy addict of hound and headlight.

Kindly, fearless, honest Ed! Gone—long since. Billeted in an antebellum graveyard behind the levee, with his friendly enemy, Old Man River, sharing eternal pact. Asleep at the bole of a gnarled cypress, where all who pass that way linger to leave the friendly words and kind thoughts they have of him. He's somewhere around, though; count on that. No doubt, in one of "the many mansions that are in my Father's house." But for happiness, old Ed didn't really need a mansion.

Toward fag-end of the shooting season the river usually reached a higher stage. With its first telltale litter of brushy driftage and foam sponge, water smashed through the old river. Its bed of willows, rank weeds and grasses became a duck paradise. From dawn to dusk, sinuous ribbons of wildfowl poured through its crescent. When the cut-off became too deep to wade, we poled across in Ed's skiff and hunted along this backwater. We had every dangerous step-off spotted and knew well enough when to take the current seriously.

For all his familiarity, Ed cherished a vast respect for the Father of Waters. His commodious house-boat was blocked up in a bank clearing from which dangerous timber had been felled against the coming of a "twister." But when high water was receding rapidly, his entire household lived more or less in mortal terror of caving banks.

"I 'member one time in pertic'ler," Ed used to relate around our camp fire while an obnoxious cob pipe fumed like a condemned fertilizer plant. " 'Twas dead o' the night, but the ol' lady was up. We all was pretty much—come to think of it. Anyways, the ol' woman was glandin' a coon I'd ketched. Naw, she warn't neither; she was preservin' some muscadines—a failin' o' mine, them muscadines. But anyways, all of a sudden it come a sorta *queswishit*. I felt the ol' boat kinda shiver an' then go to skiddin' an' slidin'.

"Yup, y'betcha I knowed what had done took place. O' cose, it scairt the livin' whey outa me, but I run to the back door—I was atrimmin' my corns at the moment—an' befo' Gawd an' my countrymen, 'bout a half acre o' our front yard was easin' into the river, an' us along with it! Things was sho' agoin' down-hill—but, gent'mens, she hit the water on an even keel an' bounced a time or two on the backwash befo' she set still. I knowed her chinks was tight; so I yells to the oldest boy. I says, 'Leave off bellerin',' I says, 'an' help yo' ma hol' them hot muscadines onto the stove.' Then I made the second kid grab a pike pole. 'Quit bawlin',' I says to him. 'She'll float. Quit tryin' to pull them breeches on backards,' I says, 'an' go to shovin'.'

"Well, we lined her back into the eddy, an' in a day or so the rise lifted us back out onto new ground. Never lost a single darn thing. Didn't even wake up the youngest baby."

Finally we planned the raid.

"De best way to git dar," evolved Horace, colored factotum of our duck club and companion on many a trip, "is to borry Mister Ed's skifft an' git a early start. Ax him to leave de boat at de haid o' de inside chute—us kin walk dat far. Den us pulls up past de Whitehall place 'bout two miles, an' shoots crosst wid de current. Dat evenin' us comes back crosst, drift all de way down an' land at Mister Ed's."

It meant a battle. In my mind's-eye I rechecked every foot of the route. But because of the birds I had watched use the place, getting there would be worth any hardship. "Ride over Sunday and ask Mister Ed to leave us the boat," I instructed. "I'll come down Monday evening, and we'll tackle the job on Tuesday."

Horace and I met to arrange final details. The boat, with two sets of sweeps, was reported ready. Two sacks of wooden goose profiles, a stubby shovel and my shoulder pack were loaded into the light buggy. In addition to tea bucket and rations the pack held camera, binoculars, 10-gauge 2's for my big double and similar ammunition for the 12-bore loaned to Horace as gun-bearer. Weather prognostication gave reasonable assurance of cooperation by the elements.

Hot Java and a snack were behind me at two-thirty next morning. Horace picked up the reins, gave Red Fox, the tall stepping mule, the watch-word, and we were off. Stabling our rig in the lee of Ed's sleeping domicile, we shouldered the load, hit a familiar trail for thirty minutes and loaded into the waiting skiff. After ten minutes' paddling, we nosed gradually out to swifter contact and the great adventure.

Stripped to rowing comfort, we warmed to the raw job. We were bucking the upper reach of a great reversed S, with two miles of hard lifting behind, when a packet rounded Walnut Light. Knowing the danger of being caught in the dark too close between wave wash and steep caving bank, we landed and yanked out. The panting monster churned past so close that we could see her rousters lying about decks and hear the lead-man chanting his fathoms. Looking after her while the waves broke, we sighted a second steamer coming up the river but apparently well down, giving us ample time to cross. We shoved off and bent silently to the oars. The weather had thickened. We were near mid-channel and making good headway.

"Gawdamighty, Mister Nash!" suddenly exclaimed Horace. "Dat big boat is shovin' blind barges widout no lights ahead—an' us is right in dey path!"

Ceasing stroke oar, I swung about. One glance told the truth. There she was, and out front, with no vestige of warning, a long line of false space and deadly black hulks angling directly at us! Too late to turn back, or dodge. The current dragged like a giant magnet. Just one chance on earth—beat her across the line of collision!

"Horace," I said, as evenly as I could, "strike a handful of matches and wave 'em—they might see an' slow down—then pull to beat hell!"

Brains and a sense of propriety never lacked in Horace. A pinpoint of light flared—and died. Meanwhile, with everything in me slowly congealing, I tried to hold on course. With a grunt Horace picked up the stroke. We leaped forward. An upthrusting black wall protruded into eye corners. Suddenly the towboat's engines shut down. They had seen the warning! In the stillness a louder rush of churning water flogged our ears. It was going to be deadly close!

A long-forgotten numbness crept into my forearms. Today's slow-motion dream films hopped madly past an imperiled brain awaiting the crash and oblivion. I saw our baby's tiny new face peeping up at me from blankets and crib, and Irma's rapt gaze. Then—somehow—I was "number two" again on Johnny Harvard's crew. Late fall—cold dusk stipling the jumpy Charles River basin—a boatload of crew freshmen battling for jobs—megaphoned voices bellowing from the launch—the Old Man himself—altogether now! The baby's face again. We've got to win—that's it—come on now—pick it up—you—number two—feather—wrists—legs—catch—drive!

We rise to meet a smashing crest—hang suspended—tilt—dip crazily and are slapped sidewinding from beneath the tow's prow as it crunches past.

Half sinking, we fall slowly aside. Horace bailing desperately with his hat. Lantern in hand, a deck-dauber races to the side-rail and roars curses. Reviving somewhat, I suspend operations to send back worse. A searchlight pries from the pilot house and holds us for a second. Engines throb, and she is back on her deadly, unthinking way. Oh, for a rifle to put a ball through her boiler!

We had drifted badly during the bailing process and found ourselves below the objective. In twenty minutes, however, we sneaked around the bar's comb and into dead water. Half a mile's easy passage along the reef took us to its base, and from the shallows roared a mass of roosting ducks and geese. Apparently, we had hit the spot.

Still a bit unstrung but recovering, we hoisted the outfit, pegged the skiff and set out to explore. A hint of dawn pallor smudged the east. Climbing to the crest, we crossed the neck, looking for human tracks. Not a trace! We found plenty of goose sign. Dead center in the open bar we dug in— twenty minutes of spelling, with the off man setting up the decoys. Our pits were thirty yards apart. A southwest breeze fanned our necks, and the decoys led back into the hollow square of a death-trap pocket.

Our first customers came from down river and the home bar. Their penciled line, looming abruptly against half-light, mounted the plateau, saw our set, pitched down and broke into a gaggle of conversation. To this day, I believe that our decoys were the first to take toll from that sand spit. Then our visitors ceased talking and sailed straight in with a roar of wing-whiff and back-peddling. Their paddles were scraping through the opening when my first swath of twos mowed down a lapped pair and raked a third skimming not two feet from the sand. With birds massed heavily over him, Horace arose and pulled down a fourth.

Hardly had we retrieved the slain when from over the woods behind us, evidently coming from some roost lake, swooped a second flock. One almost unsuspicious circle, and in they rushed! Three stayed behind. Business quieted temporarily. Meanwhile burly dark clouds ran the oncoming sun out of business. Wind freshened! Flock after flock of geese traded up-river. Shots at one outfit frequently scared off another bunch attempting to make the profiles.

Of such flights are the goose hunter's dreams made. But with sixteen down and two cripples in the river, we called it a day as far as the honkers were concerned. There was no limit in those days, but even then I did have a conscience. Few times have I ever seen greater opportunity for actual slaughter. It was coming noon. Time to eat a bite and do some exploring. It required two trips to lower the set and stow it, geese and all, in the tub. Horace boiled

the kettle in a clump of willows. We counted any number of flocks still coming to the bar while we lay there munching sandwiches.

Investigation inland revealed a promised land of sport. Within a quarter of a mile, but too far off for a shot, we flushed a gang of wild turkeys. Farther on, hidden among the cottonwoods and willows off the main bar, we
came to a stumpy, shallow lake literally alive with mallards, teal and sprigs.
What a sight it was, and all ours for the shooting! While skies darkened I
called from the bank and got down a dozen or more circling hens and drakes.

It was well past mid-afternoon when, heavily laden, we lunged from
the undergrowth and flung our bag into the boat. By now we had a load in
that craft, too. A half gale had risen. Sand spouts whirled overhead. The lagoon
was comparatively quiet, but the river beyond was a mass of seething whitecaps. Once past the rim's protection, we would be in for something. That we
knew full well, for up-current wind blows a double heavy chop. After the
morning's fright, neither of us had stomach for much more trouble. A full
mile of it lay ahead!

"Sho' looks bad, Mister Nash," opined Horace. "You reckon us kin
make it? Maybe us better try to make de other bar ahead an' walk home. I'd
ruther make fo' trips walkin' dan one swimmin'. Tell you de trufe, Cap'n, I
done jest natcherly lost my taste foh dis river. I wants to keep de ground under my feet—if I ever gits it dar agin!"

"It may get worse," I countered. "Let's get going."

Carefully adjusting the load to throw the boat's nose high, we held to
the lee of the bar and then shot from cover. Instantly we bucked a slogging
welter. Three minutes later we had lost all count of time and distance. Wind
gouged, and waves battered. It was drawing dusk. Showers of spray and water
sloshing my ankles told their own uneasy story.

"Cap'n," stuttered Horace, "dis boat is gittin' logy."

We were taking a bad beating. Just then I caught the wind-blown
"pop-poppetty-pop" of a gas engine. As we leaped from a wave trough I had
a flash of old Ed's big fishing boat careening a circle through the gloom. Then
a rain squall blotted salvation from sight. Horace yelled encouragement. Up
to us curved the rescue boat, and Ed, an oilskinned, bareheaded helmsman
hurled a hissing rope over Horace's clawing arms. In a trice it was doubled to
a thwart, and half an hour later we were fast to the dock.

All alone in the club-room, before bedtime, I was pondering things
when Horace entered. Standing beneath the swinging lamp, he shook out his
"specs" and opened a dog-eared Bible. Now I see the bulk of him, silhouetted against a dim background of gum lockers, shell boxes and stacked decoys.

Finding his place and lowering the book, he said: "Mister Nash, whin dat boat was fixin' to fly all ovah us, does you know de fust thing I thought about? Well, suh, 'twas dat li'l new baby at you' house—an'—an' po' Miss Irma."

I ceased smiling at the anticipated sermon. We used to have them of nights—everything from spiritualism to Daniel in the lion's den. How he had plumbed my own poor thoughts!

"Y'know, suh," he continued gravely, "I knows Gawd's word fum kiver to kiver, but mah favorite Gospel is de Fo'teenth o' St. Jawn. Heah 'tis now, suh." He smiled aside at me. "Whin I seed dis mawnin' how near to death us was, I begin repeatin' to mahse'f—I say—'Let not yo' heart be troubled: ye believes in Gawd, believe also in me. In my Father's house are many mansions; if it were not so, I would have told you.'"

Somehow I couldn't look up. The silver loyalty and golden faith of it all suddenly brought moisture to unstrung eyelids. On and on droned the humble Te Deum through St. John. "'I am the way, and the truth, and the life,'" Horace chanted, almost in exaltation: "'no man cometh unto the Father, but by me.'" I managed to steady and look again. Horace was saying: "I had done prayed to mahse'f—down to verse thirteen—whin I heared dem waves a-rushin' off'n de barge-boat; so I says, 'Lawd,' I says, 'what You tells us is. Whatsoever ye shall ask in my name, that will I do.' Den, as you 'members, suh, come dat big wave an' flammed us right on out o' de way o' death—whilst I was still a-prayin'."

There was triumph in his voice. He closed his Bible and, almost musingly, said, "'If ye shall ask any thing in my name, I will do it.'" Turning toward the doorway, he added gently: "An' whin us was millin' round out dar 'mongst all dem wild watahs an' de darkness, I skipped on down to verse eighteen, whar He say: 'I will not leave you comfortless: I will come to you.' An' den, suh, I looked up th'ough dem roahin' winds an' rain, an' sho' nuff, heah come ol' Mister Ed's boat!"

Maybe Horace thought I was just tired and inattentive—but I wasn't. From the clock-winding, he asked, "Does us shoot in de Teal Hole in de mawin'?"

Fighting something out of my voice, I replied, turning out the lamp, "Yes—the Teal Hole ought to be a good shoot on this wind. Good-night—and—thank you kindly, Horace."

What fired this train of reflection was the marriage of my daughter—the baby. I realize now that the average duck-shooting dad undergoes no end of self-examination as the moment nears for a one and only duckling to spread young wings for the mating migration. So, when the organ pealed its summons and the bride and I stepped off down the long aisle, I was wishing that old Horace could be among the family servants and colored friends I noted in the pews reserved for them. Up front I spotted two or three goose hunters, odd-looking in their wedding scenery.

A few moments later I had "given this woman in marriage" and re-tired to Irma's consoling presence. It was, it always is, and ever shall be beautiful—this plighting of troth sealed in Youth's perfect adoration. A wave of flowering incense off innocence! A vast organ pulsating soft allure to abiding faith. Somehow, though, I found myself peering through something away back yonder—at the murk of a dark river—death clutching in the offing—at a tiny face peeping up through pink blankets—at a mother's rapture. Then, as swiftly, dusk again—the Charles River basin—the Old Man's voice—and coxey's too—legs—drive—feather—wrists—catch—voices lost in the roar of engulfing wash—numb wrists—whitecaps—old Ed's white mane atoss—the rope's end!

Odd, how thoughts go racing. A peaceful corner of Beaver Dam in bream fishing time—flowering willows—May-pops—Horace baiting baby's hook and crying amid vast excitement, "Hold 'im, chile! Hold 'im!" as the lit-tle thing clings grimly to sawing cane, with line swishing frantically through sun-flecked waters. Good old Horace! But for him, perhaps—

Vague mist thickens. There he is again, against the lamplight, thumb-ing his old dog-eared Bible. "De fust thing I thought 'bout was dat li'l new baby—an' po' Miss Irma." Why, that's the baby, up there now—safe and sound—with Walter!

Horace's voice again: "The Fo'teenth o' Jawn—'Let not yo' heart be troubled—where I am, there ye may be also—the way, and the truth, and the life—whatsoever ye may ask in my name—I will come to you.'"

The mist is all too thick now—the old sand-bar—recurring melody from files of geese dwindling—lost—through the years.

Recessional boomed! I must have been dreaming—it must be time to pick up. Sundown and dreams. But no! For there was Irma, patting my hand and smiling the dear old smile up at me through wet, joyous eyes. Surely I had been listening to some one! And now—I know.

December 1931

Monsters Real and Unreal

HAROLD McCRACKEN

Europeans and Indians alike had fantastic ideas about North America's wildlife.

I F THERE EVER was a hunters' Garden of Eden, it was North America when the first Europeans came to explore its virgin abundance. At no time in the history of man's migrations across the face of the earth is there recorded a greater profusion of fine game than that which roamed the temperate forests and grassy plains of this continent less than three hundred years ago. Authorities estimate there were as many as 125,000,000 buffalo and millions of other varieties of large four-footed creatures—a total number exceeding the present human population of the United States. There were more deer and bear than in all the rest of the earth together—the biggest and most powerful of their kind that have lived since long before the written story of man begins.

Practically every variety in America's great profusion of game was particularly attractive to the natural instincts of the hunter—offering beautiful antlers, horns or pelts that made splendid trophies of the chase; testing the skill and courage of conquest; providing hides of fine quality for the making of clothing and other uses; and supplying good meat for food. Buffalo, deer, elk, moose, antelope, mountain sheep, caribou, bears and all the rest—here was nature's greatest development of the creatures subordinate and beneficial to man.

It is now well established that most, if not all, of the animals familiar to us today had been thriving on this continent through many thousands of years before the first Indian made his appearance in North America. We know the grizzly bear roamed from California to Maryland and Florida a million or more years ago—as long ago as the days of the saber-toothed tiger, gigantic mastodon and other prehistoric monsters that have since disappeared from the earth. Fossil remains of the grizzly have been carefully identified and dated by scientists. But to the discoverers this was literally a new world. How little they understood about it is shown by the fact that our "Indians" were misnamed as natives of India, which the explorers believed they had reached, instead of a new continent of which they had no previous knowledge. This was only the beginning of a long series of erroneous identifications, particularly relating to the wildlife of America.

We should not be too severe with our predecessors. In the sixteenth and seventeenth centuries the best European authorities had a lot of queer ideas about the wild creatures of the earth. Not only were they convinced of the existence of enormous serpents in the sea, but they honestly believed that equally strange things lived on the land. Practically every national group had its own legendary tales of fabulous creatures—the winged bull of the ancient Assyrians, the sphinx of the Egyptians, the dragons of the Chinese, mermaids, gnomes, werewolves, Minotaurs, centaurs and many other animalistic demigods of the past.

As late as 1650, or almost two centuries after Columbus sailed to the New World, the erudite Dr. Johannes Jonstonus published his *Historice Naturalis De Auibvs*—purporting to be a scholarly and comprehensive treatise on all the animals and birds of the earth, with carefully prepared pictures of the most important ones. Among those "scientifically" presented were several varieties of the "unicorn," a sort of wild horse with a long, spiral-grooved horn protruding straight out of its forehead. There was also the "martigora," a lionlike beast with a forked tail and a human head; the "gryphus," with the rear part of its body resembling that of a lion and the front part that of a giant bird of prey; and the "pelicanus," which pecked her motherly breast until the blood gushed out, as a means of feeding her baby nestlings. All of these and many other fanciful creatures were presented in a serious manner for the benefit of students of natural history, and some of them were supposed to be residents of America. That was thirty years after the Pilgrim Fathers landed at Plymouth.

There were those who believed that the mammoth (mastodon) still roamed in the western wilderness of what is today the United States. This hypothesis persisted until well after the end of the Revolutionary War and was propounded in half belief by no less distinguished an American gentleman than Thomas Jefferson. As President of the United States, Jefferson instructed members of the Lewis and Clark Expedition to look into the possibilities of mammoths still roaming in unexplored areas of the great Northwest.

"It is well known," naturalist Jefferson wrote, "that on the Ohio, and in many parts of America further north tusks, grinders, and skeletons of unparalleled magnitude are found in great numbers, some lying on the surface of the earth, and some below it. Mr. Stanley, taken prisoner by the Indians near the mouth of the Tanissee, relates that after being transferred through several tribes, from one to another, he was at length carried over the mountains west of the Missouri to a river which runs westerly; that these bones abound there, and that the natives described to him the animal to which they belonged as still existing in the northern part of their country, from which description he judged it to be an elephant."

The old tales died hard. Jefferson didn't fully endorse the idea that there were elephants in North America, but he believed it enough to publish that report as late as 1803.

In view of all the circumstances, we could hardly expect anything less than an extremely colorful background to the story of American big game, and little wonder it is that we have come to be a bit mixed up on the small matter of the proper names of some of our best-known animals. No other wild creature has been surrounded with a more extensive anthology of colorful lore and legend than the moose.

The first European to see or hunt the moose was probably the first one to land from a ship and make a foraging sortie into the forest along the coast of Nova Scotia, Newfoundland or the Gulf of St. Lawrence. Jacques Cartier, who spent the winter of 1535–36 on the St. Lawrence River, well into the interior of the continent, refers to the "dains" and "cerfz" among the various animals of the country, the meat of which he obtained from the Indian hunters. There is little doubt that the first mentioned of these was the moose, on which the natives largely depended for food and other necessities of their daily lives.

Another French explorer, Marc Lescarbot, put his name on the permanent record regarding the moose. Lescarbot's *Histoire de la Nouvelle France*, published in Paris in 1609, gives an account of all that he learned during the time he spent with the pioneer colonists on the west coast of what is today Nova Scotia. The original French edition contains a map of Port Royal (Annapolis Basin) featuring the Riviere de l'Orignac—still known as Moose River. A significant decoration is a fairly accurate drawing of the animal that gave the river its name. The map is dated 1609 and thus identifies the illustrations as probably the earliest published picture of the American moose that had been drawn from firsthand observation.

The name *moose* came into popular use by the earliest English chroniclers, who simply used the animal's Indian name—*mos, moos, mus, moosh*, in various Algonquin dialects. Samuel Purchas, the dean of all compilers of books of travel, in the 1614 edition of his *Pilgrims*, makes what is probably the first such reference (p. 755): "Captain Thomas Hanham sayled to the River of Sagadahoc in 1606. He relateth of their beasts . . . redde Deare, and a beaste bigger, called the Mus." Others shortly followed with similar references. Important among these was William Wood, whose book *New England's Prospect* was published in London in 1634, after the author's four years' residence in Massachusetts colony. It is considered the most comprehensive account of that region which had then been compiled. Wood wrote: "The beast called Moose is not much unlike red Deare, this beast is as bigge as an Ox; slow of foote, headed like a Bucke, with a broade beame, some being two yards wide in the head . . . The English have some thoughts of keeping them tame, and to accustome them to the yoake . . . There be not many of them in the Massachusetts Bay, but forty miles to the Northwest there be great store of them."

Unlike some of the other big-game animals that ranged over most sections of our country in pre-white-man days, moose preferred the cooler region where the fall seasons were frosty and there was considerable snow in winter. They were evidently very plentiful, however, in the area that is today the New England States. It has been authoritatively stated that in colonial times there were more moose than deer in the Adirondack region.

The Indians' stone-age weapons were rather inadequate for slaying an animal of such size and vitality as the moose. But it offered such an attractive supply of meat and material for the necessities of life that various equalizing methods of strategy had been developed through the ages. It should be pointed out, nevertheless, that the hunting bow and arrow of the American Indian was by no means a feeble weapon. It was in some respects more effective than the flintlocks of even the late eighteenth-century white hunters. Some of the Indians were remarkable marksmen, and they could fire a dozen or more arrows in less time than it took to reload a single-shot muzzle-loading rifle. And as every modern sportsman knows, a moose is sometimes capable of taking a lot of lead to put him down.

When the snows of winter were deep, the moose hunting of the Indians was patterned after a method they probably learned from the wolves. It suited their purpose best when there was enough of a crust on top to permit rapid traveling on snowshoes, although the crust would impede the flight of a heavy animal, which would sink to its belly as it floundered along. At these times the moose gathered together to yard up in the heavy timber, where much of the snow was caught on the trees, or in small areas where the browsing was particularly good. The Indians would sneak in close to these yarding areas, just as the wolves did, and then stampede animals out into the deep

snow. With the aid of their dogs the hunters would race on their snowshoes
to overtake the moose and dispatch them with arrows and spears.

Whether the occasion was in summer or winter, whether it was a
lone hunter or a whole village that was engaged, the killing of such preten-
tious game as moose always called for a feast on the spot. It was much easier
to improvise a primitive camp than to backpack or even toboggan hundreds
or thousands of pounds of meat to a village. The cooking methods were about
as simple as sleeping under a tree. When a fire was built, individuals could
roast their own meals on the end of a stick. A more formal procedure was to
roast great hunks of meat suspended on thongs and let them whirl slowly until cooked.

In the days before the white man, the Indians had very little incentive to kill more game than their needs of food and hides required. But the
early white traders made a market for the skin of practically every wild creature that wore fur or hair. This included the moose, and cheap French brandy
and other mediocre but enticing trade goods quickly provided the incentive
for the killing of many thousands of these big animals, the meat of which was
left to rot.

Moose hides made fine, soft leather, which found a ready market in
Europe; and the cargo records of boatloads of the hides that were sailed across
the Atlantic, along with the beaver and other peltries, indicate a slaughter that
reminds us of the later wholesale plunder of the buffalo on the western plains.
As early as 1648 more than five hundred moose hides were taken in at the
small French trading post of Tadoussac on the St. Lawrence near the mouth
of the Saguenay; and between 1645 and 1650 one French trader operating at
the head of the Bay of Fundy is reported to have handled an average of about
three thousand of these skins per year. This traffic continued for many years,
or until the moose were practically exterminated in the surrounding areas.

Legends that involved animals were extremely popular among the
American Indians in the days before the white man's coming. Practically
every tribe had its own favorite stories. These frequently included tales of
how the earth and the creatures upon it had been created; how the tribal ancestors acquired human form from some particular animal and how the habits
and characteristics of certain animals were acquired. It was only natural that
such an imposing and peculiarly shaped beast as the moose should occupy a
stellar role in the mythology of the tribes near which this animal was found.

One of the most interesting stories of how the moose was trans-
formed into its present characteristics has come down to us from the Indians
who inhabited the region of New England and Eastern Canada at the time

when the first Europeans came to that part of America. There are several versions of this story, because of the variations developed in different sections of the country, although they all follow the same basic pattern and undoubtedly come from the same source.

It seems that Moose was formerly a gigantic carnivorous creature who lived in the sea. He would occasionally come out on the land to lie in the sunshine, and he learned to feed upon the unfortunate land creatures whom he happened to meet. He was then very much larger than he is today—much taller than the tallest trees. He liked it on the land and he found the land creatures very acceptable to his hungry appetite. So one fine day he decided to make the land his permanent home. He was so big and powerful that the arrows and spears of the Indians were useless against him, and he was so destructive that all the people and other land creatures lived in a state of constant fear. Seeing what was happening down on the earth, the great Glooskap decided that something had to be done about it.

Glooskap was the omnipotent god who had created the earth and all the living things upon it. He was a good god, who believed in the proper balance in nature. He had made Moose big and powerful, so that he could live in the sea among the biggest of the whales and other mighty beasts of the water world. But Glooskap became angry at Moose for coming out onto the land; and when he came down and saw what was happening, the powerful god of all the universe immediately corrected the situation. He grabbed up Moose in his hand and squeezed him so tightly that the once monstrous animal was reduced in size so that the Indians did not have to live in fear any more. After this the Indians could hunt him with their bows and arrows, as they did the other wild creatures that provided them food and hides.

As proof of this story and the terrible squeezing which reduced Moose in size, all you have to do is look at the animal today and see what a queer shape he has. It is also a well-known fact that he still likes to wade and feed in the water, although he has not lived in the sea since that fateful day long ago.

It was a common custom among the Indians of various regions to associate incidents of their favorite legends with striking features of the local landscape. According to the orthodox old Dogrib Indians in the subarctic region between Great Slave and Great Bear Lakes, it was a fabled moose by the name of Hottah who was responsible for the existence of the Rocky Mountains that rise today between the Mackenzie and Yukon Rivers. As every intelligent Dogrib of a few generations ago knew very well, there was once an Evil One who cast his black shadow of constant fear over every living creature in their fair land. His name was Naba-Cha (the Big Man) and he lived on the west side of the Mackenzie River in a wigwam made of three hundred caribou skins. He was so large that he could step across the great river as though it were nothing at all, and each day he went roaming far and wide in search of food to satisfy his terrific appetite. For every meal he required a whole moose, two large caribou or fifty grouse, and for amusement he destroyed every village of the Dogribs he could find. He would pick up the people, one by one, and throw them far out into the Barren Lands, to die of starvation before they got back.

Sometimes Naba-Cha went on marauding trips of feasting and destruction into the lands of the other tribes, far to the south, east, north and west. On one of the journeys southward he captured a young Cree warrior by the name of Ithenhiela, who fought very desperately against the Big Man. Because of this the captive was brought home to be kept as a slave in the great skin lodge and subjected to daily torture as a special pastime.

In all the Dogrib country there was one creature who was too clever to be captured by the Evil One. This was Hottah, the moose—the cleverest of all the animals. Seeing what was happening to Ithenhiela, Hottah went to see the Indian one day when Naba-Cha was away on a trip. "Climb onto my back and I will take you to a place of safety," said the moose. "Far to the west, beyond the mighty Yukon River, you will find protection in the land that is ruled over by the good Nesnabi—who is even bigger and more powerful than Naba-Cha and the only living creature in all the world whom the Evil One fears."

Before they started out across the vast plain which in those days stretched between the Mackenzie and the Yukon, Hottah gave Ithenhiela some things to carry in his hands—a clod of earth, a piece of moss, a stone and a small branch of a tree. Then, with the Cree on his back, the moose began traveling westward as fast as he could go. They had not gone very far, however, when they saw Naba-Cha racing to overtake them.

"Throw down the clod of earth," said Hottah. And when Ithenhiela did so, big hills sprang up behind them—hills so high and wide that Naba-Cha was left far behind in his effort to get through them. But once again he raced furiously to catch up with them.

"Throw down the piece of moss," said the moose. Instantly there was a broad swamp of muskeg, through which the Evil One began floundering and falling to his knees. Finally, however, on he came after them again. When the stone was thrown down, great rocky mountains appeared—higher than the clouds and capped with white snow—the likes of which had never been known before. These great rocky mountains slowed down Naba-Cha more than any of the other obstacles had, for they were much too high for him to step over and by now he was very tired. But he finally got through. Hottah was also very tired and could not carry his rider nearly so fast as he had in the beginning. It was still quite a distance to the Yukon, and it seemed the Evil One would surely overtake them.

"Throw down the branch of the tree," panted the moose—and a dense forest of great trees sprang up just in time to save them from being captured. This delayed Naba-Cha long enough for the moose to reach the bank of the great river, and he immediately plunged into the swirling current to begin swimming across. He had hardly reached the opposite bank when the Big Man came rushing up to the spot they had recently left. But the river was too wide for him to step across and too deep to wade, and he was so tired that he just sat down on the bank.

"Hottah!" he called out across the water in the most friendly tone he could. "Help me across the river and I will do no harm to anyone." Hottah listened to him thoughtfully for a little while and then swam back to carry him across. But when they were in midstream, the moose shook Naba-Cha off his back and he was swept away to be drowned in the swirling current.

Then Hottah went on to where Ithenhiela was waiting for him. After telling the Indian exactly how to find the lodge of the good Nesnabi, the clever moose returned to his own country. And if anyone doubts the truthfulness of this story, all he has to do is travel over the same route and see for himself the hill, the muskeg, the lofty Rocky Mountains and the forest that were made to aid Hottah and Ithenhiela in their flight. The oldtime Indians would also have shown you the body of Naba-Cha, where it still lies as a hulk of rock in the middle of the deep, swirling water of the Yukon.

There was a widespread belief among the Indians that the moose was occasionally afflicted with epilepsy; that the animal could cure itself by scratching its ear with a hind hoof; and that humans similarly afflicted could also be cured by using the hind hoof in the same manner. These beliefs were held by all Indians in moose regions.

As late as 1785, the eminent English zoologist Thomas Pennant, in his erudite two-volume work *Arctic Zoology*, stated without qualification: "The opinion of this animal's being subject to the epilepsy seems to have been universal, as well as the cure it finds by scratching its ear with the hind hoof till it draws blood. That hoof has been used in *Indian* medicine for the falling-sickness; they apply it to the heart of the afflicted, make him hold it in his left hand, and rub his ear with it."

We know today that the Indian's idea of the moose being subject to epilepsy, and that its hoof could in any way cure the disease among moose or men, is little more than unrealistic legend handed down from prehistoric times. What is more difficult to understand is how the same unusual beliefs were prevalent regarding this animal's ancestral counterpart in Europe, before the Europeans knew there were such things as an American moose or Indians, or even a land of America. It is a well-documented fact that some of the most eminent medical men of Europe in the later Middle Ages endorsed the belief and employed the hooves of the European elk in the treatment of epilepsy. The great French medical authority, Pierre Pomet, completely endorsed this, as late as 1735. Does it mean that this legendary idea, as well as the story of the great deluge and others of common belief, could have been carried around the earth by the ancestors of the Indians, from the same original source of origin, just as the moose migrated from the ancient homeland of the European elk? There is, indeed, a great deal regarding the history of both mammals and men on this earth which we know little or nothing about. Big, grotesque and awkward as the moose is in appearance, his story is certainly one of the most interesting animal anthologies of legend and misunderstanding that we have today.

August 1958

Tall Tales But True

GEORGE REIGER

Conservationists can learn from the story of Pythias, who may have discovered America 1,800 years before Columbus.

S UCCESSFUL HUNTERS AND fishermen are precise observers of the world around them. They have to be in order to be successful. Yet how often is the sportsman's word doubted and his tales of adventure called exaggerations. Outdoorsmen can get so discouraged listening to the sarcastic laughter of lesser mortals (lesser, because they have not seen or experienced what we have) that we make solemn pledges, quickly forgotten, never to share our enthusiasm with anyone again, unless they were there in the first place.

However, next time you're feeling frustrated about the reception accorded your story of the mysterious fish that stripped your reel or the super-sized but unknown tracks you found on the mountain top—or some conservation problem ignored or scoffed at by officials—think of poor, forgotten Pytheas, the man who sailed to the verge of the New World. Pytheas made this journey over 2,000 years ago, but he was never given credit for it because he was later disbelieved by several prominent historians who doubted Pytheas' courage and capacity, perhaps because they themselves were deficient in both these qualities.

Of course, glory and immortality were not what Pytheas sought when he began his remarkable journey. Like most explorers, he was charged with curiosity. Gold and trade were the motives he had to espouse in order to get financial backing for his trip, but no man sailing into the North Atlantic during the very years that Alexander the Great was marching on Asia could have had greed as his primary motivation.

Why am I so certain that Pytheas was an adventurous, and not an avaricious, spirit?

154

Because he published an account of his journey when he returned. By contrast, most shrewd businessmen are secretive about their activities. Contrary to popular mythology, merchants loathe competition. The ancient Phoenicians, for example, tried to discourage people like Pytheas from sailing into the Atlantic by making up all sorts of stories about sea monsters and the possibility of falling off the edge of the world.

The Phoenicians knew better, of course. They, like Pytheas, were precise observers of nature and guessed the world was round. However, if they could terrify potential competitors into staying at home, they'd keep the eastern Atlantic trade routes all to themselves.

Pytheas was so leery of the Phoenicians and what they might do to him and his crew if they caught him poking around west of the Straits of Gibralter, that he took five sailing days to creep the 48 leagues past Cadiz, where the Phoenicians maintained a stronghold, to Cape St. Vincent, where he could dash north to England, well known to the Greek as the source of much of the civilized world's tin.

Ironically, the fantastical stories about sea serpents and a flat earth were believed by landlubbers, including most of the crowned heads of Europe, down to the time Columbus began knocking on doors to find backing for his journeys west. Thoughtful observers of nature—including many ancient fishermen, sailors, and scientists—knew the world was a globe and that the hazards of sea travel were greatly exaggerated. They also knew why they were exaggerated. After all, commercial fishermen are businessmen, too, and there is little doubt the Portuguese, heirs to the Phoenicians in sailing skills and a mania for secrecy, were catching cod off Newfoundland decades before Columbus made his more famous voyages of discovery.

By the time Columbus was thirty-one, he was a master mariner in the Portuguese merchant service, and he was doubtless familiar with his colleagues' annual expeditions to the mist-shrouded lands of the northwest Atlantic. In fact, that may have been why he chose a route due west toward Asia so as to run south of this mysterious northern land mass. In 1502, on his fourth and final journey to the New World, Columbus purposely sailed south once he reached the Central American isthmus, perhaps hopeful that he would at last make an end-run around the bottom of the "west Indian" continent.

Columbus had to seek Spanish patronage for his expeditions because Portuguese merchants, like their Phoenician predecessors, did not want the world to know about the good thing they had in Atlantic trade and fisheries. Only in recent times has fame become a synonym for wealth. Previous to the sixteenth century, fame was the kiss of death for monopoly, and monopolies were the most certain way for money-minded men to grow rich and stay that way. For that matter, they still are.

But let's return to Pytheas' journey 2,300 years ago from Massalia (Marseilles) to Thule (Iceland) and beyond the Arctic Circle toward Greenland at which point pack ice turned the intrepid explorer home again.

We only know of this marvelous odyssey through the ridicule of Pytheas' account by the lesser wanderers and chronicleers who followed him. His great literary work, *The Ocean*, was derided by people who could not imagine existence beyond the Mediterranean world, and in time this derision led to the book's extinction. Today, few modern encyclopedias carry any reference to Pytheas, although entire paragraphs are devoted to his principal critic, Strabo, who ironically enough, also becomes the principal source of Pytheas' meager immortality because of the detailed way in which Strabo picked apart *The Ocean*.

Born fully three centuries after Pytheas, Strabo was a geographer, historian, and philosopher of the first century B.C. However, as a historian, he made many mistakes because he valued Homer over Herodotus. And as a geographer, he made even more errors because he favored theory over fact.

For example, he called Pytheas a "liar" because he said he sailed six days northwest of Scotland to reach Iceland. Strabo triumphantly pointed out that since the ocean ceases being liquid at such far nothern latitudes, there is .no way anyone can sail north of Scotland—unless he has an ice boat!

When Pytheas describes the strange phenomenon of slush ice that "binds all together, and can be traveled neither on foot nor by boat" and the ominous fog "like a sea lung" in which ship, sea, and all else appear to be suspended in a void and which finally forced him back a hundred leagues north of Iceland, Strabo nearly falls out of his chair with derisive laughter over such preposterous hallucinations.

And so Strabo's account—along with those of Pliny, Servius, Solinus, and other ancient commentators—are all we have left of Pytheas' journey, which came so close to the threshold of the New World that on a clear day, Pytheas would have been able to see the mountains of Greenland from where the fog and pack ice turned him back. Today cultural memory is so distorted that people argue whether a Norseman named Leif Ericson or a Genoese called Columbus should be given the principal credit for probing at the frontiers of North America when the laurels should go to an Ionian Greek named Pytheas who accomplished this goal more than 1,300 years before Leif Ericson was even a gleam in his father's eye.

The most amazing part is that Pytheas seems to have been as good a navigator as Ericson or Columbus, and that his ship was as seaworthy as any sailed by either of those Johnny-come-latelies. Of course, Pytheas made his expedition during one of the few scientific eras in human history, while Ericson and Columbus were still bucking the superstition and technological backwardness of the Dark and Middle Ages.

Pytheas probably had some patronage from either the local Greek government or a wealthy Greek merchant in order to acquire staff and provision his ship. According to Polybius (a Greek historian who lived a century later), Pytheas was not a wealthy man and the Greek authorities at Massalia did want to find out more about the lucrative tin trade with England. At that time, the only way tin could reach Massalia was by a long overland route through France and then down the Rhone River—unless, of course, you were willing to pay the inflated rates imposed by Phoenician shippers.

From fragments of *The Ocean* that were preserved by later writers, we know that Pytheas' ship was between 150 and 170 feet long, roughly 450 tons, and her draught was 25 or 26 feet. She probably carried a crew of 50 to 70 men, and she averaged 500 stadia (500 stadium lengths) or 50 miles per day.

Pytheas' first great achievement was not in acquiring or outfitting this ship, but in determining the precise location of Massalia, his starting—hence, reference—point. This was done by erecting a large gnomon, or sundial, and dividing its compass into 120 parts. He observed the sundial's shadow at noon on the day of the solstice (either June 22 or December 22) and found that its length was 42 of his subdivisions, less one-fifth—that is 41⅘ to 120, or (to eliminate fractions) 209 to 600. He converted this proportion into 70 degrees, 47 minutes, and 50 seconds for the sun's altitude with the length of the longest day established as 15 hours and 15 minutes.

In the second century B.C., Eratosthenes and Hipparchus, two Greek mathematicians and astronomers working independently of one another, used Pytheas' calculations to find the obliquity of the ecliptic to be 23° 51′ 15″. Since local latitude can be calculated by taking the complement of this result less the semidiameter of the sun, we come up with 43° 3′ 25″—almost precisely the site of modern Marseilles' astronomical observatory.

Pytheas' next step was fixing upon the nearest star to the pole as his guide for steering the ship. Pytheas found there was no star on the pole, but three very close to it. He either used one of these or possibly something even more imaginative and precise: He may have employed a dark hole in the heavens as his reference point.

From the fragments that come down to us, most of the distances mentioned by Pytheas, his characterization of the British Celts, and his navigational plots are in accord with modern knowledge. For example, he took an observation near the island of Uxisama (Ushant) off the coast of Brittany in which 16 hours was cited as the length of the longest day, equal to 49 degrees north. This is within 30 miles of the actual latitude of Ushant.

Finally, his descriptions of promontories and other physical features were so precise we know not only that he sailed up the east coast of Great Britain on his way to Iceland "rising with immense summit," but that on Pytheas' return journey, he explored the Baltic.

And so Pytheas sailed briefly into history before being consigned to oblivion by sophomoric—and I mean this word in its ancient Greek sense of knowledgeable, but stupid—intellectuals centuries after the fact. He is remembered today only for a cluster of islands north of Scotland where he may have seen numbers of small whales. He called the Shetland Islands the *Orcas*, but the name was later transferred to the group we call the *Orkneys*.

So the next time someone doubts one of your observations of nature, or tells you that there is more than enough food in the seas to feed all the hungry people, and more than enough space in the deserts to put them, and more than enough timber to house them, and more than enough oil to warm, cool, and transport them—remember Pytheas and take comfort from the thought that being called a liar for telling the truth has happened to greater men than you or me.

June 1982

Continuum

TOM H. KELLY

Opening day of turkey season isn't a singular event but the start of a period that is whole and complete.

PROBABLY BECAUSE THEY hear so much conversation about it, one of the commonest misconceptions held by those people who are not members of the true faith is that the opening day of turkey season is a single event. They think it is whole unto itself, like a simple declarative sentence, complete with subject, predicate, and verb. Such an opinion is as faulty as the feeling that Pearl Harbor stood alone. We lost one at Pearl Harbor, we lost one big, but we made up the ground in the next four years. Pearl Harbor wasn't the war.

Opening day doesn't constitute the war either; opening day amounts to the first pitch. Baseball managers give nervous rookie pitchers, as a usual instruction: "Throw the first pitch anywhere you want and then listen to the catcher the rest of the way."

Opening day is the beginning of a period in lower Alabama that lasts forty-two days—two days longer than the flood—and is all of one piece from beginning to end.

It is whole and complete, and the fact that you happen to interrupt the continuum to work, or to marry off daughters, or to attend the funerals of close relatives, or cater to the whims of interfering vice-presidents is a private matter between you and your conscience.

I do not mean to imply that the season is exactly the same from beginning to end because it is not. There are marked differences in the actions of both turkeys and hunters before and after they establish the lek, before and after hens begin to set, before and after the leaves come out and visibility gets poor. One of the principal differences can be the weather.

Lower Alabama is 7½ degrees above the tropic of Cancer, a location that is fraught with all sorts of interesting phenomena. The weather on opening day can be almost anything.

Fortunately, I have never kept a diary. As I grow older, and as more and more of the people who used to hunt with me move across town to the Magnolia Cemetery, my memory gets better. Events take on colors they may or may not have had at the instant of their occurrence, and even if the colors stay the same, they have a positive tendency to become bolder and more vibrant over the years. Since there is no written record and since every year there are fewer and fewer people left to contradict my remembrance, I have become, in many instances, the final authority.

Opening day of 1966 is a case in point.

We had moved the previous fall, and I had a new job in a new town and no place to hunt on weekdays. All turkey hunters make arrangements to have a place to go on weekends. It may require driving 400 miles, and it may call for camping out in old farmhouses, or refurbished trailers, or staying in small-town motels. It can sometimes be horribly expensive or difficult. For example, I knew a man who once rode the L&N railroad from Evansville, Indiana, to Greenville, Alabama, one weekend a month to make drill with the A Battery of the 117th Field Artillery. He came down on Friday, after work, and went back on Sunday night.

That trip was duty, but during the turkey season he did it two out of the other three weekends on his own. Any serious turkey hunter would think this was nothing more than slightly unusual. The railroad was surely more restful than driving; you could sleep in either direction, and coming down on Friday night, before you went to bed, you could work on your yelping. You can't do this anymore because the trains don't run, not because it is too much trouble.

But all this addresses only weekends. You still need something to do two or three times a week between Sunday night and Friday night at flying up time.

I know how harsh that sounds. Everybody isn't rich and everybody doesn't live 30 minutes from the woods. I know I sound like that member of the DuPont family who said the firm shouldn't sponsor the Sunday afternoon symphony because everybody played polo on Sunday afternoon.

In any event, opening day of 1966 found me in a new place, too far from the weekend places to get there during the week, and nobody knew me well enough to deal me cards in their game. I was left with no option but to strike off into the unknown. I bought an International Paper Company hunting permit for ten dollars, noted their land ownership boundaries on a County road map copied from the plat book in the Courthouse, picked up my bat, and stepped up to the plate.

Opening morning, it snowed.

It snows in lower Alabama about every fifth or sixth year, and about twice a generation, 1½ inches will stay on the ground overnight. Mostly it comes in light flurries, melts as soon as it hits, and is of significance only to school children because the teachers usually stop classes and let the kids go out in the yard and stand around, looking. Snow on opening day has about the same probability of occurring here as does breaking the bank at Monte Carlo—but it happened.

When it got light that first morning, I was standing on the end of a ridge I had selected from a contour map in the forlorn hope that a turkey just might gobble. You wouldn't do that now at all because there are so many more possibilities, but twenty-five or thirty years ago, you spent a lot of time on strange ridges. You also put a good deal of effort into yelping at turkey tracks, or primaries found in woods roads, or breast feathers near dusting areas that had been knocked off in gobbler fights. Sometimes these were the only prospects you had. You spent a substantial amount of time listening to silence, as well. I stood on my ridge that morning watching the snowflakes, listening to silence, and thinking of the words to the song, "If My Friends Could See Me Now."

I have been on better turkey hunts. But, on the other hand, I have been on heaps worse. I have been on several that were so dull there was nothing to talk about afterward and with nothing like a snowstorm to make them stick in your memory.

Last year's opening day, by contrast, was at the other end of the spectrum. Not only did it get lively, it stayed lively, and right there at the end it got downright hyper.

To begin with, we did not have snow, we had water—all kinds of water.

Anytime after December 15, and often lasting until the middle of April, this whole area floods. The floods extend north of the confluence of the Alabama and Tombigbee for 200 miles up each stream. If you hunt anywhere along either system, you are subject to the whims of water. Every now and then the river doesn't flood at all. Some years, if all your ground is bottomland, you get to spend an entire season visiting friends, and there is every combination in between.

During normal years, turkeys will fly up in trees, sit there, and live off buds for two or three weeks. Last year, however, the water came up in December and was still there in March. Turkeys can't spend three months over water, especially if the first two months are in the period before the trees bud out. They leave the swamps and operate in adjoining uplands.

But when gobblers do come out they have a tendency to stay as close to the edge of the swamp as possible, and as the waters recede, they stay right behind them on the way back.

Some hens normally nest in the mixed pine-hardwood stands along the edge of bottoms. In prolonged floods probably a larger number than usual do this. But it appears that some hens like bottomlands and insist upon nesting there, and, while I cannot prove this, if the bottoms stay flooded long enough, do not nest at all.

In any event, by opening day of 1990, there were heavy concentrations of turkeys up and down the backwater, working along the beach as it were, and I had found two or three of them. I heard a turkey gobble out over the water on opening day, went to him, set up, yelped once, and a completely different turkey flew down in front of me from a completely different direction. I pulled the trigger at 10 minutes to 6. I went out, got my turkey, and went back to gather up the collection of nets, seats, blinds, and equipment we all carry nowadays. With the turkey slung over my shoulder, I walked down to the edge of the backwater to see how much room I had had to work the turkey I first heard gobble.

I hadn't had any at all.

The water came all the way up to the edge of the hill and there was no strip of dry ground along the edge of the backwater. There is an ancient graveyard there on the point of that ridge, and I was about 35 yards downstream from it.

I looked out over the backwater and saw a turkey, its wings cupped, sailing over the tops of the trees, coming directly to me. The gobbler pitched into a big Loblolly pine not 20 yards in front and sat on the limb, craning its neck and looking down at the ground. The bird had perhaps a 6-inch beard. I stood there with my turkey over my shoulder, silently telling this gobbler he was not going to live to be very old if he kept doing damn fool stunts like this. One morning he was going to light in front of a man who had conquered his conscience and who would drop the turkey he was carrying and roll the newcomer off the limb before he could get away. Just as I completed the thought, I heard another turkey leave the roost, fly to the point of my ridge, and pitch down in the graveyard, not 40 yards away. If you had shot the first gobbler off the limb, while you were standing there watching him fall, the second bird would have arrived just in time for you to give him the other barrel. Before I could even finish saying, "Well, I'll just be damned," at perfect spacing, the third, fourth, fifth, and sixth turkeys came from out over the backwater and pitched down into the graveyard. The timing was precisely what would have been required to shoot, break the gun, load one barrel, and shoot the next arrival. I had elected to stand on the exact half-acre that a drove of two-year-old gobblers was using as a landing area that morning. These turkeys were all roosting over the backwater, and you could hear every one of them leave the limb at about the same time the preceding bird landed.

I never saw this happen before, nor do I ever expect to see it again, and, in point of fact, I would not have been able to kill seven turkeys even if it were 200 years earlier and I was feeding the starving army at Valley Forge. I only carry six shells; two in the gun and one in each side pocket. For the first time in my life, there were more turkeys than there was ammunition. I never had the chance to fill the season's limit in 10 minutes before. I wouldn't take it even if it were offered again, but I have to admit that it is simply delightful just to have been asked.

When I broke into this league in the spring of 1938, my grandfather said it was a pity to start me. I would never have the chance to get good at it because there wouldn't be anything around to practice on in five or six years.

Everybody's grandfather wasn't old and wrinkled and full of wisdom.

April 1991

Miss Seduction Struts Her Stuff

ARCHIBALD RUTLEDGE

In the fading twilight of the Carolina swamp, a call box works its magic.

FOR MANY YEARS I have had a positive superstition about luck on the last day—sometimes during the very last hour. A thrilling and possibly dramatic experience that I had on January 2, 1933, has confirmed me in this way of thinking. True, the affair did not happen on the last day of the wild turkey season in South Carolina, for that is February 28; but it was the last day for me, as I was scheduled to leave for the North early on the morning of January 3.

That summer an old wild turkey hen raised a flock of sixteen birds on my plantation. I had had reports of them, and high hopes were mine that they would still be there on my Christmas visit. But certain turkey-minded friends and neighbors anticipated me; and while they killed only one or two of the birds, they succeeded in utterly scattering and demoralizing the flock. All through the holidays I hunted for them. Their tracks were found in the sandy roads. I once heard a hen drowsily calling at daylight; once I saw one about half a mile down an old woodland trail. But nary a shot was mine.

These birds were genuinely wild in every sense of the word: of the ancient pure wild strain, with no admixture of domestic blood—lovely bronze plumage, black heads, pink legs and a general aspect of being tailor-made. They were so keen of sight and hearing as to be able to detect a wink or a whisper at shotgun range; so silent and canny as to make an attempt at stalking a ludicrous thing. You know the feeling that I had as the precious days passed: that the game was unquestionably there, but that it was too smart to permit me to come up with it.

Finally my last day came. While I had had excellent sport with ducks and deer, it looked as if I were going to be a total washout on the turkeys. However, at about four o'clock that afternoon, with the kindly Southern sun shining genially and with no wind stirring, my three boys and I decided to try the last chance.

Scattered groups of the birds had several times been reported to me as crossing an old abandoned road—usually at about five o'clock in the afternoon, evidently on their way to roost in the great river-swamp. I had not been able to discover their bedroom, yet had a fair notion of where it likely was. I posted my boys on the road and then walked a half mile down the river-bank. My idea was to call a little in order to lure any lonely birds toward the standers posted in front of me. It sometimes happens that for weeks at a time wild turkeys will follow the same range, day after day.

At the place where I stopped, two old rice-field banks converged and met the bank of the river. It seemed a strategic spot, though I had never tried it before. All about me were giant cypresses, softly alight in the rays of the setting sun; lonely abandoned rice-fields, grown head-high in marsh; solitary pines; thickets of cane and alder and birch. Except for the firm footing on the leaf-strewn banks, the country was very wet. As I sat down to call I heard a deer tramping round in the marsh across the river, gray squirrels barking and scuttling about on the leaves, wild ducks hurrying toward the delta, and the big owls beginning their weird hooting.

At a moment when some of these sounds abated, I touched my call.

This call is one of many I have made. Most of them have had faults of tone—either squeakiness, of a tone too high-pitched, or prone to emit a sudden false note. But on account of the depth, certainty and mellow tone of this particular box, I had christened her Miss Seduction. I have tested her many times, and I have found that she will do almost anything except actually kill my gobbler for me. On several occasions she has embarrassed me by calling up old turkey hunters to me. I like them, but there's a closed season on them.

For many years I have experimented with making box calls for turkeys from all kinds of woods. Red cedar I have rejected on account of the shallowness of its tone and its inclination to squeak; seasoned poplar is excellent, as is Western fir; dried maple and holly are good. I like willow best because of the quality of the wood, the smooth texture and high tension of the grain, and the mellow tone that can be drawn from such a box. It seems a general principle that the best tone is to be had from a wood of medium hardness, such as chestnut or willow. If the wood is too hard the qualities of depth and vibrancy will be absent.

To call a turkey one will perhaps do best if he will put himself in the place of the bird and will call in such a manner that, if he were the bird, he would come. A great many things are to be considered: the time of day (of course, they call best just after and just before roosting); the condition of the atmosphere (a windy day is bad, and a rainy day not so good); the place from which the calling is done, for it should be of such a character that the bird would naturally haunt it; and then the calling itself, which is a thing to be learned rather than told of.

I may say, however, that an amateur will call too often, too loudly and with too little variation in the tone. A wild turkey is a patrician, and he does not appreciate any member of his tribe's overflowing and drowning him with too much gushing. Of course, in the mating season few birds are more garrulous than wild gobblers. But in the hunting season they are almost as silent and non-committal as they are wary.

During the next twenty minutes I called about seven times. It pays not to be too urgent. Unless I am mistaken, it is the long, sweet pleading quality of the first note that usually does the work. I had had no answer; but, as every experienced hunter knows, a wild turkey will often come silently to a call. Some answer and come. Some answer and do not come. Some do not answer and come. Some never answer and never come. Some come running; some flying; some walking fast; some stealing along furtively. I have had an old gobbler come within thirty yards of me from behind before I detected his approach.

Down went the sun, suffusing the wild, sweet world with a golden afterglow. I had heard no gun from my standers. It looked about all over. But suddenly I heard a great commotion in the marsh across the river. At first I thought it must surely be a deer jumping in to swim across. Yet when I turned quickly to look, there came a splendid gobbler, flying almost straight for my call. I knew that I ought to get my gun up while he was flying; because if a wild turkey is on the ground near you, the matter of getting your gun on him is just one of those critical things that is awfully hard to maneuver. In the two seconds that it takes you to put it on him, he's going to be executing the greatest vanishing act you ever saw.

Fifty yards from the river-bank the glistening king of the swamplands set his wings and sailed, alighting high and dry about thirty-five yards from me. I made a clean kill with 4's. Miss Seduction had done her work. In forty years of hunting this was the first time I had ever called a wild turkey across a river. And any hunter can easily understand the thrill I got out of it—especially since it was sundown on my last day.

It is not usually worth while to call from the same place after a shot has been made there. But I love the river and the swamp in those mystic fading lights, and there might be a bare chance for more sport.

It was now very dusky in the swamp. The river appeared wan and mysterious. Far up the stream I could see the lights of home shining in the twilight. Once more I touched Miss Seduction. It really seemed too late; yet while I have known some wild turkeys to take the roost long before sundown, I have known others to delay their retiring until it was almost too dark to see a limb on which to perch.

On the farther side of the old wooded bank coming down through the middle of the swamp, I had heard a brown thrasher scuffling in the leaves. This sound grew a little loud and unfamiliar. Save for his keen head, this turkey was completely hidden by the bank. But he was only thirty-five yards away, and coming closer. At the range which he had already reached, I would not have been afraid to try a chance at his head alone; but I had no shells save the two in my gun, and they were loaded with buckshot. All my turkey-shot, save the lone 4's I had already fired, I had given to my boys. Now, a man stands a beautiful chance of missing a wild turkey with buckshot, whatever the range; and to shoot at his head with buckshot is almost certainly to miss him.

The gobbler would pass me on my left. The old bank, behind the shelter of which he was walking, was perhaps of more advantage to me than to him, for I waited for him to get his head behind the bank and then got my gun up, leveling it through a small break in the dyke, across the aperture of which his majesty would pass.

The west was barely glimmering with the last streaks of day and the dusk in the swamplands was almost night when the great gobbler suddenly filled the opening in the bank. I could barely discern the white sight of my gun against his dark and splendid form. I touched the trigger, and immediately stood up.

What I saw was a big gobbler with a broken wing running for the tall marsh as if a dozen wildcats were after him on wings. I could not really lay the gun on him right, but I let drive with my last shell in his direction. Silence profound settled over the river and the swamp. It was my last shot of the hunting year.

A few minutes later I found my second gobbler, killed by a single buckshot in the neck. With my two wild turkeys over my shoulder, I was soon on the homeward road, along dim starlit paths, familiar to me since boyhood days, toward the old home that has always been to me a beloved sort of shrine for a thousand memories of the river, the pinelands, the broom-grass fields, the brooding solitary swamps and all their wonderful inhabitants.

January 1934

Mastodon and Other Rare Meats

C. E. GILLHAM

Toothsome wild tidbits from around the globe.

THERE SEEMS TO be a lot of interest lately in exotic foods. You can hardly pick up a magazine anymore without finding an article like "Luau Brunch," or "The Curries of Ranjipur." If you really crave exotic menus, however, you have to get into the nonstandard foods, which include such sensational items as boiled skunk cabbage and fricasseed raccoon. But even these sound like hotdogs and french fries next to some of the meals I've had occasion to eat.

I once put on a black tie and invited a wealthy industrialist to be my guest at the annual clambake of the Explorers Club. We didn't sit on the dais with Lowell Thomas; in fact, we occupied a table for four at the back of the ballroom in the Waldorf Astoria. I had never met our companions, but they weren't the kind of explorers who had walked anywhere. I think they'd driven a submarine under the North Pole, or something. Anyway, the four of us ate together.

The main event on the menu that night was a roast of considerable age. Seems a mastodon fell off a glacier that split in two in Spitzenbergen or some such seaport, and got trapped in a natural deep freeze. Perfectly preserved were a few hams, filets, and chuck roasts. This prime protein was rushed, air express, to the Waldorf, where the Explorers consumed it at a banquet. I doubt that the meat was anything much when it was fresh, and 10,000 years hadn't improved it any. It tasted like a boiled saddle blanket jerked off a sweating Navajo pony—both very old.

My millionaire guest was up to the occasion. He had a suite in the hotel and knew the head waiter. He ordered a fifth of very fine bourbon that marinated the antique entree already in our stomachs, and we finished the meal with prime roast of modern beef. This is only a casual observation, but

I'd say that if you must partake of mastodon, dissolve it first in sour mash. This way, the flavor will either be improved or you won't care what it tastes like.

That mastodon was undoubtedly the oldest food I've eaten, but it wasn't necessarily the oddest. Once, while enjoying an after-duck-hunt drink in Stuttgart, Arkansas, I was presented with a tin of dried grasshoppers by my host. The hoppers were crunchy and salted, and had all their original barbs, spurs, and hooks. They tasted all right, but when swallowed they took your tonsils with them, reducing even a duck hunter to a faint whisper. I'd recommend dried grasshoppers to hunters who practice game calling in hotel rooms, and to certain politicians, mothers-in-law, and wives.

Of course, grasshoppers, if you want them, can be bought in a store, which makes them a little less rare than a delicacy like pickled walrus hide. To get your teeth into this you must go to a bit of trouble. First, have an Eskimo friend harpoon you a walrus. Let him have the tusks to carve into trinkets to sell to the dudes. You keep the hide. This is 1½ inches thick and resembles a sun-dried lake bed. Hack the skin into chunks and boil it for two days at high heat. When you can stick a hunting knife into it, drain, wipe dry with a Hudson's Bay parka, and pickle in vinegar. The stuff smells like pigs' feet while it's cooking, and it tastes a lot like the pickled ones. No bones, either, which may give the walrus hide a competitive edge.

Another memorable banquet was one I shared with King William, an old Eskimo chief at Tuktoyaktuk, in the Western Arctic, many moons ago. King William was in his summer quarters of huge tents. He had his countless offspring out harpooning white whales and catching shee fish, and putting it all into the fish hole for winter. Reclining upon a couch of barrenland grizzly hides, he looked like a latter-day Genghis Khan summering in the polar regions.

The old chief was most courteous. He offered me my choice of his six wives and invited me to lunch. I accepted the latter. A woman brought into the tent a big iron pot filled with dried, boiled muskrats. When these rodents had been skinned for their pelts, the carcasses had been split open and the intestines thrown to the dogs. Tails and heads had been left on. To eat this entree, I discovered, you fish around with your fingers until you find a scaly tail. Then pull the muskrat from the pot and eat it like corn on the cob. Take the tail and hind legs in one hand, hold the head and protruding rodent teeth in the other, and start gnawing. This dish doesn't present much of a waste problem, for you eat everything but the bones and the tail.

If those muskrats sound intriguing, you should really enjoy prairie dog à la Navajo. This is a rare dish getting rarer all the time as the Government's poisoning program moves ahead. However, pocket gophers, lemming, or ground squirrels can be substituted.

There's not much work involved in cooking this dish. Trap, snare, shoot, or dig out a mess of prairie dogs, being careful not to pick up a rattlesnake or a burrowing owl while you're at it. Conk the sod poodles' noodles, then build a big fire and let it burn down to hot coals. On this bed of coals, throw the animals to be cooked—innards, hair, and all. Burn. Stir with a stick. Burn some more. When they double in size, remove. Scrape off the burned hair with a stick, peel off the skin, and salt to taste. Garnish with purple sage.

Somewhat similar in its preparation method is roast shrimp, shell and all, a specialty of my Guaymas friend, Ralph. "Ralph" is an unusual name for a Japanese, but Ralph is an unusual Japanese. So is his cooking. His roasted shrimp are good and will work as well as dried grasshoppers to clean out your gullet. Ralph's recipe is this: Get a lot of Mexican shrimp and cut off the heads. Broil in an open fireplace glowing with mesquite coals. Put on the shrimp the sweet-sour dope used by millions of Japanese. When the shrimp are dark brown and almost burned, remove and eat—shells and all. If you are as tough as Ralph, you may survive unscarred. If you do wound your digestive tract, it can be cauterized with a cocktail of tequila and tabasco, mixed 50-50 (one jigger of each). Mexican tortillas will help put out any fire that drink may start.

Marrow gut, or S.O.B., was standard eating in the old cowpoke days. This delicacy, usually excised from stolen cattle, gave many tribes of Indians the monicker of "gut eaters." In every cow there is an intestine that is choked off; it doesn't seem to do the cow much good. It is the size of a big macaroni and is most toothsome. Take it out—you need it more than the cow does. Wash thoroughly and empty out anything that might be in it, though there seldom is. Cut into 2-inch lengths and boil with a bit of rice, barley, or pinto beans. Garnish with juniper berries and serve piping hot. One bit of this can grow hairs on the chest of a salamander.

If your tastes run to more orthodox oddities, on your next grouse hunt in Scotland try potted hares à la Limey. These big rabbit-like things will come galloping, ears flopping, out of a patch of roots. They are about the size of yearling burros, and are about as hard to hit with a shotgun. Shoot a brace of them and hang them by their hind legs, but do not skin or eviscerate. The British have a tin cup especially designed to use in the hanging of hares. It is attached to the head.

When the hair of the hare is slipping and the cup is filled with liquid, skin out the animal and remove the insides. Disjoint, wash thoroughly, and pot roast—a few carrots, turnips, and spuds may be added. Don't fret over how you go about the cooking. The British are not great cooks, and anything you do will be an improvement. My first crossing of the Atlantic was in the company of Charles Dickens' 80-year-old grandson, who was making his fortieth crossing. The congenial old barrister introduced me to pink gin, which is just country gin and a dash of bitters on the rocks. Pink gin is recommended, in large quantities, with potted hair.

For those adventurers who find hare in Scotland too commonplace, here's another rare gourmet treat. For this one, go to Mexico and shoot an iguana about 3 feet long. These lizards are built like miniature dinosaurs but a good duck load of No. 4 shot will do the trick. Take out the innards, or leave them in—it doesn't much matter. Dig a pit and build a good-size fire alongside. When you have a half bushel of coals, wrap the iguana in wet leaves or moist clay. Shovel half the coals into the pit and throw in the iguana. Add the remaining coals and throw on a bit of dirt. Roast two hours. Remove the lizard from the pit, shuck off the hide, and salt and pepper. The meat is whiter than a crawdad's tail, and one doesn't even need dentures to chew it. Wash down with mescal. If iguanas are scarce, substitute a thick rattlesnake. This can be quite good too, but it's best to remove the head. Once you do, don't step on the fangs; you could lose a leg.

A lot of so-called gourmets have already put in their votes for the "ultimate" cuisine, but I'd say that if you haven't eaten moose headcheese, you haven't eaten. I discovered this delicacy quite by accident once when, after flying around over the treetops along the Little Gerstle River in Alaska, I got marooned overnight in a cabin that had a small airstrip alongside. We were hunting a murderer who had axed a couple of drinking buddies, and the F.B.I. told us that if we would fly over these woods, the murderer would get nervous and come out. Damned if he didn't, a couple of days later—and I think he got hung. Anyway, in this cabin was a Scandinavian lady named Tecla, making moose headcheese. The head was that of a cow with long ears and a bulbous nose. The hide had been removed and what was left had been scrubbed as clean as the driven snow. The moose's head was so big that Tecla had put it in a washtub out in the yard, where she boiled it until the meat fell off the bone.

The teeth, jaws, and skull were then fished out and thrown to a disappointed-looking sled dog. More cooking followed, until the chunks of meat were tender, then salt and pepper added. This mixture was put into shallow pans and placed in a cache where the bears couldn't get at it. When cooled, it was a jellied meat that could be sliced and eaten cold, or fried in grease or bear fat. Bull moose heads work just as well but Tecla said that you have to knock off the horns because they won't go into a washtub.

Not all rare dishes are delicious. Some are purely utilitarian. Take boiled owl à la Mackenzie River. If you're starving, and happen to have an owl, it's great. It will last you for days. I tried this just once—when an Indian boy and I swamped a canoe on the south shore of Great Slave Lake. We salvaged the tea pail, two wet eiderdown robes, and the shotgun after we had been rolled up in the waves into a mess of driftwood on a most barren shore. The only living creature we saw was a great gray owl. I shot it and we carefully picked it. Contrary to the kid's advice, I boiled the owl instead of roasting it on a stick in the fire. We boiled it for hours. And the longer we boiled it, the tougher that owl got. The drumsticks turned blue, and we couldn't sink a tooth into them. Carrying the owl in the tea pail, we walked in to Hay River a couple of days later and ate a 15-pound canned ham in the Hudson's Bay Trading Post.

Another time, a mob of Indians and I were floating down the Porcupine River in the Yukon Territory when a herd of woodland caribou started across the river in front of us. We killed fourteen of them, planning to take most of the meat to the hospital in Fort Yukon, Alaska. We camped on the sandbar where we killed the caribou, and I had visions of roast ribs, filets, and all kinds of delectable items. Instead, my companions set up a tripod of three poles over a whopping fire. In the heart of this blaze they suspended the unskinned head and neck of a caribou. Periodically they turned the thing in the leaping flames, and the burning hair stank to the aurora borealis.

After an hour of this primitive cooking, the caribou's eyes bugged out in the heat, giving the charred head an expression of great surprise. At last it was finished, and we fell to. The burned skin was scraped off. This was hard as a butcher's heart, but the meat beneath was tender and toothsome. Because I had shot eight of the caribou I was paid special honor by my companions; they gave me an eyeball. It might have tasted all right with a touch of salt.

I hope that these little ideas in exotic menu planning may spark some jaded appetites. I've tried all of the dishes. Not only have I survived, I still have the main part of my digestive tract. But now that the years are upon me and my travels are over, I endeavor to get by with more mundane fare. At the moment, I have a 2-inch, corn-fed T-bone broiling over charcoal, and unless a fat mastodon or a toothsome iguana comes galloping through my yard, I'll have to settle for this. I don't really care for beef—but, as the old mountain man said, "Meat's meat!"

I Don't Want to Kill a Deer

TED TRUEBLOOD

Instinct takes over when a buck's thick neck falls in a hunter's crosshairs.

I DON'T WANT TO kill a deer. I haven't really wanted to kill a deer for years. Yet I go deer hunting every fall and have, I suppose, shot about as many of them as most other men my age. If these statements constitute a paradox, bear with me.

Consider October, the hunter's moon. The heat of summer is over. The September rains have washed the haze of August from the air, and frosty nights have brought the first dusting of gold to the white-barked aspens. In all the arid West, from the Coast Range to the eastern slope of the Rockies, the shimmering, lovely days of Indian summer have laid their spell upon the land.

The early harvest is finished, but the orchards are still flecked with the rich red of late apples. The voice of the cornfield has changed from the whisper of summer to the dry rustle of autumn. The stubble, from which the grain had long since been taken, has the look of fall about it, and the young cock pheasants that it harbors are rapidly acquiring the full glory of their adult plumage.

Everywhere, especially in the cool of evening, the rich, ripe, fruity odors of the season lie heavily upon the air. Late-curing hay; grapes hanging purple from the vine; the rich earth, disturbed to yield its treasures; melons, frost-sweetened and dead ripe—all these and many others add their savor. And always, somewhere in the distance, an eager householder, unable to wait for the deluge of leaves that will come later, is burning the first sprinkling. The smoke, thin and clean, drifts low across the countryside. It adds spice to all the other mingled odors, seasoning them with the sure proof that this is indeed October.

At this time we go hunting. It is a tradition. Our preparations are

173

made pleasant by memories of past trips and anticipation of the one ahead. We are going to hunt deer, not merely kill them. The reward is in the hunt, but since there could be no hunting were there no deer, and since the logical culmination of any hunt must lie in securing its object, we will no doubt kill one.

Thus rifles and food and bedrolls and tent are loaded, and we drive away from the rich, green valley into the brown foothills and through them, winding always upward into the home of the mule deer in October. Yellow pines stand majestically alone on the south slopes, their trunks brick-red in the late sun. Aspens line the draws along the clear brooks that trickle down, and make bright splashes of yellow among the dark firs on the north hillsides.

Camp is made, water carried from the little stream nearby, a fire kindled. Soon the heartening odors of good outdoor food and coffee mingle with the tang of the smoke that rises in a thin, straight column toward the earliest stars. We eat and loaf beside the embers and plan the morrow. This first evening, loaded with anticipation, is a real part of deer hunting and we enjoy it to the fullest.

We will hunt a country we know well. It is always a challenge to explore a new area, but it is also rewarding to hunt where you know each ridge and valley, where every little bench and pocket holds its share of memories. Here beside this patch of timber I missed a big buck in 1936. With a forkhorn, two does, and two or three fawns he had walked out of the thick cover just at sunset. He was very close, and I thought, "I'll shoot him in the neck," but somehow I missed. I saw the bullet kick up the dirt behind him, a little to one side, and before I could work the bolt he leaped back among the trees and disappeared.

And down the draw from this saddle is where another fine buck eluded us by running low along the bottom, screened by alders and aspens, until he was out of range. On this bench, several deer have fallen to our rifles during the years. And down the canyon below it, where alternate thickets vie with more open browse among the boulders on the hillsides, many fine bucks have rewarded us.

There are real, as well as sentimental, values in hunting a familiar country. You know where to look for deer that are trailing through on their annual migration from the high summer range to their lower wintering area. You know the pockets where they hide during the day. You know where to look for the resident deer that spent the summer here rather than higher in the mountains. And you have learned through experience the best way to approach all these places without alarming any game that might be in them.

The alarm rang at 4 o'clock. I crawled reluctantly out of the warm sleeping bag, touched a match to the fat pine slivers in the little sheet-iron stove, lit the gasoline lantern, and dressed. Then I stepped outside. The snapping stars were so close that I could almost touch them; not even the palest hint of gray showed in the east. There were slivers of ice in the water bucket. I slopped a little into the wash pan, and by the time I had applied it to face and hands no trace of sleepiness remained.

It is during these magic hours that a hunter has the best chance to see deer undisturbed in the open. In the early morning, usually not later than 8 o'clock, they gradually feed or wander into some tight and hard-to-approach thicket where they will spend the day. About sunset they emerge to feed again.

The grass was crisp underfoot as I walked along the bench east of camp. The mountain on my left loomed black against the northern sky, and since I couldn't possibly see a deer anyway, I hurried; I had about a mile to walk and I was chilly. I wore no coat because I knew it would be warm later, but now the air was sharp.

The eastern sky grew paler, and finally there was a hint of pink and saffron to give sure promise of approaching day. Individual trees became visible on the mountainside. I knew I'd soon be able to see a deer. I slowed down and attempted to walk quietly. The spot where I wanted to be at shooting time was just ahead.

Here a little stream came gurgling down out of the hills. Its drainage was a basin, perhaps a mile long and half that wide, divided into several draws and pockets, with steep ridges between. There were bare slopes and brushy ones, dense thickets and sparsely covered benches. It had everything—food, water, thick cover, and shade. During migration the deer—which followed a course generally parallel to the river in the bottom of the valley and did most of their traveling at night along the open slopes facing it—turned into this basin to spend the day. Here, finding things to their liking, they sometimes loitered for a week or more if the weather remained pleasant.

I paused at the mouth of the basin to test the wind. It was perfect, a steady, downstream breeze. I crossed the brook and started slowly up the game trail a few yards above it on the other side. It was now light enough to shoot. I took a few careful steps, paused to examine everything in sight, took a few more steps, and paused again. I tried not to make a sound.

Time was when I hunted mule deer from the ridges. I could watch a big area and cover more ground, and there was less chance of alarming the game. Lately I've come to favor walking up a valley. I can't see so much country, but what I can see, I see better. I have to hunt more carefully, but any deer I see is usually in range.

I moved slowly along, alternately watching and walking. The predawn chill, which my brisk walk across the flat had overcome, caught up with me again. Shivering, I hung my rifle over my shoulder and put my hands into my pockets to warm my fingers. The light grew stronger, and at last the sun touched the highest tip of the high ridge on the west.

I was looking at it, anticipating its warmth—though the best of the hunting would be over by the time the sunlight reached the bottom of the valley—when I saw a movement halfway up the slope. It was in sparse brush along the point of a ridge that came straight down toward me from the peak. On the right, on the north slope of this ridge, was a dense stand of firs. On the left, extending toward the mouth of the little valley for several hundred yards, was a sparse stand of mixed snow brush, ninebark, and chokecherry, with clumps of bunch grass in the open spots.

The movement could have been made by a bird or a squirrel—or by the flick of an ear. I watched carefully but saw nothing more for several seconds. Then suddenly a deer stepped from behind a cherry bush. It was a long way up the slope. I raised my rifle slowly and looked at the animal through the scope. A doe. Does were not protected, but I had no desire to kill one, at least not this early in the hunt. Our best venison has always come from big bucks killed before the beginning of the rut.

I lowered my rifle and continued watching. Soon a second deer materialized, farther out in the brush. It was no bigger than the first, and I assumed that it was another doe or a small buck. Then, almost at the edge of the timber, a third deer stepped leisurely from behind a clump of ninebark, moving slowly toward the trees. Even before I could raise my rifle to look at him. I knew he was the one I wanted. I could tell by his size and by the way he walked that he was a big buck. I got the scope up barely in time to get a glimpse of him before he disappeared. His rack was big; certainly each antler bore the four points of a mature mule-deer buck, and maybe more.

The chill was forgotten. I sat down in the game trail and watched the edge of the timber until the sunlight reached the bottom of the valley, hoping he would come out. He didn't. The two other deer, one a small buck, went in.

Thanks to having hunted here before, I didn't have to walk on up the valley and inspect that patch of timber to learn how big it was. I knew all about it. It covered ten acres or so, from the top of the high ridge on the west to the creek in the bottom, and it ran from the crest of the hog-back down into a ravine on the north. It was big enough to hide a hundred deer, and it would be impossible for a lone hunter to push any of them out—or get a shot if he did.

There were several things I might do. I could go on hunting and for-. get about the buck. I could continue up the creek and climb the hillside to inspect a bench north of the timber in the hope that the deer might have gone on through. I could, of course, work my way into the jungle and hope for the best.

None of these possibilities seemed very attractive. I felt sure that the little band of deer had gone into the timber to spend the day. When evening came they would emerge, and with luck I might be in the right spot waiting.

Back in camp by 9 o'clock, I cut some wood, started a stew that would be ready when my partner came, and looked around for any other odd jobs that needed doing. Twenty yards from the tent, the bench on which we were camped broke away sharply to the river bottom. I walked over and looked down at the river, sparkling among the cottonwoods. Its voice, muted by distance, rose and fell softly with the vagaries of the breeze.

The jobs didn't seem very important and the blanket of pine needles on the ground was soft. I decided to sit down in the mellow sunlight and look at things. I thought about the spots where the big buck was most likely to come out of the timber and wondered whether I should go fishing—the trout season was still open. And then I decided to sort of lie back on the needles for a minute or two and put my cap over my eyes.

My partner woke me as he came in. He had seen only tracks. We ate and discussed the possibility of getting a shot at the big buck in the evening. Two of us would have a better chance than one, since there were several spots where the three deer might emerge, either to feed or to continue their leisurely migration toward the winter range.

Northwest of the patch of timber was a low saddle over which deer often crossed into the drainage of the next creek. A hunter stationed here would also be able to watch the bench that bordered the timber on the north, a likely spot for them to feed in case they decided to loiter a few days in the little valley. If they intended to continue toward the winter range, however, they would be more likely to come out of the south side of the timber, prob-ably near the spot where I had seen them in the morning, and swing around the points of the ridges that dropped sharply down toward the river.

The high point above the timber, where I had been looking at the sun-light when I first saw them, was the apex of several ridges. The good browse bordering the timber extended around to the river slope in the pockets be-tween the heads of the ridges. It would be worthwhile to watch those pockets.

We left camp in late afternoon, not retracing my path of the morning but walking up the next creek to the west. This way we could reach our chosen stations without forewarning the deer, because the breeze regularly drifted up each valley in the evening. When we were a little beyond the saddle, we climbed the hillside nearly to it. Here we separated. My companion would find a position from which he could watch the hillside, the bench on the other side, and the northern and western edges of the timber.

Gradually climbing higher, I angled back toward the southern point of the ridge, staying on the west side, opposite the timber. Eventually I reached a spot from which I could watch a couple of brushy pockets, above and just around the corner from the southern edge of the cover. I couldn't see the cover—I was afraid to go around because the upcanyon breeze might drift my scent into it—but any deer that came out should eventually wander into my view.

I had barely settled myself down to begin my vigil when I heard a shot. Just one. It was back where I had come from. It could be nobody but my companion, since there were no other hunters in the area, and one shot usually means a dead deer.

Instantly I was born by indecision. Had he killed the big buck? Should I go back to help dress it or should I stay here? Was there any chance of the buck's coming out now, assuming he was still alive? Well, if I returned I certainly would not get a shot, whereas if I stayed I might. So I leaned back against the hillside with my rifle across my lap and devoted my attention to the pockets below me. They were partly floored with grass and partly grown up to several varieties of browse. I searched them minutely and, satisfied they were vacant, allowed my attention to drift off across the valley.

This was the magic hour, when the night creatures begin to stir and game feeds in the long twilight. Instead of the keen anticipation that I should have felt, however, the ordeal of holding still bore heavily upon me. I was assailed by doubt. I sat there quietly while the sunset blushed and faded.

Imperceptibly the shadows grew thicker; it would soon be too dark to shoot. For the thousandth time I began a careful examination of the two pockets below me. And there, suddenly in full view and close, stood the buck of the morning! How he arrived unseen was a mystery, but of his presence there could be no doubt. Nor did I have any question as to his identity. He was magnificent.

He was standing broadside, but his head was turned slightly away and he appeared to be looking at something farther down the little basin, perhaps at another deer that I couldn't see in the deep shadows. Slowly, quietly I raised my rifle and eased off the safety, holding it with thumb and finger so that there would be no click.

Twenty-four hours earlier I had harbored no particular desire to kill a deer. I would hunt, yes, but I was not anxious to kill a deer. Twelve hours earlier I had seen this buck, and immediately, as though ordered by some remote ancestor whose very life depended upon the hunt, I had devoted every faculty to bringing about this very moment. Now, partly because my planning had been sound, but to a much greater degree because the buck had been unlucky enough to come into the open at this particular place and time, I was about to kill him. Without thought, without an instant's hesitation, I centered the crosshairs on his gray neck and squeezed the trigger.

October 1960

The Last Buffalo Hunt

JIM MERRITT

When the Sioux hunters finished with these remnant bison, a way of life would be gone forever.

O N THE RANGE the routine seldom varied for the buffalo hunter. Rising at dawn, he shook off the Dakota cold, then joined the other hunters in the outfit for a breakfast of bacon, sourdough bread, and coffee. There was no need to hurry. Wait for the animals to eat their fill, and many in the herd would be at rest, making even easier targets.

The October sun had burned off most of the frost by the time the hunter set out, carrying about 40 pounds of gear, including a .45-caliber Sharps rifle, 100 cartridges in two belts slung across his shoulders, and a leather scabbard containing a honing steel and a pair of knives for ripping and skinning. He worked alone and usually on foot, a stealthy approach being easier without a horse. As he neared the top of a rise, he dropped to his knees and elbows and crawled into position to view the herd spread out below him. About 10,000 buffalo, he guessed, were scattered in small groups across the undulant prairie. In the distance he could hear the familiar boom of Sharps from the other outfits working on this bright, Indian summer morning of 1883.

In the draw below him, a group of about fifty animals fed contentedly on the yellow grass. With the barrel of the big Sharps propped on a weathered buffalo skull, he estimated the distance at 150 yards. Selecting an old cow on the periphery of the herd, he took aim behind the shoulder, and squeezed off a shot. The cow shuddered on the bullet's impact but remained standing. Then blood began pumping from her nostrils, and when she dropped, the hunter knew he had shot true. The hunter had to immobilize the animal with a lung shot to keep it from running off and stampeding the herd.

Some of the others in the herd looked up at the report, and when one of them moved toward the fallen cow the hunter took aim at his second target. For the next hour he picked them off one by one. Finally, he hit a young bull in the leg. He fired again and managed to down it as it limped away, but the rest of the herd was at last alert to danger and began moving out of range. He might have pursued but elected not to. Several dozen dead buffalo lay in the short grass, and it would take the better part of the day to skin them out.

They would return in several days with a wagon to collect the hides. A few years before, when the herds had numbered in the hundreds of thousands, a hunter could work out of a single camp for months, and the hides might be left out on the range for most of the season. But a herd of this size could be wiped out in a matter of weeks. Moreover, this herd was on the move, pushed east by the relentless shooting toward the Sioux reservations along the Grand and Moreau Rivers, and the hunter would have to keep moving with it.

In the decades following the Civil War, the numbers of professional buffalo hunters who plied their bloody trade on the great prairies of the West grew to many thousands. Buffalo had been killed in great numbers earlier by such men, but the coming of railroads like the Kansas Pacific and the Atcheson, Topeka and Santa Fe provided an efficient way of transporting buffalo hides east, and once the rails had penetrated the plains, the slaughter began in earnest.

In the early 1870's the southern prairies had still been so thick with buffalo as to defy description. Each spring, massed in herds that might be 20 miles wide and 60 miles deep, they followed the ripening grasses north, moving out of Texas and the Indian Territory and into the phalanx of hunters spread across western Kansas into Colorado. At the height of the killing as many as 20,000 hunters may have been waiting for them. The hunters generally took only the hide, leaving the carcass—which on an old bull might weigh 1,500 pounds—to rot.

Mountains of pressed buffalo robes, meanwhile, crowded the freight docks of towns like Dodge City and Wichita. A good hunter could average sixty buffalo a day and might kill 3,000 in a single season. In the wake of the hunters came others to gather up the bleached bones, which were stacked by the railroad tracks in piles up to a half mile long, to be carried east for crushing into fertilizer.

By 1879 the southern herds were gone—vanished, in a wink of time, from a landscape they had dominated since the end of the Ice Age 10,000 years before. The hunters shrugged in disbelief at their own bloody efficiency, then moved into the remaining buffalo country north of the Platte.

Railroads opened up the Montana and Dakota ranges to wholesale slaughter, just as they had in the south. When the Northern Pacific pushed up the Yellowstone River in 1881, the towns of Glendive and Miles City sprang into existence as centers for the northern hunt. A typical hunter working out of Miles City might have one partner and two additional hunters hired at $50 a month each. His outfit would consist of a pair of wagons and eight draft horses, two saddle horses, two tents, a field stove, three Sharps rifles, and enough powder, lead, primers, shells, knives, and provisions to last from October to February, the season of the buffalo's winter pelage.

The first two years of concentrated hunting on the northern range were good indeed, but by the end of the third year the herds were vastly shrunken. The accounts of one New York jobber were typical, and reflected this decline: In the spring of 1881, he bought 26,000 robes and hides, and 45,000 in 1882; following the 1882–83 season, he shipped only 7,500. Hunters also noticed this precipitous drop, but many chose to ignore it. Hadn't they seen an estimated 75,000 head crossing the Yellowstone on its way toward Canada just that spring? This immense herd would return, they were certain, to supply the trade at least through another year. And so in the fall of 1883 the buffalo hunters prepared as usual for another season in the field.

Preoccupied by the killing, the hunter did not notice the tiny figures crouched on buttes to the east. Under the high October sky, the Sioux scouts listened to the distant pop of rifles carried on the wind and watched the herd drift slowly in their direction. It had been less than a fortnight since the hunt had started, but already the herd had shrunk by nearly half. Still, the appearance now of even 5,000 buffalo was a source of wonder and astonishment—a vindication, perhaps, of Sitting Bull's prophesy that *Pte*, the buffalo, would return and that the white men would vanish from their land.

The Sioux had depended on the buffalo for as long as they could remember. It was their standing crop, sustaining them with food, clothing, and shelter. Meat from the succulent hump ribs filled their bellies in summer. Dried, mixed with berries and pounded into pemmican, it carried them through the snow months. Buffalo chips fueled their lodge fires. The dressed hides of buffalo covered their tipis and were fashioned by squaws into moccasins and leggins. Untreated, a fresh buffalo skin was impervious to water and could be made into kettles or stretched on a willow frame to create a bullboat. The matted wool of a buffalo robe was their mattress and winter blanket. The thick hide from a bull's neck, hardened with glue boiled from the hooves, made a war shield tough enough to turn an arrow. They used braided hair for rope and sinew for bowstrings. Ribs became knives and sled runners. From buffalo horn—boiled until supple, then cut into strips and bound together with rawhide—they crafted bows that could send an arrow clean through a bull.

The buffalo's central importance to the Sioux and other plains tribes was not lost on those responsible for controlling Indians on the frontier. By the 1870's the first tentative steps were taken to control the terrible slaughter. When the issue was debated in Congress in 1874, however, the Secretary of Interior stated that he favored killing off the buffalo as a way of settling the Indian question once and for all. A bill to protect the buffalo passed anyway but died when President Grant refused to sign it. The following year the Texas legislature considered a similar bill and was advised by the regional military commander, General Phil Sheridan, that each hide hunter ought to receive a medal: "Let them kill, skin, and sell until the buffalo is exterminated, as it is the only way to bring lasting peace and allow civilization to advance."

Nor were the Indians flawless conservationists. But given their relatively small numbers, primitive weapons, and fondness for running buffalo on horseback—a more sporting and exciting, if vastly less efficient way of hunting them—Indians made little dent in the bison population. Blame for the buffalo's demise lay squarely with the *Wasichus*, or white eyes, overrunning their country.

For a while, the Sioux had succeeded in stemming the flow of whites through their land. In 1867 the great chief Red Cloud had soundly defeated the U.S. Army, closing off the Bozeman Trail through their hunting grounds along the Powder River. But eight years later, the discovery of gold in the Black Hills brought a new invasion and fresh conflict, culminating in the Custer debacle at the Little Big Horn.

Of all the Sioux leaders, none fought longer or more fiercely to preserve the old ways than Sitting Bull, the victor at the Little Big Horn. After the battle, he retreated with his followers into Canada. But the game proved scarce in the land of the Great White Mother, where settlers had done as thorough a job of killing off the buffalo as they had in the south. Sitting Bull's people grew hungry and weary of exile. So in the summer of 1881 he led them back across the border and surrendered at Ft. Buford on the Missouri.

The Army held Sitting Bull prisoner for two years before releasing him to the Standing Rock Reservation, where white officials hoped he would take up farming and become a model for the rest of the Sioux. (He didn't.) Soon after, in an act of cruel if naive irony, officers of the Northern Pacific invited him to speak at the dedication of their new railroad, whose construction had been directly responsible for the decimation of the buffalo on the northern plains. Accompanied by an Army interpreter, the most famous Indian in North America arrived at Bismarck and delivered a scorching diatribe in his native Lakota. "I hate the white people," he told the assembled. "You are all thieves and liars. You have taken away our land and made us outcasts." In place of these remarks, the interpreter substituted friendly platitudes. The crowd gave Sitting Bull a standing ovation.

Sitting Bull went home to Standing Rock, where the Sioux were reduced to living on government handouts of beef and flour. The White Father also delivered cattle on the hoof to the reservation; rather than slaughtering these animals conventionally, the Indians ran them on horseback, killing them with bow and arrow or with the few ancient trade guns the Army had allowed them to keep. Longhorns, however, proved a sorry substitute for buffalo, so when the scouts returned in the autumn of 1883 to tell of the herd approaching from the west, the news seemed too good to be true.

The Sioux had not seen buffalo since June of the previous year, when a large herd had appeared near the western border of the reservation. The Standing Rock agent, James McLaughlin, ordered rifles issued to the Indians and accompanied them on that hunt. McLaughlin described these events years later but made no mention of a hunt in October 1883, which suggests that Sitting Bull and the thousand warriors who accompanied him to meet the herd did so without agency permission.

A brief record of the hunt in the fall of 1883 is preserved in an account by William T. Hornaday, a naturalist and chief taxidermist at the Smithsonian Institution, who interviewed several white participants after it was over. (Hornaday became a tireless campaigner in the buffalo's behalf and played an important role in rescuing the animal from extinction.) Although no firsthand Sioux account of the last buffalo hunt exists, descriptions of similar hunts allow us to imagine it in all its ritual and excitement.

Once safely removed from agency headquarters, the hunters collected out on the prairie. They sat facing west, forming two horns of a crescent, in front of which was placed a painted stone as a kind of altar. A half-dozen scouts gathered around the stone and swore to Sitting Bull to report correctly on the numbers of buffalo they would see. The old headman sealed the oath by drawing on a pipe, then touching the earth with it and raising it to the sky in tribute to *Wakan Tanka*, the great spirit, and to the buffalo god *Tatanka*. Each scout took the pipe in his turn and repeated Sitting Bull's gestures.

The ceremony over, the warriors jumped to their feet and scrambled to their ponies. They could forget for a moment the humiliation of agency life and the likelihood that the buffalo they would soon encounter would be the last they would ever see. Finally the warriors broke away from the scouts and raced furiously back to camp.

The hunting party set out early the next morning, and it was not long before they met the scouts returning with their report. The herd was dwindling, and by the time the Sioux were upon it and had joined the white hunters in the fray it was down to perhaps 1,200 head—a little more than one animal for each warrior. Since the Army had disarmed the Sioux years before, most of them reverted to bows and arrows in this final, furious melée. In two days they finished off the entire herd.

As the Sioux hunters prepared the meat for winter, the old man who had led them watched and ruminated. The historian Mari Sandoz pictures Sitting Bull alone in his lodge, "his pipe cold beside him, remembering the great Indian and buffalo country he was born into. It was just over on the Grand River there, the year before the fire boat, the *Yellowstone*, came smoking up the Missouri. Now all of it was gone, vanished like wind on the buffalo grass. True, he had known glory, much glory, but his broad face was hard as the walls of the upper Yellowstone when he thought about it, for what is glory to a man who must see his people as he saw them now."

In their own camps, the white hunters talked about what they had seen. No lovers of Indians, they had felt nonetheless an unexpected sympathy for the Sioux in what was certainly their last buffalo hunt. There were more buffalo out there, they told themselves, but they were west of here and far out of range of the Sioux confined to their Dakota reservations. The professional hunters would not realize for another month that the buffalo they were talking about had been obliterated along the Canadian border by other white hunters and by half-starved Blackfeet and Assiniboins. The only survivors were a few strays that took refuge in the Missouri Breaks. Three years later, William Hornaday would scour these remote badlands and turn up 275 head—nearly half of all the buffalo left on earth.

Thanks largely to the efforts of Hornaday and other conservationists, buffalo would make a slow but steady comeback, from an estimated 635 in 1886 to perhaps 80,000 today. While encouraging, the latter figure still pales next to the 60 million that may once have roamed North America. The great herds that had sustained the Sioux and other plains tribes were gone forever, and with them any hope for a return to the old way of life. Sitting Bull spoke for all his people in his song:

A warrior
I have been.
Now
it is all over.
A hard time I have.

February 1986

Saga of the One-Eyed Bull

WALTER L. PROTHERO

Whether by bullet or age, the old elk's time had come.

I RECOGNIZED THE OLD bull by the odd dark patch of fur against the blond of his shoulder and, for two years now, the empty eye socket. There'd been no heavy roundness to the barrel of his body when I'd seen him early that September before the rut, only the shoulders and hips sharp in silhouette against the dusk sky, the sway-back, and the careful old-man steps back into the timber. There were still six points on each antler, but the beams were shorter and thinner.

He won't make it through the winter, I thought, almost aloud. I was convinced I'd have to get him that season, or the winter would. There'd be no next time for me and the bull.

I'd seen him first some years earlier (was it four now?) when he was in his prime. He had stood on the meadow in the gorge at dusk, Clydesdale-big and rounded, and bugle-roared at a lesser bull at the edge of the trees, the banshee scream and then the heavy, gut-deep grunts echoing between thousand-foot limestone cliffs.

Two weeks later and a few days before the season opened, I returned to find the bull gone and his big tracks leading up the gorge onto a mile-long bench, then high into a heavy mixed stand of aspens and Douglas fir on the shoulder of a big mountain. There were no tracks leading away from that blown-down, hair-thick tangle, either.

That seemed to be his routine: summering in the tangle on the mountain and then dropping down to the meadows along the creek in the gorge in the middle of September to fight and bugle and rut, and then climbing back up the mountain again in October to rest and regain weight before winter pushed him out.

I came back to hunt him first that October. I rode a mountain-wise mare up the first canyon and onto a high wind-blasted plateau and through the canyon heads and then down into one last valley, the bay quick-stepping silently on fir needles through a heavy, sunless timber to the foot of his mountain. I let the mare switchback her way up the steep flank of the mountain, stopping to blow when she needed it, until we were at the meadow below his cover. From the tracks he was coming out of the timber to feed at dusk, and I waited there and remembered his antlers, the beams as big around as a man's forearm. He came slowly to the edge of the timber almost at dark, stood a moment, then disappeared back into the gloom. Perhaps he'd scented me, or maybe he had some other way of knowing I was there. Though I had three days to hunt I didn't see him again.

I looked for the bull again the second season ten days before the hunt, and he was there, lean from rutting and fighting, and there was a black, oozing hole where his left eye had been. Apparently, he'd taken an antler tine there in a fight, and the wound had that sunken look you see in toothless old people. I left as soon as I'd found he was still there, careful not to disturb him.

When the hunt began, I waited for several days at the meadow without results. His fresh tracks were there in the grasses and mud of the seep, but he only came out of the thick trees to feed at night; he remembered too well the season before. After waiting those days, I still-hunted very slowly into the tangle of trees, stalking along a deeply tracked trail, examining antler rubs on aspen and fir saplings where the bark had been scraped higher than I could reach. The blunt hoofprints were as big as salad plates and went deep where the soil was soft. The timber reeked of his musk. It took me an hour to ease 200 yards into the tangle, looking long and hard into the shadows ahead and the sides, aware the wind was quartering into my face, listening for anything that might hint "elk." But there was nothing, only the Indian summer sun filtering through the broken canopy of autumn-dead leaves and the twitterings of chickadees searching the tree bark.

So I continued, reveling in that "action-to-come" feel; nothing is as absorbing as hunting with the certainty that something will happen. Then there was a crash as if a 10-ton boulder had rolled from the bluff above through the timber, and the brief glimpse of teak-and-ivory antlers with the sun glinting off them and the disappearing creamy, heart-shaped rump. That was the last of him that season, and I knew it as I sat on a deadfall and watched my hands shake.

I had similar luck on the last day of the following season (it was the third hunt for him—by that time I was keeping track), as I still-hunted back into the timber again and jumped him at 20 yards. As he crashed off through the trees, bowling over saplings and hurtling blowdowns, I couldn't quite get the crosshairs anywhere but on his rump. If I touched off the .270 like that, he'd get away and die miserably.

He made it through that long, hard winter and the late-coming spring, though that next September he looked poor and his antlers were smaller as I scouted before the hunt. "He's passed his prime," I told the mare as we rode to camp.

He was with two raghorn bulls that fourth season, and as they fed out of the timber on opening evening in the dusky half-light, I could just make out the old bull hanging back in the trees behind a screen of fir saplings. Then it was dark, and I stumbled down the ridge to where the mare waited in the night and chuckled softly at my approach. I waited and watched the meadow for several days, then still-hunted back into the tangle. I heard the bulls go far ahead; the wind had shifted suddenly, and that was it for the season.

The final season I scouted a week before the hunt and he was there. I knew then as I looked at the bony flanks and watched him take those old-man steps back into the timber that this would be his last year on the mountain. There was no doubt, and as soon as the first heavy snows came he'd begin that irreversible downward spiral.

The old one-eyed bull was in the meadow in the late dawn of opening day just standing in the wind. I hesitated after settling the crosshairs on that dark shoulder spot and looked up from the rifle. *You get old and you die*, I thought, but I knew it was better this way than in the winter. "It's better," I told myself aloud, perhaps rationalizing just a bit, the sound of my voice as soothing as if someone else had confirmed it, too. I pressed the trigger and the bull hunched and sagged forward.

I walked up to him. Though he was still a six by six, the antlers were no longer the massive, heavy-beamed rack they were two years earlier. *Maybe I shouldn't have shot him; maybe I should have let him have the rest of the fall until the snows got too heavy*. But then I saw him in my mind lying in the belly-deep, blue-cold snow, like that bull I'd watched die in Yellowstone. He took six days to do it, weakening all the time until he was too feeble to keep the coyotes from eating at his haunches and the magpies away from his eyes.

"It was right to shoot him," I said to myself. A heavy, deep bugle and then the grunting of a prime bull floated up from that sunless timber at the base of the mountain, and in my mind I could see the bull in the gloom of the trees with beams as big around as a man's forearm.

January 1991

Knife Against Fang

FRANK C. HIBBEN

Old Ben Lilly had never known a mountain lion to turn and fight, but this one was different.

T HERE'S ONLY ONE panther that ever fought against me," Ben Lilly said in his quiet manner. "She jumped for my throat. I had only a knife to defend myself with. It was close—and then there was a lava ledge—and the dogs. . . ."

The old man's voice trailed off. Already his blue eyes were dreamy as his mind turned back across the intervening years. For a long time he was silent. He had obviously forgotten that I was there.

The people in Silver City, New Mexico, had said that old Ben Lilly was as nutty as a Christmas pudding. "But he's the greatest bear and lion hunter that ever lived in these parts," Forest Ranger Henry Woodrow had added as we talked of the man. Ben Lilly was a legend in the southwest and had been ever since that day so long ago in the Louisiana cane-brakes when he had told his wife he was going out to shoot a hawk that was bothering her chickens. He was gone two years. "The hawk just kept going," he replied when asked about the beginning of his career.

Throughout the rest of his life Lilly hunted in the western United States and in Mexico. He killed bears and lions for pay or he hunted them because of an inner urge that seemed to press on him like a consuming passion. No one man had ever killed so many black and grizzly bears; no one hunter had ever brought so many green-eyed lions to their end as Ben Lilly.

But in 1933, Ben Lilly himself was close to the end. When I visited him to ask details about some of his hunting exploits, he was at the Poor Farm near Silver City, and his mind was obviously wavering between sanity and those empty voids unknown to ordinary men. Ben Lilly was courteous enough when I questioned him. He started walking as we talked. Without food or other preparations for an extended stay together, we climbed into the foot-hills of the

Mogollon Mountains near the Poor Farm. We were gone three days.

In these mountains Ben Lilly had a cave complete with a few fragments of moldy oatmeal, a battered skillet and a Bible. With these implements we lived very well as Ben Lilly talked.

The old man leaned back against the rough rock of the cave. His clothes were baggy and his trousers were tied at the ankles with old pieces of buckskin to keep out the draft. He wore a round and battered hat that might have been the equipment of some pious but poorly-dressed country preacher. Even Ben Lilly's face, as the firelight played upon his features, seemed benign. His full beard gave him a patriarchal appearance.

After a few moments of silence Ben Lilly again began to speak. His pale eyes stared back through the years to that time when he and his dogs were young and they were on the trail of a certain lioness in these same Mogollon Mountains. The old man not only told the story to me; he relived it himself. His flow of words wove a spell that belied distance and the passing years. Soon I also forgot the rugged cave where we sat. The dancing firelight formed itself into the scenes that Ben Lilly described. I did not hear the poor-wills that called from the dark ridges below the cave. I did not hear Ben Lilly's story. I saw it happen.

Four spotted hounds sat in a semicircle on the far side of a campfire. Their long ears drooped disconsolately as their nostrils drank in the satisfying odors of frying meat. December is a hard season, even in the southern regions of the Mogollons of New Mexico. The dogs' tails were wrapped tightly around their hindquarters to try to protect those exposed portions of their anatomy, chilled by the cold winter wind that swept down the Gila Valley.

Ben Lilly smiled knowingly at the fixed attention of his four canine companions. With the tip of his peculiar knife he flipped out some scraps of lion meat from the sizzling grease of the skillet that he held. When the pieces had cooled a little, he fed them to the hounds. For himself, he filled an old tomato can half full of a dark liquid that he had brewed from the dried leaves of the wild-cherry tree. The vile stuff gave off an odor like the water from a cedar swamp.

"We'll get the she-panther and the kittens tomorrow," he told his dogs with quiet finality.

The hounds did not change expression, but continued to gaze with mournful eyes where the last of the lion meat still sizzled in the crooked skillet.

The next morning, as Ben Lilly and his four hound companions left their beds in the pile of leaves within the lava cave, they started out confidently up the main valley of the Middle Fork of the Gila. It was a wild and beautiful country at the bottom of this deep canyon, rendered even more so by the frost crystals that glittered on the rough stone and even on the needles of the scattered pine trees that grew along the river. The canyon was narrow here, flanked on either hand by rough cliffs of lava rock. On the vesicular surfaces of these stones, all sizes of green, orange and snuff-colored lichens had found a purchase. Alligator-bark junipers curled in gnarled and distorted forms from the lava ledges. Mountain mahogany bushes and dark green firs covered the slopes in those places where their roots could find a precarious footing.

As Ben Lilly left the small rincon where his camp was located a group of white-tailed deer jumped into motion across the canyon. The frightened animals climbed a talus slope amid the sound of falling rocks that rolled beneath their frantic hoofs. Ben Lilly glanced at the deer briefly. Although he must have seen thousands of the animals during his long career in these wild mountains, he could still appreciate their beauty and the grace of their movements.

Gazing at the deer, Ben Lilly leaned his .30-30 against a rock fragment and called one of his hounds to his side. Taking a short length of an old lariat rope from his pocket, he tied one end of the piece to the hound's collar and the other to his belt. With a dog fastened to him, he used the ears of the hound to supplement his own. Thus fitted for the chase, this strange assortment of hounds and the bearded man in the baggy clothes set off up the canyon of the Gila.

In a short distance they began to climb a spur point where a pile of broken talus rock formed a natural ladder by which the canyon cliffs could be surmounted. Scarcely pausing for breath in the almost vertical ascent, these hardened hunters climbed ledge after ledge until they stood on the very top of the rock cliffs on that side of the river. It was along these same ledges that a certain female lion had left the tracks of herself and her two kittens a few days before.

The loose hounds sniffed eagerly along the rim of the rock. They seemed to anticipate that they were close to a kill. One of the dogs barked briefly at an old scrape beneath a juniper at the very edge of a cliff. But the pile of dirt and dead twigs that had been heaped there by lion paws had been made by a male. Perhaps it was the same luckless lion they had killed three days before.

Ben Lilly, with the dogs close around him, skirted the cliff for a mile or more. They circled out around the narrow crack of a side canyon that broke the solid edge of the parent mesa like a tear in a piece of brown cardboard. Ben Lilly even turned away from the river cliffs and made a traverse through a shallow, wooded valley. Here the deer tracks seemed to cover every foot of ground. There were old beds and other sign that the deer used this wooded place. But nowhere did the keen nose of any hound point out a spot where the paw of the lioness had stepped, nor did the equally keen eye of old Ben Lilly see any sign that the female had been there.

"I was sure she had those kittens somewhere around this side canyon," Ben Lilly said to his hounds or to himself. "Perhaps we'd better have another look."

As the cold sun of that winter morning gradually rose over the ridges to the east of the river a slight breeze sprang up. It was often so when the growing light had melted the frost crystals and warmed the southern slopes. It was this slight breeze, although a lifeless and impartial thing in itself, that located the lioness.

Suddenly one of the hounds ahead threw his nose into the air and wriggled that sensitive organ back and forth with an amazing mobility. At first the dog did not seem to be sure. Then he gave a short bark. There is an intimate connection between a hound's nostrils and the barking mechanism. This circuit is also joined at the other end of the animal to the mysterious contrivance that wags a hound's tail.

The hound tied to Ben Lilly's belt also showed signs of agitation and strained to be off with the other dogs. Curiously enough, the loose hounds had bounded back in the direction of the same narrow side canyon that the hunters had circled only a short time before. On the edge of this cleft in the lava rocks the two lead hounds stopped and began to bay furiously. The faint movement of air that came up over the dark-shadowed ledges below was bringing to them the smell of lion, and from the action of the hounds the panther was close.

Ben Lilly lay on his belly among the barking dogs and looked over the edge of the rock, down into the darkness of the cleft. Apparently sunlight never penetrated into this narrow place, even at midday. As it was early morning, the shadow between the lava walls was so deep that he could scarcely make out any details. He could see dimly a series of ledges below him, each one of them representing the surface of some ancient lava flow that had hardened there in geological ages past. But nowhere on these projections was there the tawny form of a female lion. Only once, in a momentary gap in the uproar of the dogs around him, Lilly thought he heard the spitting of a cat, but his hearing was bad, and he was not sure.

To one side, along the edge of this narrow crack in the cliff, was a sloping place where the water poured off the top of the mesa when the snows melted in the spring. Here the rock was stained by the descending waters, but the action of these same floods had made a place where an agile man could climb down.

Ben Lilly untied the hound from his belt so that the eagerly straining dog would not jerk him from a precarious footing on the smooth rock. Holding his rifle in one hand, he began to descend. As he dropped down onto the first of the lava ledges his eyes became accustomed to the gloom. He turned and helped his dogs down, one after the other. The hounds still barked incessantly, although their exuberant canine spirits were somewhat dampened by the danger of the depths that they sensed below them. Hounds are afraid of heights, and these dogs were no exception.

But the heady smell of lion body odor again came to their eager dog noses. Old Bugle, the most audacious of the hounds, ran along the surface of the ledge to where it disappeared around a shoulder of pitted rock. The other dogs, taking heart from the first, also ran forward, although noticeably pressing close to the parent cliff on the right hand and avoiding, even in their enthusiasm, the crumbling edges of rock that marked the boundary of the ledge and certain oblivion in the unknown depths at the bottom of the cleft.

A few yards beyond, Ben Lilly again came among his dogs. The ledge had stopped as abruptly as it had begun, the end marked by a crack that had broken the horizontal strata in some cosmic shift of long ago. But along the fault made by this breakage there was a narrow trail again leading downward. As before, Lilly helped his dogs descend the break and get onto a wider ledge below. These lava terraces were like the balconies in an old-fashioned theater, each one hanging out over the one below in a descending series.

Ben Lilly thought, as he came onto the lower ledge, he saw on the lava rock signs that humans had been there before. The dark stone was worn in places, as though sandaled feet had smoothed the footholds as ancient people passed up and down that precarious trail. At one place where the slanting lava left no foothold at all, a small masonry wall made of lava fragments set in adobe mortar had been substituted to fill in the gap. On the rock beside the narrow trail that led to the ledge were some colored glyphs of dim red and yellow paint scarcely visible in the gloom.

But Ben Lilly had seen such signs in the Gila country before. There was hardly a side canyon or cliff cave in this rough terrain that the ancient inhabitants of the Mogollon region had not utilized for precarious dwellings or hidden mountain sanctuaries.

On the lower, broader ledge Ben Lilly again fastened the hound to his belt and, with his dogs before him, doubled back along the lava terrace toward the head of the cleft. Even this deep, between the confining rock walls, a few sickly bushes and a small tree grew from the scant earth caught in cracks of the rock, and reached upward to get what light they could. Bracing backward against the pull of the dog at his waist, Ben Lilly followed his other hounds along the ledge.

Here and there bastions of rock from above made any straight progress impossible, nor could the hunters see for any distance in front of them. Only the insistent lion smell that apparently pervaded the narrow place kept them going at all. The clamor of the dogs between those confining walls would have been deafening to a man with ordinary hearing. As it was, Lilly had no difficulty in telling that his hunting hounds were close to the quarry. None of the dogs had shown any inclination to track, although from time to time one of them put his nose to the rough rock and indicated by renewed barking that a panther had stepped there not long ago.

Suddenly there was a roar of sound between the lava walls. The dog on Lilly's belt jumped with the rest of the hounds, almost jerking the hunter from his feet. The three other dogs had disappeared around a projection of rock. On the other side of this their frenzied barking was quickly mixed with the snarls and spitting of cornered cats. But these noises of beleaguered animals were diminutive and high-pitched. They were not the sounds of a lioness that, with full-throated growls, defends her young.

"Kittens!" said Ben Lilly to himself.

The captive dog at Ben Lilly's belt surged forward, his hound claws raking the rough rock. He was frantic to join the other dogs in the attack on the young of the lion family. A hound is a docile and soulful-eyed animal under most conditions, but when he smells lion close before him his whole character changes in an instant. The hound becomes a demon, with flashing teeth and half-open mouth, whose only purpose is to sink those fangs into soft lion flesh and kill if he can. Ben Lilly knew well what was happening on the other side of the rough lava rock. His hounds had trapped the lion kittens in a rock hollow where their mother had left them. In a few moments the dogs would kill them both.

Ben Lilly shifted his short rifle under his other arm and walked slowly forward. Even this veteran hunter, who had witnessed a hundred primitive sights such as this one, was reluctant to round the rocky projection and come upon the scene of the massacre of a panther family. Not so the dog that strained against the short piece of rope at his waist. This hound, in his canine way, was all eagerness to be a part of the same bloody business.

Without explanation, the pull of the tugging hound suddenly ceased. The dog stood quiet for an instant, apparently listening. The hound's head turned around as he looked back along the ledge in the direction they had come. Again the dog bayed fiercely and lunged at the rope, but this time backward, away from the snarls and mouthed growlings of the other hounds where they finished the lion kittens.

When the captive dog charged around him, the sudden change in direction of the short lariat as it snapped backward spun Lilly around like a top. For a moment he tottered and threw out the hand that held the rifle to balance himself. The dog before him still strained forward, with all four legs steeply braced. The hound's ears were laid back as a fighting dog's are when he gets ready for battle. His nose and his whole body pointed back along the ledge. But Ben Lilly did not need this canine sign-post. Not twenty feet away, belly down on the bare rock, was a full-grown panther.

If these had been Asiatic tiger cubs that Ben Lilly had found in that rocky crack in the Gila cliffs, he might have been more cautious. Or if he had been dealing with African lions or with any of the other great cats, he might have expected trouble. As it was, however, he never thought about panthers being dangerous. The mountain lion always runs when pursued by hounds with men at their heels. On many previous occasions Ben Lilly himself had trailed female panthers with kittens by their side. Never once had these she-lions stayed to protect their young. Each time they had fled ignominiously.

But Ben Lilly did not think of these things as he stood there stock-still and stared at the lioness, for it was a she. The panther facing him was long and slim, with a narrow neck and smallish head. In the few seconds that Ben Lilly appraised her she made no move. Curiously enough, the green eyes that burned so brightly there in the dim light were not fixed on the dog that growled and snapped so close before her, but on the face of the man. As the she-lion stared so intently straight into the eyes of Ben Lilly her long tail twitched back and forth a little against the rock behind.

Who can say what might have happened there on the rock ledge if Ben Lilly had slowly raised his short rifle and fired? He feared that the hound surging against the rope at his waist would jerk at the crucial instant that he shot. He slowly reached behind him with his free hand and drew from its sheath the home-made hunting knife that he carried at the back of his belt. Still moving with deliberation, he brought the keen blade around and with one swift, upward motion severed the rope that held the hound to him. The dog, pulling so eagerly, was suddenly loosened, and shot forward as though propelled from behind. This was the movement that exploded the issue.

As though the sudden advance of the hound had tripped a trigger somewhere beneath her, the lioness leapt with all four feet. The latent energy of those soft cat paws carried her straight forward, but not upon the hound that charged beneath her. Instinctively Ben Lilly brought his rifle forward, but too late. Perhaps the action saved his life. His groping thumb never pulled back the hammer, nor did the swerving barrel ever straighten out toward the chest of the panther that came at him like an arrow.

The leap of the lion struck the gun in mid-air and knocked it back against Ben Lilly's face. The impact of the hard barrel on his cheek-bone was paralyzing. At the same instant Lilly felt the sting of sharp claws on his shoulders. He went down like a frail stalk before a blast of wind. The useless gun clattered to the rock and bounced from the ledge into the shadows below. Ben Lilly saw lion teeth before his throat. As the panther knocked him sprawling he had no time to wonder why he did not feel the biting pain of those teeth or the rake of claws in his own belly.

In the next instant a weight moved from his chest. The lioness had bounded beyond him after knocking him down. Perhaps he hadn't been the target of the attack at all—had only stood in the way. It was her kittens—The other dogs beyond. . . .

Ben Lilly half raised himself on one knee. His cheek was laid open and he still was half stunned. The lioness had leapt on him and over him so quickly that the single hound that had precipitated this whole affair scarcely had time to turn around and follow the panther as she passed.

Automatically, as Ben Lilly rose from the hard lava rock, he picked up the short-bladed knife that had been brushed from his hand by the onslaught. He turned to look for his hat. Dazed as he was, he froze in mid-motion. There was the panther behind him. She was ready to attack again, and crouched on the flat rock as before, with her feet underneath her. Lilly, still on one knee and with one of his eyes almost closed from the gash on his cheek, for the first time in his life was afraid. Slowly he began to back away. Even the hound beside him seemed to feel fear. There was something unnatural in the fanatical eyes of that panther lying on the ledge.

Without warning she leaped again with the same spring-uncoiling speed as before. This time there was no doubt that Lilly was her target. She was going to kill him. Lilly knew this. It was plain in the green eyes as she came toward him. The panther's mouth opened. Lilly half rose to meet the attack. Instinctively he raised his left arm to ward off those awful teeth from his throat. With his other hand he struck out blindly with the four-inch blade of his home-made knife.

The raking forepaws of the lion went wide of their mark. For an instant she seemed to hang there in mid-air with no support. Then she slumped sideways. The knife in Lilly's hand was twisted from his grasp as she fell. The straight steel blade had ripped away half of the panther's throat. The very fury of her own attack had pressed the weapon home.

Lilly felt the sting of pain in his thigh where the flailing hind feet of the struggling beast had jerked away his clothing and cut deep, parallel grooves in the flesh beneath. Weakly he leaned against the lava wall behind him, panting as a man does when his breath is almost gone. He watched as the lion before him slowly rolled to her feet and crouched to spring again. She jumped—straight at his face. He could not raise his arm—his knife was gone. There were widespread paws and an open mouth. Then the brown body twisted and fell away.

Ben Lilly stared dumbly as the she-panther thrashed and twitched on the ledge before him. Dark-red blood pumped in ever-diminishing spurts from the severed vein in her throat. In a moment the white fur of the female's neck was matted with wet blood. Then the hounds came to worry the carcass.

After some time Ben Lilly knelt to skin the lioness. He wondered what it was about this particular panther that had caused her to attack a man so viciously. She looked the same as any other that he had killed, as far as her dead body went.

From the belly of the carcass Lilly cut strips of lion fat, mixed them with urine and applied them to the painful scratches in his own flesh where the lion's claws had marked him. This done, he finished the skinning. As he came to the neck he saw how the blade of his knife had cut the she-lion's lifeline. If the thrust had been a fraction to either side or had missed the throat of the panther entirely, his own body would have been lying there in sticky blood on the dark rock. It would have been the mad lioness standing over him, not he over her. Ben Lilly knew well that of such accidents are the heroes or the victims of the wilderness made.

February 1954

Crazy Caribou

FRANK DUFRESNE

The big herd appeared out of nowhere—then vanished like the wind.

BY THE TIME I decided I didn't want to go caribou hunting with Wild Pete Bogey it was too late to quit. I was strapped in a bush plane alongside the old flying prospector and we were a hundred miles out of Fairbanks, threading our way among the turbulent air currents of the Crazy Mountains. All at once Pete yanked the ship around in a tight, diving turn.

The yellow four-seater went tumbling through the skies in a violent skid and my head went into a spin. My stomach started pushing up into my throat and my feet felt as if they were going through the floorboards. Gunny sacks of camp gear began jumping like grasshoppers. Gold pans, shovels, tin pots, and a frying pan flitted about the cabin like butterflies. A wooden box came tumbling at me end over end.

"Grab it!" yelled Pete, wrestling at the controls. "Then read the label."

I caught the box and hugged it close, my eyes no more than six inches away from the red-stenciled letters: DYNAMITE. The plane leveled off for a moment. Pete gestured. I had time only to glimpse a great silver-maned caribou bull as we whizzed over its back almost close enough to tick its antlers with our tail skid. Then Pete gunned the motor and hauled back on the stick as though he were operating a steam shovel. We zoomed for the clouds with the speed of a rocket heading for orbit, then swung off in a wobbly circle and came swooping back.

Through the smudged window on my side of the cabin appeared a pinwheel of blue sky, white snow peaks, jagged canyon walls, and then a flat stretch of gray. Pete eased up on the throttle, and then there was a smashing impact, a screech of rubber on gravel, followed by an interval of silence. The box tore loose from my arms and started to sail. I snatched it back and was clasping it fervently to my breast when the plane thumped again and lurched to a halt on a windswept hogback.

"Wal, there's ya caribou," said Pete, pointing down the valley. "Go git him!"

I muttered under my breath, "You asked for it," because I'd been warned about this zany character and his mad flying.

Wild Pete Bogey's squat figure, his bald head with its big red ears, and his scraggly gray whiskers had made this oldtime gold prospector a well-known man around Fairbanks. Pete panned for gold in the summer and trapped furs in the winter. When he couldn't mush a dog-team any more on account of having his toes frozen off in a blizzard, he bought himself a beat-up plane of early vintage. And this, according to the local newspaper, made Pete Bogey the oldest student pilot in Alaskan history.

With complete disregard for life and limb—his own and others—Pete zoomed joyfully over the town's cabin tops, striking cold fear in every other pilot who had to use the same field. When the day came for him to take off on his first prospecting trip to the Crazy Mountains, one would get you five that he'd never come back, except possibly sewed in a sack. But in a few days I spotted the yellow wings on his plane as he came yawing in over the tamaracks and bounded down the runway like a snowshoe hare.

Out stepped Pete, his whiskers whipping in the prop wash and his big red ears fairly flapping with excitement. He'd struck it rich, he told me. It was hard rock stuff and he'd have to go back to do some blasting to find out how many millions he was worth.

I gave the old prospector a lift back to town in my pickup, and next morning hauled him and his paraphernalia back to the airfield. I helped him fill his tanks with gas, spun the wooden prop for him, and told him I hoped to see him again when I got back from a caribou hunt I was making along the highway. Above the roar of the engine I heard Pete's voice bawling out a command.

"Caribou, ya say?" He was leaning out the door of his plane. "Hop in, boy. I'll drap ya right down where ya can shoot a bull, and we'll have it back here before sundown."

I don't know why I do things like this, but in the next moment I was belted down next to old Pete and we were tearing down the strip like a scared cat. An hour later we were down in the Crazy Mountains and Pete was pointing out the caribou bull.

I unshackled myself from the seat and stepped down to the ground, feeling lucky to be alive, wishing I were back in Fairbanks, and wondering how long it would take me to walk home if I never saw Pete Bogey again. Pete jerked his thumb at a boulder just off the ridgetop. "Drag the carcass up here, and I'll be back for the pickup in three, four hours. Good luck, son, spin the prop."

I watched him out of sight, then started looking for the caribou. It had moved about half a mile into the wind. My scent hadn't reached it, and it was busily thrashing its antlers against a willow bush to free them of shedding velvet. The rutting season was coming on. It was the time of year when the caribou congregate, and as I started my stalk I wondered why this bull was all alone in the mountains.

Between bouts with the willow bush the caribou would raise its nose to sniff the breeze, toss its great rack, then stand motionless as a bronze statue, facing a narrow pass to the northeast. Soon I discovered what was holding the big stag's attention. Two or three miles distant, like little paper cutouts against the skyline, a band of caribou emerged from a draw and moved our way in a snakelike file.

While the lone bull was questing the air and filling its flaring nostrils with the scent of its own kind I crept within easy rifle range and quietly levered a cartridge into the firing chamber of my .30/30 carbine. Stretching prone and resting the worn octagonal barrel across a bed of reindeer moss, I centered the bull's shoulder in the buckhorn sight and started the slow trigger squeeze.

The shot was never touched off. There was a clatter of rocks and a piglike snort behind me. I swung around, hackles on edge, thinking it was one of the savage Toklat grizzlies so plentiful in these Crazy Mountains. Facing me was a spraddle-legged caribou calf, and behind it another group of cows and yearlings. They had appeared out of a steep canyon as if by magic.

Before they were gone, still another bunch came pushing out of a willow thicket to make a beeline for the same ridge. Among them were several fine males, some of them fully as big as the lone bull.

The willow patches disgorged more and more batches, and when I stole a look at the mountain passes I saw even greater numbers. A steady stream of swaying antlers began flowing down the slopes until the hillsides seemed to be alive. The ridgetop where I had a rendezvous with Wild Pete Bogey in a couple of hours had become, all at once, a crossroads for all the caribou herds in the Yukon.

I dropped off the ridge into a narrow box canyon and stepped behind a boulder, hoping to witness the caribou parade unseen. But almost immediately the vanguard of another band veered off the spur and came clattering into the slot, filling the alley from wall to wall with rolling stones and dust clouds.

Grunts and groans and snorts of cows and young stock blended in a wild chorus. Beneath these sounds were the queer, clicking noises peculiar to caribou and reindeer in motion, a rhythmic popping of tendons in their toggle-jointed hoofs as they surged by me and fought their way up a steep rock slide out of sight.

Straight through the gully they came now, jammed antler to antler, the fawns running under the protective bellies of the cows. Some of them passed within the length of my .30/30. And then, suddenly, a rack of horns with the widest spread and greatest number of points I had ever seen loomed before me.

I had stepped partly clear of the boulder shield when I glimpsed the antlers rising above the herd. The gray avalanche split apart just enough to avoid contact with me, but the animals continued to force their way past without a break in the ranks.

And then occurred the kind of incident that makes a man wonder if he's reading the right books. The bull showed fight. It braked to a dead stop right in my face, its reddened eyes rolled wickedly, and an enormous set of antlers hooked at me. Before I could make up my mind to shoot pointblank out of the churning masses there was a pile-up of caribou behind the great herd boss, and he was rammed past me to be lost forever in a welter of flying feet and showering gravel.

An hour passed. Then another, and finally the herd began to show signs of thinning. Numerous good bulls were still trotting by within easy shooting range, but I let them pass until I could make the climb unhampered to the hogback where I was to meet Pete Bogey. I had it all figured. I'd be taking my pick out of a herd totaling many thousands. I'd drop my bull where the flying prospector could park his plane alongside and help me heave it aboard.

There were only a few stragglers left in sight when I mounted the ridgetop. One of them was a fleet little calf racing panic-stricken ahead of a lame cow. Behind the cow were four black and three gray timber wolves closing in for the kill. I emptied the magazine at them, and while only one shot drew blood, the fusillade turned the brutes away. They fled into a gully and vanished, and in that moment so did the last of that great caribou migration.

I couldn't believe it at first. I clambered desperately to a high knob and scanned the Crazy Mountains in all directions. It wasn't any use. In all that vast wilderness there wasn't a caribou in sight.

I was still sitting there on the ridgetop, holding my head, when I saw the glitter of afternoon sun on yellow wings and heard the drone of Pete Bogey's plane. He crashlanded as usual and I got in and buckled myself in the seat beside him, saying nothing.

"Lost ya caribou, eh?" observed Pete, and slued the ship around for takeoff.

He seemed to be all wrapped up in his thoughts. We were halfway back to Fairbanks before he gave me the bad news about his million-dollar gold strike. He'd touched off the dynamite, he said, and it must have blown his rich pay streak to hell because he couldn't find it any more.

The plane was yawing all over the sky as he waved his arms and shouted his loss. His flying was bad enough without my diverting his attention with any more bad news. I decided to wait until we landed before I told him I'd lost a sight more than one caribou. I'd lost nearer to fifty thousand of them.

January 1960

Alaska Peninsula

DUNCAN BARNES

This wilderness can dwarf a man, a grizzly, or a trophy caribou.

I N THE SHADOW of an active volcano named Veniaminof, the narrow trails cut deeply into the boggy tundra of the Alaska Peninsula, stretching off into the distance and marking the migratory routes followed since time immemorial by one of the world's greatest herds of barren ground caribou.

Wedged between the Bering Sea and the North Pacific, the Alaska Peninsula is a weather factory as fickle as any on the North American continent. Hunting out of a one-room shack on Fracture Creek one morning in early October, guide Tom Hundley, of Palmer, Alaska, and I kept a weather eye out and recorded the following:

Dawn—salty wind about 35–40 mph: temperature 19°F.

9 A.M.—sleet storm slants out of the West.

10 A.M.—sleet turns to windblown rain.

11:30 A.M.—Sun bursts out, skies turn blue, temperature rises to high 60's. Clouds of bugs, including mosquitoes, rise out of the tundra flats.

2 P.M.—Skies turn gray, wind starts to honk, temperature drops like a stone.

5 P.M.—Temperature hovering at 20°F, wind howling. We pass on the evening ptarmigan shoot and opt for double chicken noodle soup and early bed. The cabin shakes and groans in the teeth of the gale.

The caribou are oblivious to the "squirrely" weather that almost constantly buffets this wild, lovely piece of real estate dominated by the 8,225-foot Mt. Veniaminof. They move in small groups and large bunches— thousands of animals migrating northward against a backdrop of dwarf birches and alders turning gold and russet in the early autumn. Even if a hunter misses the height of the Peninsula migration, as I did, he still has the opportunity to look over hundreds of animals and plan a stalk that will put him close enough to a trophy bull without spooking the animal's harem. It is a unique part of the North American hunting scene.

One comes into this country between bouts of weather in a Super Cub with a hot 150-horsepower engine and huge 30-inch, $3,000-a-set tundra tires, flown—"worn" is more accurate—by Keith N. Johnson, a master guide/outfitter who logs hundreds of hours in the fall flying everything from gasoline to granola, and especially caribou antlers and meat, plus hunters and guides, through his piece of the Peninsula.

Johnson's headquarters are at Wildman Lake, a speck on the aeronautical chart south of Port Heiden. This is grizzly bear country, and there is bear sign everywhere—half-eaten silver salmon along the riverbanks, miniature craters created by grizzlies digging for pikas, piles of crowberry-stained bear droppings.

At the dirt airstrip in Port Heiden, the attendant told us about a grizzly—a "teenager"—that had chased an Inuit girl who was riding her bicycle on the outskirts of town. The bear gave up after a while.

"Probably just a smart-aleck yearling griz acting curious, is all," Johnson said as I squeezed into the back seat of the Super Cub. On the dashboard behind the controls was a sign: *IF IN DOUBT, DON'T*. A few minutes later, flying on the deck—"If I get up higher than 400 feet, I get a nosebleed"—Johnson dropped the starboard wing so we could get a clear view of a big sow grizzly and her two cubs moving along the edge of a muskeg bog where thousands of ducks, geese, and swans took to the air at the sound of the approaching plane. On the far side of the bog, a wide beach sloped down to the Bering Sea. The black volcanic sand was crisscrossed with the tracks of grizzlies, big and small.

Johnson's outfitting area is strategically located; through it passes the bulk of the northern Peninsula caribou herd, some 20,000 to 25,000 animals migrating north to their wintering grounds near King Salmon. "The Peninsula herd consistently produces good trophy heads," says Johnson. "We've got mild weather, temperature-wise, long grazing and growing seasons, and lots of groceries, and all that equals big-horned caribou." The Number 13 barren ground caribou in the Boone and Crockett Club's *Records of North American Big Game*, an incredible set of antlers, was taken from one of Johnson's camps by Ken Higginbotham in October 1984. Johnson admits that's a selling point. . . .

"To my way of thinking, the real appeal of this country is the opportunity to study lots of game, try to pick the best head, and then make as perfect a stalk as possible," says Tom Hundley. "When the migration is at its peak, you can occasionally get out in front of a bunch of animals spotted from a distance. But forget about trying to catch up with them. A caribou's normal walking gait is roughly equivalent to that of a man running, and you can't run very far in spongy tundra with a rifle and a pack. Fortunately, a caribou bull stays so busy during the rut, rodeoing cows and trying to keep his harem together, that it's usually possible to make a good stalk if you dope out the situation correctly."

No small part of the challenge is judging the sheer mass of a big caribou bull's antlers, trying to sort out and separate points, shovels, length of top tines, antler spread, palmation, and so forth. All bull caribou look big, even after studying hundreds of animals through spotting scopes with an expert like Hundley providing the commentary—"decent left top, but kinda stinky on the right," "one decent shovel, but the other's just a dagger," "symmetrical rack but sorta puny. . . ."

"In the simplest terms, you look for big tops or wide, heavy main beams," says Hundley. "A good double shovel rack is very special, but a good single shovel will often outscore a double." Johnson's guides work hard to put their sports on bulls that score at least 350 B&C points, and most do better than that. It's a game of ambush, with lots of walking, glassing, and deciphering antlers, often through a spotting scope at great distances. And just when you see that "monster," Hundley looks, shakes his head and negates the deal quietly—"decent spread, but no height; gone by his prime, not a shooter."

As the hunt progresses, so do encounters of one sort or another with grizzlies. Sitting atop a bear dig that looks as if it had been excavated by a backhoe, we eat blueberries and glass small groups of feeding caribou. Five miles to the northwest, as the raven flies, the Bering Sea shimmers on the horizon. In the muskeg swamp to our east, turned crimson by the recent frosts, a big blond grizzly lies next to a caribou carcass he appropriated from Hundley and his last client, Dale Vander Yacht. They had shot the bull at twilight, taken the head and cape, and then, faced with a long hike back to camp in the dark, had opted to spend the night at the edge of the swamp. By morning the grizzly was already "working" the carcass, feeding on it heavily and then burying it.

So there was the blond bear in the swamp, another pretty big boar between us and the caribou we were studying through binoculars, and a sow and one cub working westward beyond the caribou. "Now look at this fellow coming up our trail," Hundley said. There was a boar of, oh, 800 pounds or so, moving up the cinder blow toward our grassy hummock. He didn't take our wind until he was within about 80 yards, and then he stood tall on his hind legs for a long moment before he loped away, cutting an impressive swath through the alder swale.

In the two days we spent hunting out of the Fracture Creek cabin, Hundley and I did not find the right trophy bull. But we did lose track of all the grizzly bears we saw. The second night in camp, while Radio Moscow extolled the good life in the Soviet Union, we feasted on sautéed mallard and ptarmigan breasts shot at dusk, and filleted for breakfast two nice Dolly Varden trout we caught in a tundra pond. About 2 A.M., something big enough to wake us both from a sound sleep bumped against the cabin wall. "You got four possibilities," Hundley said. "A caribou, a moose, a grizzly, or a Sasquatch throwing a full 50-gallon fuel drum. Course, the Sasquatch is just a sourdough's tale."

The next morning Johnson swooped in with the Super Cub and moved us to a tent camp in higher country. We flew across the muskeg swamp right over the blond grizzly, which was lying alongside his buried caribou. On the second pass, the bear rose up on his hind legs and pawed the air. Really. Over the roar of the engine, Johnson identified the bear as a mature grizzly pushing 1,000 pounds. "When a bear gets that big, he's not afraid of anything, including airplanes," Johnson shouted.

At first light on the following day, Hundley picked up a big white-maned bull grazing with an impressive group of ladies on a rolling stretch of wide-open tundra cropped as close as a well-tended putting green. It was a classic stalking situation, and we went for it immediately, gulping down a quick breakfast and then plunging down the mountain, across the valley, and up through a thick stand of birch and alders, flushing three big flocks of noisy ptarmigan and praying they wouldn't spook the bull's sentinel cows.

For almost 20 minutes we bellywalked uphill, pushing rifles out in front and dragging packs behind us, trying to press ourselves nosedown into the tundra. Finally we could see the tops of the bull's antlers shining in the sun against the snow-covered slopes of Mt. Veniaminof. But he was surrounded by alert cows, forcing us to backtrack downslope and try again from another angle. This time we found an opening through which I was able to shoot, using my pack for a solid rest. The .270 Nosler put the bull down, quickly. By the time we got to him, we could already hear the hoarse croaking of ravens flapping above us in the thermals, waiting to claim the carcass. The bears would not be far behind.

The weather was closing in when Johnson arrived in late afternoon to take the first load of caribou meat and the antlers, tied to the struts, back to the lodge. He returned for me and a second load of meat and then went back for Hundley. The wind was honking. Johnson has a sixth sense about the wind; he likes to be on the ground when the gusts reach 40 mph. He and Hundley made it back to the lodge, but it was close. By the time the plane was "tied for wind," there were gusts in excess of 50 mph.

"Remoteness and the weather are what keep this country unspoiled," Johnson says. "It's just too far from Anchorage (550 miles) for the weekend prop jockeys, and those who try it run the risk of weather and running out of gas, two pretty strong deterrents for a pilot." Another is the difficulty of finding a "runway"—a cinder blow or a short stretch of hard tundra—as well as a lee in which to pitch a tent so the wind can't get a real grip. "The wind and rain may be blowing sideways, but as long as you can stay warm in camp, cook a little, and dry your britches out, you'll be having fun," Johnson says.

In spite of the weather, you'd have to work at not having fun in this country, even after your bull is down. There is a late run of spawning silver salmon in the Ilnik River that tends to concentrate bears, mink, foxes, otters, gulls, eagles, and ravens. Dolly Varden trout, arctic char, and rainbow trout follow the salmon upriver, gorging on roe and milt. It is a tableau that fits the country and the visiting angler perfectly.

And there are flocks of ptarmigan, turning white as winter approaches, that flush from clumps of wildflowers called Eskimo cotton, and provide sporty wingshooting. Johnson will even tuck you into his Super Cub and set you down on the hard, black volcanic sand beach beside the Bering Sea, where you can wander among the grizzly tracks and the bleached whale and sea lion bones, scavanging Japanese glass fishing floats and watching seals feeding in the crashing surf.

Back at Wildman Lake, Keith Johnson will regale you with stories about bears and caribou and moose and salmon, and flying. The bear stories are fascinating; the flying stories make everyone laugh, nervously. Even when he is full stride into a story, Johnson keeps a weather ear cocked for the wind; when a strong gust buffets the lodge, he disappears outside to check the Super Cub.

Inevitably, someone will ask Johnson what is the single most important lesson he has learned from flying around the Alaska Peninsula.

"It's right there on my dashboard," Johnson shoots back.

IF IN DOUBT, DON'T.

November 1988

Brown Bear The Hard Way

BOB BRISTER

*They had killed the huge boar grizzly, and now, on the snowswept tundra,
its home and hide saved their lives.*

HAP MATHIS WAS breaking trail through a dense alder thicket
when suddenly he dropped to one knee and flipped the sling
of his .458 off his packboard in one swift, smooth motion.
A few yards ahead was something big and dark in the
brush. Instantly I had the two-power scope on it, and when I started laughing Hap looked around incredulously.

"It's no bear," I told him, "just a pile of dirt."

From our position, the mound looked almost exactly the size of a big,
dark Alaska brown bear. But Hap still wasn't laughing.

"Start backing up the way we came," he whispered. "Get to that
clearing over there, and be ready to shoot in a hurry if you have to!"

Backtracking uphill through dense alder bushes is not easy, and when
we finally made the clearing I pantingly demanded to know what all the excitement was about.

"If there had been a bear working on that new den in there, he just
might have showed you," the oldtimer grumbled. "You live around those big
devils forty years like I have and you just may change some of your Texas ideas
about bears. Two guides got killed not far from here a couple of years ago because they stumbled upon a bear working on his den. Both had rifles, too, and
got off a shot. But at the range we walked in on that den, one shot ain't likely
to stop a big bear in time."

He handed me his binoculars, and I could make out the dark hole in
the side of the steep, alder-thick ravine. The dirt around it was fresh, with
some huge tracks not yet covered by the light mixture of snow and rain
which had been falling all morning.

"Brownies are strange bears some ways," Hap mumbled around his ever-present pipe. "Let's just sit here a minute and see what happens. My judgment tells me there's a bear right here close someplace, and he's probably seen us close to his den. If so, he ain't gonna like it; a bear knows he's helpless when he goes into hibernation, and he just doesn't like the idea of any two-legged critters knowing where his hideout is. You see the size of those tracks in that fresh dirt?"

For half an hour we sat there, watching the alders and the slope below which led down to a gurgling, snow-fed creek called "Hot Springs." We were near the base of white-capped Mount Peulik on the Alaskan Peninsula some eighty miles from the little fishing town and U.S. Air Force base at King Salmon. On the other side of the mountain, nearly twenty miles away and a hard day's walk up and down dozens of brushy ravines and hummocks in the tundra, was our base camp—outfitter Ray Loesche's snug, isolated cabins on the shore of Lake Ugashik.

It had all started back in my home town, Houston, Texas, when one of my hunting partners, Houston architect Kenneth Campbell, invited Alaskan guide Ray Loesche and me to the same informal dinner at his home. Loesche was in Texas at the time booking hunts for the following year, and during the evening he mentioned a particularly big brown bear which he'd seen several times from the air in a little valley where no plane could land.

That sort of bear—and challenge—appealed to me. And in the comfort of Kenneth Campbell's living room I decided that backpacking in after an old monster that had been isolated for years would be a wonderful idea.

Now, shivering, wet to the skin, I pondered the radio reports we'd heard that morning of an incoming blizzard. In late October in that part of Alaska, we were asking for trouble.

Ray Loesche had not exactly liked the idea, but Hap Mathis, then his assistant guide, is an oldtimer in his 60's, a native of Alaska, and he helped me convince Loesche that it was a now-or-never situation; if the blizzard was very severe the bears would go into hibernation and the object of my hunt would be covered over in snow.

Hap and I packed bedrolls, food, a small tent, and some emergency rations. Even if we got holed in for a few days, we could walk in around the base of the mountain. With a little luck we could find that big boar of Hot Springs Valley and be on our way back before the bad weather ever hit. It all sounded so simple.

The walk in had taken almost all day because I'd persisted in stalking some caribou for pictures, and when we finally made Hot Springs Creek we were both tired and the weather was already starting to change. We'd stashed our heavy gear, including the food and bedrolls, in a little ravine near the creek and had gone on upstream looking for bear sign before making camp.

That was a bad mistake, and I made another when I killed more time by demanding to take pictures of the bear's den. Hap finally relented but first made me fire a couple of shots in the air to make sure the bear wasn't in there. The two shots reverberated up and down the valley—and nothing happened.

So we walked carefully down to the den and I realized just how large an Alaskan brown bear's winter residence can be. From the tracks, this was obviously a big boar, and Hap showed me how he'd selected the exact spot in the steep bank of the ravine where snow would pile up heaviest. Thus, the entrance would be protected through the winter by several feet of snow.

With gun shouldered, I eased into the gloomy interior, stopped to let my eyes adjust, and realized that the den enlarged to a circular "room" somewhat larger than the entrance. The bear had been working on it that day, judging from the loose dirt that fell on me every time I bumped the ceiling. It was still damp where his giant claws had scraped out earth and roots. Hap was outside clamoring for us to get started, and when I came out of the den I carefully flipped on the rubber scope cover to keep out the snow and rain.

We walked straight down to the creek, forced our way through the dense alders, and found we'd picked a spot too wide to jump. Hap went one way to look for a crossing, and I went the other.

I'd gone maybe 25 yards when there was a sudden, deep-throated "Wuuuff" and a huge, dark mountain of fur rose up above the alders. He was so close I could see his hair rippling in the wind, and in that split second he dropped down out of sight again and I could hear alders crashing.

Instinctively I'd flipped the rifle sling upwards and off the packboard, and took a precious second to clear the scope—all the time thinking I'd muffed my chance at the biggest bear I'd ever seen.

Then suddenly an alder swayed and the next instant a dark shape was crashing through like a freight train, heading straight for Hap. I filled the scope with brown hair and brush and shot, and with a roaring, snarling, ground-jarring crash the bear rolled and broke brush, biting at the wound. When he came up, as if in slow motion, I saw him turn and come for me, and the gun seemed to fire itself head on into the bulk of brown hair and exploding brush. He rolled like a monstrous ball into the opening beside the creek, snarling and biting at his shoulder, and in the same instant was up and coming again. The bolt worked, slammed shut, and I knew it would be the last time; I'd have to save the shot until I could put it between his eyes at pointblank range. With only the creek and 10 yards between us I could see nothing in the scope, could only point the gun as a shotgun, holding for his head. And as the gun bellowed the bear jumped the creek and I knew I'd hit low. But then he hesitated, shuddered, and slowly collapsed like a huge brown tent into the edge of the creek.

Hap came ripping through the alders, pipe smoking like a chimney, yelling and slapping me on the back. "By God, I never saw a bolt-action fired like a machinegun before;" he whooped, "and thank God for it . . . I couldn't shoot with the back of that fat Texas head in my sights the whole time!"

It was then, for the first time, I realized what had happened in that time lapse of seconds. The bear had apparently been in the thicket beside the creek, stalking us or perhaps just hiding and believing at the last moment we'd found him. At any rate he had charged Hap, giving me that first crossing shot, which apparently had been a good one. When he'd rolled and turned for me, I'd stepped to the right from behind an alder to shoot . . . and Hap said at that instant I almost lost the back of my head—he'd been already starting to squeeze off his .458 when I popped out in front of him.

We both sat down, shivering suddenly from the combination of excitement and cold, and it occurred to me that we were being rather confident. There was a giant bear lying less than ten steps away which hadn't yet been proven dead or alive. "Don't worry about that," Hap chuckled. "I saw the fur fly that last shot; you made a perfect neck shot, best there is on a bear that close. Who taught you to do that?"

I told him I'd held between the eyes and missed when the bear jumped, and he shook his head. "At that angle," he said, "you'd better be glad you missed; a bear's skull is thick and the slug might have glanced off with his head down and coming; lucky or not, you got him in the right place."

We eased up to the bear and Hap poked his eye with the .458. But it was all over. Judging from his position and the entrance holes of the bullets, my first shot had taken him in the shoulder, the second had gone through his leg and then into the chest as he rolled and roared coming up for me, and the third broke his neck. Neither of the first two would have stopped him in time, Hap decided.

"Look at those worn-down teeth," he whistled. "Now he's an old one for sure! See those porcupine quills in his lips and tongue? There's reason enough right there for him to be in a bad humor. He must have been having a tough time getting food to take on a porcupine."

I pulled open the huge jaws and saw that the bear had indeed been in pain; his teeth were worn down and rotting with cavities, and two big porcupine quills were imbedded in his tongue while several more quills stuck in his lips.

"But look at this if you want enough reason for him to be mad at two-legged critters," Hap was saying. On the side of his head the bear had a long, ugly bullet scar. The shot had creased his jaw, then plowed into the top of his back—just missing the backbone.

With a sudden chill I wondered whether that hunter is still alive. From the angle of the shot, the bear had to be coming head on. Had the shot turned him, or had this been the same giant bear that killed those two guides two years before? One of them had gotten off a shot.

"You better quit speculating about that other hunter and worry about us," Hap grumbled. "It'll be dark before we're done skinning him, and it ain't gonna be easy as you think to find our gear down there."

I offered to walk down the creek, find the equipment, and get a fire started so we'd have no trouble finding it. The snow was beginning to stick to the ground, and the thought occurred to me that it could cover our little spike camp in a matter of minutes. But Hap shook his head. "Your friend here will weigh close to 1,400 pounds," he said. "I can't turn him over to skin him by myself, and unless we get this hide off him right now, we'll never get it off. It's gonna be freezing on him as soon as his body heat leaves him."

Hap seemed maddeningly slow with the skinning and fleshing tools, but he reminded me that the more fat he could get off the hide the easier we could carry it out. "If I do a real good job," he puffed, "the hide will still weigh over a hundred pounds, maybe a hundred and a half."

When he finally rolled up the dark rug and lashed it to his packboard, I argued that I should carry it; Hap is twenty years my senior. But he grumbled that Texans know very little about Alaskan packboards, and puffing his pipe like a bandy-legged steam engine, he made the last moments of daylight count. It was pitch dark when we reached the bend in the creek near our spike camp, and Hap wasn't sure if it was upstream or down from us.

Rather than take a chance on getting separated in the dark, he kept the flashlight and stayed put to signal me back to him while I took off upstream looking for our tiny pile of equipment. I began falling through the ice of little swamps and stumbling into hummocks and holes in the tundra called "tules" until my legs began to get rubbery. Still no sign of the equipment. The falling snow had covered everything—it was a futile search.

When I gave up and turned to go back to Hap, I expected the wind to be at my back. It was the only reference point I had in the dark to maintain direction. Instead, it was blowing straight into my face. Was I lost that easily? Then I realized the wind had a different, ice bite to it. The blizzard had arrived, and instantly I knew Hap and I could be in serious trouble. We were both wet, and the weather forecast had called for the temperature to drop down to zero.

Snow began blowing almost horizontally with the rising wind, and I had trouble making out even the outline of the brush. I was tiring fast from the repeated falls and trip-ups in the dark. I fired a signal shot and listened; if I could get the exact direction to him some precious steps could be saved. For nearly five minutes there was no answering shot, and a sort of numb panic gripped me. Why didn't he answer? Was the wind so strong he couldn't even hear the rifle? All I had was a metal match to start an emergency fire, a couple of candybars, and a soaked-through parka that was beginning to freeze stiff on my back.

Then I heard the heavy boom of the .458 straight ahead. I lunged through the brush, falling and getting up again, and finally saw the beam of Hap's flashlight probing up against the clouds like a miniature searchlight. The old trapper and woodsman had known I probably couldn't see the flashlight because of the brush and the ridges, but I could see that beam against the low clouds and sky.

When I reached him, utterly exhausted, Hap was shivering on his knees, trying to start a fire. The wood was wet, now frozen, but he had used a hatchet to cut some of the larger alder trunks and then split them open to get the wood in the very middle of each tree. He had his "fire insurance," a two-inch stub of a candle, lit and had made a pyramid of shavings and tiny sticks. But every time the fire would try to flame up the snow would put it out.

I took off my parka and made a windbreak of it, using my body to shield the wind and the parka to keep off the snow. The tiny blaze flickered and with numbed fingers we tried to whittle more dry sticks. For the first hour the fire was only a smoking, smouldering hope. But finally it was large enough to begin drying out the larger limbs. I looked at my watch and it was almost midnight. We had seven more hours until there would be daylight enough to find our sleeping bags and food.

The exertion of fetching and chopping wood began to take more and more effort; the temptation was just to lie down and go to sleep. Twice the hatchet slipped out of my numbed fingers and once it glanced off the knee of my hip boot. How stupid can fingers be just because they are cold? I found myself talking out loud to them.

Our clothes had begun freezing on our backs, and we dragged the bear hide to the fire, thawed the leather thongs binding it to the packboard, and rolled it out on the ground, hair side up. Then we wrapped ourselves up in it together to utilize our combined body heat and the thick hide's insulation to break the cold.

I had begun shivering uncontrollably, which Hap said was because of the exhaustion of nearly three hours of stumbling in the snow and tundra hunting for our gear. He told me to try to sleep, and finally in the protection of the hide some of the shivering began to subside. I woke up sometime later, checked to see if the fire was still alive, and tried to get up to put more wood on it. I couldn't move at all!

Hap awoke with my movements and helped me rock the hide back and forth; we were mummies in a frozen bearhide for a moment or so, but then the hide cracked loose and we pryed it apart. The rest of the night we took turns chopping alder limbs, devoting half of them to the fire and the other half to building up a lean-to shelter for snow to bank against.

The wind kept howling higher, scattering our fire, so we began lying beside it on our sides to shield the fire and to warm one side while the other froze. Twice I got too close and the collar of my down jacket caught fire and burned my neck. I didn't realize it until I smelled. it.

When daybreak finally came, 2 feet of snow covered the ground and the odds of finding our food and equipment had gone down with the temperature. Nothing looked the same, and we were so tired there could be no staggering around with a 150-pound bear hide.

"We've got to find some kind of shelter," Hap decided. "We can't travel until this blizzard quits."

Then I thought of the bear's den. It was close, and it would be warm and big enough for both of us. Also, the carcass of the bear was close and it would certainly be enough to feed us. We left the hide by the remains of the fire and marked it by hanging my blaze-orange hiking pack atop a close-by alder bush. Then we walked across the ridge and found the den.

We were so cold we just walked in—probably too fast—but there was no bear, and for the first time we were protected from the wind. Instantly we started warming up and feeling better. Hap cut some wood and we made a fire at the entrance, then found there was enough of a chimney effect at the entrance that we could bring the fire inside. We moved several burning sticks in, and for the first time in hours got thoroughly, smokily warm.

Hap thawed the tough, red meat we'd hacked from the frozen carcass and we roasted it until it was burned on the outside. He said most bears have trichinosis, and the heat kills the germs. With or without germs, it was delicious; twenty-four hours had passed since we had eaten anything but a candybar each.

By midafternoon it was obvious the blizzard would be a two- or three-day affair and we'd have to spend another night. Shortly before dawn the wind changed, and we knew it immediately, because suddenly the den was full of smoke.

"We're rested and full of grub as we're ever gonna be," Hap decided. "Let's just go get that bear hide and start for base camp; longer we wait the deeper the snow's gonna be."

I asked about our sleeping bags.

"Hell with them," he grinned. "We'll mail yours to you next spring. We got all the load we can carry in this snow and the shape we're in now."

As soon as it was light we started out, and I was glad there were only a couple of feet of snow. Everything was covered over and it was like walking in the dark again; we couldn't see the holes in the tundra. I was also glad there were two of us; when one fell down the other could pull forward on his packboard to get him up again. Without help, I don't think either one of us could have made it.

Finally we cleared a ridge and could see the blue expanse of Lake Ugashik below. Our base camp cabins were tiny, dark dots against the snow. They looked close, but there were half a dozen creeks and ravines with steep, brushy sides to be crossed and we were getting very tired. Again I had that strange sensation of just wanting to lie down in the snow and go to sleep. We stopped to eat our last candybar and Hap developed leg cramps when he tried to get up with the bear hide. I switched packs with him and realized what a terrific load this 60-year-old man had been carrying all along. He had to be tough!

The last few hours are not clear; just an interminable expanse of snow, stopping to breathe on the ridges, wanting to lie down and sleep. Hap was worrying we couldn't make the cabins by dark, but I was too tired and cold to worry. We just kept walking.

Kenneth Campbell had been outside in the yard of the cabin making some pictures of the trophy moose rack he'd killed and happened to see us coming across the willow flats. Thinking we'd had our sleeping bags and food along, he started yelling and joking at us from a distance . . . and then he saw the looks of us.

Only a few yards away were those wonderful warm cabins, hot coffee, whiskey, and food. It was all over . . . that long, cold, hard night of the bear.

December 1971

Tenderfeet and Bears

RUSSELL ANNABEL

The ways of bruins can be mysterious to humans, and vice versa.

HOMESTEADERS, TROPHY HUNTERS, tourists and assorted tenderfeet going about their lawful occupations in the Northern wilds often assert plaintively that the ways of our Alaskan bears are whimsical and erratic to the point of outrageousness. I suppose they are quite right; I have felt the same way about the brutes. But in simple justice to the bruin tribe let me state that the animals must themselves be pretty dog-goned baffled by the antics of some of the humans they meet. Consider a little after-supper episode that took place last autumn at my backwoods headquarters in the Susitna Valley.

It was one of those pitch-black September evenings, with a scatter of high stars over the cottonwoods and the smell of snow on the wind whining off the ghostly loom of the Alaska Range. My wife Dell was doing the supper dishes and I was putting some new babiche filling in a pair of webs when we had a visitor. The chap's name was Sullivan. He was a burly black-Irish construction-camp foreman, fresh up from the States and eager to make friends. As he felt his way up the dark trail through the trees he was burdened with a portable phonograph, a stack of swing records and a layer cake he had wangled from his camp cook—all set for a convivial evening.

As Sullivan approached the cabin door a tall, indistinct figure emerged from the gloom and moved forward as if to intercept him. Naturally supposing it was I, the Irishman attempted to make conversation.

"Sure an' it's a black, threatenin' night," he observed heartily. "D'ye think it's gonna snow?"

"*Whuff-huff-whowff!*" the other rasped.

"H-how was that again?" Sullivan asked, stiffening. "I don't think I—"

"*Grrrr-RUFF!*" the bear promptly interrupted, popping his teeth like

217

a trap springing shut.

That was plenty for Sullivan. He burst through the door at such a wild, headlong gallop that he tripped over a chair and came down with a joist-shaking crash amidst the wreckage of the phonograph, the records and the layer cake. Although he had one leg through the rungs of the chair, he leaped up nimbly to gaze pop-eyed at the oblong of blackness beyond the open door and bellowed:"Bear! Shoot him, somebody, fer the love o' Hivin!" His entrance had been so violent and unexpected that Dell had dropped and broken a cherished willow-ware platter she was wiping, and our mop-headed sheep-dog puppy, Punkins, had shot under the couch, where she was now enjoying a noisy attack of hysteria.

Dell made the first rational remark. Grimly regarding the broken platter, she said, "If that fool bear scares another tenderfoot, I'm going to beat his ears off with a skillet."

I explained to Sullivan that the bear was just a fat, lazy oaf of a black, one of the dozen or more that made their homes along our creek; that the animal had formed the habit of coming to the cabin at night to forage for such food scraps as Punkins hadn't cleaned up; and that, while he was embarrassingly inquisitive and greedy, he apparently was harmless. This was lost on Sullivan; I might as well have saved my breath. The guy patently preferred to believe that he had escaped death or mutilation only by virtue of a superior set of reflexes. This had been his first encounter with a wild bear, and he wasn't going to be cheated out of his right to make something of it. Scraping cake frosting off his chin with one hand and gesturing dramatically with the other, he told us what had happened.

"There we stood in the dark," he said, "so close together that I could've spit in his eye, an' him growlin' an' gnashin' his teeth like the divil himself. Quick as a flash I realized—" It was the birth of another of the thousands of slam-bang man-meets-bear yarns that are now coming out of this wilderness, and I will bet that after a few rehearsals and some polishing it will be a honey.

The incident had its typical aspects. Four or five years ago, when unprecedented hordes of home-seekers, construction men, trappers, prospectors and ragtag-and-bobtail adventurers of all stripes began pouring into the Alaska wilds, a state of undeclared warfare developed between the newcomers and the bears of the Territory. Virtually every man who journeyed beyond the end of a village sidewalk carried a high-powered rifle and was filled with a mighty yearning to kill a bear.

To the old-timers, myself included, it looked as if the bears were going to take their final shellacking. We were about ready to write them off as a bloody sacrifice to that much discussed but seldom defined thing called progress. But to our astonishment, the bears did all right for themselves. While most of our other big-game species have rapidly worked backward toward the past tense—was—the bears have demonstrated an unsuspected ability to share their wilderness freeholds with humans and still keep their hides out of drying frames.

Of course, their enemies continue to increase; there actually are powerful political lobbies that seek their extermination—a matter I will discuss later. But the bears' talent for surviving the encroachments of civilization also seems to be increasing. It now looks as if they will be around for a long, long time.

There are today around 20,000 giant brown and grizzly bears and 75,000 blacks in the Territory—which makes Alaska the only country under the sun in which the bruin population outnumbers the permanent human population. As can be imagined, with such a number of temperamental bears using the salmon streams, berry patches and pea-vine meadows along with an army of gun-toting tenderfeet, some rare bits of guerilla activity occur. It is a dour and unimaginative chechako indeed who, returning to town from a sojourn in the wilds, doesn't have a choice collection of hair-raisers to tell about bears.

One result is that the black bear is fast becoming legendary as a camp-thief and cache-robber who could teach even the wolverine some tricks. The newcomers are just finding out what woodsmen always knew— that the black is a burglar by birth, training, preference and ancient tribal custom. They are discovering that he has larceny in his heart from the day of his birth, and would rather risk his pelt to steal a meal than gain one honestly fishing salmon or grubbing roots—and that in most cases he gets away with it.

For example, there was an incident that took place during a sheep hunt which Tex Cobb and I made in the Chugaches with Harvey Wells, a recently arrived Government employee.

A rainstorm of near cloudburst violence had caught us at timber-line and forced us to take shelter for the night in a temporarily abandoned prospector's cabin. It was the usual high-country set-up: a little sod-roofed cabin on a strip of tilted red-top meadow above a tumbling creek; a stilt-legged Siwash cache in the dooryard, the logs weathered to the whiteness of bone; some brush dog shelters; a tunnel in the mountainside with a trail leading up to it.

While Harvey inspected the cache and speculated as to what kind of ore the prospector had hoped to find in the bowels of the mountain, Tex and I rustled wood and water, built a fire in the rusted Yukon stove, cleaned the squirrel and porcupine dung off the table and shelves, and cooked supper. Rain continued to roar on the roof, a steady, battering torrent, cold and dispiriting, without a break in the leaden clouds, as if it were the beginning of a second deluge.

When I woke at daybreak next morning, it was still raining. I was wondering whether I should get up and build a fire or declare a holiday and stay in bed another hour when there was a sudden, heavy, inexplicable thump in the yard. I woke Tex and Harvey, who sat up in their bunks, listening. Presently the thump was repeated, and this time was followed by a hoarse, hog-like grunting. The three of us hit the floor simultaneously, eased across the room, and stepped outside. After one look I wished I had crawled under my bunk instead, for the scene out there in the rainswept clearing was such a one as nobody ought to have to behold while standing barefoot and in his underwear in a cloudburst before breakfast.

A bear—a big, glossy, shanty-rumped black—was looting the cache. Harvey had carelessly left the pole ladder leaning against the front of the structure, and the bear had climbed it and managed to claw the door open. Working with one paw while he held on with the other, he had thrown out a sack of sugar, a bale of moose jerky, a keg of salt, salmon bellies and two cases of 60 per cent dynamite. At the moment he held a third case of dynamite under one foreleg and was about to drop it on top of the others.

We stood rooted to the ground in a paralysis of horror. The dynamite was venerable stuff that had been frozen and thawed so many times that its paper covering had absorbed the nitroglycerine, making it dangerous no matter how carefully it was handled. In fact, powder like that will sometimes explode when two sticks of it are pulled apart, as the ghosts of a good many miners would ruefully testify.

"Fer Gawd's sake," Tex bawled, presumably on the theory that in the circumstances anything was worth a try, "don't drop that! Put hit back!" The final exclamation point stuck in his epiglottis.

Startled silly, the bear let out a moan and jerked around to face us so violently that he overbalanced the ladder. With the case of dynamite still clutched under his arm, the unhappy beast rode the ladder desperately as it swung outward in a slow, teetering arc. Tex, Harvey and I took off. The laws of gravity and momentum being what they are, we didn't have much time to hunt cover, but we made the most of what we had. Neck and neck, we plunged over the ten-foot creek bank into a flooded devil's-club patch and flattened ourselves among the thorns.

I heard the ladder crash down across the woodpile, and heard the bear emit a bawl of pain and protest. Then there was silence save for the sound of something rolling briskly down the slope toward us. This object proved to be the case of dynamite. It tumbled over the bank, caromed off a rock, and came to rest among the devil's-club ten feet distant. Tex took his hands from over his ears. Harvey swallowed hard, obviously trying to force his heart back into position. I started breathing again.

Back at the cabin, while we were helping one another pick out thorns, Harvey said, "But why would a bear steal dynamite?"

"Son, hit goes like this," Tex informed him somberly. "All bears are teched; an' to figger out why they do the things they do, a man would have to be as teched as they are, which ain't possible."

That bears have a proprietary attitude toward their favorite salmon-fishing riffles, and actively resent being interfered with on them, is a fact that many a tenderfoot has lately discovered. As a case in point, take something that happened two years ago during a hunt that "Starvation" Smith and I tried to make with a hay-and-feed dealer named Bill Jackson. We were back-packing into the Talkeetnas for moose, and had made our second camp at the upper forks of Goose Creek when the hunt blew up like a pup tent in a tornado.

The trouble began when Jackson, a man with no luck at all, bit into a .22 bullet embedded in a piece of fried spruce-grouse breast and split one of his molars to its roots. The resulting toothache was such a blazing, four-bell horror that the poor dude spent the night pacing back and forth, wringing his hands and groaning. Starvation, worried and sympathetic, offered to try to pull the tooth with a pair of pliers he carried for skinning fish and de-quilling dogs, but Jackson waved him away with a shudder.

"Just get me out of here," he moaned. "Head for the nearest dentist, and don't stop until you plant me in that chair."

We broke camp in the first light and took a short cut back to the railroad. Eleven hours later, having spent the day floundering through sundry bogs, blowdowns, birch jungles and beaver swamps, we reached the railroad at the mouth of the creek a few minutes before the biweekly southbound passenger was due. Since it is necessary to flag the train when you want it to stop between stations, Starvation and I left Jackson at the bridge with our gear and hurried up the track to a point where the engineer and fireman couldn't fail to see us. We could already hear the train in the distance and were congratulating ourselves, as we got out our bandannas for the flagging operation, on having made such a timely connection.

Meanwhile, unbeknown to us, strange things were happening back at the bridge. As Jackson told it later, he was pacing the bridge ties, holding his throbbing jaw and wondering if the pain was going to drive him nuts, when he saw something flopping below him on the grassy creek bank. It was a salmon, a bright, fresh-run silver. This was so extraordinary, as the fish was a good ten feet from water and there were no anglers visible on the stream, that Jackson said he thought at first his agony was causing him to see things that weren't there.

Presently, however, pulling himself together, he concluded that it was a fine, fat fish, no matter how it had gotten there, and that it shouldn't be wasted. So he hastened down the bank, clubbed the salmon to death with a piece of driftwood, and turned to go back up to the track with it. At this juncture, behind him, the backwoods quiet was abruptly shattered by a roar with enough decibels in it to lift a man's hat. Jackson said he did a double-take, and felt a deep freeze start at his belt buckle and work south.

The grizzly that had risen on his hind legs out of the frosted red-top, he said, looked as wide as a barn door and half as tall as the trees. Starvation and I later recognized the animal from his description. He was a shaggy, sinful old scoundrel, well known in these parts: genuinely big, about a nine-footer, with a sinister mask-like brown patch across his muzzle and a pelt bleached by time and weather to the color of oat straw. An ancient bear, a patriarch in the valley, he had probably fished here each summer since cubhood—since before the railroad was built—and so wasn't disposed to let himself be shoved around without at least expressing his sentiments. No doubt he had caught the silver salmon shortly before our arrival, and had been lying in the grass guarding it when Jackson came down and appropriated the fish. I imagine he thought, with reason, that if Jackson wanted a salmon he ought to go catch one.

Anyway, Jackson didn't need 20-20 vision to see that he was in a bad spot. He left the fish hanging in the air and fled at top speed in the direction he happened to be facing, which was straight out across the 50-foot-wide creek. A moment or two later the passenger train arrived. Starvation and I loaded our gear aboard and then, aided by the conductor and brakeman, began looking for Jackson. When we sighted the dude, he was just making a landing, churning in to a brushy cut-bank with a vigorous six-beat crawl, 150 yards downstream.

The conductor held the train while he made his way up through a wild-rose jungle to the track. I don't think I have ever seen an angrier pilgrim or heard more inspired profanity. He had lost his hat, barked his shins on a rock, got water in his ears and thorns in his hands, and was shivering and out of breath and mad at himself, us, and the entire race of grizzly bears.

"Yer toothache," Starvation said wonderingly as Jackson stalked past us to the coach steps, "musta got better, huh?"

Jackson paused in the middle of a complicated apostrophe to grizzly bears and their ancestors all the way back to the Pleistocene, glared briefly at us, and growled, "What toothache?" and I still think he actually had forgotten all about it.

As I said, almost every tenderfoot in Alaska nowadays has a bear yarn or two to tell, and many of them should be preserved for posterity. But there was a fighter pilot named Les Willard up here three years ago who had an experience which, for special rib-tickling reasons, tops any I have come across to date. "Beluga" Johnson and I had taken Willard down Cook Inlet in June for a week of king salmon and eulachon fishing, and were making our headquarters at Beluga's cabin.

On this particular afternoon Beluga and I had busied ourselves digging a sack of razor clams while Willard did battle with the giant kings that were hanging around the mouth of a near-by freshwater slough. Toward evening, our clam-digging having been halted by the incoming tide, Beluga and I headed up through the sawgrass to start supper. Willard saw us come off the mudflats and yelled that he would join us as soon as he licked the king salmon he was fast to, or busted his tackle, or was pulled off the bank. It had been a fine day, and Beluga and I were commenting gratefully on how well the weather and the fish had cooperated when we came in sight of the cabin. Beluga gazed in silence for a moment, then groaned as if he had been stabbed through the liver. Hitching up his boots, he made for the cabin at a lumbering, ding-toed lope.

"As our friend the pilot would say," he gritted over his shoulder, "we hev been foiled by the fickle finger o' fate."

You could tell at a glance from a distance of fifty yards that the cabin had been raided by bears. Closer inspection revealed that the culprits were a pair of brown bear cubs, yearlings. The two must have had previous experience, because this was no mere amateurish job. They had pulled down shelves, broken open grub containers, overturned the table, smashed the kerosene lamp, and bitten holes in my waders. They had ripped Beluga's sleeping bag to tatters and scattered the feathers like a snowdrift, eaten a gallon of hot-cake syrup, and tipped over and spilled a drum of green boat paint. On past occasions cubs of various species of bear had wrecked my camps, but few had been as thorough and workmanlike as this pair of juvenile delinquents.

A half hour later, as Beluga and I were glumly cleaning up the debris and wondering how beans would taste flavored with green boat paint, Willard came sprinting up the trail. He was red-faced and excited, panting as if he had used up all the oxygen for yards around.

"For gosh sakes, I just saw the damnedest thing!" he shouted when he was still a stone's throw distant. "You wouldn't believe it! Two little bears passed me on the beach, right back there"—he gestured with his casting rod to show us where—"and one of them was green and the other had white feathers growing all over its head."

You can't blame newcomers for getting the eerie feeling now and then that the bears are the ancient gentry up here, temporarily out of power but organizing for a comeback. The attitude of the big beasts toward humans is a bizarre mixture of resentment and habitual arrogance tempered by the timidity which high-powered rifles inspire. They look at you menacingly, seemingly remembering the old days when they bossed the trails and the miserable spear-armed savages were delighted to give them all the room they wanted. You get the impression that it gripes their guts to run from you, and that they'd almost, but not quite, rather try to bat your head off and accept the consequences. They seem free of a persecution complex only when they are clowning, putting on a show for themselves and such witnesses as may be on the scene. As an example of their flair for buffoonery, take something that Tom Wilson and I saw a pair of grizzlies do one morning at Brooks Lake, down on the Alaska Peninsula.

I had flown to the lake with Tom to prove to him that, in the stream connecting the two lakes, 30-inch rainbows are common and that a competent, hard-working angler can count on taking 36-inchers. We landed toward mid-afternoon and fished until dark, then went down to the mouth of the unnaturally clear, sedge-bordered stream and made camp on the wide beach of the lake. Tom had already hooked, fought and beached or lost so many big fish that he had the equivalent of a Charley horse in his right arm, but he made me promise to wake him at daybreak so that he could get in a full day along the stream tomorrow. It turned out, however, that it wasn't necessary for me to wake him. The aforementioned pair of grizzlies took care of that detail.

The sun had just topped the peaks when a basso profundo roar and a wild splashing in the water jerked us upright in our sleeping bags. The bears were on the beach about a hundred yards distant, scuffling at the water's edge—wrestling, belting each other around, and roaring happily, like a pair of spring cubs. They were at least eight-footers, with beautifully matched pelts, very dark brown and thick, each pelt set off spectacularly by a broad streak of light yellow, a sort of mane, that reached from the ears back over the shoulder humps. As Brooks Lake is in Katmai National Monument, the animals were of course protected; so Tom had to content himself with enjoying their performance. All in all, it was quite a performance, with a climax to make your eyes bug out.

After an exchange of playful roundhouse swings, any one of which would have folded a man up like an accordion, the nearer bear ran across the beach to a boulder—it was a sizable boulder, about the size of an apartment refrigerator—and pretended to take shelter behind it. The other bear pursued him, whiffing in simulated rage, his big flat feet making the loose gravel fly. Whereupon the first bear picked the great rock up and flung it a dozen feet through the air. The rock struck and rolled, and both bears lunged after it, keeping it rolling for some distance along the beach by slapping it, like a pair of kids banging a basketball around.

Tom blinked and shook his head as if to clear his vision. "I don't believe it," he said. "It ain't so. An elephant couldn't toss that rock around."

It was a gag, all right, but a good one. When the bears had moved on about their business, we pulled on our shoes and wasted no time in going up the beach to examine the rock. It proved to be a chunk of pumice that had been spewed up by one of the many volcanoes in the area. I could lift it myself. In fact, it floated when we rolled it into the water. But it had been a marvelous prop for the bears' act. With a little stretching of the imagination, you could almost believe that they understood its value as such.

Sportsmen in the States will no doubt be startled to learn that there are politically potent groups in Alaska that have tried long and earnestly to bring about the extermination of the Territory's brown bears. The first of these was a group of ranchers on Kodiak and lower Cook Inlet who sought to have the animals outlawed and a bounty placed on them, claiming that they were killing stock. Fortunately this attempt met such vigorous opposition, spearheaded by Stewart Edward White, that the ranchers were glad to drop the matter. Now, however, another and more serious effort is being made to get the bears classed as vermin and destroyed, this time by the salmon-canning interests.

A memorial to Congress was introduced in the last session of the Territorial legislature stating that brown bears eat salmon on the spawning grounds and so are a "continuing factor in the face of ever smaller salmon runs." Some thoroughly screwball statistics are cited in an effort to show that more than 31 per cent of the salmon in the streams are destroyed by brown bears before they have opportunity to spawn. Opponents of the bill countered with the argument that, inasmuch as there are approximately one billion pounds of salmon in the streams at spawning time and only around 6,000 bears in the area, each bear, including cubs, would have to kill daily more than 1,000 pounds of fish.

Ridiculous as the whole thing sounds, it should be remembered that these same interests once succeeded in getting a bounty of 1½ cents per tail placed on trout in Alaska, and kept the fish outlawed for a number of years at taxpayers' expense, simply because they eat salmon eggs and it was feared they were a menace to the annual runs. Also it should be recalled that, despite the protests of ornithologists all over the nation, these same people lobbied for, and obtained, a bounty on the American eagle, their argument being that the eagle was a fearsome threat to all salmon!

What has been done to the trout and the eagles could conceivably be done to the brown bears if sportsmen and conservationists fail to keep an alert eye on the strange political maneuvers in this part of the world.

The way the sourdoughs feel about the bears up here, it is anybody's privilege to cuss the brutes and make dire threats to their continued existence; among some of us this is one way of blowing off steam after finding a cache robbed or a cabin looted. However, we certainly don't want anybody to become overwhelmed by their eloquence to the point of sponsoring legislation against bears. Because, aside from their tourist appeal and other important economic and esthetic considerations, the bears add a color and interest to the wilds that no other beast could supply. The back country would be very dull indeed without them. Besides, the incoming armies of tenderfeet wouldn't feel that they were on an authentic frontier if they didn't get into a brangle with a bear now and then.

You could ask Elmer Brown. Elmer is a homesteader, an ex-mathematics professor and a tenderfoot among tenderfeet—a veritable type specimen of his kind. He came north last year with his wife Marge, filed on 160 acres of birch bottom land, and managed to erect a two-room house before the first frosts. Naturally, he wanted to follow local custom and kill a fat bull moose for his winter's meat; he confessed he had been daydreaming about it all summer. So, one September day when the birches had turned yellow and the snow-line was creeping down the peaks, Tex Cobb and I went out with him and helped him find a good one, and then aided him in dressing out the carcass and carrying it to the cabin. As it was too late to go home when we had finished, we accepted Elmer's invitation to spend the night.

Punkins was with us, and around nine o'clock, when Mrs. Brown was getting out a late supper for us, the pup bounded up suddenly and went over to the door, growling. Before Tex or I could stop him, Elmer opened the door and let the dog out. Pandemonium instantly ensued in the yard. It was a dark night, but the sift of starlight was strong enough to reveal a medium-sized bear, apparently a black, walking across the yard on his hind legs and carrying a quarter of Elmer's moose meat.

Punkins was raging about the animal, squalling her head off. She had the bear at a disadvantage, because to strike back at her he would have to drop the moose meat, which he obviously did not want to do. He must have realized, however, that his position was so tactically unsound that his life was in peril, for he presently made what he apparently regarded as a compromise move—he dropped the meat and sought refuge where he could watch it.

"Where is he? Where'd he go?" Elmer shouted, dashing out of the door with his moose rifle.

"Well, you can believe it or not," Tex said, "but he's on top o' yer house."

The bear, with Punkins yelling at his heels, had fled around behind the house, where he had leaped onto the roof of a low shed in which Elmer stored his tools, and from there had climbed to the peak of the house itself. Elmer lined his .30/06 as best he could in the darkness, and blazed away. The first shot went into the attic, but the second gave the bear a mortal wound. Falling backward, the animal rolled down the farther side of the roof, clawing off a sheet of tarpaper, breaking the radio aerial, and knocking off the stovepipe as he did so. He landed rump first in a hogshead that Elmer had placed under the eaves for a rain barrel. I had dimly heard stovepipe clatter down inside the house as well as outside, and now a cloud of smoke came billowing through the open door.

Mrs. Brown shouted; "Elmer, I think the house is afire! Bring some water!"

"I can't, dammit," Elmer shouted back desperately. "The rain's in the bear barrel—I mean, the barrel's in the bear rain—aw, use the fire-extinguisher."

Well, the house wasn't afire, and by midnight we had the stovepipe back up, the radio aerial repaired, and the bear carcass hung up with the moose meat. I sort of gathered that Marge Brown was pretty dismayed by it all, but Elmer said it was absolutely the best day of his life. It was just exactly, he said, the sort of frontier fun he had hoped to find when he quit teaching kids about logarithms and came north.

Which is what I meant about tenderfeet and bears. They are naturals together, like hot dogs and mustard. I hope we always have plenty of both around.

April 1950

Where Trees Grow
Too Close Together

KEITH McCAFFERTY

The ruined shed was little bigger than a coffin, and before the night was over it might become one.

THE GRIZZLY BEAR is believed to be among the few mammals besides man which commonly dies in its sleep. Winter takes it in the end, although its fate is not that of deer shrunk to skeletons by March, nor of bighorns drowned by avalanche. It may be that a bear nearing the end of life takes to its den early one fall, and pulling up winter for its funeral shroud, lies entombed there forever.

In the Rocky Mountain West, the grizzly has made its final stand in a handful of retreats: in Yellowstone National Park, in a slender finger of Canada's Selkirk Range that juts into Washington, and in the high country of northwestern Montana, principally Glacier National Park and the Bob Marshall Wilderness. Some grizzly researchers believe the last bear to grace this country will leave its skull in a den in the Bob Marshall Wilderness, and that its bones will be finished by the rodents in time for our generation to be the voice of its history.

In the Bob Marshall Wilderness native trout teem in three forks of the Flathead River; green, transparent races of water that vein a vast roll of mountains where every other feature of land has been named for its bears: Silvertip Mountain, White Bear Creek, Grizzly Gulch.

This area used to be a favored hunting ground of timber wolves. A few can still be heard in its forests. It also was the winter haunt of pine marten trappers, just of few of whom remain.

The marten trappers were a colorful lot who defended individual creek drainages as vigorously as did the old boar grizzlies that ransacked their camps. Like the bears, they were victims of progress, finished four decades ago by Russian sable farms that exported domestic furs thickened in Siberia.

Blackened scars where traps were notched into the trunks of trees blemish the older stands of lodgepole pine in the Bob Marshall to this day. Tiny log cabins the trappers built are less noticeable. Most have returned to the forest floor, although a scattering still stand, banked back into the sides of ridges for insulation. These "cabins" were little larger than coffins, and the trappers heated them with body heat. They remain as testament to a hard way of life that has all but disappeared from this country.

This is a story told by one of the last marten trappers. He is my age, thirty, but already an old hand in the wilderness. He has run a trapline up the headwater tributaries of the South Fork of the Flathead River since he was seventeen years old.

Shortly before I met him, the trapper had the misfortune of stepping on one of the decaying, nail-quilled bear doors that are strewn about various cabins constructed by the Forest Service for backcountry rangers. I had come into the Bob Marshall with a party of three to measure the spring snowpack for government records. We had traveled 90 miles by snow cat to the wilderness boundary, and gone on skis from there. The last 2 miles of the 20 we skied trailed the lopsided dinosaur waddle of snowshoe tracks. I knew whoever was up ahead had a bad left foot.

The trapper, hunched under the bulk of his pack, looked like he had journeyed to this place from somewhere considerably farther north. He had tangled hair down to his coat collar, a winter's growth of thin beard, a hawk nose. He was not a big man, yet his handshake brought blood to the tips of my fingers. His eyes, clear and green, moved as deliberately and as carefully as his speech, which sounded like that of an older man.

"I don't want to make trouble for you," he said. But he said he had been on the bad foot for a week, and the pain which radiated from the deep puncture the nail made grew worse by the hour. The nearest passable road was still on the far side of a broad belt of mountains that avalanched frequently this time of year. This was no small predicament, and the trapper well knew it.

Our party had the key to an outpost ranger cabin that sat over the river on a bench of timber, near the junction of the South Fork with Big Salmon Creek. We had to dig out the door through 3 feet of snow. The mattresses hung up under the ceiling in looping hammocks of rope. On the slab pine floor the mousetraps were all long sprung and the mice collected in them had rotted away, leaving miniscule skeletons, puffs of fur, and threads of tails.

We walked around inside like crabs on blistered feet, banging the pots for our supper. The trapper sat beside a big barrel wood heater, his boots and stag shirt dripping off 60-penny nails driven into the log center beam, his foot soaking in a dishpan of melted snow.

There is an unspoken code in the backcountry that no one broaches the subject of grizzly bears until a suitable interval has passed. To speak of the grizzly too soon is a sign of insecurity. We had pumped up a lantern going into that night. But the circle of light dimmed considerably before we heard the trapper's story.

He said that years ago, a grizzly bear stole an elk he had shot for winter meat. That fall he was guiding elk hunters for an outfitter who took a string of mules up the South Fork of the Flathead. The outfitter packed out Thanksgiving week, hurrying to beat the snow out of the mountains. He left the guide his best wishes. For the trapper it would be his first winter alone in the wilderness.

The bear raided the trapper's camp the following week. It took a beaver he'd left lying on top of a skinning table; stuck its head inside the tent flap to get it. It jerked the elk out of the tree where it hung nose up with a rope around its antlers. The trapper had slept through the night; he read the story in the snow in the morning. He followed bear tracks to the river. It was a grizzly all right, its long claws biting into the snow inches from the impressions of the feet. Under a heaping of branches the trapper found the torn, bloodied carcass of the spike bull elk. He caught himself staring at a heap of dung that spread a brown pillow in a pool of water isolated from the current of the river.

The bear had crossed the river and lumbered up a steep slope of lodgepole. An hour later, still following but long after the weightless feeling of his purpose had dissipated in fear and sweat, the trapper for one long moment let his mind float away from the odor that tainted the forest in the grizzly's wake. This time the sight was of his sagging tent, far below on the opposite bank, and in a clearing the reddened trough in the snow the bear had made dragging the elk to the water's edge.

He had just gained the ridge when he turned to look back. In that moment the bear, which must have been lying in the shintangle, rose to its height. The trapper later recalled that when the bear put its nose on man scent the hair of its thick neck rose like a cat's. And he had heard the hissing of his own hair as it stood against the crown of his hat.

Then in an instant the bear was down on fours, bulling through the matchstick lodgepole and gone out of sight over the ridge. The trapper never hesitated. He turned and ran, dodging through the close trees in the thicket, coming off the mountain in a flood of adrenalin to lurch against the river and stagger to the giddy safety on the opposite bank. He sat down, sucking air. His Springfield rifle was held in gripped fists, at the ready, forgotten at his moment of opportunity.

With little forethought and no real experience the trapper had set out to kill a grizzly bear. "It was the rug," he would say. "I'd always wanted a grizzly bear rug." And a little of the morning's instant courage lingered even after retreat, a thrilling, insane urge to bend once more to the tracks.

But it had been foolhardy to take a bear to task in such tough country. The trapper knew it. He faced the fact that whatever return of confidence he enjoyed with the sun up and the bear gone would desert him utterly at the close of day.

Downriver an old plank shed had weathered the snows of too many winters. There were the remnants of a corral; a few crossed logs deteriorating over the cleared ground. The trapper had this shed in mind as he heaved at the corpse of the elk. Even with its hindquarters eaten the elk was a burdensome animal which hugged the snow as the trapper worked. It took hours to move it to the higher ground. He finally dropped it outside the shed's solitary window, a black, square hole that had been crudely barred with twisted strands of barbed wire in an attempt to keep out the bears of a former era.

Quickly the trapper retraced his steps to the tent. He packed his backpack with food, sleeping bag, lantern. He had a side of bacon for cooking grease and he packed it. Upon his return to the shed he pried a nail from a plank of wood, and stepping on top of his elk for height, nailed the bacon outside and just over the top of the window.

He figured to fire on the bear soon as it stood up to take down the bacon.

It was either a brave or foolish thing to have done. But at the time the trapper felt certain the bear would return, if not that night the next, and it would keep returning until one of them was dead. He dreaded this uncertainty as much as he feared the bear.

The shed itself offered little protection against a grizzly bear. The trapper had to prop the door with axed sections of a lodgepole snag just to keep it from falling in the wind. Inside, he sat on a cut stump, facing the door. He drank coffee he made over a fire built on earth exposed by some charred floorboards. There were blackened rings where others had built fires inside this tinderbox. It was not something to make a practice of, but the trapper knew how desperate men could be in this country.

The stars came out; they shone through the window and separations in the shed walls. He thought the stars were peculiarly beautiful; remembered precisely how they had appeared to him. He fell asleep looking at them.

When he woke up the stars were gone. The night was black and the river which murmured him to sleep, despite the coffee, had a new cadence he sought to place. The window over his head was a solid square. It was blacker than the room. The trapper did not move once his eyes opened; nor did he take his eyes from the window. Breath, not wind, blew in through the window, and the trapper, wide awake, felt his body break into sweat.

He had fallen asleep with his hand on his rifle but the trapper did not dare lift it. He feared that the slightest movement on his part would trigger the bear, there all along, so close he could have touched it with an outstretched arm.

Many minutes passed. Then abruptly the tiny shed flooded with starlight and the trapper heard a heavy dragging noise as the bear moved the elk away from the window. A bone cracked outside the shed door. The grizzly began to eat, 6 feet of air and 1 inch of wood from the ridiculously small hole at the muzzle of the rifle which now swung like a compass needle to every snuffing grunt, every underwater rumbling of the bear's great belly.

Now the trapper only wanted it to be over. He pointed his rifle at the window during maddening periods of silence. Hours passed; the trapper wondered if the bear had forgotten the bacon. Then there was lingering quiet. The trapper heard the bear's heavy tread. The light went out of the window.

In the confined quarters of the shed, the report of the rifle was deafening. The trapper threw the bolt of the Springfield, his finger on the trigger. But there were no clues at all. The sky framed the window as it had before. The river murmured through the vast emptiness of the night, smothering all sounds from the forest.

At dawn the trapper removed the braces from the door. Out on the snow was his elk, a torn drag of spine with mangled flaps of skin fanned over its bones like a wedding train. Even the head was missing. (The trapper found it later in a clump of aspen saplings, tossed many feet apparently, for no tracks approached the trees.) A riot of snow showed the path the bear had taken to the river after his shot. Above the window the slab of bacon was still nailed to the shed. Below it the huge tracks of the hind feet cut deeply and the snow had iced under them.

The trapper didn't have to look far to see what happened. The bullet had cut a hole in the braided strands of wire crossing the window. He looked for cut hair, speckles of blood, and found nothing to indicate that the bear had been hit. The trapper imagined his bullet must have deflected enough to miss it entirely.

Once again he found himself standing at the river. On the far bank he could see where the bear had shaken itself before entering the forest. This time the trapper allowed himself no illusions of following.

The bear never returned. The trapper stayed the winter, but moved back into his tent only when he felt sure that the grizzly had gone to its den. The trapper caught beaver until the river froze in its backwaters. He continued to take marten in the creek bottoms through March, when their lustrous chocolate fur began to thin and lose its value. Then he wrapped his Springfield in the fabric of his tent and pitched it high in a tree, where it would stay safe until his return the following fall.

Ten years passed. The trapper never did get his rug. In fact, he said he didn't see much sign of grizzly bears anymore. He said he wouldn't shoot one now if he had the chance.

"But that was a real silvertip," he said, "a really big bear. I'll never forget him."

So that was the story.

Like the best of stories it had been unexpected, and I don't believe there was a man among us who did not wish it was his story to tell, who was not reminded of probings into wilderness which paled in comparison. No doubt we all seek places where the air is soured by bears and trees grow too close together.

In the morning we saw the trapper off. He said he could make it back downriver to the wilderness boundary on snowshoes. We'd catch up in a day or two, then we'd all ride the snow cat to Hungry Horse where a doctor could attend to his foot.

In the interim there was our work, my part of it being to ski to the inlet of Big Salmon Lake where I hoped to find open water and perhaps a cutthroat trout or two for our supper. Part of the trail wound up from the river, passing through a thicket of lodgepole pine. In the thicket, shafts of light escaped through the tree trunks, striping the snow abstractly.

"Trees no bigger around than that," the trapper had said, making a circle with his thumb and finger to describe a country where his hair stood on end. Now, it seemed to me a measure of grizzly bears that you felt their presence even when snow covered the dens, the graves in a foretold future.

I cast out, and while the fly settled and the rings spread from the center of the pool to the ice at its edges, I searched among the trees on the shoreline for any sign of movement.

September 1984

When the Eiders Flew

C. E. GILLHAM

On the Bering coast, survival for man and beast rode with the sea ducks gliding out of the pale sky.

W E CROUCHED BEHIND great ice slabs piled up on the shore by the Bering Sea, and I noticed that Toolgak, my Eskimo companion, was shivering in the blasts of wind out of Siberia, almost due west. When an Eskimo shivers there's a reason, and in Toolgak's case it was starvation. Beneath the clothing that made him look as round as a gasoline drum was a torso weighing less than 110 pounds. I shivered too, though I was wearing two-piece cashmere underwear that had set me back twenty-eight bucks, and over it pants and parka of feathers topped by a windbreaker.

The month was March, but no ice had moved and there were no leads of open water from which seal or walrus could poke their heads. Except for a lone white-fronted goose that we'd seen three days earlier, not a living creature stirred in the Alaskan Arctic. Our hope of obtaining food had long since dwindled, and as we crouched there I bitterly reviewed the sequence of events that had brought me to this pass.

Only a short time before, the Government had ordered me to Hooper Bay, one of the most isolated areas of the Bering coast, to study waterfowl. When I left Illinois the feel of spring was in the air and I smelled the odor of newly turned earth, an aroma that only farm boys appreciate. An airliner deposited me in Anchorage, Alaska, where I bought 300 pounds of grub—then discarded all but a small portion of it so that Gren Collins could fly me to my frozen outpost. We didn't make it; I was grounded forty-two miles from Hooper Bay in Chevak, an Eskimo village of five igloos. The place was wrapped in ice, and except for the presence of some starved dogs near the snow mounds I might never have recognized this as the dwelling place of people.

My only white predecessor to study the area's wildfowl had been Frank Dufresne. Working as fur warden at Nome, he had invaded this foggy coast of high tides and mud and brought back information about rare Emperor geese and Steller's eiders. More important, he reported the presence of waterfowl that flew the Pacific flyway. To prove he was a mortal man he sank a powerboat, fought mosquitoes, and had a hell of a time getting his outfit out of the country.

Now the second white man was here, and the mounds of snow erupted some thirty Eskimos who offered me shelter. But the stench of the igloos was unbearable, so I hired a dog team and slept in an inactive trading post.

Then, as sometimes happens unexpectedly in the far north, the temperature moderated. The ice thawed, and in order to have good sledding I left at midnight, with a full moon, driving a team of five lank Malemutes. I actually ran behind them for forty-two miles, according to my maps—a figure I remember because it was also my forty-second birthday.

Arriving half dead in Hooper Bay, I was given something to eat from the meager stores of the lone white occupant, Father Fox. The people in this village were starving—a few children had died. The average annual family income was less than $200, and this year had been a bad one. There had been few fish, the seals were not abundant; the White Father in Washington had not realized their plight, so no aid had been forthcoming.

Maybe I am a sucker, but little scurvy-ridden kids looking like miniature skeletons have all my sympathy. My half bushel of potatoes went immediately, doled out one to a family, to furnish vitamins when eaten raw. My sugar went the same way, but I retained a ham and carefully marked it off with my hunting knife into sixty divisions—two months of breakfasts.

Squaws, men, and kids were hunting ptarmigan with bows and arrows. There weren't two boxes of shotgun shells or fifty rounds of .30/30's in the whole village of three hundred people. Toolgak was an Eskimo chief and a shaman, or medicine man. He personally took me to the Bering Sea so that his family might enjoy the results of my half case of shotshells and the sixty rounds of .30/06's I had brought with me.

The temperature dropped to minus 40 degrees as we hid behind the ice cakes, a natural blind. The dog team had been tied up, and the kayak we had brought on our sled, hoping for a breakup, was safely stored out of their reach, for they would have eaten the sealskin covering from it in a matter of seconds.

I glanced at my companion. His hands clutched a cheap single-barreled Winchester 16-gauge, and in his pockets were eight hand-loaded brass cartridges, the only munitions between him and starvation. The shells were carefully loaded with soft shot, 3 drams of powder, and a top wad of shaved wood, tamped and packed. There would be no top-wad interference here; the stuff would scatter ahead of the lead and let a lethal pattern go through.

The ice groaned, accompanying the moaning of the husky dogs. Actually, these poor animals gave me as much distress as the starving kids. Like catfish, the dogs seemed all heads. Even the furlike hair couldn't hid emaciated bodies. Their ribs protruded and their eyes were the saddest I had ever seen. Pulling the empty sled with the light kayak aboard was almost more than they could do. Frequently they fell on the hard-packed snow, and only the cursing, beating, and urging of Toolgak kept them staggering onward to the Bering coast.

The sun was a miserable thing. It hung only horizon-high and had no more warmth in it than a yellow dog skin. Inside polar bear mitts, my fingers were blue. I wondered if I could pull a trigger if the opportunity presented itself. Toolgak had no gloves. His hands were shoved under his parka and he leaned forward on them like a man in prayer. I could see no sign of breathing beneath his padded parka, and I nearly panicked. Could he be dead?

I fully believed I was frozen myself, and at the time I didn't give a damn. I saw the old chief bow his head lower. Ice froze to the wolverine-fur trim of his parka. Was the old man praying? If so, to whom? Certainly he was not a disciple of Father Fox, for Chief Toolgak was a shaman. He worshiped Eskimo gods.

Suddenly Toolgak sat upright and wiped the ice from his parka hood. His narrow Oriental eyes shone like black beads in a snowbank. Then, as if by some prearranged signal, the five sled dogs lifted their wide muzzles and howled in unison. It was the most mournful sound I have ever heard—even now, years later, I can still hear their wail. Somehow these animals sensed a change in their lot—and God knows it is a poor one. Even in good times their only reward is barely enough to eat.

Toolgak pointed a trembling finger. "They are coming. The life of our people. The first ducks of the spring."

And they were. I rubbed my eyes with the white bear mitts. Had this old shaman prayed these birds in? Strange things happen in the Arctic, especially when one is with a medicine man. I had witnessed dances to bring seals, walrus, or a salmon run. They often lasted for twenty-four hours and usually worked successfully.

Long lines of eiders—kings, common, and Pacific—approached the point where we shivered behind our ice cakes. Never in my life did I lift a gun with more resolution, and that includes World War I. Slipping the mitts from my hands, I raised the old pump gun and wondered, *Is it so cold that the firing pin will break?* Then in deadly earnest I zeroed on three tough sea ducks, tripped the trigger, and saw two plunge to their death. Frozen hands, arms, and shoulders? They didn't bother me. I jacked the pump three times and dumped three more Pacific eiders that weighed almost 6 pounds apiece. One, wing-tipped, fell among the tethered sled dogs. It was devoured to the last feather, and even the blood splotches on the snow were carefully licked up.

Toolgak? He didn't miss. His handload accounted for two eiders. He reloaded quickly and brought another spinning to the earth. What wonderful wingshots are starving Eskimos! That old man could take the Grand American if the stakes were as high as they were at that moment.

We loaded the sled with eider ducks and helped the Malemutes pull the sled, kayak, and birds. I took a picture of the three wobbly lead dogs, each fortified by part of the eider duck it had consumed. Their paws left bloody prints on the frozen ground. A high wind blew the buckshot-like snow, and Toolgak's old weathered cheeks were as red as fire. Mine were bleeding.

We returned to the village, the old shaman and I, like conquering heroes. Then, two days later, the Bering Sea's ice broke. Seals and walrus appeared and again all was well in Eskimo Land.

The eiders were eaten, all but the feathers. Even the paddle-like feet were roasted on driftwood fires, and little moon-faced children chewed the skin from them and left only the bare white bones. And the sled dogs? They ate the bones. They ate the bills and the guts of the eiders, and they ate two sealskin-covered kayaks.

The message here? Perhaps there is none. But maybe when you pick spring flowers and mushrooms or dig a mess of sassafras and smell the sweetness of fresh-turned loam, you will think of what the arrival of the warmer season means to those tough, unconquerable people in our new state. For the Eskimos still await the coming of fish, seals, walrus, and the first ducks of spring—as Toolgak and I did twenty years ago on that day when the eiders flew.

February 1964

All for the Love of a Lady

BRIAN O'BRIEN

Ewart Grogan would do anything for Gertrude—even trek the length of Africa.

C APTAIN DUNN, ON shooting leave far up the Nile from his post in the Sudan, stared as a small party straggled out of the wilderness that stretched unmapped and virtually unknown thousands of miles south to the Cape of Good Hope. The leader seemed European. His boots were held together by string; a broken hat was tilted over his bloodshot eyes. He wore a tattered jacket and trousers—hacked off at the knees. One arm hung useless and he gripped an empty pipe between haggard, unshaven jaws.

"How d' you do?" was all that Dunn could think of saying.

"Pretty fit, thanks." The stranger saluted weakly. "How're you?"

Dunn began to feel like Livingstone greeting Stanley.

"Er—have a drink? Lunch is almost ready."

Not until his famished porters were eating did the young man sit down. Dunn watched the carefully restrained knife and fork until his politeness gave way.

"I say," he burst out. "D'you mind telling me where the devil you've come from?"

"Oh, sorry. Name of Grogan. I've just come from the Cape."

"Good God Almighty!" said Captain Dunn.

The year was 1899, and the man was Ewart S. Grogan, the first person to travel the length of Africa. His journey had taken him through fearsome desert, mountains, and jungle teeming with wild beasts, hostile tribes, and diseases unknown to science. And, as Cecil John Rhodes commented: "The amusement is that a youth from Cambridge should have succeeded in doing what the ponderous explorers of the world have failed to do."

That youth, when I met him in 1960, was 87 and the most impressive personality in East Africa. His sardonic, gray-green eyes matched his voice, which had the intimate softness that accompanies a funny and slightly improper story. His white hair was plentiful and he sported a piratical little beard. He was square-shouldered, slim as when he made that epic journey, and still walked with an easy, cat-footed lunge.

Since 1904, when he settled in Kenya, Grogan had opened hundreds of square miles to agriculture. By means of wooden pipes and elephant-proof dams he tapped the melting Kilimanjaro snow to irrigate several thousand acres around his home in Taveta. His vision in building the first wharves at Kilindini made Mombasa the finest port in East Africa. As president of the Colonist's Association he was a gay and irreverent fighter against the administration. Seizing on a flaw in an unjust mining ordinance, he staked out the whole of Nairobi one night and claimed it for his own. The government found, to its dismay, that his claim was legal.

"Change the law," Grogan said, "and I'll give you back your town."

The Mining Act was promptly amended.

During the Kaiser's War he earned the D.S.O. and Belgian medals as intelligence agent behind the German lines. In 1939, promoted to lieutenant colonel, he was sent to observe the Congo situation. The Belgians were ready to turn over their vast resources to Hitler. Irritated that his superiors ignored his warnings, Grogan signaled: "A show of force is necessary, if only an obsolete warship and an admiral with red whiskers!"

The affronted War Office finally sent a mission influential enough to postpone the collapse of the Congo.

Though flippant with those in authority Grogan was tenderness itself to the young. When his wife, to whom he had been devoted for forty-two years, died during the war he built a children's hospital in Nairobi and named it Gertrude's Garden, in memory of the "the mainspring of my life."

He was a permanent member of the Kenya Legislative Council until he retired in the mid-1950's. But, a settler at heart, he still kept a critical eye on the administration, "like a humble old owl that sits in the roof and hoots occasionally." His hoots are delightedly printed in the East African Press.

I had the good luck in 1960 to be seated beside him on a B.O.A.C. Brittania in flight from London to Nairobi. The hostess told me that the Airways had invited him to be the first passenger to fly the length of Africa, the journey he had once made over land. I asked what had decided him to make that amazing trek.

"Well," he shrugged, "I'd always wanted to shoot an elephant."

His real reason came out during many conversations I had with him at his home under Kilimanjaro.

Sent down from Cambridge at 19, he wandered off to Africa, served in the Matabele War, and was posted to the escort of Cecil Rhodes on his daring peace mission to the Matabele. He listened, entranced, to the great man's dream of opening Africa with a railroad from the Cape to Cairo. One of the proposed routes was up the western fork of the Rift Valley and down the Nile. What an adventure to explore that unknown valley! Grogan knew enough about surveying to run a traverse. Maybe he could help man the course of the road. But before he could offer himself to Rhodes he came down with a fever and almost died. He was invalided home, and might never have returned to Africa had not a Cambridge friend, Eddie Watt, invited him to recuperate on his family's farm in New Zealand.

There Grogan met the true inspiration for his journey, Watt's sister Gertrude, a pretty, blue-eyed girl with shining brown hair and a beguiling smile. Grogan, who had never taken girls seriously, found that there could be no one else for him. He promptly asked her to marry him. To his awed delight she consented. He dashed off to find her stepfather, a Mr. Coleman, who was not amused.

"Infernal cheek!" he huffed. "Sent down from Cambridge! No job, no prospects! Drifter! Certainly not! Get off and do something worthwhile before you think of my stepdaughter!"

Grogan did some thinking then and there.

"Suppose I was first to explore Africa from the Cape to Cairo," he said. "Would that be worthwhile?"

"Stuff and nonsense! Even Stanley couldn't do it without an army. You're a fool, sir!"

"Nevertheless," Grogan held his temper, "I'll have a go at it. And if I succeed I'll be back!"

"He's right, you know," Grogan later admitted to Gertrude. "Have to prove myself. I won't hold you to your promise, of course. And I gave my word I wouldn't communicate with you unless I'm successful. I'll send you a cable as soon as I reach Cairo. Then, if . . ."

"You'll succeed." Gertrude said. "And I shall be waiting."

With her picture in his pocket he took the next ship home, his purpose to plot the route and collect data for the Cape to Cairo Railway. He was more than pleased when Arthur Henry Sharp, Gertrude's sporting uncle, volunteered to go with him.

They bought small tents and camp cots, spare boots, changes of clothing, one heavy rifle, two .303's, revolvers, ammunition, some old trade muskets, camera, surveying instruments, boxes of beads and rolls of calico for barter, a few staples—they planned to live off the land—a bottle of quinine for fever and one of permanganate for antiseptic. Thus equipped they set off lighthearted as schoolboys on vacation.

They landed in Cape Town late in 1897. Grogan was 22, wearing a wide hat, tweed jacket, and trousers tucked into marching boots. His excitement was hidden under a casual, you-be-damned manner. Sharp, in his 40's, with beard, moustache, florid face, and hat cocked over one eye, looked like the Prince of Wales, soon to be Edward VII. By narrow-gauge railway, oxcart, and muleback they reached Beira, at the end of the Rift, after several weeks and had to wait several more for their gear. They decided to try their guns. Sharp was nearly killed by a buffalo and Grogan almost got his head blown off by a careless gunboy. Finally they started north, ignorant as babes of what lay ahead. They went up the Shire and Zambesi Rivers in paddle boats and canvas, and when they couldn't go by water they went by mule carts and on foot. When they reached Lake Nyasa they paddled in dugout canoes to its north end.

Now the real march would have to begin. All food and equipment for the long journey had to be carried and porters were needed. But for weeks no carriers could be found, for it was planting time. Finally Grogan strolled into one of the Watonga villages and, through an interpreter, shouted—"Hear me. Follow me and I will show you wonders; mountains that spit fire; peaks so high their water turns to stone; white men's ships bigger than a town; a great river that has no end."

The Watonga listened with interest. A trip with such a fine liar should prove interesting, said their chief, Makanjira. He volunteered with four more. It was a start, but not till the rains came, putting an end to the planting, were they able to set off with a safari of 150.

It had taken Grogan and Sharp a year to get to this point, and they now struggled through torrential rain into the western fork of the Rift. Streams were flooded, paths were nonexistent. The porters moaned, for there was no fire in that sodden land to cook their food. Somehow the party came to Lake Tanganyika, loaded men and food into canoes, and reached Ujiji, where Stanley had found Livingstone twenty-seven years before. Both Grogan and Sharp were sick with fever, and they paid off all but the Watonga, then collapsed. It was a month before they were fit to go on.

"You can't," the German officials at Ujiji told them. "Kivu is our farthest post. Beyond are impassable volcanoes, wild beasts, cannibals."

"We're going anyway," Grogan said.

With Manyema porters supplied by the Germans and new provisions, supplied by Arab traders, they pressed on over 7,000-foot cliffs, washed-out trails, and lake swamps. Every night, before sleeping, Grogan gazed at Gertrude's picture; sometimes, with fever on him, he talked to her. Sharp went down with sunstroke. The Manyema chose this time to mutiny. Grogan snatched a hippo-hide whip and lashed them into line. Then he plastered Sharp's head with mud and led him, half blind, to the end of the lake.

As soon as Sharp was fit they moved on, camping in dripping forests, Grogan patiently plotting his traverses. His foot became infected with jiggers. He dug them out with a pocketknife and was dosing the wound with permanganate when Makanjira, the Watonga headman, reported elephant. Grogan hefted the double rifle that fired 4-ounce slugs and limped off with the devoted Watonga through thorn, swamp grass, and bush. Soaked and feverish he came up with the herd, fired both barrels, and was knocked flat on his back. When the smoke cleared one elephant was down. He saw two others lift the stricken bull with their tusks and lead him, between them, away. Then he fainted.

Two days later, the party reached a plateau where bananas and corn grew and long-horned cattle grazed near Ruanda villages. A chief, Ngenzi, offered to conduct them through his country, and for days they had plenty to eat and drink. Then, beside Lake Kivu, the camp was looted of spare clothing, money, and instruments.

While Sharp held Ngenzi at gunpoint Grogan, with the Watonga, rounded up a herd of cattle, held off a mob of spearmen with revolver shots, and demanded the return of the plunder. After some days a few rags were brought in, but the instruments, useless to the thieves, had been thrown over a cliff. Sick at heart, they booted Ngenzi out of camp with his cattle and moved on by prismatic compass, the only instrument left.

Several days later, gaunt with hunger, for the Ruanda would sell them no food, they reached the Mfumbiro volcanoes, the first of the wonders Grogan had promised the Watonga they would see. Sharp, sick and hopeless, talked of going home. To give him a chance to rest, Grogan left him in a base camp and set off with the Watonga and twelve porters to seek routes through the mountains. Climbing the 2,000-foot western wall of the Rift they encountered terrified natives fleeing east. These people moaned that the Baleka had come out of the Congo, looted their villages, and were hunting them to eat them.

The porters muttered uneasily but Grogan laughed them on. At the top of the escarpment they were halted by the sight of a smouldering village guarded by painted spearmen.

"Baleka!" Makanjira slid Grogan's rifle into his hands.

The cannibals charged, screeching. Grogan shot the leader. The rest came on. He dropped three more before they retreated.

By the time their survey of the volcano country was finished their food was gone and there was nothing they could eat in the gutted villages. They marched for five days on green bananas and a few pumpkins before they reached the base camp, half dead with dysentery.

They had found a way through the mountains to flat country. On their right was the Uganda border, and ahead was Lake Edward and what is now the Queen Elizabeth National Park. Here Grogan killed his first elephant, welcome food for the men. But Grogan's pride in the achievement was reduced by the queasy effect of a stew made from part of the elephant's trunk.

They moved on through endless herd of elephant, buffalo, hippo, and Uganda kob, but Grogan's foot had turned septic again, and he couldn't hunt. Sharp, despondent over the two-year neglect of his business, his nerves on edge, talked of nothing but home. Sick and tattered, their bodies and clothing showing the effects of 18 months hard travel, they somehow managed to toil up Lake Edward where a missionary tended Grogan's foot. There they divided the gear and Sharp left for Mombasa and a ship to England.

Grogan was deeply depressed. There were still thousands of miles to go. Could he make it alone? He took out Gertrude's picture, cracked and stained from much handling. Gazing at her steady eyes his problem became simple. If he gave up he could never face her again. Life without her was impossible. Therefore he *had* to go on. So he bathed, shaved, and called his men together, then with the Watonga and thirty Manyema, marched around the Mountains of the Moon and down into the Semliki Valley.

There he found villages looted bare by Congolese mutineers, and shot elephant and buffalo to feed the famine-stricken locals. He kept the ivory to help pay his expenses. Proceeding north, Grogan and his band struggled up the west bank of Lake Albert, through fever swamps, often wading under 3,000 foot cliffs, until the lake funnelled to a forest-lined river. The Nile, at last! The worst was over—he hoped.

Three days later Grogan marched up the hill to Wadelai, 300 feet above the river. He paid off the Manyema, left his ivory to be sold, loaded the Watonga and the gear into a tippy canoe, and started gaily down the Nile.

It soon became apparent that the worst wasn't over yet. Masses of tightly packed vegetation called sudd hampered their progress, and later rapids forced them ashore. Here Grogan found porters and the party marched for ten days through mosquito swamps and thorn bush till they reached the end of the rapids. There Grogan got hold of an ancient boat which carried them through slimy lagoons, where snakes writhed and a hippo charged them, until at Bor the Nile became completely blocked by a wilderness of sudd.

By this time Grogan was a fearsome sight. His face, long unshaven, was swollen by mosquito bites, his last shirt had disintegrated, his boots were falling apart. Thorns had left gaping holes in jacket and trousers and his foot had gone bad again. He managed to collect nine bearers here—including a lunatic, a Dervish deserter with a lame leg, and an idiot boy. With the gear reduced to the bare necessities, the motley party moved out by compass through the most dismal country Grogan had yet seen. By day stinging flies tormented the group. At night Grogan fired reeds and they crouched in the smoke to escape the insects. One morning a porter was found stung to death by mosquitoes.

They were now in the steaming swamps of Dinka country, where the 7-foot, naked natives smeared themselves with a paste made of urine and ashes as protection against insects. Grogan made a Dinka chief some presents, and in return he offered to show the safari a "shortcut." This turned out to be a labyrinth of bog and elephant grass, where the guides abandoned Grogan's party, then perched on nearby bluffs to wait for them to die. Shouting, cursing, and singing half deliriously, Grogan led his men through several miles of warm, neck-deep slime till finally they came to solid ground.

Ahead of them now was an endless waste of thorn and low bush, no villages and no food. That day the lunatic porter deserted with the tent. Grogan shot a hippo and the men chewed raw meat, for there was no wood for fires. This assuaged their hunger, but thirst was still a danger, and their tongues were swollen with drought when at last the river reappeared, clear and limpid, so beautiful Grogan named it the Gertrude Nile. And for the first time in weeks they drank all they wanted, wallowing in the precious water.

But soon the river disappeared again, and studying his map, Grogan decided that if he kept to a northerly course he would meet it again near the confluence of the Sobat River. So carrying all the water they could they struck out over dried lagoon beds and stretches of hot shale broken with infrequent patches of bush. This route led them straight into ambush. A porter went down with a spear through him; three more dropped under Dinka clubs, and the rest bolted. Grogan fired his rifle into the attackers, but when he had emptied it, a 7-foot giant charged him. He took a paralyzing blow on his arm, jammed the empty rifle into the Dinka's belly, and while the man was recovering, fumbled a shell into the beech and shot him. The Dinkas retreated. Grogan called his men out of hiding, dressed the wounded, buried the dead, and limped desperately on.

All their water was lost in the fight. Two of the wounded porters went off their heads, another simply disappeared. Grogan threw away more gear. His arm ached sickeningly and his foot was swollen purple. He managed to knock down two storks, which they ate raw. Then he opened his last box of shells and found them corroded and useless.

The carriers were thoroughly discouraged, but Grogan urged them ahead, shouting, "On! Plenty of water ahead."

Sullenly they moved, halting every few miles to rest under the pitiless sun until Grogan pricked them on with a Dinka spear.

"Up," he muttered through caked lips. "March or you'll bloody well die!"

In the afternoon they found a puddle crusted with salt and sucked it dry. That night, while they writhed with dysentery, lions prowled around the camp in the moonlight. Without shells, Grogan could only watch helplessly, but at last they lounged away.

"It's a good sign," he confided to Gertrude's picture. "I'll get through, old dear." Then he went to sleep.

He doesn't know how long he limped ahead of the nine men left, but at last they saw ahead of them green brush, and something swaying above it.

"Trees, *bwana*," Makanjira mumbled. "Water."

Grogan shook the fog from his eyes.

"It's a mast," he croaked. "A flag!"

Through the quivering heat haze he made out white-robed figures. A Sudanese soldier challenged, and behind him Grogan could see the river and a boat tied to the bank. Pulling himself together, he demanded, "Whose boat is that?"

"Captain Dunn, *effendi*. Come!"

Three days later, shaved and dressed in clothing borrowed from Dunn, Grogan was delivered at Fashoda (now Kodok), where Hayes-Sadler, military governor, listened in astonishment to his story.

"Well, young fellow," he said, when it was finished. "You can let the lady know you're safe now. Military telegraph here, you know."

"Can't." Grogan smiled. "Have to wait till I get to Cairo."

The carriers were paid off and sent back to Bor, but the Watonga, eager for more of the wonders they had been promised, accompanied Grogan to Khartoum. There he reported to Sir Francis Wingate, the Sirdar, whose launch carried the party to Abu Hamed, where the Watonga saw their first train. Makanjira eyed it with alarm, then slid the rifle into Grogan's hands.

They rode the train to Aswan where a steamer took them to Cairo. Two and a half years after setting out to travel the length of Africa, Grogan had completed his task. He hurried to a cable office.

"Have reached Cairo," he wrote. "Anxiously await your answer. Make it yes. Love, Ewart."

After several suspenseful days came the reply:

"My feelings unchanged. Am waiting for you. Love, Gertrude."

January 1968

On the Ivory Trail

BWANA COTTAR

as told to EDISON MARSHALL

A braggart and con artist spins a tale of adventure.

I AM AN AMERICAN. Sometimes I think that half of the adventures and troubles of my life are due to my nationality. Our countrymen have never taken very kindly to too much law, especially if the law was made by someone else. Yet I emigrated to an English colony in Africa where law is god—where I ran into it and fell over it, and now and then broke it, nearly every day for twenty years.

I grew up a husky sort of fellow, weighing two hundred pounds. They were putting up too many fences, building too many roads, and passing too many laws out in Texas and Oklahoma where I used to range; so in 1910 I migrated to East Africa. In those days there was a breed of men out there I could understand. They were Englishmen, yes, but the kind of Englishmen that settled America in the sixteen and seventeen hundreds. They were dying off fast, many of them under the feet of elephants, but while they ran the country it was a real country.

I might as well begin with a *shauri*—the Swahili word for almost any kind of doings—out in the Belgian Congo. Now, the Belgian Congo was originally supposed to be international territory—made so by our explorer, Stanley—but in our usual weak-kneed fashion we let the King of Belgium take it for his own. Moreover, he claimed all the elephants feeding in those great black forests, no matter from what part of Africa they had originally wandered. If a man hunted or killed them, the penalty might be anything from six months in a native jail—give me six years in Hades in preference!— to a bullet in the back by a deputy and a lost grave in the bush. But I remembered what Stanley had done, and without any pangs of conscience I crossed the frontier hunting ivory.

My outfit was light compared to those of modern sportsmen, but complete enough to give me a decent amount of comfort in those vast, lonely forests. It included Kamau, my cook. Kamau was an excellent camp cook, but, like most men of his trade, whether black or white, he was inclined to be stout. I have never figured out whether stout men naturally take to cooking, or whether cooking and the impulse to sample his own concoctions naturally put flesh on a slim cook's bones.

With my small outfit I went deep into pygmy country and engaged a whole tribe to help me track elephants. At this game they were expert. The only pay they desired was to feed full of the fallen giants, which they did a-plenty. Still they remained lean and thin, not at all like Kamau, who gloried in parading his shiny black bulk around my camp-fire.

I had pitched camp about two hundred yards up-wind from the pygmy village. Those who know African villages will appreciate my foresight in pitching upwind instead of down-wind. Every day twenty or thirty of the little pygmy women came over to my camp and stood around admiring Kamau. They would feel his oily skin and give little grunts of delight. They would thrust their tiny fingers into his ribs and paunch, according to the pygmy idea of flirtation.

All this went to Kamau's head. He fairly swelled and strutted, assuming that the ladies' admiration was due entirely to his masculine charms. In vain I tried to warn him.

One evening I came back to camp hungry for some of Kamau's good chow. But Kamau was not in sight! I looked in the dust and found his huge footprints, flanked on each side by a tiny pair of footprints, headed toward the pygmy village. It was plain that two of the little Jezebels had him by the arms, leading him home.

With deep misgivings I started to follow. When the breeze shifted into my face, I suddenly remembered—and at first I did not know why—the barbecues I used to attend in Oklahoma. There was something in the air that recalled a good fat porker sizzling on the spit.

I sat down on a log. It never pays to hurry Africa. The pygmies seemed oddly shamefaced. They stayed in their huts and peered at me from under the thatch. But I began to find evidence to piece out the story.

First, a woman who had been especially ardent in her admiration of Kamau darted between two of the huts wearing a familiar garment. Instantly I recognized it as Kamau's *shuka* (wrap). Then I saw an old hag, plainly a witch doctor, anointing her lean body with oil and making faces like a sick monkey. Finally, I noticed a *toto* (baby) sitting on the ground at my feet, gnawing a bone. The more I stared at that bone, the less I liked the look of it. So I called out the little four-foot chief and made him stand before me.

"You've eaten my cook," I told him.

"Oh, no! We wouldn't eat the great Bwana's cook."

"Where is he, then?"

"We haven't seen him."

But I persisted with the charge, pointing out the *shuka*, the anointing with Kamau's fat, the bone and the roast-pork aroma in the air. The weight of evidence was too much and finally, after many protestations of innocence, he broke down and confessed.

Yes, they had eaten the great Bwana's cook. They were very, very penitent, because they knew it was very wrong, and they would restore him if it were in their power. But the truth was, they had admired him so much, and had felt him so many times, and had lusted for his chops so many nights that finally they were just obliged to eat him!

Mind you, this happened only a very few years ago, among the Ituri Forest pygmies. And don't think they wouldn't eat him just as cheerfully today if the chance offered!

Is it wrong to kill elephants? The sentimentalists will tell you so—as they sit at table over their roast turkey and big juicy steaks cut from an innocent old cow-brute that never did any one any harm in his life. They could live on herbs and rice if they liked, but they don't. After dinner they go in and have a nice game of billiards with ivory balls—and they don't buy any pianos with imitation ivory keys. As long as they are accessories to the fact of elephant killing, I don't think they have much to say.

I was in the Belgian Congo when the King of the Belgians closed the Ivory Trail. It still ran on through Kenya and Uganda and up to Somaliland and Ethiopia, and down to the waters of the great Zambezi; but in the Belgian Congo it was closed for the white hunter apparently forever.

The lure of the big tusks had drawn me again over the border, an outlaw in dead Leopold's dominions. On the banks of the Semliki, near where it flows into Lake Albert, I built a shack to store my supplies. Two other ivory poachers were operating in the vicinity, one an American named Pickering and the other an old Dutchman named Broom.

Pickering and I saw a good deal of each other. We laughed together at the underground warnings we had received from the Belgian government—that if we were caught we would be shown no quarter. Who were these thieving "long noses" that they could drive us from the heritage of the pioneer? We hadn't crossed three oceans, walked thousands of miles of veldt and lived for years in the fever-haunted jungle, only to be cheated of our prize.

I felt fairly secure, as only the river separated my camp from the comparative safety of the Uganda territory, but I worried about Pickering and Broom, who were several miles inland.

As the situation became more threatening day by day, I moved most of my heavy supplies, including two heavy rifles, tent, ammunition and trade goods, to safety across the river. I could not take the ivory, because it would certainly be stolen by Uganda natives.

I had hardly returned to the Congo shore when a native came with word that our Bwana Broom, the Dutchman, had been killed by an elephant.

I trekked to the nearest village and demanded that they tell me what had happened to Bwana Broom. One of them offered to show me Broom's grave. On the way we found the tracks of a great herd of elephants and the single track of a white man. But it was going the wrong way to be Broom's. Suspicious and depressed, I trudged on.

I did not know Broom well. He was a stolid, stupid old creature. Yet when white men are so few, they should be friends; and in the jungle one mourns the departure even of an enemy. Besides, there was a wrong feel in the air. The smell of the decaying vegetation seemed to stifle me; I had a presentiment of evil. But I cussed aloud—and trudged on.

Soon we found where a bleeding body had been dragged across the trail. Following the red splashes on the leaves, we found the half-dead body of an East African native, obviously one of Broom's men. He was unconscious, but we made camp and did our best to save him.

The native had a deep, wide-gaping wound on the thigh, and there was a bullet hole in his arm. An elephant made the first—but as sure as God, a military rifle, not an elephant gun, had inflicted the second.

That night will linger long in my memory. The native raved and wept, trying to tell us what had befallen his master. The wild elephants tooted and yelled. A leopard coughed—like a buck-saw going through a tough board—just beyond the firelight. I felt that enemy eyes were peering at me from the thickets.

In the morning I left the wounded man in the care of two of my boys, and continued the search. The elephants had made a tunnel through the thick jungle, and as we passed under the dark arch we knew we were nearing the end of the road for poor old Broom. There was human blood on the trail, and human footprints were everywhere.

The blood-spoor led us on a hundred yards farther. Here the elephants had apparently gone mad—tearing up trees, plowing the ground with their tusks. Human tracks were everywhere. Who could have been here after Broom's death?

We found his hat, his rifle and several empty shells, and in a few minutes more a shallow, hastily constructed grave. Above it was a cross made with two sticks, tied with a handkerchief—where some pious Belgian had tried to atone for the murder of a fellow white man.

For Broom had been murdered. I dug him up to see. It was not a pleasant job, but I did it. And no old savage forest bull, fighting for his life had done that job! He had been shot in the back by a military rifle, and his head cut off with a *panga*.

And presently I saw through the whole brutal story. His headless mangled body had been dropped before a feeding herd of elephants. Smelling his blood, they had trampled him almost out of human likeness. A fine end for a grand old hunter like Broom! But the history of the Ivory Trail has ever been stained with blood.

The pastoral tribes up on the northern frontier had been killing elephants and caching ivory since time out of mind. I wanted some of those tusks; but how to get them, and then how to export them through the British customs, was a problem that would tax the best powers of any bwana of the Ivory Trail.

Finally another old-timer and I worked out a crafty scheme. He sauntered into Nairobi and gave a newspaper reporter a tall yarn about "elephant graveyards." You know the story—how no one ever finds the skeletons of elephants that have died a natural death because, when they felt the end was near, they all trekked off to some lost burial ground and laid down their bones with their pals.

Of course, this is one of the grandest myths in Africa. The real truth is, first, that elephants very rarely die of sickness. Most big wild animals are healthy, because they live natural lives; and elephants being sort of animal Methuselahs, most of the old bulls, wearing big ivories, very rarely die of old age either, but sooner or later get a bullet in the brain. Besides, the jungle makes quick work of any kind of skeleton, hiding it under vegetable mold and rotting away the bones. However, I have found such skeletons, not once but several times.

Yet my old friend's graveyard story made quite a sensation. He followed it up like a good publicity man, and in two weeks the whole country was excited about dead elephants. So it did not look at all suspicious when I organized a safari to hunt an elephant graveyard of my own.

But what was I to do with the ivory when I found it? I couldn't ship it or sell it without government permission. And the government would pay white men only two shillings a pound for graveyard ivory. However, they would pay natives five shillings a pound. You bet I would make sure that all my ivory was found and turned in by natives.

I loaded my porters with trade goods, cheap but bright. Just how I meant to use these in finding elephant graveyards I did not explain to the government. Then I hit for the frontier, and put up a shack near a swamp, close to a native village. Of course, an elephant graveyard would naturally be in a swamp.

Before long the natives began to bring in some of their caches of ivory, trading it for beads, cloth and copper wire. Still there was not much profit here. The stuff was costing me nearly two shillings per pound.

When my trade goods were exhausted—and I had an elephant graveyard well started in the swamp before my shack—I decided to get a few more tusks in a regular way—with my old level-action .405. But I needed the cooperation of the old village chief.

No, his elephant hunting days were over. He had six wives to support him, and saw no sense whatever in risking his bones under the feet of the wild bulls. And next month he would acquire a seventh wife, very young, very lovely by African standards.

At this point I mentioned the wonderful *dawa* (medicine) that I had brought with me. It would make an old chief young again.

His wrinkled old face lighted up. Yes, he would go with Bwana to kill an elephant. He proved a good tracker—we added two fine tusks to the graveyard—and then, around the camp-fire, talked of ivory and youth.

Finally we struck a deal. He would exchange ten tusks from his store for one bottle of *dawa*. True, they proved a scrawny lot—I had failed to stipulate the weight of the tusks, and the old villain took advantage of my oversight. The ivory was, however, well worth the bottle of good tonic, mostly alcohol, that I gave him in exchange.

Now would he take all my ivory to the government, get five shillings a pound, and turn the money over to me? He feared the District Commissioner—one such had thrashed him once—and for a long time we could not strike a bargain. But in the meantime he had tried the *dawa* and found it very good.

At last he came to terms—for five bottles of *dawa*. Then we resurrected, out of the swamp, the biggest African "graveyard" in the history of the territory. His tribesmen transported 2,500 pounds forty miles to market—for ten shillings' worth of tonic. In the end I found I had a clear profit of nearly $2,000—not bad for one little fib about elephant graveyards.

In the north of Uganda in 1918, I fell in with a band of Somali Arabs. They were collecting ivory and trading to the east of Karamaja along the border of Uganda and Kenya Colony.

Man dear, what a pack! What a camp to brighten the eyes of a silly old adventurer like me!

There were only a few firearms in camp, rusted and ill-kept, but there were plenty of sabers, bows and arrows, dried-skin shields and wicked-looking knives. And when I had taken a good look around, you couldn't have pried me away with less than six good tusks! I made up my mind to join these desert bandits for a month or two and just enjoy myself.

You can never tell about Africa. It belongs to the devil. Just as I was daydreaming of a month of adventure my mouth suddenly felt furry, my thoughts began to tangle up like wet line when the angler gets a backlash, and a chill stole over my body.

I ordered my canvas water-bag filled and hung up in the shade. Then I got out my medicine box and took a big dose of quinine. But I couldn't keep the medicine down—a symptom I knew only too well. I was in for a siege of "black-water fever," one of the deadliest maladies known to man and the scourge of Africa.

Old Fundi used to tell me about demons. That day I believed him. Only a demon could set such a trap as now had me by the heel. There is only one effective treatment for black-water fever, and that is plenty of good fresh drinking water—and I was far out on the Great Thirst. There was no doctor, no nurse, no shelter but a thin tent in the intense heat. It looked as if my jig was up.

In a chill, with my teeth chattering and grinding, I swam again the Semliki River with Belgian bullets screaming overhead. I died of thirst in the desert not once but a score of times—a score of wretched lives, crawling upon one another. I was chased by raging elephants. I dug up and reburied old Broom, over and over, for an eternity. Finally I was fighting the Arabs, shrieking like a banshee.

My shout brought my boys in a troop. They stood dejected and self-pitying at the door of my tent.

"What is to be done, Bwana?" came Fundi's voice.

"What is wrong?" I asked.

"Our food is gone, the Arabs are going to move, and a lion has killed one of your mules."

It was just what could be expected of Simba at a time like this. He never misses a chance.

I learned that I had been ill a full week. But the Arabs had stood by me better than I had expected. Perhaps it was pity for a down-and-out bwana—more likely, the legend of his prowess and the fear that he could still rise and shoot.

The old sheik informed me that he desired to move camp, but would wait until I recovered or died. The latter was most likely, he told me cheerfully. "What white man had ever recovered from so severe an illness?"

After days of illness and danger, Bwana Cottar was finally able to continue the journey east toward Somaliland.

Our destination was 600 miles across the uncharted sands. None of us had ever passed this way: the only known water was at Marsabitt, two hundred miles eastward. I wondered how many of us would get through alive.

The desert gave way to ridges of rock, separated by valleys of drifted sand. Soon these hills grew to bare, sun-baked mountains.

About five o'clock we pitched camp at a small spring, an old watering-place for sheep. About the ridges giraffes and antelope were grazing on the scanty desert shrubs. To avoid scaring game and elephants bearing ivory, I had camp pitched almost a mile from the water.

Our ivory store was increasing, but our food was getting short. We had plenty of goats and sheep, but the long dry march had made them almost unfit for food, and camel milk was becoming scanty and bad. I started out with the little .303 to shoot a buck for meat.

I was hardly a mile from camp when I found myself in one of those suddenly violent shoot-for-your-life *shauris* that make Africa so terrible and so grand. Without the slightest warning, two rhinos rose from behind a big rock and charged me.

My mule bolted. The sight of those two prehistoric brutes with their dragon heads and leveled lances was too much for his calm mule nerve. But a rhino is incredibly fast. Before the mule got his feet under him, one of the monsters had closed in.

I shot straight and fast, but the bullets were too light to stop the beast in time. I saw the big evil head go under the mule's belly, and he was fairly hoisted into the air. The next instant I was on the ground, my right leg pinned under the mule's body.

Man dear! The mule was mortally wounded, the rhino was fighting mad, and I was a prisoner. But when the brute lowered his point to charge again, I managed to twist my body, get my gun up, and finish him off with a shot to the brain.

But this was only the beginning of one of the worst *shauris* of my life. In the next few seconds I made two discoveries that fairly raised the hair on my head. One was that my rifle was empty. The other, that my spare cartridges were in a pocket beneath my body, and though I tugged like a bear in a trap I could not get at them.

The sun was already low. A great ball of burnished brass, it dipped into a red and purple cloud. Away to the north an elephant bugled. A mile south I could hear through the still air the blubbering of camels, the shrieks of children and the bleating of sheep about our camp. Flocks of pigeons and doves darted past on the way to the spring.

Sundown! And maybe sundown for old Bwana Cottar too, and the most devilish finish the desert could contrive. Just as the flaming rim winked the last time the low, rumbling grunt of a lion sounded from a ravine.

The tropic night seemed to fall much more slowly than usual. But at last the shadows hid the fire-scorched rocks and sun-blistered shrubs. Then came the hyenas! I knew they would come—ghouls of the desert. They always come to the dead, the dying and the helpless.

They crept clear up to the head of the dead mule and chattered, howled and snarled. Nor would they satisfy their ravenous hunger on the dead rhino. The inch-thick hide was too tough for them until the sun softened it.

Desperate, I twisted my imprisoned foot from the boot, but a stone, buried in the sand, caught on my ankle and tore the flesh. Further struggles were too painful for the present. Meanwhile the hyenas were attacking the head of the mule, not eight feet from my face. For a time I hoped that they might drag the carcass off my leg and free me—a strange trick of fate, to be freed by the devil pack—but they only grew bolder.

By ten o'clock they were feeding all around me, and snarled only when I shouted and waved my arms. In an extreme of terror I tore my coat and managed to reach my ammunition. Great God, what a relief! But my fingers were almost dead from the chill of the desert night and the long cramp, and at first I could hardly feed the magazine.

One of the brutes came up behind my head and, sniffing at my face, gave an ear-splitting howl. Twisting about and nearly breaking my imprisoned leg, I shot the brute dead.

The beasts scattered, but almost instantly came creeping back. I knew they would. They would never forsake the warm feast. And now they tried to drag the carcass away, but they only drew it farther on my leg, imprisoning me all the tighter. I was forced to lie flat on my back, one knee hard against the dead mule's shoulder.

For one of the few times in my life I contemplated putting myself out. A shot to the brain—if I could manage it in my half-paralyzed condition—to save the agony of cruel claws and foul teeth: I tell you it was a comforting thought. And I felt for my long, keen knife. I would hardly feel its razor edge as it raced across my throat.

But the nearing grunt of a lion wakened again the lust to fight—and live. I tell you, lions have always moved strangely through the destiny of Bwana Cottar. I got ready. I have always advocated small-bore guns—perhaps because of my confidence that I could place the bullet just where I desired— but how I longed that night for my big .470 with its dull, monotonous boom!

I waited till the big black-maned brute was hardly ten feet away, and then shot for his head. Instantly he bounded past me, his mane erect, with a roar that chilled the marrow of my bones. The sound came rolling and echoing back from the hills, and with it the hiss of another bullet that I sped after him.

The hyenas now cleared out. Only the jackals and the little desert foxes were left. I did not fear the jackals, but for some reason the hungry, feeble yapping of those little foxes caused chills of ice and fire to chase each other up and down my aching spine. Pinned down under a dead mule, helpless and in agony, I was in no position to fight even the meanest and smallest of the desert folk.

I was still weak from the fever. I felt my sense slipping away. Little deliriums came and passed. Great eyes gleamed from the darkness—millions of needles were being driven into my flesh. And then, after a nightmare eternity, it was gray in the east.

I came wide awake. I could smell decaying flesh. Just as quickly in the desert putrification would spread to my own body. But I had the knife and, by God, I meant to use it, but not yet, on my own throat.

I began the most gruesome task of my life, not excepting the post-mortem of old Broom. Lump by lump I cut away the flesh and unjointed the bones of the mule. A great wave of exultation surged through my veins as I thought of freedom.

But a sting on my back turned it to a wave of horror. The brown ants had come. I knew they would. They always do come to the carrion feasts of the desert.

There was a brown ribbon advancing across the sand—countless millions of little killers. They could clean my bones and the mule bones almost in a space of minutes. But with the strength of fury and despair I threw sand at their ranks, and made them swerve. Presently the pieces of mule I had cut away came to brown crawling life.

Lord God, wasn't this enough? But one troop of the desert ghouls had not yet come. And I knew they would come! They always do, when the feast is spread on the sands. I heard a flapping swoop of wings.

Above my head appeared what looked like a squadron of aeroplanes, all nose-diving toward me. I closed my eyes and covered my face with my hands as the long-beaked grisly band lighted all about me. They were the king vultures.

Heaven only knows how they had assembled so quickly. Birds soaring far off must have seen the first swoop of some telescope-eyed watcher high above me in the sky. At least a hundred of the foul birds were flapping about my head.

With the fierce hunger of the desert, they began to attack the carrion, casting sidelong glances at me with their bright little eyes. But they were cowards and I kept them away by waving my hands.

The sun rose and poured its searing molten gold into my face. A greater koodoo—graceful, strong, sleek, fleet of foot and free—strolled by on the way to the spring. To be free! I felt I could never ask for any other blessing.

Presently I saw the great spiral horns of the koodoo go high in the air, and he stood at attention. He was staring down the valley toward my camp. Hope raced to my heart.

An instant later the filthy vultures hopped up, with a great thunder of wings, and took flight. The koodoo darted away.

I could see bobbing heads coming up over the hill. At the head of the line came Fundi and all my boys.

The air was full of "Bwana! Bwana!" Old Fundi caught me around the waist and held me upright. I was saved!

After a few more days of rest, the expedition was ready to head off across the desert again.

The morning air was cool and swift, more exhilarating than elsewhere in the whole world. Soon the whole camp was astir. Smoke from dung fires was curling up: a leopard coughed out there in the grayness as he retreated toward his lair. But we did not get away without trouble. Africa was on the job, as usual. We thought we had caught her napping, but we were mistaken.

As the men were packing one of the kali-broken camels the beast suddenly leaped to his feet, breaking with one surge of his mighty muscles the ropes that confined him, and dashed after one of the men. The man ran for his life—few animals in the world are as dangerous as an enraged camel—but not quickly enough. The brute sank his teeth into the man's hip and swung him into the air.

The man would have been killed in five seconds more. The beast would have stamped and bitten him beyond recognition. But I had just picked up my old .405 and, firing from the hip, I shot the brute dead. As he dropped his jaws opened, so that the man fell clear.

When we were packed up, we headed due east toward Marsabit, two hundred miles as the crow flies across howling desert. But no crows flew over that waste of sand and barren rock. The only life out there was a few antelope, clumsy puff-adders, deadly coral snakes and big black desert scorpions that could sting like the devil's pitchfork. Man dear, what a country! The men who lived out there partook of the nature of the desert—simple but subtle, forever deadly and untamed.

The little vegetation that exists is thorny and ferocious. The nights are cold, but the sun bursts up as from an erupting volcano, without warning, without twilight, with cruel heat and blinding light. At least there are no insect pests. Not a fly or a midge, or even a mosquito that can survive arctic ice, can endure the Great Thirst.

All that day we bore eastward without a pause for food or rest. There was not a cloud in the sky, not a breath of wind, no sound but the everlasting "crunch, crunch, crunch" of hoofs on the sand and the squeak of saddle leather and the grating of ropes on chafing backs burned hard in the terrible heat. But there was a spring somewhere ahead of us, if we could just find it. If we found it—and if sheep had not drunk it dry—we would drink tonight. If we did not find it, we would not drink. Our precious stores of water must be saved for an extreme emergency.

The fact that I am telling this shows that we did find water. But before that hideous trek was over, most of our camels and sheep fell exhausted on the sand and had to be put out of misery.

When we had lost all track of time, seemingly a party of ghosts doomed for eternity to pace an endless desert, we looked ahead and saw an enchanted lake gleaming in the moonlight. Man, dear!

Again we heard the wind soughing through trees. The air was perfumed by flowers, toads croaked, a water bird called to its mate. And then there was a stampede such as I had never seen and hope never to see again.

A rhino and a band of water-buck that had been drinking at the lake were almost run down by our thirst-maddened animals. Horses, camels, sheep and men plunged into the water; the smaller beasts were trampled under the feet of the larger ones. It was all we could do to save the desert children in our party from the plunging, frantic hoofs. As it was, most of our sheep were drowned or trampled to death.

But at last peace was restored. Morning found our camp pitched, the smoke rising up from the dung fires, and our bellies full. Lord, deliver me from any more such journeys! I would sell my ivory and then return to Nairobi. There I would fawn upon newcomers from England for some underling job to keep my body and soul together.

"Bwana?" It was Fundi's voice.

"What do you want?"

"Look, Bwana. *Tembu*."

He pointed up the hill. There, on their way to the feeding grounds, shuffled and lumbered along a big herd of elephants. The ivories of several big bulls caught and reflected the morning sun.

Fundi grinned and pulled his ear. He understood his old Bwana better than that old Bwana will ever understand himself! Well, we be two men.

December 1938–April 1939

The stories Ewana Cottar told Edison Marshall took place in 1910, when laws against killing elephants were aimed not so much at saving scarce animals, as at preserving a valuable commodity—ivory—for its legal owner, e.g., the King of Belgium. When the stories—told in a five-part series—first ran, *Field & Stream* stated that the magazine didn't "excuse or condone the acts of the man. We report the fearless nerve, the deadly aim and the savage code of this African pioneer who knew no law of the jungle but his own." Such tales of derring-do were staples of many adventure magazines in the 1930s and '40s. But the profound changes Africa underwent starting in the 1950s affected both the stories, the nature of the safaris, and the attitudes of the hunters themselves. The Bwana Cottar story and the three Africa hunting pieces that follow it reflect these changes, and provide a valuable insight into the history of both outdoor writing and a part of the world still undergoing great changes.

Death in the Morning

WARREN PAGE

The Cape buffalo had killed without reason, leaving the hunter with a head full of questions.

THE MAN WAS dead. He had been gored, trampled into the red sand, tossed like a bundle of rags, ripped again and again by black horns. He was bloodily, messily dead—destroyed by a bull buffalo in an utterly senseless attack.

Now, it isn't often that an African buffalo charges a man for no reason at all. Yet one had murdered this native without provocation. The evidence was still clear in the sand. During the night the buffalo herd had moved up from the river, through the crop fringe of the native shambas, and on into the hills. But one bull had dropped out of the herd and stood for hours in a patch of bush not far from a footpath that meandered among the huts. In the freshening dawn the native and his brother had come along that path. And then—for no reason at all and from at least sixty yards—the Cape buffalo had rushed him, smashed him.

The tracks were clear—deep-cut marks of spread hoofs. Here the bull had angled out of his hideaway and rushed down on the hapless native with the power of a locomotive. Then the prints blurred into the smears of brutal murder, finally showing clear again where the buffalo had slowly returned to his hideout, leaving behind the bloodied bundle that had, only moments before, been a living man.

As I've said, this kind of blind, insensate attack doesn't happen often, even among game animals as massively dangerous as the Cape buffalo. When one does charge, it is usually because it has been wounded—has good reason for attacking man. José Simoes, the safari outfitter who was studying the scene with me, agreed with me on that. Only once or twice in his years of hunting Mozambique, first for meat and later with clients, had he run into a situation like this.

José had been one of the professionals back when meat hunting was big business. In those days there were between forty and fifty working hunters, each with a trained squad of some thirty natives, who hacked away at the vast herds roaming the Marromeu and Cheringoma plains below the Zambezi. José had had his close calls in the course of shooting hundreds of buffalo, many of them with an ordinary .270 and soft-points, in order to provide sugar-plantation workers with meat. It had been dangerous work.

"It was not the danger that stopped me, though," he said. "The buffalo is not usually like this, a murderer of unarmed men, but honest and brave like a Miura fighting bull in facing his equals. I have dared buffalo to come and fight me because I knew we could do fair battle together, but this is pure murder."

As a guide, José displayed that combination of guts and stubborn—even foolhardy—courage that the Scandinavians call *sisen*. This I knew, for he'd been alongside me in one scrap with a pair of black Mozambique bulls, and there was no questioning his bravery—or that of Juan Cazadore, the long-limbed black gunbearer he had assigned to me. Juan and I, looking for a 50-incher to outdo the pair of 46-inch trophies I'd taken in Kenya, had also met the bulls of Portuguese East Africa. We'd run into no crisis—merely a stroke of bad luck. The trio of oldsters we'd found had run behind a big clump of bush, and when they reappeared I broke the neck of the wrong bull—not the 50-plus giant I had marked earlier. The kill had one broken horn, more than a foot of it having been smashed off in some herd fracas, yet the horns were still almost four feet in spread.

It was the government, José told me, that had put a stop to the practice of running the black Marromeu herds with trucks, as our Sioux once ran the bison of North America on horseback. It was government action, inspired by José's conservation-minded friends, Dr. Palhinha and Senhor Tavares, that had reduced the number of meat hunters from forty to twenty, then to eight, and eventually eliminated the practice. Economics had helped. The stiff restrictions of 1954 limited the buffalo and elephant kill to thirty tons of meat, and required a tag of 100 escudos, or $3.30, for each animal. The tariff was four times as much for an elephant worth less than $100 at railhead. These restrictions, plus the rising prices of trucks and supplies, had put the casual meat hunters, and finally many professionals, out of business. It was, I knew, a source of great relief to José, both as a person and as a safari outfitter, that the buffalo herds were scattering and growing ever thicker over the rich graze and parklike forest that covers much of Mozambique. He respected buffalo. But from the evidence before us, this was murder, an unprovoked charge on a defenseless black.

"Hard to understand," I offered. "Sometimes they won't charge even with reason!"

"That is so," agreed José as he studied the clues in the sand.

There had been several buff dropped by my rifle up on Mount Kenya, I recalled. None of them had charged, nor had the second bull of the pair that Bob Kuhn and I took on the Rift Valley escarpment. Maybe I'd also been lucky with the brave bulls in Tanganyika, and certainly we'd been fortunate with two in the impenetrable thickets beyond the Mara. My friend Bob Johnson had faced a charge on our '58 hunt and lived to tell of it. Somehow or other, in my hunts in British Africa, and in French- and Belgian-controlled areas as well, the buffalo I'd met and shot at close quarters in densest cover, though dying bravely enough, had never seen fit to charge. Which was all right too.

But commonsense indicated that my string of good fortune must have an end. There had been times enough when buffalo, unwounded and unseen until the last moment, could have committed murder with me or anybody else as the victim. They didn't—so why had this bull rushed down on a native who bore neither weapon nor malice? That was a puzzler for both José and me.

The night before, on the way back to Simoes' North Camp, we had come back emptyhanded from hunting a kudu area. The camp needed meat, and just at dusk José had taken a chancy shot at a reedbuck. Perhaps it had been hit, perhaps not, but the little buck couldn't be trailed in the darkness, which drops over equatorial Africa like a curtain when the sun goes. So at first morning light José sent Juan Cazadore, a superb black tracker usually assigned as gunbearer during my safari, to investigate while we organized for the new day's hunt.

It is to Juan—afraid of no animal, few men, and, judging by the number of his wives, no woman—that the rest of this story belongs. Carrying into the dawn light the 5-shot Cogswell & Harrison .375 that had been on his shoulder during the days when he and José had hunted buff and meat elephant together, Juan had hiked the straight half mile or so to the last trace of the reedbuck.

As he sought its blood spoor he heard the dead man's last scream, the affrighted howls of his brother, and the bellowing of the blood-mad buffalo. Quickly he ran the five or six hundred yards to the scene. There the murder evidence became as clear to him then as it was to us now, an hour later. And then Juan had taken onto himself, alone, that part of the white man's burden that involves the execution of animals dangerous to the unarmed blacks.

Juan told his story simply. He was sure from the tracks, he said, that the bull had gone back into the very clump of brush from which it had made the fatal rush. But no blotch of black hide was visible, no stir of movement. José circled at fifty yards, deliberately gave the hidden bull his scent, but the buffalo refused to stir from cover. José knew what he had to do. With no one to back him—just his rifle and its full magazine—he worked into the tangle of a fresh-felled tree that had been burned off its stump by the natives in clearing the area, and stood by its trunk.

Then he shouted at the buffalo, taunted it as a matador in a bull ring of Spain cries "Toro!" until finally the brush parted and a ton of black fury, its horns already blood-tipped, launched itself at him.

It took every shot from Juan's .375 to stop that charge, and he hit the bull hard every time—in the head, in the shoulders, and finally in the spine. It lay before us now, a black hulk only five steps from where Juan had stood, perhaps fifty from the huddled body of the black it had earlier smashed into death.

There was little more we could do. "I must send the truck to notify the D.C. of all the details," said José, "and we will take this man to the village of his father for burial. That is all."

But it wasn't really all. There remained points on which I for one will forever wonder. Why should a buffalo in the prime of life, accustomed to the villagers' activities, unwounded, bearing no evidence of illness, charge down on that defenseless African to gore and stamp him flat? What murderous instinct had prompted the bull hiding in the bush by the path that morning? I doubt we'll ever know the answers. The ways of Africa, its animals, and its people are often strange indeed.

September 1961

The Elephants of Chirisa

BOB BRISTER

It's hard to hunt a beast of such unfathomable intelligence and loyalty to its kind.

THE TRACKS ARE the size of small washtubs, and we have been following six hours since the chill of dawn. Now sweat trickles, the canteen is out of water, and September sun beats down like a blowtorch.

It is dry season in the Chirisa Safari Area in Zimbabwe, and little puffs of dust float up from each step of professional hunter Chris Hallamore ahead of me.

I do not like the looks of that dust. Sometimes it floats back as it should, but then it drifts to right or left. Eddying air currents have fatally altered the course of a lot of elephant stalks.

The three bulls have moved fast and steadily, from the sandy river climbing into rugged highlands, then into a brushy plateau of chest-high yellow grass crisscrossed by steep canyons and gullies. Elephants seem to know wind plays tricks in canyons.

Somehow they knew we were behind them.

At one narrow place in the trail where a rock ledge overhangs a drop of maybe 100 feet, a freshly uprooted tree lies across the ledge like a barrier. Not a leaf has been eaten. I have seen trees shoved across roads, clearly on purpose, since no others in the area were felled, and I have seen the wreck of a hunting car in Botswana that trip when the young bull stepped out of ambush and rammed a tusk through the cab, overturning it, and then crushed it as he fell from hunter Dougie Wright's brain shot . . .

Chris Hallamore is tapping his sock filled with fireplace ashes. One bit of dust blows one way, the next another. "They seem to know where the wind eddies like this; they can't see well but they can pinpoint us if they can get the slightest smell. We'll have to go very slowly from here. Watch me; if I suddenly drop to the ground, you do the same."

Like the heat haze shimmering over the long grass, my mind keeps shifting and wavering. . . .

On four safaris I have tracked elephants, including that time in Kenya crawling into the huge herd on the Athi River with David Lunan so close that, with heart in throat, I noticed toenails on the "tree" beside me in the thick grass just before cows and calves stampeded all around us. Maybe I took more risk than those with the rifles because I had the movie camera for the TV film. By the time my partner Harvey Houck shot the big bull with the long, curving ivory, the young bull with him charged me instead of the guns because he heard the camera. . . .

All those miles, and blisters, and chances, but never with the rifle in my hands. Now I have the heavy Ruger .458 with its 510-grain solids and its razor-sharp Leupold scope set on 2½ power so I can count every wrinkle in a bull elephant's trunk . . . and I am having misgivings because this trip I have learned a lot more about elephants. No more fear or awe of them—there was always that—but now mystery and new respect for an intelligence I cannot fully comprehend.

At the Chirisa Wildlife Research Station and its vast surrounding safari area, new things are being learned about elephants. Forty-seven of them are being radio-tracked day and night as biologists and scientists study their movements, their habits, why some learn to become crop raiders or dangerous elephants while others do not.

We had visited the research station, seen the 12-foot neoprene collars used to attach the brightly colored radio transmitters behind the heads of dart-drugged elephants. Each unit sends out a different beep, and with three-directional receiving towers, the location of each animal can be pinpointed within a few yards. Scientists from around the world come here to study the elephants, with much of the program expense financed by the U.S.-based Mzuri Foundation, a hunters' group. The area is literally overrun by elephants crowded out of other areas by an increasing native population.

Yet relatively few elephant permits are issued for safari hunting in an area as vast as some states and so overpopulated with elephants that rangers have been methodically culling entire family groups. They may take another 1,000 before destruction of habitat is brought under control.

Why not let safari hunters do that culling? The bull license in my pocket cost $3,200; enough to pay for an anti-poaching patrol. Elephants killed by the wardens and patrols are worth much less, and the men doing that job do not relish it. The animals are located and harassed by aircraft into ambushes; fully automatic FN assault rifles cut loose on cows, calves, the whole herd. Meat stripped from their bones brings $9 a gunnysack to natives. Ivory and hides sold to traders bring far less than safari income generated for management. Why not safaris for full-time culling?

"Because," says bright, highly dedicated director of the research station Tony Conway, "we have learned the hard way that the elephants can communicate. One reason we use trained culling crews is that we must kill entire family groups. If even one is permitted to escape, word is immediately out among the other elephants and after that it becomes much more difficult, and dangerous, for scientists to approach them for observation or for our crews to cull them. We cannot take those chances with human lives; there are just too many elephants here and too many natives on the surrounding tribal lands."

We went to an "elephant graveyard," big as a small city dump, where stripped carcasses of literally hundreds of elephants lie bleaching in the sun. Out of the rubble poked the small, round feet of calves alongside those of big bulls.

"I know how you feel," said Tony Conway softly as we stood there. "It is a terrible thing, if you like elephants as I do. I've lived around them, worked with them, most of my adult life. The more I understand them the more difficult it is to kill them, but it must be done if they are to survive here."

He showed me a huge map dotted with different-colored pins. "These are surrounding tribal lands," he explained. "Natives are attempting to grow crops. Here we are, in the heart of the wild area left. These pins represent poachers' camps we have apprehended, these are some we haven't gotten to yet. Poaching is mostly with wire snares.

"Here is the leg bone of an elephant; see how the snare cut completely through it and the bone calcified around it. This elephant must have lived in constant pain, and she was a very dangerous one that had to be destroyed. Once an elephant is hurt by a snare, or wounded by some primitive native muzzleloader, the odds are much higher for that one to be a dangerous elephant.

"In this area every safari hunting party is required to have one of our game scouts along, armed with an assault rifle. It is added protection for the hunters. We realize the value of safari hunting—it provides the funds we must have to deal with the poachers and to manage and study the elephants.

"I visited your country recently," Conway added, "and I couldn't believe some of the so-called documentaries on your American television, nor the attitude of some people toward hunting here. They do not seem to realize that safari hunting is the most realistic, practical hope for the survival of many African species in countries where no other monetary support for game management exists. We have more game, of all indigenous species, here in Chirisa now than existed forty years ago, and this is designated as a safari area. By contrast, look at Kenya where the government stopped safari hunting and the elephant was almost decimated from the land by poachers. You must write some of this when you return. Or send some of your television people here. We can show them the real world of the African elephant in the wild."

When we were riding back to camp, 3 hours over rough country, I asked veteran professional hunter Sten Cedergren, who spent years guiding safaris in Kenya before moving to Zimbabwe, if he accepted Conway's views.

"About Kenya elephants and poachers, yes," he said. "About elephant communicating, yes. I have watched them, whole herds on different sides of a high ridge, out of sight of each other, suddenly begin moving at the same time to meet at the same place. As if they knew what the others were thinking."

"They do it by telepathy," says professional hunter Gary Baldwin, a native of Rhodesia and now Zimbabwe. "They have developed senses over the centuries man cannot fully understand. Yet they do some things that are so stupid for their survival. Look out there."

We were passing what appeared to be the path of a tornado; large trees were uprooted, others stripped of limbs or broken halfway to the ground. Yet most of the bark and leaves remained. Elephants that shoved over those trees took only a few bites and then shoved over others. If they are so intelligent, can they not see they are destroying their future food? A tree requires years to grow but one elephant can shove down a small forest in a day.

One of the most important things being studied at the Chirisa Research Station is which bands of elephants move around most, create the most crop or habitat destruction. Perhaps by concentrating upon those bands for culling, there could eventually be a resident population able to live within its own habitat. . . .

My mind reverts instantly to reality. Something has moved.

"Shhh," says Chris Hallamore, on his knees testing the wind. "He's right there. Young bull. Don't look at him. We'll have to go completely around. The wind is changing. I think they somehow knew it would. They're waiting for us right there, and they have the wind. Hurry! We have to cross that canyon and come up on the other side."

We follow him doggedly, thirsty and tired. My wife Sandy's normally olive complexion is pale, and Kasare, our native Green Beret game scout who has become a trusted friend, is carrying her cameras over one shoulder, the assault rifle over the other.

Suddenly he leaves the trail, circles wide, and motions to Chris.

The elephants have moved, silently as ghosts, and somehow Kasare has anticipated that and crossed their new track. We could have been walking right into them. Again we circle, and in the heat my mind wanders. . . .

It had been the cold, windy dawn before, scouting for fresh tracks, when we met a ragged apparition of a man in the road, frantically waving us down. At first we thought he was a native; his European features were smutted by campfire ash, his clothing singed, eyes blank with cold-numbed terror.

His name was, and is, Gabriel Stoltz, and he has every reason to be terrified of elephants. I had already heard his life story from the hunters and park rangers. His father had been a ranger and elephant-control officer at Wankie National Park. One night when Gabriel was fourteen, news came that a tourist vehicle had been found inside the park overturned and crushed, its occupants dead. His father, Wilhelm Stoltz, left at first light with his elephant gun and two trackers. That night young Gabriel saw his father's body rolled into a blanket because there was not enough left to carry. The two native trackers were dead, but their bodies were unmolested. From the huge tracks and other indications, a great head had crushed Wilhelm Stoltz into the ground, time and time again.

Three years later, the body of Gabriel's uncle (for whom he had been named) was found cut almost in half, gored by an elephant.

Now, still a young man, he was showing us the remains of his fire where he had lain in the sand trying to keep warm after his vehicle broke down, and the huge elephant tracks around it. He said they had come screaming and trumpeting and pounding the ground and he had climbed a tree where he'd shivered through the rest of the night. The fire had died but the elephants had stayed for hours.

Could it be true that elephants never forget? That they can communicate past happenings in faraway places? Could they somehow have known that this was the son of Wilhelm Stoltz, the man some older Wankie elephants hated and killed?

Ridiculous. Wankie is many miles away. But then, why did elephants so uncharacteristically come to a fire, pounding and trumpeting? Rhinos come to fires, the natives say, but not elephants. And why had they kept Gabriel Stoltz up that tree, in terror, until they heard our vehicle approaching?

We had been unable to track them then; they were headed for the boundary of tribal lands not far away, and the trackers said they were traveling too fast. If an elephant walks fast, a man must run.

This morning we had picked up the tracks crossing the same road, returning, and they were apparently the same three bulls, one much larger than the others. . . .

"Don't move!" commands Hallamore. "Slowly sit down below the grass."

From the corner of my eye I have already seen the giant gray mound move; incredible how something so mammoth can be so invisible until it moves—an elephant is so big it looks like the landscape.

Hallamore in one smooth movement is up a tree, climbing hand over hand to the top, then dropping lightly to the ground. He can be an incredible athlete when he is close to game and the hunting instinct lights his eyes.

"The other two are ahead," he whispers. "Can't make out which is the big one; they're facing away into the wind. We'll circle; stay bent over, watch every step, no camera clicks, no sneezes. We'll act as if we are just passing by the other way. They can't see well, but they can make out movement."

We crouch, crawl, stop to rest, and Chris opens the bolt of his battered .375, checking the chambered round. I do the same.

We sit with rifles across knees, inching forward on hands and butts to keep heads higher in the grass. We can see the vague, gray blobs. Finally, when they loom like gray mountains over us, we must slowly stand to judge the ivory. It is impossible to realize how big they really are until you are looking up at them, 11 feet tall at the shoulder, maybe 11,000 pounds. I can feel the sheer exhilaration of closeness to wild and dangerous creatures, but also other feelings entirely different from those I've had with less perilous game.

Cape buffaloes have been excitement and danger, cunning and willing to ambush and kill you until their last death bellow. But there has been no remorse for them.

The big cats have seemed so aloof, impersonal, uncaring for me or anything else, killing machines that play with victims and sometimes begin eating while the prey is still alive.

But this is different.

It is one thing to see the bones of a thousand elephants bleaching in the sun, to know the old crop-raiding bull would soon be dead anyway. It is something else entirely to realize you are about to be personally responsible for the end of a creature from another time, about your own age, with a degree of intelligence and loyalty to others of his clan that man cannot completely comprehend.

"Hold halfway between the ear and his eye," Hallamore is whispering, "Be absolutely sure. The instant you shoot, that young bull on the right probably will charge. I'm watching him; you must watch only the big bull. If you miss the brain, he'll get up; put another one instantly into the heart. Are you ready? I'm going to move to the right, so he will turn his head and give you a better angle and then we can see that other tusk better."

He takes two steps and suddenly the bull's trunk snakes up into the air like a huge rubbery antenna, scanning the sky, then pointing straight at us.

"Now!"

The trigger squeezes and the sound and jolt are distant, as if someone else has done this and time freezes into slow-motion frames as the bull slowly, ponderously sits down backwards, then rolls over. The ground jars and dust rises.

All hell breaks loose; both small bulls are coming, the one on the right fast with ears against his head, trunk coiled.

Kasare knows instantly he means business. The FN chatters in ear-splitting bursts, inches over the bull's head, and Chris has the .375 pointing upward at the huge, bulging forehead.

At 10 yards the young bull skids to a stop, trunk lashing and swinging, ears now flare forward in confused bluff. The bull on the left comes up beside him, growling like a huge dog.

Kasare cuts loose again over their heads, and perhaps it is a sound they remembered. They shuffle off, tails upraised and switching in anger, back to the dead bull. Defiantly they stand beside him like sentinels, refusing to let us come closer. Flies buzz, and the long grass rustles in the wind. Nobody speaks.

And then, as if by some signal, the two young bulls turn and melt into the brush.

I do not think I will ever kill another elephant.

June 1982

The Lion Hunt

GENE HILL

Sometimes, the best trophy is the one not taken.

THE BEST AFRICAN trackers are by nature quiet, matter-of-fact professionals dealing in a world that most of us will never understand. When an experienced tracker sees something of extraordinary interest, he nods his head in that direction or sometimes makes an undemonstrative pointing gesture, as if slightly embarrassed to show you the obvious. So when our man spotted the huge redheaded lion, he casually touched me on the shoulder and whispered, "Simba."

Someone once remarked that you will never forget your first lion in the wild; that may be the understatement of this century, at least. My first lion was not only the biggest, most ferocious lion anyone had ever seen, it was red-maned—not pink or strawberry, but *red*! It was *my* lion and I can see it right this minute as vividly as ever, an incredible, mythical sculpture of arrogant power out for an afternoon stroll, exhibiting himself for adulation and fear in his kingdom. We stopped the hunting car and watched him disappear into some scrub. Never once did the lion so much as acknowledge our presence with a glance; his majesty did not wish to waste time on the likes of us.

The traditional hurried conference took place and this time it was really hurried since our hunter, David Ommanney, knew exactly what he was doing and neither Jim Rikhoff nor I had the faintest idea. Up until now I hadn't considered a lion and Jim already had a very nice one from an earlier safari. Now that we had one virtually sitting on our doorstep, and with nothing better to do, we decided to have at least a good look at it.

"Our doorstep" turned out to be a private farm that bordered our hunting block and the manager, a Scot named Jock McDonald, knew the redhead all too well; in fact, he'd been providing his dinner for quite a while. Not only did he want the lion off the farm, he pleaded for us to do it and sweetened the offer by telling us we could take anything else as well. Everything had fallen into place. Except for a few insignificant details, the lion was as good as ours.

Earlier in the day I had taken a good eland and much of the morning had been devoted to talk of eland steaks, eland roasts, eland hash, and the proper wines. Now I was about to offer up a hind quarter, which I did gladly in the spirit of the great lion adventure. Ommanney supervised the hanging of the meat and then spent a couple of hours building the blind. He walked around it from every conceivable angle, adding a branch here and a tuft of grass there, making us sit inside to be sure we could see out and nothing could see in. When the hide was finally finished, it was perfect—virtually unnoticeable, the best I have ever seen, before or since.

At camp that night we tossed a coin and Jim won, or lost (it's still debatable), but he was to be the savior of Jock's cattle. The good news was that I didn't have to get up at 3 A.M. and sit in the dark with the mambas and army ants, with Ommanney forbidding you to do anything but breathe, and to do that very quietly.

I heard them all getting ready and blissfully went back to sleep for about 3 minutes before my gun bearer came in with a cup of tea, handed me my clothes, and told me to hurry. It was at least a mile from where we left the truck to the blind, and since we were more afraid of Ommanney than the lion, we were *quiet*. Pictures of teachers taking the third grade to the zoo passed through my mind, but if I had giggled, David would have strangled me.

At first light we could see that the lion had come to the bait and we were positive he was *right here* and would be back feeding any minute. But as hunting so often goes, the lion had other ideas. We had a late breakfast and talked for the rest of the day about the lion. I shot a Thompson gazelle for supper and we all went to bed early. I tossed and turned all night thinking about the wounded lion stories I'd heard; it was not unlike being in the trenches with an attack scheduled for dawn.

For the next two days it was the same story. The lion fed a little during the nights but had other errands to attend to at dawn. Then on the third morning there was something different in the air. We sat in the blind totally alert, with that strained composure you get when you know something is there—that strange blend of anticipation and fear of being both the hunter and the hunted. Suddenly where there had been no lion there was one. The cold light glinted off his red mane. He turned and stared into our souls for a second and then he was gone. It was almost unreal.

At full light Ommanney whispered, "He's there, in that little thicket;

let's go shoo him out like a rabbit." I was only carrying a camera and the idea of the lion/rabbit exercise gave me considerable pause.

"What if I see him?" I asked.

"Shoot!" David said. Then he looked up at the sky for a second and said, "I'd guess about F-8 at 125th of a second."

Thus comforted, I followed Jim and David, at a decent distance, into the thicket. In terms of sheer reluctance, I've never been able to top this one. I wondered how bad it would hurt and how they'd get me to the hospital in Nairobi.

After the longest half hour of my life, it was decided that the lion had run off. I had been released from death row. I wanted a cold beer and so did Jim. Ommanney, honoring tradition, had a cup of tea and we sat and chatted about the lion. David was strangely happy and I finally realized that he had never really wanted to shoot the lion. He talked about the beast's prime condition and the fact that Africa *was* lion and not cattle. We felt that we had played the game and had fairly lost—but the only thing we'd really lost was a kind of remorse, the strange sense of hollow victory that troubles the heart when you take such a fine animal.

David cut the rope that held the haunch and we left it there, suddenly feeling very good about ourselves, about lions, and about Africa.

The other day Jim and I were talking about our lion and just the conversation made us feel young and strong again. That's part of the enduring magic of the animal. Jim said that it must have been the lion's lucky week. I have been thinking about that, and now I'm sure it was just the other way around.

October 1990

The Old Man and the Boy

ROBERT RUARK

*The Old Man's remarks made the Boy sense time in a new way, and
a day on the marsh would never be the same.*

THE OLD MAN squinted at the sunny summer day, the washed sky
lightly fleeced with cloud. He filled his pipe and lit it with great
care. Then he puffed it into strong coal and pointed the stem at
me.

"I don't care very much for you today," he said.

"What have I done bad now?"

"Nothing," the Old Man answered. "But you will. And that's got
nothing whatsoever to do with the reason I'm not particularly fond of you
today."

The Old Man raised me to be polite; so I was polite. "Why?" I asked.

"Because you're a boy," the Old Man said. "And I am an old man. And
there are days when an old man looks at a boy and realizes what it is like to
be a boy. And that makes the old man mad, because he can't ever be a boy any
more."

Privately I reckoned that this was as useless a piece of confab as the
Old Man ever unloaded. I didn't say anything at all.

"It's envy, of course," the Old Man said. "Just pure jealousy slightly
complicated with rheumatism, sciatica, and the knowledge that all roads point
only to the grave. I apologize for bringing up the subject. But I would like to
leave you with one thought: Don't look forward to next Christmas. You'll just
be six months older, and you can't get those six months back. And try to train
yourself to milk the most out of any experience you're having at the moment,
whether it's being kept after school or having the measles. Most of the things
you do, you do only once, the right way, including whooping cough. I'll see
you around."

275

The Old Man stuck his pipe in his mouth and stumped off. He was seldom if every surly, but he was plainly what he called "ungruntled" today. He hadn't been really well for a long time, and I guess being sick was riding his nerves pretty hard.

All of a sudden I felt mighty miserable. You know how it is when you get used to a person—you can't see them change—and I was so used to the Old Man it never occurred to me that he was getting older all the time, and feebler, and maybe a little bit crankier. But now I watched him walking down the street, and he walked slower, and his feet sort of dragged, and his shoulders hunched more, and the thought suddenly struck me: He's getting *old* and so am I. It had never occurred to me, in a life where I waited for school to close, or Christmas to come, or the bird season to open, that I was merely marking time between one date and another, and wasting the hours in between. It never occurred to me that as the Old Man got older, so did I. All of a sudden the sun wasn't quite so bright, the sky was not so lovingly lined with soft cloud.

The Old Man used to say that most people looked but never saw anything. "Most people go through life," he told me once, "stone-blind with their eyes wide open. Anything from a chinch bug to a clam is interesting if you will really look at it and think about it." I was now beginning to understand what he meant.

I dived under the house and got the oars. I went to the attic and collected the cast net and a light fishing rod and the tackle box. I shouldered the lot and headed for the river. It never occurred to me that everything I did was dictated by something the old gent had told me. "Son," he would say, "when your heart is sick and you got some thinking to do, there ain't no substitute for a boat and a fish pole. Water eases the mind, soothes the eyes, calms the nerves, and you can always eat the fish."

I got into the boat and rowed out across the channel, the sun sparkling off the jolly little wind-tossed wavelets, and the smell of salt water and steaming marsh strong in my nose.

I don't know if you've ever been lucky enough to smell a salt mud marsh on a fresh summer's day, but this here Chanel No. 5 I read about can't smell near as good as just plain channel with the wind blowing off the marshes, fetching the smell of mud with a little bit of the cedars and cypress that line a sound mixed up in sun and grass and plain old mud full of sand-fiddler holes, oyster beds, and rotting clams. I never thought too much about a marsh, but it's really the richest piece of real estate in the world.

The life you don't see that goes on in a marsh is fantastic. I loved to hear the bongo booming of the bitterns you never saw, and the cawing of the crows, and the occasional shrill scream of a lesser hawk as it swooped low and graceful over the tips of grass, looking, always looking, for something to swoop on and seize. The yellow-green of the marsh was spotted with great white herons, blue herons, and a rather droopy-looking heron we called a "cranky." The brilliant red epaulets of the blackbirds looked like rubies scattered in the grasses.

Just off the sand bars, in the mud, I drove an oar into the bottom and tethered my boat to it. Then I took the cast net and waded around until I saw a school of shrimp making little pops of water; two casts got me four or five dozen baits. A school of mullet was jumping—rather big ones, ten, twelve inches long—and the cast net took care of supper, even if I had no luck with the rod.

It was the time of year for soft crab, and I found half a dozen with my feet. A boy with nimble toes will always stumble over a clam or so, and by the time I got ready to unleash the boat, I had it pretty well stocked with crabs and kicking shrimp and mullet and big, blue-purple, white-lipped clams.

Don't let anybody kid you about a fishing hole. You can throw a bait all day long in ordinary water and get nothing but exercise, but if you know a deep sinkhole or an old wreck or some barnacled pilings, according to what you're looking for in the way of fish, you've got it fixed when you first drop your line. I rowed the little skiff to a hole I knew that was as certain a source of supply as a deep freezer, which had not at that time been invented. This hole was populous with blackfish and perch and an occasional trout—nothing grand, maybe, but powerful nice for the pan. I fished as happy as a boxful of birds for two hours, and filled the crocus sack I kept tied over the stern of the little boat. A half-pound of fish on a tiny rod seemed as big as a marlin in those days, and a two-pound weakfish was a whale.

In the boat's locker I always kept a frying pan, some cornmeal, salt, pepper, and vinegar. Driftwood was no problem on a sand bar, and I had myself a North Carolina approximation of a shore dinner when the fish quit biting and my stomach started to growl. There is nothing really wrong with soft-shell crabs, fresh clams, and fish that don't stop kicking until they feel the flame, not if you are a boy and starving and all by yourself in a boundless burning sweep of sand and marsh and sky and water.

When I washed the skillet clean with sand and salt water, wiped the grease off my hands and face, stomped out the fire, and got back into the boat, the tide was running strongly out, and shoving the skiff along was a job for a whole set of galley slaves. The sun was hitting like it always hits around three or four, hotter than the noonday sun, and by the time I got back to the shingle I was pouring sweat.

It was a simple enough matter to drag the boat up on the shingle and then walk down to the pier for a fast jump into the water. When I collected what was left of the fish and clams and crabs and shouldered the oars and the rowlocks and the cast net, I was just about barely able to make it to the house.

The Old Man was sitting on the porch, smoking his pipe and rocking gently in his favorite chair. He looked like he felt better. He looked younger. "What you been doing?" he asked unnecessarily.

"I went out in the boat," I said. "I went fishing."

"See anything interesting you want to tell me about?" he asked.

"Nothing very much," I said. "It was just the same old thing, marsh, water, fish, birds—same old thing."

"I am not being rude when I call you a little liar," the Old Man said. "It is a term of respect, not to say endearment. I apologize for this morning all over again, and I am no longer jealous of you because I am not a boy. Go wash the mud off you and come to supper. We're having steak, as I figgered you've had a bait of fish for one day."

The Old Man smiled. "I really wouldn't want to be a boy again." he said. "It's too much work."

July 1954

Of Miracles and Memories

BILL TARRANT

A man's relationship with Pup won't last forever, except in a special dimension.

OLD GUN DOGS have stood the test of time and event and circumstance. They come now, slowly, and lay at foot or close to side, jowls flat, eyes faded with the fog of cataract, their muzzles and paws white or speckled salt and pepper. But they come. They want to be close.

They are great treasures, these old dogs. For they are more than themselves lying there. They are us. Parts of us. A hill climbed together and the crimson leaves of sumac danced in the morning sunlight. The well looked in and the rock dropped and the chill of the dark hole seemed forever before the splash was heard.

They are sweaty palms, for you were hosting your boss and he'd never gunned over a trained dog before, yet Pup was so birdy you couldn't be sure he'd hold for shot and wing.

They are the iced mace of wind thrown by bad-dad winter, off to the north, blowing the redleg mallards off their last haunts. Blowing them south, flying like buckshot. And you're gripping Pup and whispering, "No head up," and you fit the duck call to your lips. It is cold and you know it will freeze to the skin. But you call. And the lead hen throws her body high, looking down and back, seeing the iced-in blocks pointing bill-up to the slate sky.

And now they come, shingles rippled loose from some old barn and the wind is driving them crazily toward your decoys and you stand and the old gun barks and the dog launches. He's breaking ice and standing high in the water, though his feet don't touch bottom. And you wish you'd never shot. For nothing can live out here. Not even Pup in the prime of his life. Yet he clamps the big bright drake and spins about, throwing water with his whipping tail, and comes for you—the drake covering his face—so he must

279

swim by instinct, for he cannot see.

You're out of the blind now and running the bank, yelling out. And the retriever comes to shore, not stopping to shake, and heads straight for you. But the black dog turns instantly silver. The water has frozen that fast. And you take the duck and the dog shivers, his teeth chattering, and the pelvic-drive muscles convulse. Then he spins in the tall yellow grass; he runs and rubs the side of his jowls in the mud and stubble.

No duck is worth this—remember saying that?—and the two of you go back to the house. Back to the towel you rub Pup with and the fire you sit before while the wind makes a harmonica of your house-siding and whomps down the fireplace to billow the ashes.

But the duck *does* lie on the sideboard by the sink. You entered nature and went duck hunting and tricked the wild fowl to your trap and the dog closed the door.

Still you're sorry you went, but years later when the smell of that day's wet fur is forgotten and even the curled tailfeathers from the mallard have long been blown from the fireplace mantle, you'll remember. You'll remember that retrieve and old Pup will come to side and you'll fondle his ears and the memory of that cold day and that single duck will become the most important thing that ever happened in your life.

For Pup is dying.

And you can't see him, but you have to smile and call him to you. It may be the last time you ever touch his ear. But that's just part of it. You're dying, too. Pup will just go first. As he always went first in the field and at the blind. You followed him, not the other way around. It was he who entered the unknown and learned its bareness or its bounty.

And you love the old dog, for he lived your life. He was the calender of your joy. Why, you could leap the stream when you got your first pup. Remember? And you could hunt all day. Cold? Bosh! And the apple in your pocket was all it took to fuel you from Perkin's fence to Hadley's barn—a limit of bobwhite later.

But now the arthritis hobbles you. And the cold. It seems to come and sit in your bones like an unwanted stranger.

So you don't call just Pup to side, you call your life. You run your fingers through your past when you fondle his ears.

And you stand and go to the gun case. Why, the bluing's gone from that old Superpose. Then you remember when you bought it: long before Pup ever came into your life. And look at that duck call. There's no varnish left on the barrel. And the barrel is cracked! And the string that holds it. . . .

It was a country store back in the hills. You stopped for a loaf of bread to feed Pup. And the duck call was just in your pocket, just out of its cardboard box. And you asked the proprietor for a piece of string and he went to the meat counter and drew off a yard of it. You were always going to get a bona fide, braided lanyard.

But that's like life. You were always going to. . . .

And there's Pup. He was not a going-to. Not a put-off-till-tomorrow. Pup was planned and bought and trained and taken to field. That happened. And the million dollars was never made, and you never became branch manager, and your kids didn't make it through college. But Pup did all you imagined for him.

Pup was your one success.

And he is dying.

How many pups ago was it your sweater fitted loose on your belly and your belly was hard like the barrel of a cannon? But look at the sweater now. Stretched tight and tattered and faded. Why do you still wear it? There are Christmas sweaters still in their box: on the shelf in the closet.

And the boots. Remember? They had to be just so. But look at them now. Toes out, scuffed, heels run over. And yet you shuffle about in them.

Is it because you're holding on to the past? Is it because looking back down the road means more than looking on up ahead? Is it because the birds you went with Pup to get were got? And now? What do they say? A bird in the hand is worth more than two. . . . Maybe that's it. Pup made you a bird-in-the-hand man.

Others, in those days, may have been two-bird hopefuls. But you and Pup did it. You went. No sunshine patriots then. No sir. That bird was in hand.

He's got bad teeth now, you know? Pup has. And let's admit it. His breath stinks. And look at him, great blotches of hair hanging here and there—like some derelict mountain sheep that's taken to roadside begging. And he does little but sleep—and pass gas. He does lots of that.

There are pups to be bought, you know? Why, ads are everywhere. And some say gun dogs have gotten better than ever. Or at least the training methods have gotten so sharp you can even bring a mediocre pup along.

But, no, it's always been you and Pup. And you'll wait till he's no more. But have you ever wondered? What will you be when he's gone?

If he was the best part of your days, then what will there be when he's dead and buried? What will there be of you? Some grumpy old mumbler who sits by the fire and harrumphs at those who come to be kind?

No, not at all. For you were a gun dog man and you went to field.

Your Pup was the best gun dog you ever saw. And you watched the flash of the great black dog as he leaped through bramble and you saw him once atop the hill—how far away was he on that cast? A half mile! And all you must do is close your eyes or, better yet, just go to the window and watch the falling leaves. Pup's out there. He's by the gate, see him? And he's leaping that way he always did, urging you to get on with it. And he darts now, to the field, and sniffs the passing mice, the dickey birds.

And then you're with him, the weight of the gun reassuring in your grasp and your stride is strong and the wind bites your cheek but you laugh and blow the white steam of cold. Always you can do this, just standing at the window—for you did this.

What of the smell of straw at the old duck blind and pouring the coffee from the Thermos. Then learning how to pour the coffee from the steel cup so you could put the cup to your lips. And you never knew why the pouring made the cup manageable.

And the pride in your decoys, watching them run to the end of their cords and spinning about, ducking their heads and bobbing to drip water from their bills.

And off to the left, in that stand of multiflora rose—hear him! The cock pheasant *car-runks*. Bright as brass he is. And you could heel Pup out of the duck blind and go get him, but you like his sass. You like his arrogance. And anything that gaudy can live out there in the back of your place.

And what of the morning you and Pup were sitting there? Duck hunting, for you, didn't mean shooting ducks. It meant being there. Hearing the rustle of your heavy canvas pants and the tinkle of the dog whistles and calls as they danced on your chest. Blowing in cupped hands, beating them against the sides of your chest. And standing and stomping on the wood pallets you brought in, for the water rose with the late rains. And yet for that moment you and Pup were silent and the redtailed hawk landed, right above both of you, on a naked limb.

And you were ornery. Jumped up, you did, and yelled, "Hey Hawk!" And the hawk was so discombobulated he hurled himself to the air with a great squawk and left a white stream all over your blind as he beat his departure. But it was still funny and you sat in the draping of hawk feces for that morning and laughed.

Not another single living thing had that moment but you and Pup and the hawk, and the three of you made it momentous forever. Now the hawk is gone and Pup is going, but that memory makes you all vibrant and alive. And in a way it makes you important. Who else ever had an exclusive moment?

And if Pup had not taken you to field, you'd not have had it. So he lies there now, that generator of meaning and memory. That's what a gun dog comes to be for us. An enricher of life. Something to take ordinary moments and make them miraculous.

That's why the love for Pup is so great. What matter if he passes gas and has bad breath and moans in his sleep. He's earned his transgressions. And he tells us of our own end, for sharing the best with him, we must now share the worst with him, and we lie there, too.

But dog men push that away. Their Pup was a springer spaniel, you know. Oh how happy he was afield. Why the stub of his tail couldn't be tallied as it wagged. And it wagged that way when idle or working. He was just that happy. And he made the man happy. For happiness is infectious and there's no known cure. Not even disaster. For you'll walk around the knowledge of disaster to peek in memory of that happy tail.

And that man's Pup was a beagle, a mellow-voiced ground snorter if ever there was one. The bow legs, all that massed muscle. And how he used to launch the rabbit and then dart out in pursuit, giving the man instructions—loud instructions!—on when to shoot.

But that's not the Pup I was thinking of. No, that Pup was your cocker with thick hair the color of wheat tassels and he'd rut to launch the bird, down in the mud, going under the highwater log. And up he'd come with that smashed face, little mud balls hanging from his silver whiskers, and in a turn—which was more like a complete flip—he'd tell you with his body signal there was nothing down there and you'd best be off.

But who am I to talk like this? You know your Pup better than I ever could. For there were just the two of you and, oh, maybe a hawk! And what happened can never happen again. No man and dog could ever be that rich again, that lucky again, that blessed again.

Yet, each year several million new pups are taken into American homes, into American hearts—all on the knowledge there are some miracles and memories left out there, yet.

August 1983

A Hunter's Story

JOHN BARSNESS

He took to the trail as a child, and as life passed he found that nothing else mattered.

H E BEGAN HUNTING back in the time when men first learned to fly. Seven decades later, when I began hunting with him in the Missouri Breaks, he still had not accepted winged humanity, was convinced that every Piper Cub droning above the juniper hills was determined to drive the deer from his land, his black eyes tracking the plane across the sky like a young jack rabbit watching a red-tailed hawk.

They were the same hills he'd hunted since he was a child, when his mother, half-Assiniboine and half-Scot, drove the wagon across the high winter prairie to a coal vein eroding from a cutbank near the Dakota border, winter fuel in a treeless land. They rode wrapped in Pendleton trade blankets, and when a cottontail ran from the wind-carved snow, he would jump down from the wagon and follow the rabbit to its burrow and stamp the hole full of snow, knowing (because his mother told him so) that the rabbit would leave by another entrance and seek the sun. On the trip back, late in the afternoon with the brittle sky the same white of the hills, the rabbits would run up the hillsides and stand confused by their snow-stamped holes and his mother would lean one elbow on the wagon seat to steady the single-shot .22. When he was six or seven and could hold the little rifle she let him shoot sometimes, but he always helped gut and skin the carcasses and pack them frozen in a barrel in the barn. Sometimes there would be smoke in the distance from a coal vein struck by lightning the autumn before, and it seemed strange to his child-mind that the fire didn't freeze during blizzards like the cattle they sometimes found standing upright after storms.

He told me his father was a métis horse trader from the Cypress Hills of Saskatchewan who believed in fast horseflesh and fat cattle, who could see nothing of value in rifles but the death of wolves. He would not allow his son to hunt when fences needed fixing, and fences always needed fixing. So the son told the teachers at the Indian school that he was needed at home, and told his father at home that he was needed after school, and by the age of eleven was breaking horses for ranchers around town, riding his black gelding 30 miles between jobs. By his twelfth birthday he owned a Winchester .30/30 with a 26-inch octagonal barrel and broke horses during summer for a ranch 100 miles up the Missouri. They gave him a $1 gold piece for each greenbroke cowpony, and everyone knew they could afford it because they had made their fortune robbing trains back in the 1890's. The railroad they'd robbed ran through towns named Glasgow, Malta, Havre, Harlem, and Zurich, tank towns named by the railroad baron's daughter who'd spent a year in Europe, then traveled west in her private car, bringing the names with her.

At age fourteen the young horsebreaker was sent to boarding school in Kansas and learned of cities on the other side of the world that were named after water towers in Montana. He knew from pictures in the books that the rest of the world was no place to live, and spent his time with sharecroppers on the edge of town, running hounds after raccoons and drinking Kansas corn. The boarding school presented him with a train ticket home after one semester, and he was never happier than when he saw through his Pullman window a gray mule deer moving across the Montana dawn. He swore he would kill one, though they were scarce, and all the while he was riding home from the train depot with his father, who told him he would never amount to anything but a lazy hunter, he thought of hills where mule deer dance. He saw the shape of a certain horizon in his mind and rode there that evening with his .30/30 and killed a forkhorn buck under a rising moon.

When he came home with the buck behind the cantle his father told him to leave. He said he loved his father but could not help hunting, and even seventy years later he bit hard on his pipe when he told me the story. He said that he became very unhappy then and did too many things: drank whiskey and broke horses for gold to buy whiskey, and fought anyone who would fight. Finally he met a woman from the city who made him less unhappy so he married her. She did not like him hunting either and instead wanted more money to buy city things, so he rustled cattle at night until a friend he trusted said he would soon be strung up. His wife wanted more than he could give her and took her revenge by burning his clothes after he undressed at night. He began drinking again and would come home and shoot at the flies on the ceiling with his Colt. This stopped his wife from burning clothes, but she also stopped other things and went back to the city.

The day she left he took his .30/30 and rode down to the Missouri bottomlands, which in those days were covered with brush and timber as far as he could see from the bluffs above the river. The sun went down and the moon came up; he left his horse tied to a box elder, and he told me many years later that he still didn't know why he went down there so late but that a white deer walked between the trees through the moonlight and he followed, toward the river, seeing white antlers and white legs between the trees but never enough for a shot. He followed close to the river and could hear the current under the cutbanks. Then a breeze came down from the bluffs and he heard strange clickings and scrapings in the trees above and looking up toward the moon he saw feathers lifting and then falling around skulls and scaffolds in the branches of the trees, and heard dry leather scrape against bark. He stepped back in the shadows and something hard and white touched his cheek and he turned and ran though the cottonwoods, fearing dead grandfathers, falling over things he would not look at, picking himself up on bloody hands until the willows held him tightly with wild thin arms. He wouldn't open his eyes and yet he saw the white deer again, running toward the moon, and he fell to his knees and crawled after the deer, under the willows, until the riverbank broke and he fell down a sandy cutbank to the mud on the edge of the Missouri and saw across the water the white deer swimming, moon on his antlers and moon on the waves behind.

He'd dropped his .30/30 somewhere in the woods and would not go back. He had left his desire for whiskey back there, too, and knew that he was done with whiskey and stolen cattle and most things from the city, but that he still needed a rifle and a good shotgun, also. He broke horses again until he felt that he'd broken the madness still left in him, and bought another rifle, one of the .30/06's that hunters said could shoot as straight and far as a wolf running, plus a Winchester pump shotgun, and married a woman who could make star blankets and bead white buckskin. She did not want many city things, and his jobs breaking horses and stretching barbed wire kept them in flour and cloth and shells for his guns. They had three daughters, and in the summer and fall during the drought years, when the prairie blew for days and carried the antelope and grass away on its breath, he and his family would go to the mountains where the women picked huckleberries and sold beadwork in the tourist stores while he hunted, never carrying a compass but following instead glimpses of a white deer through dark trees. He was never lost, he said, just late sometimes, and then he would sit under a tree and eat a piece of loin or heart from the elk he'd killed and wait until the white deer came by again. He said his daughters never did understand such things, though they ate the elk, and until they noticed boys and needed to smell nicer, they helped tan the hides. They wanted to ride the highways in automobiles and do other city things, but in later years when they'd grown and run away with men from the city and then come back home without their men but with grandsons, they brought him broken-winged birds and asked his help, as if they knew a knowledge of death could help life. His grandsons listened to him (as I did a few years later, following his pointing pipe through the Missouri hills), listened to how he killed the elk whose antlers lay on the dogpen roof, the old bull he'd killed on the mountain the Assiniboine called Thunder because of the clouds that always ran through its scalp. He told about falling across a rock slide in the wind of a thunderstorm and breaking nothing but the rear sight from his rifle, and how he'd climbed to the ridge where his horse had run in the lightning and the bull was lying under the only tree on the ridge, a stunted fir; he'd walked up behind rocks and swung the rifle as the bull ran like sage grouse flying, and broken the elk's neck in front of the shoulders. He told about how he killed the mule deer as big as a yearling steer—his grandsons did not believe it, he knew from their eyes, and he grew suddenly angry, remembering how it had taken all one day to lower the buck off the steep mountainside, the cowhide rope around his waist to keep the buck from sliding off into the canyon below, down to a barren ridge where he let the horse drag the deer down in the night. But he forgave his grandsons because they were young and would sometimes ride with him in the old Chevrolet pickup he now hunted from on the prairie. They shot the young sage grouse that stood under the sagebrush along the coulees with their great-grandmother's .22, and he showed them how to gut grouse quickly without a knife, but they were bored with dead things and wanted to find more live things to kill. He tried to explain that other moments were possible, but did not have the words, not because of any lack of education but because of the repetitive stubbornness between youth and old age, where grandsons never want anything but the high ridges and grandfathers have lost the memories of all the valleys and draws. As he grew older he circled the places he remembered best, the coulees near home, and left the mountains to the young men who would not climb them. He forgot to grow bitter because he kept these places in his mind.

He still went out in the mornings before everyone else and sometimes would kill a buck or catch a large fish while others slept, not because of any particular skill but because the sky still held wonder and the prairie still seemed unknowable. He remembered his youth more clearly than his old age, and the horizon still seemed the same horizon he'd envisioned when he'd stepped off the railroad with the names of distant cities. He began to forget the names of his great-grandchildren, but during the times he had the strength for his grandsons or me to take him back in the hills he could still find the trails where he'd driven stolen cattle, where he'd killed the buck with antlers as long as wagon spokes but only two tines. Often he was very tired and would sit smoking his pipe while around him people whispered strange words like Alzheimer's and wondered if he heard, but he listened only to sounds and not words, because in the mountains and pale coulees he had never heard words and knew that forgetting now and remembering when was just the calling of the white deer and the moon.

March 1987

Fishtail Poker

FRANK DUFRESNE

*The sourdoughs thought they knew a sucker when they saw one, but the
horn-rimmed biologist turned the cards on them.*

IT'S ALL RIGHT now, I hope, to tell about a small band of old sourdoughs who took part in the strangest hoax ever perpetrated in Alaska.
Most of the characters involved in this bogus fish deal have long since
gone on their last stampede. They've left the fabled trout waters of the
wild Iliamna for a place where the fishing may be even better for them, and
where they won't have to play any more shenanigans with a gullible government. After twenty-five years it should be okay to reveal how this group of
oldtimers finally had the rug jerked out from under them when the Territorial Legislature stopped shelling out a 2½¢ bounty on Dolly Varden trout tails.

When the black news reached the Iliamna settlers they all blamed the
Juneau lawmakers for their hard luck. But that wasn't the whole story. It was
just the ending. Their real trouble started months before in a poker game.

It was the queerest, the wildest, game I ever saw in all my Alaska travels. Outside Sam Foley's log cabin trading post that long ago night chained
malemutes howled their sorrows at a ragged half moon riding across the broken clouds. Salmon thrashed in the spawning riffles in Sam's creek. You could
hear the crazy shrilling of loons in the cove, and if you pushed open the slab
door sagging on its bear-hide hinges you might pick up the "Whuff!" of a
grizzly up around the bend chasing salmon. Wild, did I say? There wasn't another roof for thirty miles up or down the Iliamna Lake shore. That's why a
half dozen boat travelers crowded into Sam Foley's little fur-trading post that
night. We wanted to escape the jabbing hot needles of a billion mosquitoes.
The poker game came later.

Loner Bill Hammerstone, with tobacco-fouled whiskers hiding a
dirty wool shirt all the way to the belt-line of his seal-skin britches, started it.

Nicoli, the one-eyed half-breed from Koggiung, sat in and so did Pegleg Pur-kee and trader Sam. None of them had any money, but they had something just as good in those remote parts. They had fishtails.

When turned into a deputy collector for the Territorial bounty, Dolly Varden trout tails were worth 2½¢ each. Strung forty on a coil of bailing wire and dried in the smoke around the summer fish camps, each hoop was good for a dollar in such limited trade as went on all over the Iliamna wilderness in those days. Ten hoops bought a gunny of flour. Another ten could be bartered for a sack of sugar, and with this potent combination properly blended the shaggy-haired pioneers had the makings of a few johns of pop-skull hooch. Of course they could buy other items, too, like paystreak bacon and dried beans, woollen longjohns, beaver traps, and .30-30 cartridges. The hoops were like money, only freer, because when they were gone a man could always rustle up a few more fishtails with his seine. Bush pilots accepted them as fare for plane hops. Holy men left the settlement churches on Sunday fes-tooned with fishtail bracelets and smelling like sin.

I was humped under a sputtering gasoline lantern scrawling field notes when my partner for the trip invited himself into the game. C. Wardsworth Thatcher was a chubby, horn-rimmed biologist from the States, and I figured that what he didn't know about Alaska-brand poker would fill a bigger book than the one he told the sourdoughs he was planning to write on Alaska fishes.

"Didn't fetch any fishtails with me," he apologized. "Just silver, paper dollars, stuff like that. . . ."

Bill Hammerstone stroked his boar's nest of whiskers, and his preda-tory gray eyes under hooded eyebrows reminded me of a tom lynx sizing up a fat young snowshoe rabbit. "Sit in, son," he invited as he shoved his up-ended cartridge box along the puncheon floor to make space at the table. "Y'couldn't be in nicer company."

Of that I had my doubts. Not only were these old reprobates reckless poker players, but they'd also learned to read the cards on Sam Foley's dog-eared, greasy deck almost as well from the back as the front. Still, I guessed it was none of my concern. The government had asked me to take C. Wardsworth Thatcher along on my next patrol trip to the Iliamna region, but they hadn't said anything about being his guardian angel. If the fishery scien-tist got himself picked clean in a backwoods poker game, I figured it was his own hard luck.

At first it looked as if C. Wardsworth would be down to his pin-feathers in a hurry. I stole a look now and then, and every time I did he was shoving out good currency and not a hoop of fishtails was coming his way in exchange. After a while he must have smelled a rat—or three of them. He called for a new deck. Bill Hammerstone bawled his objections, said there wasn't another pack of cards within a hundred miles, and glared ferociously at me when I dug into my duffel bag and tossed in a fresh, sealed pack. It wasn't long afterwards that C. Wardsworth Thatcher started raking in a few fishtails.

At the time it didn't mean much to me one way or the other. I had troubles of my own. The Alaska Game Commission was more than merely puzzled; it was frustrated by the great preponderance of Dolly Varden trout showing up in the Iliamna region. In other parts of the Territory this red-spotted cousin of the eastern squaretail shared normal distribution with rainbows, cutthroats, lakers, and grayling. I'd been asked to find out why the Dolly Varden had become so thick in the Iliamna watersheds that it had been judged a menace to the commercial salmon fisheries, from which most of Alaska's taxes were collected. The Dolly had been accused of following migrating salmon up from the Bering Sea to the river spawning beds and gorging on eggs and newly hatched fry. Canners had passed laws classifying it as a predator and they were contributing toward payment of a special 2½¢ bounty to wipe out the beautiful varmint.

It hadn't worked out that way at all. The more Dolly Varden trout tails the residents turned in for bounty, the more they seemed to swarm in the rivers. Locals were seining slithering boat loads, snipping off the tails, and boiling the carcasses in big iron pots for sled-dog feed. The bounty hunters were doing all right for themselves and their dogs were growing fat as seals, but there wasn't any sign that the Dolly nuisance was being eradicated. The situation had become a first class mystery, and I hadn't done anything to solve it in my interviews with the oldtime settlers and Eskimo tribes.

"Just keep that bounty money rolling," was all Sam Foley could contribute. Pegleg Purkee and halfbreed Nicoli agreed, but big Bill Hammerstone didn't think the government was doing enough.

"Y'ought to up the 2½¢ bounty," he growled as he sluiced tobacco juice at a knot-hole in the floor of the trading post. "Quit splittin' pennies. Y'ought to double it to a nickel a tail."

It had me stumped. On three rivers reported to be "infested" with Dolly Vardens, where heavy bounty payments had been made, I fly casted bright streamers, strips off my red felt hat, and clusters of fresh salmon eggs—all prime Dolly lures. I dredged the pools with hardware. Everything worked. I never caught so many fish in my life, and I'll always remember the Iliamna as the greatest angling water in all of Alaska. Mostly they were enormous rainbows, lake trout long as a pair of waders, grayling, and northern pike. Only three were Dollies.

"You're not fishing right," hinted C. Wardsworth.

I found an old piece of seine at an Eskimo fish camp and a couple of moon-faced youngsters helped me pull it across the river pool out front. We netted a couple of suckers; also a dozen young salmon and small trout. There were no Dollies. The only clue I picked up at the Eskimo camp was a trout that had missed the dog-cooking pot and fallen on the ground. Though it was covered with bluebottle flies I could see that its tail had been snicked off. I also observed that it was not a Dolly Varden trout but a protected rainbow.

This lone clue got lost in the shuffle when Johnny Walatka, the famous bush pilot, told us that most of the trout-seining was now going on below Iliamna Lake in the Kvichak River. It took C. Wardsworth Thatcher and me a couple of days to buck a hundred miles of lake whitecaps to the outlet village of Iguigig, local government center. Johnny had been right about the seining, though we were too late to see any of it done. The Dolly Varden seiners had turned in their hoops for Territorial warrants, and all the dried fishtails had been burned in the presence of witnesses so they couldn't be cashed again. Everything had been handled neatly by the village official. It was almost too neat.

We cranked up the outboard motor in our long, open boat and started our return voyage up the lake for the portage to Cook's Inlet to catch a mailboat back to Juneau. We'd used up our time. I didn't know any more about where all the Dolly Varden fishtails were coming from than I had at the beginning of the trip. The only thing I'd found out for sure was that nobody wanted to talk about it. The scattered homesteaders would gab with us for hours on every subject save one—fishtails.

If it hadn't been for our chance stopover at Sam Foley's trading post we might never have cracked the nut. And even then the case of the fake fishtails would have remained one of the great unsolved mysteries if C. Wardsworth hadn't got lucky in that poker game.

Behind his horn-rimmed glasses, the biologist eyed his shaggy-faced opponents cautiously. He'd figured out by now that they were all in cahoots against him. But with a fresh deck of cards he'd whittled down the odds, and was taking his share of the pots. Between pauses in scribbling my field diary I began to note a pattern in his play. He was being cagey about it, but it was now beginning to show through. He was pushing silver when he lost; pulling in fishtails with his winnings. When the game broke up halfbreed Nicoli, Pegleg Purkee, trader Sam and long-whiskered Bill Hammerstone were all jingling silver coins, and C. Wardsworth had his pockets turned wrongside out. But it was a fair exchange, because now he owned two gunnysacks full of dried fishtails.

Next morning he toted them out to our open boat and mounted guard on them all the way back to Juneau headquarters. When I saw them next, one of the hoops had been unstrung and the tails spread across a laboratory table. C. Wardsworth was studying them intently through a magnifying glass and jotting the results on a kind of scorecard he'd made up.

"This is what I meant by fishing 'right,'" he reminded me, checking his observations with technical sketches in a volume on fishing nomenclature. "Take a look at this one."

I did. "It's not a Dolly," I said.

It wasn't, and neither were most of the others. Meticulously, C. Wardsworth keyed them all out right down to the last shriveled tail. A sample hoop of forty tails contained fourteen rainbows, five whitefish, six lake trout, two pike, two grayling, one sucker, seven fingerling salmon, *and three Dollies*. Another hoop was almost all immature sockeye salmon, the very species the bounty was being paid to save!

Like all bounty systems, the 2½¢ price on Dolly Varden tails had proved a costly fizzle. I thought of Bill Hammerstone and all the other old-timers who would be jolted out of their improvident socks when the Legislature acted. They'd survive the shock. Things were changing fast in Alaska. Johnny Walatka was ferrying in plane loads of sport fishermen from all over the States. In their camps, with their boating and guiding, the shaggy characters of an earlier era would soon be making a site more than 2½¢ on every trout.

January 1963

Bingo

GENE HILL

A story of a fat man, a fat Lab, and the love between them.

THEY WERE BOTH too fat. He had a big safety pin, the kind used for a horse blanket, holding the front of his hunting coat together, and under the coat an old red-and-green wool shirt threatened to throw its buttons. His black Labrador wheezed and whistled from the effort of walking up to the line where the judges were waiting, and when he removed her collar, her neck fell to double in size. As they stood there listening to the explanation of the test, the fat black dog snuggled so close to her master's leg that she seemed to be leaning on him for support. He let his arm drop and she put her nose in his palm and closed her eyes. A minute ago I had been ready to laugh at these two, but now I had to turn for a minute—something seemed to have gotten into my eyes.

The test wasn't easy. The first bird was a rather long mark across a weedy channel and the second mallard an even longer marked single deep back among dead timber. A couple of the younger dogs had finished the series but none without a lot of whistles and hand signals. On a rating of one to ten, the best score I had given was a generous five. A lot of duck hunters would have used a boat rather than send a dog through the stumps and snags, and I wouldn't have blamed them. What we judges had meant to be a hard marking test turned out to be one that depended a lot on pure heart; "want to" was what we ended up grading the dogs on. Most of them didn't have a lot of it.

The fat dog's name was Bingo, and somehow I got the picture of the two of them eating popcorn together and watching game shows on television. I imagined them sitting side by side at the local bar, drinking beer and watching baseball. What I couldn't imagine is one ever being more than 3 feet from the other if they could help it.

Much to my surprise and delight, Bingo did a pretty respectable job. You could hear her for half a mile, huffing her slow way through the lotus pads and pickerel weed. At first I was worried that she'd drown or have a heart attack, but she was too fat to sink and seemed more than delighted to do something that her boss wanted done. Bingo wrestled her belly over the bank, took a half dozen deep breaths, waddled over and picked up the duck and swam back. Her master hadn't used one whistle or so much as moved a hand. It took forever, but Bingo was showing the skinny Labs a thing or two and the crowd loved every long, worried minute of it.

She finished her retrieve with a lovely little flourish, walking around behind and sort of adjusting herself and then sitting practically on his foot and offering him the duck as if it were a crown. As one of the senior judges, I was supposed to be the very model of impartiality and decorum, but I put my notebook under my arm and joined the gallery in a spontaneous minute of applause. Then I wrote "10" next to Bingo's name on my scorecard. By now she'd recovered her breath and her handler signaled that he was ready for the next test. He had Bingo lined up perfectly and she glowed with anticipation at the shot. The bird boy threw the shackled duck and Bingo slid into the water with a very audible sigh of pleasure and began paddling toward the swamp.

You look for a lot of subtle things when you're judging a trial. You get so you can sense indecision in a dog, or reluctance. Some dogs are too bold and don't use their head, just crash on until they stumble over a bird or get handled to it. Others are too tentative, continually asking their handler, "Am I doing this right?" I don't like either one. What I like in a dog is a mixture of confidence, common sense, and obedience; about in that order. I'm big on a good dashing water entry, an aura of determination, and a feeling that a dog wants to please rather than do the job like an automaton. I like to see more of the pure dog than just the result of training.

I'd gotten away from field trials for a while because I felt that a lot of the judging was unrelated to hunting situations, and there was a laziness that ended up with the tests being too hard rather than being fair, and having a few more dogs come back in recalls. I'd run a lot of dogs and had a very sensitive feeling about the work and companionship part of it; I hated to drop a dog too quickly. I'd lost a couple of first-place ribbons because of what I felt was a lack of understanding of the dogs' problems in certain situations. I felt that a lot of judges had never really done enough gunning or worked enough with dogs to be able to get a good handle on borderline judgements.

But, at the bottom, the whole thing is for the dog, not the convenience of the gallery or the handlers or the judges. You get to feeling sorry for dogs that have handlers who are too harsh on them—and almost as often, for handlers who have dogs that are too good for them. I'd been one of the latter a couple of times and am still a little embarrassed about being obviously dumb when I should have left it all to the dog. But here I was trying to keep a good balance between my head and my heart and worrying about poor old Bingo running into an underwater log or limb and getting disoriented, or worse, hurt.

Bingo had been her perfunctory self in our other series in the morning, taking forever and looking anything but stylish or fiery, but somehow she always got the job done. Other dogs were faster, more elegant, or more exciting, but where they'd overrun a bird, then circle for a minute trying to find it, Bingo would walk up to exactly where it was, pick it up, and come back. One of the gallery remarked that watching her was "as exciting as seeing a guy lay brick." That may be, but the brick got laid, and laid right. And after all, this was just a fun interclub trial, not a big regional AKC sanctioned affair. We were supposed to be judging hunting retrievers, not watching a track meet. And as much as I like a dog that can zip out and zip back in, I also respect the old workman who gets it done right the first time.

Bingo was not going to be placed first or second. Those places had already been established by a couple of dogs that were clearly "big trial" contenders, dogs that shouldn't have been in this trial at all. It was just that their owners were ribbon-hungry and liked to show off a bit when the chance came along. But a third here was not to be taken lightly. There were plenty of old campaigners doing their stuff, and a couple of up-and-coming dogs that had it all on any given day.

Sometimes in competitions, a great and certain knowledge spreads among the judges, the spectators, and the contestants that a prize is deserved, regardless of what the rules or the score are. And there was poor old Bingo, looking like the kid at the picnic who had unexpectedly been asked to join the games and said, "Why not?"

Well, not to prolong what you've already guessed. Bingo did it all, and we gave her the ribbon for third place with as much pleasure and sense of rightness as I can ever remember.

At the little awards ceremony, her master poured her tiny mouthfuls of beer from a long-necked bottle, and Bingo seemed rather self-satisfied. I was somewhat in love with her by now and more than a little envious of her owner. When it was his turn to come up and get his ribbon we all burst into a few minutes of applause and cheering that we had held, pent up, for some time. He took the ribbon and waited until we'd quieted down, then bent over and fastened it to Bingo's collar, played with her ear for a second and, speaking for both of them said, "Well, as they used to say, the show ain't ever over until the fat lady sings."

Then he and the fat lady went over to his truck. He lifted her into the front seat and gave her the last swallow out of the beer bottle, handed the empty to a friend who came to say good-bye, and they drove off.

I watched the truck disappear as it turned through a stand of pines and, through the rear window, I could see them sitting shoulder to shoulder. For a moment I thought about love. Not the kind that they sing about or the kind that disgraces a bumper sticker, but the kind that means you'll put your arm in the fire. The kind that becomes a Navy Cross or Silver Star—or a ten-cent pink-and-silver ribbon. The kind that you don't talk about. The kind that is just there, like earth.

I wasn't the only one watching the truck fade away. Half a dozen of the crowd had moved off by themselves and were watching it too. I wondered what we all felt in common, and I think it was sorrow. Suddenly we all knew what it was we had been looking for for so long, from some one or something . . . and we felt that it had passed us by.

November 1984

Tommy's Fiddle

NORMAN STRUNG

The best teachers aren't always found in a classroom.

H E CALLED IT a Stradivarius. It wasn't, of course, but it was a
fine, old fiddle that I suspect was crafted by a settler newly arrived in the American West who longed to bridge the gap between the rough frontier and the Old Country. Tom didn't
know where it came from, only that it had been in his family when they emigrated south from Canada. I preferred to believe it was traded for some other
object of hand manufacture—traces, or a saddle, or a plow struck from the
belly of a glowing forge.

The fiddle was Tom's most prized possession. He stored it under his
bed, and whenever he went hunting, fishing, or visiting he placed the cased
instrument in a secret compartment in the trunk of his old Studebaker.
Though it accompanied him everywhere, he didn't play it all that often. Being a shy man, and self-conscious of his lack of education, his spirit usually
needed to be liberated from a bottle before he would touch bow to string and
make music.

That was how I met Tom. I had rented a college apartment above his,
and one day, while I was attempting to make sense out of some dreary ab-
stract of literary theory, the lilting melody of a lively fiddle invaded my
thoughts and refused to be evicted. After 15 minutes of dubious effort, I
closed the book, reached for my banjo, and began to play along.

Within a dozen bars there came a dull tapping at my feet, a signal that
for many years to come would be an invitation to hunt and fish and be taught
the secret places and rites of a West that even then was fast slipping away. Tom
rapped on his ceiling with a broom handle and yelled, "Hey kid, you're pretty
good. C'mon down."

What songs we played that afternoon! "Soldier's Joy," "Wildwood

Flower," "Wreck of the Old 97" . . . and as would be expected, between the runs and riffs and the sweet, clear notes, we got to know each other a bit. I was a student of literature with an untutored passion for the outdoors. Tom seemed to have been everything one could be within the limiting confines of small Western towns: cowpoke, carpenter, plasterer, and farmer; yet all of them were nothing more than semiprofitable pastimes that financed his hunting and fishing trips and his love of whiskey and music.

Tom was not exactly an alcoholic. He was not a social drinker or even a regular drinker. It was my habit to have a drink before dinner, and when Tom was around, I'd offer him a glass. Most of the time he'd turn it down with a contemptuous wave of his hand. Tom, like other native sons of the West that I have known, did not view drinking as a social event. He viewed it as an opportunity to get rip-roaring drunk and raise hell, and once every three or four weeks, determined by some mechanism of time or taste that was beyond my reckoning, he would open a bottle and throw the cork away, and all that were present were welcome to join him.

It was on that kind of night that I first met Tom. I cannot say with certainty what quality of music we were making when I finally excused myself and crawled up the stairs. Certainly it was loud, and it sure sounded good to us. What did not sound good to me was the thump of Tom's broomstick under my bed at 5 the next morning.

"C'mon down, kid. Did you forget we're going elk hunting?"

I was terribly hung over, but Tom's eyes were as bright and clear as that chilly snow-tinged dawn. He had made a breakfast of venison, fried eggs, hotcakes, sausage, and toast that I couldn't bear to look at. Although he weighed all of 140 pounds soaking wet, he said something about the need for nourishment in the mountains and ate it all. I didn't know then that I was looking at the tip of an iceberg.

Tom was nearly fifty. I had just passed my twenty-first birthday. By all rules of logic and conditioning it was he that should have had trouble keeping up with me, but that was not the case. He set a deceptive pace over hill and dale. He didn't seem to be moving fast; in fact, at first I found myself stepping in his heels. But like a good walking horse, he never broke stride or rhythm no matter how rough the terrain, and within an hour he began to pause every 15 minutes to wait for me to catch up. And there I'd find him sitting on a rock, puffing away on one of the Camels that he usually chain-smoked.

I don't know how much country we covered that day, but it was surely the longest walk I'd every endured. Tom's strategy was to climb high, then hunt down in a zigzag course that led us along the edges of parks and open meadows, then upon reaching a creek bottom, to climb high again. I was so exhausted by the afternoon that I never would have seen the elk if I had been alone. Suddenly Tom froze, slipped his rifle off his shoulder, and hissed, "There they are!"

Two bull elk grazed at the edge of a meadow. We were headed downhill, I had caught my breath, and I managed to shoot straight. The two bulls fell within 50 yards of each other.

As a seasoned veteran of exactly two deer kills I was embarrassed to admit that I didn't have any idea how to go about dressing out an animal the size of a cow, but with no more than an occasional "hold that leg" and "grab the hide here," Tom had both animals cleaned in a half hour. "Now just wait here. I'll be right back," he said, and walked off with that mile-eating gait.

And he was—riding a horse he'd borrowed from the rancher at the head of the canyon. We skidded both animals out to Tom's car by sundown.

That was another thing about Tom. He seemed to know everybody, or at the very least, he always knew somebody who knew somebody. As a result, we had entree to every farm and ranch in the valley; to prime stretches of trout streams so far from public roads that they were never fished; to brushy coulees next to fifty-bushel-an-acre wheatfields that crawled with pheasants; and to canyons and mountains loaded with deer and elk, but blocked to public access by private lands. Tom shared them all with me.

I didn't know why Tom took such an immediate liking to me—I couldn't possibly reciprocate with anything other than my music. Perhaps, at first, it was curiosity over my seemingly contradictory combination of a bookish nature and an unquenchable thirst for the sporting life. I can recall Tom being awed by the fact that I was writing a book. Whether it was good, bad, published, or unpublished did not matter; he was taken by the idea that I could conceive of such an act. Eventually though, we were bound by the mutual recognition, respect, and pleasure derived from the relationship between a promising student and his mentor.

The things I learned from Tom during the twelve years I knew him should rightly fill a book. On a grand scale, he taught me to be a competent and caring sportsman and even how to build a log cabin—my present home. On a smaller scale, each day with him brought new delights of practical and sometimes arcane knowledge that I still use today: the way to fill a woodbox fast is to gather wrist-thick wood that can be chopped with two swings of an ax; a loose axhead will firm up solid if left overnight in a waterbucket; and no matter how dog-tired, cold, and hungry you are, you always unsaddle, brush down, feed and water your horse before retiring to the warmth of the cook tent in hunting camp.

There were also fun times with Tom, times when I either laughed at his corny jokes (his favorite response to just about anything I might say was, "That's what she said, and now she can't button her overcoat . . .") or his original perceptions of a world beyond his grasp.

One day he stormed into my apartment with a newspaper. "Ahah Mr. Perfesser," a name he had given me shortly after I accepted a teaching position at the university, "Look at this. I told you all that messing around in space was screwing up our weather and our hunting to boot! It says so here, plain, it's them jet streams that are doing it."

After glancing at the article, and hearing Tom's reasoning, I realized he'd confused a term for upper air patterns with jet contrails.

And on an April day when we were planning to fish the next morning, the time of arising a bit muddled by the arrival of Daylight Savings Time, he pulled me aside and whispered—even though there was no one else in the room—"Tell me something about this damned Daylight Savings Time. They take an hour away from you in the spring, then they give it back in the fall, right?"

"Sure," I said. "That's roughly the idea."

"But where does the hour go in the *meantime*?" he asked with the urgency of a man on the edge of a great discovery.

Tom had his darker side, too, as we all do; moments of sadness and bitter reflection. Marveling over books in my library whose very titles he could not understand, he allowed as how he didn't get much schooling because he had to help with the family farm that was later lost in the Great Depression.

There were also references to two wives who ran off—one with a gambler, the other with a drummer—and a severely retarded child ("I could never understand it," he confided to me once. "There was never any bad blood in the family . . .").

Tom was also capable of anger, but he was hardly short-tempered. In my haste to follow him to a fishing hole, I once failed to thoroughly latch a gate. When we returned, the gate still stood, but I was lectured for the half-hour ride home on all the possible consequences of my error: stock on the loose, bulls breeding at the wrong time of year, the posting of No Trespassing signs, and probably worst of all in Tom's mind, us being considered city-bred people. Another time, exasperated at the long shots I was taking at ducks, he "accidentally" dropped a full box of shells into soupy mud. "That just leaves us ten, kid, so we gotta make 'em count." I waited for the ducks to come closer, and learned one of my most important lessons about wing-shooting—at 35 yards, you hit what you aimed at, and left no cripples.

Only once was Tommy genuinely angry with me. It was when I became angry at a sixteen-year-old on his first hunting trip who gutshot an animal. After consoling the youth and telling him he did just fine for his first deer, Tom strode over to me and hissed between white lips, "You're gonna ruin hunting fer that kid's life if you keep up like that. You got to teach kids, not bully 'em. Don't never forget that you were a young punk once, too." Since that day, I never have.

The end came swiftly for Tom, and for that I'm grateful. One year he was climbing mountains and making music and the next year he could not even take the moderate cold of a well-made duck-blind or the warming bite of a shot of bourbon. There was something in my mind that said Tom was eternal, so I didn't worry; I just told him he would be better next year, and that he would hunt and fish and play again.

"If I could just get back up into those mountains one more time," I overheard him tell a friend that fall.

I received the letter in New York the following January, sent to me by a distant relative who had found my temporary address among Tom's belongings. Emphysema, colitis, and finally pneumonia had felled him in a veteran's hospital. He was buried in a cemetery that overlooked his family's old homestead. From his grave you can see the Madison Valley, and the Spanish Peaks beyond.

I don't know what became of his fiddle. I wish he would have willed it to me, and I think he would have if he had known the value I placed on it. But never mind. On cold winter nights when the snow curls like smoke around the eaves of my cabin, if I listen very carefully I can still hear Tommy's fiddle, ringing out as clearly as the stars shine in the coal-black sky.

July 1985

The Road to Tinkhamtown

COREY FORD

A lilac bush and some crumbling foundations marked the grouse cover of dreams,
where the dog's bell beckoned for the last time.

IT WAS A long way, but he knew where he was going. He would follow the road through the woods and over the crest of a hill and down the hill to the stream, and cross the sagging timbers of the bridge, and on the other side would be the place called Tinkhamtown. He was going back to Tinkhamtown.

He walked slowly at first, his legs dragging with each step. He had not walked for almost a year, and his flanks had shriveled and wasted away from lying in bed so long; he could fit his fingers around his thigh. Doc Towle had said he would never walk again, but that was Doc for you, always on the pessimistic side. Why, now he was walking quite easily, once he had started. The strength was coming back into his legs, and he did not have to stop for breath so often. He tried jogging a few steps, just to show he could, but he slowed again because he had a long way to go.

It was hard to make out the old road, choked with alders and covered by matted leaves, and he shut his eyes so he could see it better. He could always see it when he shut his eyes. Yes, here was the beaver dam on the right, just as he remembered it, and the flooded stretch where he had picked his way from hummock to hummock while the dog splashed unconcernedly in front of him. The water had been over his boot tops in one place, and sure enough, as he waded it now his left boot filled with water again, the same warm squdgy feeling. Everything was the way it had been that afternoon, nothing had changed in ten years. Here was the blowdown across the road that he had clambered over, and here on a knoll was the clump of thornapples where a grouse had flushed as they passed. Shad had wanted to look for it, but he had whistled him back. They were looking for Tinkhamtown.

303

He had come across the name on a map in the town library. He used to study the old maps and survey charts of the state; sometimes they showed where a farming community had flourished, a century ago, and around the abandoned pastures and in the orchards grown up to pine the birds would be feeding undisturbed. Some of his best grouse covers had been located that way. The map had been rolled up in a cardboard cylinder; it crackled with age as he spread it out. The date was 1857. It was the sector between Cardigan and Kearsarge Mountains, a wasteland of slash and second-growth timber without habitation today, but evidently it had supported a number of families before the Civil War. A road was marked on the map, dotted with X's for homesteads, and the names of the owners were lettered beside them: Nason, J. Tinkham, Allard, R. Tinkham. Half the names were Tinkham. In the center of the map—the paper was so yellow that he could barely make it out—was the word "Tinkhamtown."

He had drawn a rough sketch on the back of an envelope, noting where the road left the highway and ran north to a fork and then turned east and crossed a stream that was not even named; and the next morning he and Shad had set out together to find the place. They could not drive very far in the jeep, because washouts had gutted the roadbed and laid bare the ledges and boulders. He had stuffed the sketch in his hunting-coat pocket, and hung his shotgun over his forearm and started walking, the setter trotting ahead with the bell on his collar tinkling. It was an old-fashioned sleighbell, and it had a thin silvery note that echoed through the woods like peepers in the spring. He could follow the sound in the thickest cover, and when it stopped he would go to where he heard it last and Shad would be on point. After Shad's death, he had put the bell away. He'd never had another dog.

It was silent in the woods without the bell, and the way was longer than he remembered. He should have come to the big hill by now. Maybe he'd taken the wrong turn back at the fork. He thrust a hand into his hunting coat; the envelope with the sketch was still in the pocket. He sat down on a flat rock to get his bearings, and then he realized, with a surge of excitement, that he had stopped on this very rock for lunch ten years ago. Here was the waxed paper from his sandwich, tucked in a crevice, and here was the hollow in the leaves where Shad had stretched out beside him, the dog's soft muzzle flattened on his thigh. He looked up, and through the trees he could see the hill.

He rose and started walking again, carrying his shotgun. He had left the gun standing in its rack in the kitchen when he had been taken to the state hospital, but now it was hooked over his arm by the trigger guard; he could feel the solid heft of it. The woods grew more dense as he climbed, but here and there a shaft of sunlight slanted through the trees. "And there were forests ancient as the hills," he thought, "enfolding sunny spots of greenery." Funny that should come back to him now; he hadn't read it since he was a boy. Other things were coming back to him, the smell of dank leaves and sweetfern and frosted apples, the sharp contrast of sun and cool shade, the November stillness before snow. He walked faster, feeling the excitement swell within him.

He paused on the crest of the hill, straining his ears for the faint mutter of the stream below him, but he could not hear it because of the voices. He wished they would stop talking, so he could hear the stream. Someone was saying his name over and over, "Frank, Frank," and he opened his eyes reluctantly and looked up at his sister. Her face was worried, and there was nothing to worry about. He tried to tell her where he was going, but when he moved his lips the words would not form. "What did you say, Frank?" she asked, bending her head lower. "I don't understand." He couldn't make the words any clearer, and she straightened and said to Doc Towle: "It sounded like Tinkhamtown."

"Tinkhamtown?" Doc shook his head. "Never heard him mention any place by that name."

He smiled to himself. Of course he'd never mentioned it to Doc. Things like a secret grouse cover you didn't mention to anyone, not even to as close a friend as Doc was. No, he and Shad were the only ones who knew. They had found it together, that long ago afternoon, and it was their secret.

They had come to the stream—he shut his eyes so he could see it again—and Shad had trotted across the bridge. He had followed more cautiously, avoiding the loose planks and walking along a beam with his shotgun held out to balance himself. On the other side of the stream the road mounted steeply to a clearing in the woods, and he halted before the split-stone foundations of a house, the first of the series of farms shown on the map. It must have been a long time since the building had fallen in; the cottonwoods growing in the cellar hole were twenty, maybe thirty years old. His boot overturned a rusted ax blade and the handle of a china cup in the grass; that was all. Beside the doorstep was a lilac bush, almost as tall as the cottonwoods. He thought of the wife who had set it out, a little shrub then, and the husband who had chided her for wasting time on such frivolous things with all the farm work to be done. But the work had come to nothing, and still the lilac bloomed each spring, the one thing that had survived.

Shad's bell was moving along the stone wall at the edge of the clearing, and he strolled after him, not hunting, wondering about the people who had gone away and left their walls to crumble and their buildings to collapse under the winter snows. Had they ever come back to Tinkhamtown? Were they here now, watching him unseen? His toe stubbed against a block of hewn granite hidden by briars, part of the sill of the old barn. Once it had been a tight barn, warm with cattle steaming in their stalls, rich with the blend of hay and manure and harness leather. He liked to think of it the way it was; it was more real than this bare rectangle of blocks and the emptiness inside. He'd always felt that way about the past. Doc used to argue that what's over is over, but he would insist Doc was wrong. Everything is the way it was, he'd tell Doc. The past never changes. You leave it and go on to the present, but it is still there, waiting for you to come back to it.

He had been so wrapped in his thoughts that he had not realized Shad's bell had stopped. He hurried across the clearing, holding his gun ready. In a corner of the stone wall an ancient apple tree had littered the ground with fallen fruit, and beneath it Shad was standing motionless. The white fan of his tail was lifted a little and his backline was level, the neck craned forward, one foreleg cocked. His flanks were trembling with the nearness of grouse, and a thin skein of drool hung from his jowls. The dog did not move as he approached, but the brown eyes rolled back until their whites showed, looking for him. "Steady, boy," he called. His throat was tight, the way it always got when Shad was on point, and he had to swallow hard. "Steady, I'm coming."

"I think his lips moved just now," his sister's voice said. He did not open his eyes, because he was waiting for the grouse to get up in front of Shad, but he knew Doc Towle was looking at him. "He's sleeping," Doc said after a moment. "Maybe you better get some sleep yourself, Mrs. Duncombe." He heard Doc's heavy footsteps cross the room. "Call me if there's any change," Doc said, and closed the door, and in the silence he could hear his sister's chair creaking beside him, her silk dress rustling regularly as she breathed.

What was she doing here, he wondered. Why had she come all the way from California to see him? It was the first time they had seen each other since she had married and moved out West. She was his only relative, but they had never been very close; they had nothing in common, really. He heard from her now and then, but it was always the same letter: why didn't he sell the old place, it was too big for him now that the folks had passed on, why didn't he take a small apartment in town where he wouldn't be alone? But he liked the big house, and he wasn't alone, not with Shad. He had closed off all the other rooms and moved into the kitchen so everything would be handy. His sister didn't approve of his bachelor ways, but it was very comfortable with his cot by the stove and Shad curled on the floor near him at night, whinnying and scratching the linoleum with his claws as he chased a bird in a dream. He wasn't alone when he heard that.

He had never married. He had looked after the folks as long as they lived; maybe that was why. Shad was his family. They were always together—Shad was short for Shadow—and there was a closeness between them that he did not feel for anyone else, not his sister or Doc even. He and Shad used to talk without words, each knowing what the other was thinking, and they could always find one another in the wood. He still remembered the little things about him: the possessive thrust of his paw, the way he false-yawned when he was vexed, the setter stubbornness sometimes, the clownish grin when they were going hunting, the kind eyes. That was it; Shad was the kindest person he had ever known.

They had not hunted again after Tinkhamtown. The old dog had stumbled several times, walking back to the jeep, and he had to carry him in his arms the last hundred yards. It was hard to realize he was gone. He liked to think of him the way he was; it was like the barn, it was more real than the emptiness. Sometimes at night, lying awake with the pain in his legs, he would hear the scratch of claws on the linoleum, and he would turn on the light and the hospital room would be empty. But when he turned the light off he would hear the scratching again, and he would be content and drop off to sleep, or what passed for sleep in these days and nights that ran together without dusk or dawn.

Once he asked Doc pointblank if he would ever get well. Doc was giving him something for the pain, and he hesitated a moment and finished what he was doing and cleaned the needle and then looked at him and said: "I'm afraid not, Frank." They had grown up in town together, and Doc knew him too well to lie. "I'm afraid there's nothing to do." Nothing to do but lie here and wait till it was over. "Tell me, Doc," he whispered, for his voice wasn't very strong, "what happens when it's over?" And Doc fumbled with the catch of his black bag and closed it and said well he supposed you went on to someplace else called the Hereafter. But he shook his head; he always argued with Doc. "No, it isn't someplace else," he told him, "it's someplace you've been where you want to be again." Doc didn't understand, and he couldn't explain it any better. He knew what he meant, but the shot was taking effect and he was tired.

He was tired now, and his legs ached a little as he started down the hill, trying to find the stream. It was too dark under the trees to see the sketch he had drawn, and he could not tell direction by the moss on the north side of the trunks. The moss grew all around them, swelling them out of size, and huge blowdowns blocked his way. Their upended roots were black and mis-shapen, and now instead of excitement he felt a surge of panic. He floundered through a pile of slash, his legs throbbing with pain as the sharp points stabbed him, but he did not have the strength to get to the other side and he had to back out again and circle. He did not know where he was going. It was getting late, and he had lost the way.

There was no sound in the woods, nothing to guide him, nothing but his sister's chair creaking and her breath catching now and then in a dry sob. She wanted him to turn back, and Doc wanted him to, they all wanted him to turn back. He thought of the big house; if he left it alone it would fall in with the winter snows and cottonwoods would grow in the cellar hole. And there were all the other doubts, but most of all there was the fear. He was afraid of the darkness, and being alone, and not knowing where he was going. It would be better to turn around and go back. He knew the way back.

And then he heard it, echoing through the woods like peepers in the spring, the thin silvery tinkle of a sleighbell. He started running toward it, following the sound down the hill. His legs were strong again, and he hurdled the blowdowns, he leapt over fallen logs, he put one fingertip on a pile of slash and sailed over it like a grouse skimming. He was getting nearer and the sound filled his ears, louder than a thousand churchbells ringing, louder than all the choirs in the sky, as loud as the pounding of his heart. The fear was gone; he was not lost. He had the bell to guide him now.

He came to the stream, and paused for a moment at the bridge. He wanted to tell them he was happy, if they only knew how happy he was, but when he opened his eyes he could not see them anymore. Everything else was bright, but the room was dark.

The bell had stopped, and he looked across the stream. The other side was bathed in sunshine, and he could see the road mounting steeply, and the clearing in the woods, and the apple tree in a corner of the stone wall. Shad was standing motionless beneath it, the white fan of his tail lifted, his neck craned forward and one foreleg cocked. The whites of his eyes showed as he looked back, waiting for him.

"Steady," he called, "steady, boy." He started across the bridge. "I'm coming."

The Contributors

Russell Annabel lived in Idaho and wrote regularly for *Field & Stream*, *True*, and other publications for many years.

Havilah Babcock was born in 1898 and for many years was the chairman of the English Department at the University of South Carolina. He began to write for *Field & Stream* in 1934 and for the next thirty years was a regular contributor. His five books include *Jaybirds Go to Hell on Friday*, *My Health Is Better in November*, *Tales of Quails 'n Such*, and *I Don't Want to Shoot an Elephant*. He died in 1964. *The Best of Babcock*, a collection of his outdoor writing edited by *Field & Stream* editor Hugh Grey, was published in 1974.

Duncan Barnes, *Field & Stream*'s editor since 1981, grew up in southern New York State. After graduating from Dartmouth College, he wrote about the outdoors for the St. Petersburg (Florida) *Times* and *Sports Illustrated*, and was editorial director of Winchester Press.

John Barsness lives in Townsend, Montana. His books include *Hunting the Great Plains*, *Montana Time*, and *Western Skies: Bird Hunting in the Rockies and on the Plains*.

Robert M. (Bob) Brister, a native Texan, was born in 1928 and has written for *Field & Stream* since 1971. The outdoors editor for the Houston *Chronicle* for almost forty years, he is a lifelong hunter and angler who has won hundreds of awards at competitions ranging from bait casting to skeet, trap, sporting clays, and live-bird shooting. His books include *Shotgunning, The Art and Science*, and two short-story collections, *The Golden Crescent* and *Moss, Mallards, and Mules*.

Nash Buckingham was born in 1880 and grew up in Tennessee. A champion amateur boxer as well as a conservationist and newspaperman, he was one of America's best known and beloved outdoor writers. His books include *De Shootin'est Gent'Man*, *Ole Miss!*, *Tattered Coat*, and *Game Bag*. His first article for *Field & Stream* appeared in 1913.

Russell Chatham, a writer and painter, grew up in San Francisco and lives in Livingston, Montana.

Ralph D. Conroy is an ardent outdoorsman, freelance writer, and photographer. He is married and has two children and one grandchild. He and his wife, Jeanne, shoot the sporting clays circuit. He works as a civil servant in Pittsfield, Massachusetts.

Byron W. Dalrymple was born in Michigan and attended the University of Michigan. In 1944, after spending four years in New York City and five years in Hollywood writing music for radio and films, he became a professional writer and subsequently moved to Kerrville, Texas. In the years since, he has written twenty-eight books, contributed chapters to thirty others, and wrote and produced thirty-three nationally distributed TV films, mostly about the outdoors. His five thousand magazine articles appeared in *Field & Stream* and many other publications. He died on September 27, 1994 at the age of eighty-four.

Robert H. Davis, a noted humorist of his day and a regular contributor to *Field & Stream*, edited *Munsey's Magazine* and was a member of the Anglers' Club of New York. A tongue-in-cheek biography of him published in a 1912 issue of *Field & Stream* called him the "greatest living authority on Black Bass" and "a champion of the wooden worm and plaster of Paris minnow."

Frank Dufresne was born in 1896 and raised in New Hampshire. After fighting as an infantryman in World War I, he moved to Alaska, where he lived in the 1920s and '30s and wrote articles for many popular magazines of his day, including *Field & Stream*, *Collier's*, and the *Saturday Evening Post*. For a while he directed the Alaska Game Commission. His biography, *My Way Was North*, was published in 1966, and a book, *No Room For Bears*, was recently reprinted.

Corey Ford was born in New York City in 1902, attended Columbia University, and became one of America's best known humorists and writers, whose articles appeared in *The New Yorker*, the *Saturday Evening Post*, and other publications. His more than thirty books included histories and several collections of "The Lower Forty," his column for *Field & Stream* about a fictional "shooting, angling and inside straight club." He died in New Hampshire in 1969.

C. E. Gillham was from Illinois. He sold his first article to *Field & Stream* in 1928 and was a regular contributor until his death in the early 1970s.

Arthur Gordon, the author of a dozen books and many magazine pieces, is a fifth-generation Georgian who still lives in his hometown of Savannah. A graduate of Yale and Oxford, he spent many years in the magazine business, being successively the managing editor of *Good Housekeeping*, editor of *Cosmopolitan*, editorial director of *Guideposts*, and a staff writer for *Reader's Digest*. He met his wife, Pam, in London during World War II while serving as a major in the Eighth Air Force. They have five children. Surf-fishing remains a favorite pastime. "The fishing isn't what it used to be," he says a bit glumly, "but then, what is?"

Zane Grey was born in Ohio in 1872, attended the University of Pennsylvania, and became a dentist, then a successful novelist. He eventually wrote fifty-four novels, the most famous of which, *Riders of the Purple Sage*, was serialized in *Field & Stream* in 1912–13. A pioneering sportsman and a great saltwater angler, he also wrote six books on his hunting and fishing adventures. He died in 1939.

Roderick Haig-Brown was born in England in 1908 and as a young man moved to British Columbia, where he was a logger, guide, trapper, civil magistrate, educator, conservationist, and the author of twenty-four books, many about the outdoors. He died in 1976.

Frank C. Hibben, a 1933 graduate of Princeton, earned a Ph.D. at Harvard and for many years was a professor of anthropology at the University of New Mexico. He is an expert on early man in North America and a hunter who has pursued game on four continents.

Gene Hill, a former advertising executive and a graduate of Harvard University, lives in Arizona. His column, "Hill Country," has appeared in *Field & Stream* for more than twenty years.

Tom H. Kelly, a professional forester, was born in Mobile, Alabama, in 1927, and educated in his home state, where he still lives. He has written one book, *Tenth Legion*, and his magazine writings have been collected in two anthologies, *Dealer's Choice* and *Better on a Rising Tide*. He has contributed to *Field & Stream* since 1978. Kelly says that he "fishes lightly, hunts doves mildly, ducks regularly, and, since 1938, turkeys compulsively."

Nick Lyons lives in New York City. A graduate of the University of Pennsylvania and a former Professor of English at Hunter College, he has written or edited twelve books, including five on fishing, and is the founder of the sporting-books publishing house of Lyons & Burford.

Gordon MacQuarrie was born in Wisconsin in 1900. After graduating from the University of Wisconsin in 1923, he became a newspaperman, first at the *Superior Evening Telegram* and then the *Milwaukee Journal*, where he was the outdoors editor. His popular Old Duck Hunters stories ran in the 1930s into the 1950s. He died in 1956.

Keith McCafferty was born in 1953 in Steubenville, Ohio. He has written articles and stories for many outdoor and literary magazines, including *Field & Stream*, *Gray's Sporting Journal*, *American Country*, *Fly Fisherman*, *Game Journal*, and the Chicago *Tribune*. He is currently working on a collection of his stories and a children's book to be illustrated by his eleven-year-old son. He lives with his wife Gail, son Tom, and daughter Jessie in Bozeman, Montana.

J. I. (Jim) Merritt, a contributing editor of *Field & Stream*, lives in New Jersey and has written for the magazine since 1985. He is the author of *Baronets and Buffalo: The British Sportsman in the American West*.

A. J. (Albert Jules) McClane, for many years *Field & Stream*'s fishing editor, joined the magazine in 1947 and was a regular contributor until his death in December 1991. His monumental *McClane's Standard Fishing Encyclopedia and International Angling Guide*, first published in 1965, has been through many printings and sold well over a million copies.

Harold McCracken, an author, archaeologist, explorer, and for many years the director of the Buffalo Bill Historical Center, in Cody, Wyoming, was born in Colorado in 1894. A graduate of Ohio State University, he was an authority on topics ranging from the Alaskan brown bear to western art. He died in Wyoming in 1983.

Warren Kempson Page was born in 1909. A graduate of Harvard University, he served as a naval gunnery officer in World War II and became *Field & Stream*'s shooting editor in 1947. Over the next twenty years he hunted all over the world. A pioneer benchrest shooter, he was a founder and president of the National Shooting Sports Foundation. His books include *The Accurate Rifle* and *One Man's Wilderness*. He died in 1977.

Datus C. Proper, a graduate of Cornell University and a former officer in the State Department, lives and writes in Belgrade, Montana. He is the author of *Pheasants of the Mind*, *What the Trout Said*, and *The Last Old Place*.

Brian O'Brien lived in Connecticut and wrote several articles for *Field & Stream* in the 1950s and '60s, including "The Big Safari."

Walter Prothero was born in 1951. A former contributing editor of *Field & Stream*, he has hunted in the Rocky Mountains, and in Mexico, Alaska, and Africa. Trained as a game biologist, he has also taught writing at the college level and is the author of several books, including *Stalking Trophy Mule Deer*.

George Reiger lives in Locustville, Virginia. He is a 1960 graduate of Princeton and a former naval officer who served as a translator during the Vietnam War and later at the Paris Peace Talks. Reiger has written the "Conservation" column for *Field & Stream* since 1972 and is the author or editor of many books about the outdoors, including *Wanderer on My Native Shore*, *The Wings of Dawn*, *Profiles in Saltwater Angling*, and *The Undiscovered Stories of Zane Grey*.

Robert Ruark was born in North Carolina in 1915. After serving as a naval officer in World War II, he became a newspaper columnist and popular novelist. His most famous book, *Something of Value*, was based on the Mau Mau uprising during the 1950s in his beloved Kenya. He wrote frequently on big-game African hunting, which he described in *Horn of the Hunter*, *Use Enough Gun*, and other books, but he is best remembered by outdoorsmen for his popular "The Old Man and the Boy" series, which ran in *Field & Stream* from 1953 through 1961. He died in 1965.

Archibald Rutledge began writing for *Field & Stream* in 1918 while living in Mercersburg, Pennsylvania, where he continued to reside until the 1940s, when he moved to Spartanburg, South Carolina. His last article for the magazine, "The Way of the Wild Gobbler," appeared fifty-two years later, in the seventy-fifth anniversary issue. He died in 1973.

Burton L. Spiller, the "poet laureat of the ruffed grouse," wrote for *Field & Stream* for more than thirty years. He died in 1973.

Hart Stilwell was from Brownsville, Texas. His first article for *Field & Stream*, a piece on fishing for sea bass, appeared in 1933. He went on to write nearly two hundred articles for the magazine over the next three decades. He died in 1962.

Norman Strung grew up in Brooklyn, New York during the 1940s, and spent his adult years hunting, fishing, and writing in Montana, where he died in 1991.

William G. (Bill) Tapply, a resident of Acton, Massachusetts, grew up hunting and fishing all over New England with his father, H. G. "Tap" Tapply, and other legendary sportsmen such as Burt Spiller, Corey Ford, Lee Wulff,

Ed Zern, and Harold Blaisdell. A retired public-school history teacher, he now writes mystery novels and hunting and fishing essays. He continues his lifelong pursuit of ruffed grouse and brook trout throughout New England.

H. G. "Tap" Tapply, who lives in Alton, New Hampshire, wrote "Tap's Tips" and "The Sportsman's Notebook" for *Field & Stream* in the 1950s until his retirement in 1994.

Bill Tarrant, a former Marine and a veteran of the Korean War, is a native Kansan who became an industrialist, a professor, a public-relations counsel, the mayor of the United States' 50th largest city, and the chairman of the board of Wichita State University. All of which he left behind at age 37 to enter the outback and become a dog writer. He wrote for seven years without selling one word. Since then, he has become the first person to be named Writer of the Year by the Dog Writers of America. He is also a recipient of the Deep Woodsman Award from the Outdoor Writers of America for the best outdoor story of the year in all media. He lives with his wife, Dee, and a houseful of dogs in Sedona, Arizona.

Florence A. Tasker was one of numerous women explorers and sportswomen who wrote for *Field & Stream* in its early years.

Ted Trueblood grew up on a farm near Homedale, Idaho, and began writing for outdoor magazines in 1931, the year he graduated from high school. He worked as a newspaperman in Idaho and Utah and became fishing editor of *Field & Stream* in 1941, and again in 1944. After two more years of commuting to New York City from the suburbs, he quit urban life for good and returned to Idaho, where he lived and continued to contribute articles as an associate editor. He died in 1982.

Ed Zern was born in West Virginia in 1910 and grew up in Pennsylvania. His seven books about the outdoors include *To Hell With Fishing*, *To Hell With Hunting*, and *How to Tell Fish From Fishermen*. His column, "Exit Laughing," was a mainstay of *Field & Stream* from 1958 until his death in 1994.